The Computer Boys Take Over

History of Computing

William Aspray, editor

The Computer Boys Take Over

Computers, Programmers, and the Politics of
Technical Expertise

Nathan Ensmenger

The MIT Press
Cambridge, Massachusetts
London, England

First MIT Press paperback edition, 2012

This book was set in Sabon by Toppan Best-set Premedia Limited.

Library of Congress Cataloging-in-Publication Data

Ensmenger, Nathan, 1972–
The computer boys take over : computers, programmers, and the politics of technical expertise / Nathan Ensmenger.
    p.   cm.—(History of computing)
Includes bibliographical references and index.
ISBN 978-0-262-05093-7 (hc. : alk. paper)—978-0-262-51796-6 (pb. : alk. paper)
1. Computer programming. 2. Computer programmers. 3. Software engineering—History. 4. Computer software—Development—Social aspects.
I. Title.
QA76.6.E58   2010
005.1—dc22

                                                            2009052638

The MIT Press is pleased to keep this title available in print by manufacturing single copies, on demand, via digital printing technology.

For Deborah and the boys

Contents

Acknowledgments

This book represents the culmination of a long period of research, writing, and intellectual exchange that has benefited enormously from the contributions of numerous historians from around the globe. The history of the computing community, although small in number, is great in spirit, and is as welcoming a collection of scholars as I have ever encountered.

Two of the senior members of this community have proven particularly supportive of me and my work. William Aspray has served as an adviser and mentor from almost the beginning of my career, and has been unfailingly generous in his time, energy, and encouragement. The late Michael Mahoney, whose wit and erudition will be sorely missed by the community, also served as a model of unselfish scholarship. It would be impossible to detail the many ways in which both of these scholars have informed, and continue to inform, my own thinking and scholarship.

This book started as a dissertation, and owes much to the friends and advisers who guided it through its earliest incarnations. Emily Thompson, Robert Kohler, and Walter Licht served as patient readers of many, many early drafts, and without their kind and enlightened counsel this project would never have made it past its infancy. Josh Buhs, Thomas Haigh, Atsushi Akera, and the rest of my graduate school cohort listened for years to my vague musings on the eccentricities of early computer programmers, and their feedback helped refine my thoughts and arguments. Edward Bell and the rest of the crew at E. J. Bell and Associates, by providing me with frequent opportunities to pick up consulting work, made it possible for me to finish graduate school without going under financially.

My colleagues at the University of Pennsylvania have been patient and gracious sounding boards and mentors. Ruth Schwartz Cowan, who served as the chair of the department for most of the formative years of this manuscript, allowed me time and space to balance my research and teaching. Susan Lindee has continued that tradition. Both of them have provided much support and encouragement. Janet Tighe has served as a fount of wisdom and sanity for almost a decade. John Tresch and Beth Linker have struggled alongside me in the trenches as my fellow junior faculty members. My other senior colleagues have been endlessly giving of their advice and solicitude. I appreciate all of them greatly.

There are far too many archivists, librarians, and fellow historians who contributed to this project to identify them individually here. The Charles Babbage Institute, however, cannot go unmentioned. Not only does the Babbage hold the vast majority of the source material used to construct this history but also it serves as the center of gravity of the entire history of the computing community. It also provided generous funding in the form of the Tomash Fellowship in the History of Information Processing. Tom Misa, Jeff Yost, and Arthur Norberg have all served as trusted friends and advisers.

Finally, like most academic book projects, this one has absorbed more than its share of my time and energy outside the office. Many thanks to all of my family. My parents, Elisabeth and Stephen, made possible so many opportunities in my life. My wife, Deborah, has been a constant companion and source of loving support, and has been endlessly forgiving of my need to stretch the project out with "just one more" revision. My three sons, Asher, Tate, and Tucker, made the process bearable by providing joy, motivation, and strength each day.

1

Introduction: Computer Revolutionaries

To be a good programmer today is as much a privilege as it was to be a literate man in the sixteenth century. This privilege leads the programmer to expect recognition and respect on the part of society. Unfortunately, such recognition is not always realized.
—Andrei Ershov, *Aesthetics and the Human Factor in Programming*, 1972

The Computer People

Chances are that you or someone close to you makes their living "working with computers." In the decades since the 1950s, the technical specialists most directly associated with the electronic digital computer—computer programmers, systems analysts, and network and database administrators—have assumed an increasingly active and visible role in the shaping of our modern information society. All but the smallest organizations now have their own information technology departments filled with such specialists, and in many cases they represent some of the organization's most valued—or at least most highly paid—employees. In the United States alone there are more than three million professional computer experts; the total worldwide estimate is nearly thirty-five million.[1] There are now more people working in computing than in all of the other fields of engineering and architecture combined. In recent years, "computer people" have become some of our wealthiest citizens, most important business leaders and philanthropists, and most recognized celebrities.

It is likely, however, that unless you yourself are one of these computer people, you have at best a vague notion of what it actually means to work with computers. Even compared to other esoteric scientific or technical disciplines, the work of computer specialists is opaque to outsiders. Their activities are often regarded by nonpractitioners as being at once too difficult and technical to be understood by mere mortals, and too trivial and tedious to be worth the effort. The specialists themselves talk about what they do as being a mysterious blend of art and science, high tech and black magic. Many of the colloquial terms that are frequently used to describe these experts—"hackers," "wizards," "cowboys," or "gurus"—reflect the ambivalent fusion of wonder, awe, and suspicion with which they are generally regarded.[2] That so many of these computer specialists seem unwilling (or unable) to communicate to others what it is they do or how they do it only exacerbates the apparent impenetrability of their discipline.

But while you might not know much about what it is that these computer specialists do, you probably can at least imagine what they look like: the stereotype of the scruffy, bearded, long-haired programmer, wearing (inappropriately) sandals and a T-shirt, has been a staple of popular culture since at least the early 1960s.[3] He (always a he, at least in the stereotype) is usually curt, antisocial, and more concerned with maintaining the integrity of the "system" than in being truly helpful to the end user.[4] So recognized is this stereotype that a high degree of proficiency in computer programming has been linked with mild forms of Asperger's syndrome and autism—the so-called geek syndrome or engineer's disorder.[5] Regardless of the scientific validity of this particular diagnosis, the more general association of computer programming ability with a specific personality type—eccentric, arrogant, and antisocial—has a long and well-established history, and continues to define how computer specialists are seen by their colleagues and contemporaries. The archetype of the modern American "nerd" is no longer the engineer or scientist but rather the computer specialist.[6]

However little you might know (or care) about the habits and character of the computer people, you can at least appreciate their contributions to contemporary society. The products of their labor are everywhere around us. We live in a society that has been so thoroughly computerized that even the most basic human activities involve us in constant interaction with computers and computer-based technologies. Most obvious are the "personal" computers that many of us rely on daily to do our work, help us study, allow us to create and access entertainment, and facilitate communication with friends and family. Less visible, but no less significant, are the millions of other tiny computing devices that lie hidden, embedded within other products and technologies, quietly gathering data, controlling processes, and communicating between components. Your automobile almost certainly has its own computer (in fact, probably several), as does your cell phone, digital camera, and television. Even more intangible are the ways in which the electronic digital computer has transformed how we perceive and interact with our environment. In fields as diverse as molecular biology, anthropology, ecology, physics, cognitive science, economics, and medicine, the electronic digital computer has been widely adopted, not only as a useful tool for gathering and manipulating data, but also as a fundamental metaphor for understanding ourselves and the world around us. In fact, it would be difficult to identify a single aspect of contemporary social, economic, political, or cultural life that has not been profoundly influenced by computers and computer-based technologies—and by extension, the computer specialists who designed and developed these technologies.

Despite their omnipresence in contemporary popular culture and sizable representation in the modern information economy, historians have thus far devoted little attention to these ubiquitous but mysterious computer specialists. There are, of course, whole shelves of books devoted to the small number of inventors and entrepreneurs—Bill Gates, Steve Jobs, and Larry Ellison, in particular—who have managed to translate their computing expertise into fabulous wealth and personal celebrity. There is also considerable literature on the intriguingly subversive subculture of teenage computer hackers. Since the late 1970s, these geeky adolescents have been alternatively hailed as the heroic harbingers of the coming "computer revolution" or castigated as dangerous cyber-criminals.[7] But neither of these groups is representative of the larger computing community. Little has yet been written about the silent majority of computer specialists, the vast armies of largely anonymous engineers, analysts, and programmers who designed and constructed the complex systems that make possible our increasingly computerized society. Even basic demographic information about them can be difficult to come by.

To a certain extent, this curious neglect of the computer people, at least in popular histories of technology, is simply the result of the conventions of the genre. Compared to the celebratory and sensationalized accounts of genius inventors, important "firsts," and machines that "changed the world" that generally dominate such histories, the stories of merely average computer workers would seem at first glance mundane and inconsequential. Even sophisticated academic histories of technology have difficulty incorporating the actions and agendas of nonelite actors, such as end users, operators, maintenance workers, and other "invisible technicians."[8] The stories of such actors are also surprisingly difficult to document: technical specialists and other midlevel laborers rarely leave records, or at least the kind of records that are useful and accessible to historians. And since the community of specialists associated with the computer encompasses a broad and diverse range of occupational categories—from academic computer scientists to corporate computer programmers to machine operators and maintenance workers—they are an especially difficult group about which to generalize. It is not altogether startling, therefore, that many conventional histories of computing focus on easily identifiable pioneers and isolated incidents of technological innovation.

A subtler and more significant explanation for the lack of attention paid to computer specialists has to do with the inherent bias in the traditional emphasis of the history of *computing* on the history of the *computer*. Or to be more specific, on the history of a particular type of computer: the electronic, programmable, digital computer. Most histories of computing begin and for the most part end with the invention of this particular artifact. The development of the first modern electronic computers in the late 1940s is typically regarded as the seminal moment in the birth of the modern information age, the culmination of all the innovations in information technology that preceded it, and the precursor and enabler of all that would come after. Once the electronic computer had embarked on its seemingly inexorable march toward Moore's law—toward ever-smaller, faster, and more affordable computing power—the eventual "computerization" of all of society was both desirable and inevitable.

This focus on the invention and perfection of the technology of electronic computing makes for a clear and compelling narrative, and provides a straightforward and largely technologically determined explanation for the emergence of the electronic computer as the defining technology of the modern era. In doing so, however, it downplays or disregards the contributions of the majority of the computer people. Whatever it is that they really do, the typical computer specialist has almost nothing to do with either the design or construction of actual computers. There are certainly engineers and technicians whose primary responsibility is building computers, but they are an increasingly rare breed, and are generally concentrated in a small number of large and highly specialized computer manufacturers. The vast majority of computer specialists, from the earliest days of commercial computing to the present, spend little time interacting with—and probably understand little about—the inner workings of an electronic computer. Their association with the computer is much more tenuous and abstract. For them, the computer is not the primary object of interest but simply a tool with which to build other tools. In other words, the computer people are mainly concerned with the application of computers (and computer applications), not the computer itself.

To the degree that the history of modern computing has been dominated by the history of the computer as a machine, physical artifact, and tangible "thing," the work of the average computer specialist can indeed be regarded as merely marginal. But from the broader perspective of the history of computerization—of the rise to dominance of the electronic computer as the defining technology of the modern era, our chosen tool for approaching almost every problem, social, economic, and political, and the fundamental metaphor through which we understand ourselves and our environment—then the computer people are those individuals most directly responsible for bringing about what is arguably the most profound social and technological development of our times. They did so not as inventors from the traditional mold but rather as the developers of the software (broadly defined to include programs, procedures, and practices) that integrated the novel technology of electronic computing into existing social, political, and technological networks.

In many respects, it is the history of computer software and not of the computer itself that is at the heart of the larger story of the great computer revolution of the mid- to late twentieth century. What makes the modern electronic digital computer so unique in all the history of technology—so powerful, flexible, and capable of being applied to such an extraordinarily diverse range of purposes—is its ability to be reconfigured, via software, into a seemingly infinite number of devices. In fact, it is this ability to be programmed via software that has come to encapsulate the essence of modern computing: for a contemporary computer scientist, a computer is simply a device that can run a certain kind of software program. Whether that computer is electronic, digital, or even material is irrelevant. What matters is that it is programmable.

From a certain modern perspective, the significance of software seems obvious. Software is what makes a computer useful. Software transforms the latent power of the theoretically general-purpose machine into a specific tool for solving real-world problems. A computer without software is irrelevant, like an automobile without gasoline or a television set without a broadcast signal.[9]

Software is also how most of us experience the computer. Although we might speak casually about "using the computer," as if the computer was a specific, singular type of machine, most of us interact with the computer not as one device but instead as many. Simply by installing new software, we can allow our computer to serve alternatively as an email application, video game console, digital photo album, or electronic diary. It is software that defines our relationship to the computer, software that gives the computer its meaning. We might not know what kind of computer we are using or who manufactured it but we generally know what software we are currently using. Software is the interface between computer and society.

By allowing the computer to be perpetually reinvented for new purposes, users, and social and economic contexts, software has transformed what was originally intended primarily as a special-purpose technology—essentially a glorified electronic calculator—into a "universal machine" that encompasses and supersedes all others, the central metaphor that informs our most fundamental conceptions of ourselves and our environment, and the embodiment and enabler of our highest cultural and political aspirations. Historically speaking, it has been software that defined what a computer was and what it could be used for, software that provided the crucial link between the technology of computing and its larger socioeconomic environment. And so when people talk about the larger process of the computerization of modern society, or speak of the computer revolution transforming the ways in which they work, live, consume, recreate, and engage in social and personal relationships, they are really talking about the history of software.

But what exactly is software? Most of us today tend to think of software as a consumer good, a product, a prepackaged application. We purchase (or download) a copy of Microsoft Word, Mozilla Firefox, or World of Warcraft; install it; and use it. In this sense, software resembles other, more familiar mass-market manufactured goods: someone, somewhere, produces some computer code, and that computer code in turn transforms, temporarily, your computer into a word processor, Web browser, or a gateway into the mythical world of Azeroth. Software, in this context, is simply the set of instructions or "code" that controls your computer—plus, perhaps, the physical media on which those instructions are encoded (a CD or DVD, for example), and possibly the printed manual that accompanied it.

Historically speaking, however, software was not something that was purchased off-the-shelf, nor was it a single application or product. Rather, it was a bundle of systems, services, and support.[10] When a firm in the 1950s wanted to computerize its accounting operations, for example, the software that it had to develop included not only computer code but also an analysis of existing operations, the reorganization of procedures and personnel, the training of users, the construction of peripheral support tools and technologies, and the production of new manuals and other documents.[11] The concept of software encompassed all of these meanings and more. It was not until the late 1960s that software became a product that could be purchased separately from a computer, and even then software as code represented only a small component of a larger software system of services and support. To this day, the vast majority of software is custom produced for individual corporations in a process that resembles more the hiring of a management consulting firm than the purchase of a mass-market consumer good.[12]

Although the idea of software is central to our modern conception of the computer as a universal machine, defining exactly what software is can be surprisingly difficult. It was not until more than a decade after the development of the first electronic computers that the statistician John Tukey first applied the word software to those elements of a typical computer installation that were not obviously "tubes, transistors, wires, tapes and the like."[13] Although Tukey clearly intended these other elements to include primarily computer code, by defining software in strictly negative terms—software was everything not explicitly understood to be hardware—he left open the possibility of a broader understanding of software that would quickly be adopted throughout the nascent computing community. For example, just a few years later the head of the newly established University of Michigan Computing Center declared that software was essentially everything associated with computing that wasn't the computer: for the user of the center, "the total computing facility provided for his use, other than the hardware, is the software."[14] The implication was that most users could not or did not distinguish between the elements of the software system: tools, applications, personnel, and procedures were all considered essential elements of the software experience.[15] By the end of the decade the term had been expanded even further to include documentation, development methodologies, user training, and consulting services.[16] In this broader conception of software, the true complexity of software development as a human activity becomes apparent. Unlike hardware, which is almost by definition a tangible thing that can readily be isolated, identified, and evaluated, software is inextricably intertwined with the larger sociotechnical system of computing that includes machines (computers and their associated peripherals), people (users, designers, and developers), and processes (the corporate payroll system, for example). In this sense, software is an ideal illustration of what the historians and sociologists of technology call a sociotechnical system: that is to say, a system in which machines, people, and processes are inextricably interconnected and interdependent. As the sociologist John Law has suggested, the "heterogeneous engineering" required to assemble such complex systems blurs the boundaries between the technological and organizational, and typically creates a process fraught with conflict, negotiation, disputes over professional authority, and the conflation of social, political, and technological agendas.[17] Nowhere is this more true than in the history of software.

Software is perhaps the ultimate heterogeneous technology. It exists simultaneously as an idea, language, technology, and practice. Although intimately associated with the computer, it also clearly transcends it. For the most part software is invisible, ethereal, and ephemeral—and yet it is also obviously constructed. Certain aspects of software, such as a sorting algorithm, can be generalized and formalized as mathematical abstractions, while others remain inescapably local and specific, subject to the particular constraints imposed by corporate culture, informal industry standards, or government regulations. In this sense, software sits uncomfortably at the intersection of science, engineering, and business. Software is where the technology of computing meets social relationships, organizational politics, and personal agendas. All technologies are to a certain extent social constructions, but in the case of software, the social dimensions of technology are particularly apparent.

Consider, for example, the aforementioned computerized accounting system. Much of the process of computerizing the accounting department happened without any reference to an actual computer. The vast majority of the work involved documentation and analysis: the crucial step in designing the new system was understanding the old one, and then modifying it to fit the requirements of the new computing mentality. Existing processes needed to be studied, charted, and analyzed. Clerical workers had to be interviewed, accounting experts consulted, and departmental managers informed and placated. Reports needed to be written, flowcharts constructed, and product specifications developed. The translation of established work flow into terms that could be understood or implemented by a computer generally required the modification of related systems and practices. Often entire departments would need to be restructured to accommodate the new procedures.

Only after all this study and analysis could the design of the software even be considered. And since the development of new software frequently required the purchase of new hardware and peripherals, another set of actors—vendors, sales engineers, and technicians—would have to be brought in. After the software design architecture had been established, it would be turned over to the programmers. Although programming is usually thought of in terms of the translation of a design architecture into the coded language that a computer could understand, in fact, most programs were written in a higher-level language that a *human* could understand. Only later would this human-readable program be compiled into a lower-lever machine language meant only for a computer. Once these various versions of the code were written and compiled, the software application would still need to be installed, tested, and debugged. At each step a different set of users, experts, and technicians would be involved.

After the software had been tested and debugged (and possibly redesigned and reprogrammed), another series of documents—user manuals, training materials, and marketing materials—would have to be developed. Everyone involved in the accounting system, including not only those who interacted directly with the computerized system, such machine operators and clerical staff, but also higher-level managers or those members of other departments who needed to engage with or at least understand the new system, would have to be trained. The system would also have to be "operated" (a function that would eventually be taken over by yet another piece of software, called an operating system). Finally, the software would need to be continuously maintained—not because the software application would "break" but because the context in which it was used, or the other systems that it interacted with, included such nontechnical systems as corporate accounting policies and governmental regulations, would change over time. As much as two-thirds of the cost of a software system was incurred *after* the software was developed and operational.[18]

Viewed from this historical perspective, it is easy to see the significance of software in the history of computing. Software was an ever-expanding category that grew not only in size and scale but also in scope. As the nuts and bolts of computer hardware became faster, more reliable, and less expensive—and therefore increasingly invisible to the end user—the relative importance of software became even more pronounced.[19] In effect, for most organizations, by the end of the 1960s software had become the computer: software, rather than the computer, had become the focus of all discussion, debate, and dissension within the computing community.

The heterogeneity of software, its inherent messiness, and permeability, are everywhere apparent in the historical documents. Compared to the history of computer hardware, which is characterized by regular and remarkable progress, the history of software is replete with tension, conflict, failure, and disillusionment. The first commercial computers had been out for only a few years when the availability of useful and reliable software was identified as one of the critical bottlenecks hindering the expansion of the industry.[20] Unlike computer hardware, which was constantly becoming smaller, faster, and cheaper, software always seemed to be getting more expensive and less reliable. By the early 1960s industry observers and corporate managers increasingly warned against a growing "software gap" as well as a sense of "frustration," "disenchantment," and "disillusionment" with electronic computing provoked by problems associated with the rising costs of software development.[21] By the end of the decade many were talking openly of a looming software crisis that threatened the health and future of the entire commercial computer industry. For the next several decades, corporate managers, academic computer scientists, and government officials would release ominous warnings about the desperate state of the software industry with almost ritualistic regularity.[22] In fact, what is most striking about much of the literature from the supposed Golden Age of the computer revolution is how contentious it is, how fraught with anger and anxiety. In an industry characterized by rapid change and innovation, the rhetoric of the software crisis has proven remarkably persistent. The Y2K crisis, the H1-B visa debates, and recent concerns about the loss of programming jobs to India and Pakistan are only the most recent manifestations of the industry's apparent predilection for apocalyptic rhetoric.

To many observers of the computer industry, reconciling the two dominant but opposing views of the history of computing—the glorious history of computer hardware and the dismal history of computer software—often has been difficult, if not impossible. The seeming paradox between the inevitable progress promised by Moore's Law and the perpetual crisis in software production challenges conventional assumptions about the progressive nature of computer technology. This is perhaps the most significant lessons to be learned from the history of software: *There is no Moore's Law for software technology.* But the real problem with software is not so much that it is "hard" (as computer scientist Donald Knuth famously declared) but rather that it is inherently contested; the problem was generally not that the software itself did not work but instead that the work that it did do turned out to have undesirable side effects for the organizations that used them.[23] Computerization projects created "unusual internal implications," "placed stress on established organizational relationships," and demanded "skills not provided by the previous experience of people assigned to the task."[24] Such projects generally crossed organizational boundaries and disrupted existing hierarchies and power relationships. Information technology, as Thomas Whisler observed, tended to "shift and scramble the power structure of organizations among the various functional departments."[25] What might on the surface appear to be disagreements about the particular technical challenges associated with software development were in reality local disputes about organizational power and authority and, more significant for this purposes of this book, about the peculiar character of the people involved with software development. Ostensibly debates about the "one best way" to manage a software development project, they were in fact a series of highly contested social negotiations about the role of electronic computing—and computing professionals— in modern corporate and academic organizations.

This is a book about the history of software, and the intersection between the history of software and the larger social history of the computer revolution of the mid- to late twentieth century. It is a book about how software gets made, why, and for what purposes. Of particular concern is the series of software crises that plagued the computer industry throughout its early history, and the way in which these crises highlight the heterogeneous nature of software development. Rather than treating the software crises as a well-defined and universally understood phenomenon, as they are usually assumed to be in the industry and historical literature, this book considers them as socially constructed historical artifacts. It interprets debates about the core problems facing the software industry—and more important, claims about how it could best be resolved—within the larger context of the struggle for control over organization power and occupational authority. Specific claims about the nature and extent of the crisis can be used as a lens through which to examine broader issues in the history of software—and from there, the larger social history of computing. As with all crises, the software crisis can be used to reveal the hidden fault lines within a community: points of tension between groups or individuals, differing perceptions of reality or visions for the future, and subtle hierarchies and structures of power relationships.

The focus of the book is on the consultants, analysts, programmers, operators, and other technical specialists who build software, and the ways in which these specialists constructed for themselves a unique occupational identity based on their control over the nascent technology of electronic computing. Earlier in this book these specialists were referred to as computer people; from here on out, they will be called by the name given to them by their contemporaries: namely, the "computer boys." This was in part a term of endearment, in part a disparagement, and in either case, a fairly accurate representation of who these people were: young, male, and technologically inclined. This is not to say that there were not many female computer specialists. In fact, the computing professions, at least in the early decades of commercial computing, were surprisingly accepting of women. It was only later that the computing occupations became highly masculinized. This book tells a portion of that story.

The book traces the history of the computer boys as they struggled to establish a role for themselves within traditional organizational, professional, and academic hierarchies. It focuses on the tensions that emerged between the craft-centered practices of vocational programmers, the increasingly theoretical agenda of academic computer science, and the desire of corporate managers to control and routinize the process of software development. It describes the ways in which conflicts within the computing community played out in the development of professional societies, programming languages, computer science curricula, and corporate training and recruitment programs. Seen from this perspective, what are dismissed as merely internal debates about the technical features of programming languages, the inclusion of a specific course in a computer science curriculum, or the imposition of software engineering methodologies for managing development projects are revealed rather as strategic moves in this negotiation over professional status and identity.

A central theme of the book is that computer specialists possessed skills and abilities that transcended existing boundaries between scientific, technical, and business expertise. As the electronic computer moved out of the laboratory and into the marketplace, it became an increasingly valuable source of professional and institutional power and authority. In their role as mediators between the technical system (the computer) and its social environment (existing structures and practices), computer programmers played a crucial role in transforming the computer from a scientific instrument into a powerful tool for corporate control and communication. As such, they also served as a focus for opposition to and criticism of the use of new information technologies. To many observers of the computer revolution of the mid-twentieth century, it seemed as if the computer boys were taking over—not just in the corporate setting but also in government, politics, and society in general.[26]

By virtue of their control over the powerful new technology of electronic computing, however, computer specialists were granted an unprecedented degree of independence and authority. Their work brought them into conflict with established networks of power and authority. This was particularly true in the corporate environment, where the incorporation of new forms of information technology "placed stresses on established organizational relationships."[27] The systems they developed often replaced, or at least substantially altered, the work of traditional white-collar employees.[28] As the computer transformed from a tool *to be* managed into a tool *for* management, computer specialists emerged as powerful "change agents" (to use the management terminology of the era). Faced with this perceived challenge to their occupational territory, traditional white-collar employees attempted to reassert their control over corporate computerization efforts. The result was a highly charged struggle over the proper place of the programmer in traditional occupational and professional hierarchies.

Finally, this is book about the invention of the computer user. Historians have long suggested that technological innovators, including the designers of electronic computers, also invent the kind of people they expect to use their innovations.[29] The two acts of invention are in fact inseparable: assumptions made about who will be using a technology, how, and for what purposes inevitably influence its eventual design. This means that the invention of the user, like the invention of the technology itself, is a highly contested social process involving conflict and negotiation. The emergence and transformation of the computer boys as the dominant group of computer users provides a fascinating glimpse into the social and cultural history of the computer, the development of technical communities and distinctive subcultures, the relationship between science and craft in engineering practice, and the role of technical elites in modern corporate hierarchies. These are central research agendas in the labor history, business history, and the history of technology to which we as historians of computing are well suited to contribute.

Note that the principal group of computer specialists who this book deals with is computer programmers. Programmers were not, of course, the only computer boys attempting to lay claim to the professional status and authority conveyed by the electronic computer. Systems analysts, operations researchers, management consultants, and data processing specialists, among others, were all associated with the emergence of the nascent technology. In many respects, the term computer boys came to refer more generally not simply to actual computer specialists but rather to the whole host of smart, ambitious, and technologically inclined experts that emerged in the immediate postwar period. But computer programmers were the original and exemplary computer boys, and the term programmer was applied by contemporaries to the entire range of specialists involved with computing in this period. As much as the various computer specialists themselves worked to differentiate themselves from each other—systems analysts usually saw themselves as being distinct from programmers, and many academic computer scientists had no time at all for occupational programmers—they were generally all lumped together by outsiders as programmers.[30]

A Brief History of Programming

The story of the computer boys begins, intriguingly enough, with a group of women. These women, generally referred to by contemporaries as the Electronic Numerical Integrator and Computer (ENIAC) "girls"—were female "human computers" recruited by the male ENIAC engineers/ managers to "setup" the general-purpose ENIAC machine to perform specific "plans of computation." The ENIAC, which was the most widely publicized of the wartime experiments in electronic computing, contained many (but not all) of the architectural elements of the modern computer: it was digital, electronic, and programmable. And so although the idea of the computer program had not yet been developed, the women of ENIAC are nevertheless widely celebrated as the world's earliest computer programmers.

It is no coincidence that the first software workers were women. The use of the word software in this context is, of course, anachronistic—the word itself would not be introduced until 1958—but the hierarchical distinctions and gender connotations it embodies—between "hard" technical mastery, and the "softer," more social (and implicitly, of secondary importance) aspects of computer work—are applicable even in the earliest of electronic computing development projects.[31] In the status hierarchy of the ENIAC project, it was clearly the male computer engineers who were significant. The ENIAC women, the computer programmers, as they would later be known, were expected to simply adapt the plans of computation already widely used in human computing projects to the new technology of the electronic computer. These plans of computation were themselves highly gendered, having been traditionally developed by women for women (human computing had been largely feminized by the 1940s). The ENIAC women would simply set up the machine to perform these predetermined plans; that this work would turn out to be difficult and require radically innovative thinking was completely unanticipated.[32] The telephone switchboardlike appearance of the ENIAC programming cable-and-plug panels reinforced the notion that programmers were mere machine operators, that programming was more handicraft than science, more feminine than masculine, more mechanical than intellectual.

The idea that the development of hardware was the real business of computing, and that software was at best secondary, persisted throughout the 1940s and early 1950s. In the first textbooks on computing published in the United States, for example, John von Neumann and Herman Goldstine outlined a clear division of labor in computing—presumably based on their experience with the ENIAC project—that clearly distinguished between the headwork of the (male) scientist or "planner," and the handwork of the (largely female) "coder." In the von Neumann and Goldstine schema, the planner did the intellectual work of analysis and the coder simply translated this work into a form that a computer could understand. Coding was, according to von Neumann and Goldstine, a "static" process—one that could be performed by a low-level clerical worker. Coding implied manual labor, and mechanical translation or rote transcription; coders were obviously low on the intellectual and professional status hierarchy. It was not unreasonable to expect that as was the case in the ENIAC project, most of these coders would be women.

To the surprise of engineers and managers at the ENIAC and other wartime computing projects, however, programming turned out to be much more difficult, time-consuming, and expensive than had originally been imagined. What had been expected to be a straightforward process of coding an algorithm turned out to involve many layers of analysis, planning, testing, and debugging. For many, this unanticipated and unwelcome divergence between expectation and reality was already a crisis in the making. For others, the discovery of the hidden complexities posed a stimulating intellectual challenge. For the computer scientist Maurice Wilkes (one of the authors of the first computer programming textbook), it was a little bit of both. "It had not occurred to me that there was going to be any difficulty about getting programs working,"

Wilkes recalls of his experience programming the EDSAC (Electronic Delay Storage Automatic Calculator—arguably the world's first electronic, digital stored-program computer). "And it was with somewhat of a shock that I realized that for the rest of my life I was going to spend a good deal of my time finding mistakes that I had made in my programs."[33]

Wilkes might have been one of the first to recognize the inherent difficulties of computer programming, but he was hardly the last. Particularly in the pioneering electronic computing projects of the late 1940s and early 1950s, involving as they did custom-built prototype machines that were highly idiosyncratic and unreliable, programmers were required to be at the same time scientists and tinkerers. Many of these early programmers were in fact migrants from scientific and engineering disciplines. They acquired a reputation as being both geniuses and mavericks; as John Backus, the inventor of the FORTRAN programming language later described this period, programming in the 1950s was "a black art, a private arcane matter . . . in which the success of a program depended primarily on the programmer's private techniques and inventions."[34] This reputation would later come back to haunt the industry: the need to transform the black art of programming into the "science" of software engineering became a major theme of the software crisis rhetoric of the next several decades.

In the meantime, the computer itself was gradually being reinvented as a business technology. The focus of electronic computing shifted from scientific and military agendas (which emphasized mathematics and highly optimized code) to electronic data processing (EDP) and information management (in which more commercial considerations of cost, reliability, generality, and the availability of peripherals dominated). As general-purpose electronic computers became less expensive, more reliable, and better integrated into existing business processes and information technology systems, they were adopted by a larger and more diverse range of companies. Most of these companies did not possess large engineering or even data processing departments, making the availability of high-quality applications programs and systems tools even more essential (and conversely, their deficiencies even more noticeable). At the same time, the scale and scope of computerization projects increased dramatically. Whereas the first generation of commercial computers were generally used to replicate existing data processing applications, by the 1950s computers were being used for less familiar and more ambitious purposes, such as management planning and control.

Prior to the invention of the electronic digital computer, information processing in the corporation had largely been handled by conventional clerical staffs and traditional office managers. There had been attempts by aspiring "systems managers" to leverage expertise in the technical and bureaucratic aspects of administration into a broader claim to authority over the design of elaborate, custom information-processing systems.[35] In certain cases, strong-willed executives were able to use information technology to consolidate control over lower levels of the organizational hierarchy. For the most part, however, the use of such technologies did not contribute to the rise of a class of technical professionals capable of challenging the power of traditional management.[36]

As more and more corporations began to integrate electronic computers into their data processing operations, however, it became increasingly clear that this new technology threatened the stability of the established managerial hierarchy. Early commercial computers were large, expensive, and complex technologies that required a high level of technical competence to operate effectively. Many nontechnical managers who had adapted readily to other innovations in office technology, such as complicated filing systems and tabulating machinery, were intimidated by computers—and computer specialists. Many of them granted their computer specialists an unprecedented degree of independence and authority. The increasing centrality of the electronic computer to the economic, social, and political life of industrialized nations also started to raise profound questions about the qualifications of computer workers. Who were these computer boys who were not just processing the payroll but also radically reshaping organizations? Despite their relatively low status in the managerial hierarchy, they seemed to exert an undue degree of power and autonomy. What were their qualifications? They were increasingly responsible for constructing systems that were increasingly mission and safety critical. But who were these people? Were they scientists, engineers, or technicians? Should they be required to be college educated, certified by the state, or members of a professional society?

The "Labor Crisis" in Programming

One of the immediate implications of this transformation and expansion of commercial computing was a sharp increase in the demand for business programmers. At the first-ever Conference on Training Personnel for the Computing Machine Field, held at Wayne State University in 1956, industry observers warned of an imminent shortage of the kinds of programmers required by the rapidly expanding EDP industry: "The development of these machines is resulting in even greater recognition of, and paying a greater premium for, the man who is above average in training and mental ability."[37] By 1961, industry journals such as *Datamation* were using crisis rhetoric to describe the looming "programming gap" that threatened the "bright and rosy future" of the industry.[38] A year later, Daniel McCracken talked about the "software turmoil" that threatened to set back the industry. By the mid-1960s, it was widely estimated that there were at least a hundred thousand people working as programmers in the United States alone, with an expected immediate demand for at least fifty thousand more. "Competition for programmers has driven salaries up so fast," warned a contemporary article in *Fortune* magazine, "that programming has become probably the country's highest paid technological occupation. . . . Even so, some companies can't find experienced programmers at any price."[39]

The burgeoning information technology labor shortage of the late 1950s (to apply yet another contemporary term anachronistically) was complicated by the general lack of consensus about what skills and characteristics were required of a good programmer. The problem was not just simply that demand for programmers far outstripped supply. In fact, numerous attempts to ramp up the supply of programmers, either through in-house training programs, private vocational training schools, or academic computer science programs, generally failed to alleviate the growing crisis. A 1968 study by the Association for Computing Machinery (ACM) Special Interest Group on Computer Personnel Research (SIGCPR) warned of a growing *oversupply* of computer personnel: "The ranks of the computer world are being swelled by growing hordes of programmers, systems analysts and related personnel. Educational, performance and professional standards are virtually nonexistent and confusion growths rampant in selecting, training, and assigning people to do jobs."[40] In part this critique reflects the immaturity of the industry, and the lack of established institutions for educating and certifying programmers. That similar critiques have continued to plague the industry to this day suggest a deeper structural problem worth exploring. As with various other iterations of information technology labor shortages (past and present), the problem was not so much an absolute shortage of programmers but rather a shortage of a *particular kind of programmer*. What this particular kind of programmer might look like—what skills they need to possess, what level of professionalism they aspire to, what wages they require, and how willing they are to conform to the managerial goals of the corporation—is the real question underlying many of these debates about labor shortages and other programmer personnel crises.

One of the perennial problems facing the computer industry, in the 1950s and 1960s as well as the present, was defining precisely what characteristics or training made for a good computer programmer. As was mentioned earlier, programming was frequently seen as a black art whose success or failure was dependent on the idiosyncratic abilities of individual programmers. This notion was reinforced by a series of aptitude tests and personality profiles that suggested that computer programmers, like chess masters or virtuoso musicians, were endowed with a uniquely creative ability. Great disparities were discovered between the productivity of individual programmers. "When a programmer is good, he is very, very good. But when he is bad, he is horrid," declared one widely quoted IBM study of programmer performance.[41] The same study introduced the meme—which despite the original study's serious methodological limitations and a general paucity of follow-up empirical research, continues to be repeated—that a good programmer was at least twenty-five times more efficient than his or her merely average colleague. Whether the exact ratio of performance was precisely twenty-five to one (or a hundred to one—another commonly quoted figure) did not much matter. What did matter is that whatever its deficiencies, this study and others seemed to confirm plentiful anecdotal evidence that good programmers appeared to have been "born, not made."[42]

It should be noted that computer programming is not by any means the only technical occupation in which elements of both art and science are seen as being inextricably intertwined. There is a large literature in the history of science and technology that describes the role of intuition, tacit knowledge, and craft technique in many technical industries.[43] Computer work is different in the degree to which this blurry boundary is perceived to be a central contributing factor to an ongoing crisis.

The administrative and managerial problems associated with finding and keeping the "right" programmers was complicated by both the newness of the discipline and the extent and duration of the early computer revolution. The nascent computing professions were so pressed for resources that they had little time to construct the institutional framework required to produce and regulate software development. Almost from their very origins university computer science programs were criticized as being too theoretical in focus, too concerned with "playing games, making fancy programs that really do not work, [and] writing trick programs" to "discipline their own efforts so that what they say they will do gets done on time and in practical form."[44] In fact, this focus on theory served computer science well as a disciplinary strategy in the modern research university; if it did not satisfactorily meet the needs of industry, then so be it. Professional certification programs run by the professional societies—such as the Certified Data Processor (CDP) program offered by the National Machine Accounting Association (NMAA, or later the Data Processing Management Association, or DPMA)—also proved unsatisfactory for various reasons.[45] The computer programming business appeared to many to be a free-for-all in which "anyone with ten dollars can join the ACM and proclaim himself a professional computer expert."[46] The competing pressures to regulate the industry while at the same providing enough programmers to meet constantly growing demand proved difficult to balance.

Perhaps the most important reason why the "personnel problem" dominated the industry literature during the late 1950s and early 1960s has to do with a fundamental structural change in the nature of software development. It was clear to most observers during this period that not only were many more programmers required to meet the demands of a rapidly expanding industry but also that the type and range of skills required of programmers had changed and expanded dramatically. The mathematical training essential for scientific programming was seen as being increasingly irrelevant in the business context, which stressed the application of specific knowledge, training in systems analysis, and the ability to work well with others. New programming languages were developed that highlighted the specific needs of corporate programmers: legibility, ease of use, continuity with older data processing systems (as was the case with RPG), and the ability to be read and understood by corporate managers (an ostensible selling point of COBOL, for example).

A Crisis in Programmer Management

The increasingly widespread use of the word software—which as we have seen, included not only computer code but also the tools and processes used to create it—emphasized the systemic dimensions of computerization projects. Describing the products of computerization as software—as opposed to applications or programs, for instance—implied a much larger organizational role for computer personnel. As Willis Ware argued in a 1965 editorial in the trade journal *Datamation*, "It is clear that only a part—perhaps a small part, at that—of the programming process is involved with actually using a language for writing routines." And since the rest of the work involved required "intellectual activity, mathematical investigation [and] discussions between people," Ware maintained, there was no easy fix to the programming problem. "All the programming language improvement in the world will not shorten the intellectual activity, the thinking, the analysis, that is inherent in the programming process."[47] Many companies did attempt to formally differentiate between programming tasks and systems analysis, but in practice these distinctions proved difficult to maintain.[48]

The merging of computer programming into systems analysis aggravated the training and personnel problems of many corporations. The principle difficulty, contended Daniel McCracken, "seems to be that systems work is not so much a body of factual knowledge, as an approach to problem solving—and no one knows how to teach the problem solving approach." Perhaps even more than programming ability, the skills associated with systems analysis were difficult to teach: "All that we seem to be able to do is let the coder work with an experienced systems man, and hope that some of the skills get transferred by osmosis."[49] At the least they were clearly not easy to replicate on the scale required by the growing industry.

The increasing inclusion of computer personnel as active participants in all phases of software development, from design to implementation, brought them into increasing contact—and conflict—with other corporate employees. As software projects expanded in scope to encompass not only traditional data processing applications (payroll, for example) but also management and control, computer personnel began to encroach on the domains of operational managers. These managers resented the perceived impositions of the computer boys, regarding them as threats to their occupational status and authority.[50]

The growing use of computerized "management information systems" corresponded with a general shift in management practices in the postwar period. The Second World War had produced a series of "management sciences"—including operations research, game theory, and systems analysis—all of which offered a mathematical, scientific approach to business management. Many of this new breed of management consultants were already familiar with the computer from their experience with the military and pushed heavily for information technological solutions to perceived management problems. And because these computer-based solutions were extremely capital intensive, they were generally pitched to and approved by high-level executives—in many cases without any input from the midlevel managers whose work would be most affected by their implementation.

The combination of "professional management" and computerized management systems threatened to remove power from the hands of local managers. In a widely cited 1958 article in the *Harvard Management Review*, Harold Leavitt and Thomas Whisler predicted that within thirty years, the combination of management science and information technology would decimate the ranks of middle management and lead to the centralization of managerial control.[51] Whisler would later suggest that EDP specialists were the direct beneficiaries of such centralization, which occurred at the expense of traditional managers. He quoted one insurance executive who claimed that "there has actually been a lateral shift to the EDP manager of decision-making from other department managers whose departments have been computerized."[52] Or as one Wharton MBA graduate warned his colleagues in a 1965 article, "As the EDP group takes on the role of a corporate service organization, able to cut across organizational lines, a revolution in the organizational power structure is bound to occur."[53] In a 1971 book describing *How Computers Affect Management*, Rosemary Stewart argued how computer specialists mobilized the mystery of their technology to "impinge directly on a manager's job and be a threat to his security or status."[54]

In addition to this direct threat to their occupational authority, traditional managers had other reasons to resent EDP specialists. "Computer people tend to be young, mobile, and quantitatively oriented, and look to their peers both for company and for approval" suggested a 1969 *Fortune* article explaining why "Computers Can't Solve Everything": "Managers, on the other hand, are typically older and tend to regard computer people either as mere technicians or as threats to their position and status."[55] As the persistent demand for qualified computer personnel pushed up salaries and created considerable opportunities for occupation mobility, computer personnel acquired a reputation—deserved or otherwise—for being flighty, arrogant, and lacking in corporate loyalty.

As might be expected, the perceived impositions of the computer boys prompted a determined response from midlevel managers. By the end of the 1960s the management literature was full of reports of a growing crisis in "software management." An influential 1968 report by McKinsey and Company suggested that most computer installations were unprofitable—not because the technology was not effective but rather because "many otherwise effective top managements . . . have abdicated control to staff specialists—good technicians who have neither the operation experience to know the jobs that need doing nor the authority to get them done right."[56] The secret to "unlocking the computer's profit potential," according to the McKinsey report, was to restore the proper balance between managers and programmers: "Only managers can manage the computer in the best interests of the business. The companies that take this lesson to heart today will be the computer profit leaders of tomorrow."[57] The combination of new software development methodologies and stricter administrative controls promised to eliminate management's dangerous dependency on individual programmers.

By accusing computer specialists of being self-interested peddlers of "whiz-bang" technologies, or referring to electronic data processing as "the biggest rip-off that has been perpetrated on business, industry, and government over the past 20 years," managers were as much playing organizational politics as they were responding to any real crisis.[58] In their representation of programmers as shortsighted, self-serving technicians, managers reinforced the notion that they were ill equipped to handle big picture, mission-critical responsibilities. By redefining contemporary understandings of the nature and causes of the software crisis, turning the focus of debate away from "finding and caring for good programmers," and squarely toward the problem of programmer management, the McKinsey report (among many others) also relocated the focus of its solution, removing it from the domain of the computer specialist and placing it firmly in the hands of traditional managers.[59]

The growing management frustration with software systems cannot, of course, be attributed solely to organizational politics. There is no question that in this same period the costs of software increased dramatically. In the internal language of the discipline, an "inversion in the hardware-software cost ratio curve" occurred in the mid-1960s that clearly demanded a managerial response.[60] Put more simply, the cost of the actual computers went down at the same time that the cost of using them (developing and maintaining software) went up. By the middle of the decade the expenses associated with commercial data processing were dominated by software maintenance and programmer labor rather than equipment purchases. And since the management of labor fell under the traditional domain of the midlevel manager, these managers quickly developed a deep interest in the art of software development.

At the same time that the costs of software were visibly rising, a series of highly public software disasters—the software-related destruction of the Mariner I spacecraft, the IBM OS/360 debacle, and a devastating criticism of contemporary EDP practices published by McKinsey and Company—lent credence to the popular belief that an industry-wide software crisis was imminent. The industry literature from this period is rife with scandals, complaints, laments, and self-recriminations.

This all suggests that by the mid-1960s, the rhetoric of crisis became firmly entrenched in the vernacular of commercial computing. All of the elements of the subsequent debates had been articulated: a widespread critique of the artisanal practices of programmers; the growing tension between the personnel demands of industry employers and the academic agenda of university computer science departments; emerging turf battles between technical experts and traditional corporate managers; and a shared perception that software was becoming increasingly expensive, expansive, influential, and out of control. The culmination of this period of tension was the 1968 North Atlantic Treaty Organization (NATO) Conference on Software Engineering, widely regarded as one of the seminal moments in the history of modern software development.[61] By defining the software crisis in terms of the discipline of software engineering, the NATO conference set an agenda that influenced many of the technological, managerial, and professional developments in commercial computing for the next several decades. In the interest of efficient software manufacturing, the black art of programming had to make way for the science of software engineering.

The NATO conference has achieved almost mythical status in the literature on software development. Not only did it deeply imprint the discourse of software crisis on the consciousness of both the computer industry and the broader public; it also introduced a compelling solution. The general consensus among historians and practitioners alike is that the NATO meeting marked "a major cultural shift" in the computing community, the moment when computer programming "started to make the transition from being a craft for a long-haired programming priesthood to becoming a real engineering discipline."[62] The call to integrate "good engineering principles" into the software development process has been the rallying cry of software developers from the late 1960s to the present.[63] By defining the software crisis in terms of the discipline of software engineering, the NATO conference set an agenda that substantially influenced many of the technological, managerial, and professional developments in commercial computing for the next several decades.

And yet, despite the consensus reached at the NATO conference, the crisis continued to rage on. Although the specifics varied over time, the core issues remained the same: a perceived shortage of a certain type of "qualified" programmer; calls to replace "pseudo-artists [programmers] by engineers and to treat programming as a normal branch of engineering"; and rising costs and increased incidence of failure.[64] In 1987, the editors of *Computerworld* complained that "the average software project is often one year behind plan and 100% over budget."[65] Two years later the House Committee on Science, Space, and Technology released a report highly critical of the "shoot-from-the-hip" culture of the software industry. Later that same year the Pentagon launched a broad campaign to "lick its software problems" that included funds for a Software Engineering Institute and the widespread adoption of the ADA programming language.[66] The list of critical reports, denunciations of contemporary methodologies, and proposed silver bullet solutions continued to grow. And yet, in the words of one industry observer, by the mid-1980s "the software crisis has become less a turning point than a way of life."[67] In the late 1990s the Y2K crisis called new public attention to this long-standing debate; in many respects, however, it added little to an already-established discourse. It is a rare article on software engineering that does not make at least a token reference to the ongoing crisis. The legacy of the past continues to shape the possibilities of the future.

Computing as a Human Activity

It is tempting, from the vantage point of the early twenty-first century, to view the widespread adoption of the electronic computer as an uncomplicated and technologically determined process, driven by the growing informational demands of modern scientific, corporate, and governmental organizations along with the obvious superiority of the general-purpose, programmable digital computer as a tool for managing and manipulating information. Indeed, from a modern perspective, it is difficult to imagine a more obviously useful and desirable technology. The inherently protean nature of the electronic computer—its ability to be easily reconfigured, via software, to accomplish an almost infinite number of applications—combined with regular and impressive improvements in the underlying hardware makes the computerization of modern society seem, in retrospect, overdetermined, almost inevitable.

But like all great social and technological innovations, the computer revolution of the previous century didn't just happen. It had to be made to happen, and it had to be made to happen by individual people, not impersonal processes. One of the most significant and lasting insights of recent scholarship in the history of technology is that technological innovation is as much driven by social processes as by inherent technological imperatives. That is to say, there is never a single, ideal type toward which any given technology will inevitably evolve. Specific technologies are developed to solve specific problems, for specific users, in specific times and places. How certain problems get defined as being most in need of a solution, which users are considered most important to design for, what other technological systems need to be provided or accounted for, who has the power to set certain technical and economic priorities—these are fundamentally social considerations that deeply influence the process of technological development. Nowhere are the social dimensions of technological development more apparent than in the history of computing.

If we take seriously the notion, foundational to the history of technology, that the things that human beings build matter—that the vast technological systems that we construct to understand and manipulate our environment both reflect our social, economic, and political values, and constrain them—then it is absolutely essential that we understand how these systems get built, by whom, and for what purposes. If there was indeed a computer revolution of the mid- to late twentieth century, then computer specialists were its primary revolutionaries; it behooves us, therefore, to understand something about who they were and what they hoped to accomplish.

2

The Black Art of Programming

When a programmer is good, he is very, very good. But when he is bad, he is horrid.
—IBM study on programmer performance, 1968

An Unexpected Revolution

One of the great myths of the computer revolution is that nobody saw it coming—particularly not the so-called computer experts. In one widely repeated but apocryphal anecdote, Thomas Watson, the legendary founder and longtime chair of the IBM Corporation, is said to have predicted as late as 1943 a total world market for "maybe five computers." The story of this wildly inaccurate forecast, alternatively attributed to Watson, the Harvard professor and computing pioneer Howard Aiken, or the Cambridge professor of computer science Douglas Hartree, among others, is generally mobilized as a kind of modern morality play, a cautionary tale about the dangers of underestimating the power and rapidity of technological progress.[1] Similar tales (similarly apocryphal) are told about a series of unimaginative computer industry executives—from Digital Equipment Corporation's Ken Olsen to Microsoft's Bill Gates—whose alleged lack of imagination prevented them from fully appreciating the transformative potential of computer technology. Such stories are a staple of popular histories of the electronic computer, which generally privilege dramatic change—sudden, unanticipated, and inexorable—over continuity.

In reality, many of the predictions made by contemporaries about the revolutionary potential of the electronic computer were, if anything, wildly optimistic. Almost before there were any computers—functional, modern, electronic digital stored-program computers—enthusiasts for the new technology were confidently anticipating its influence on contemporary society. As early as 1948 the cybernetician Norbert Wiener was predicting a "second industrial revolution" enabled by the electronic computer.[2] A year later, the computer consultant Edmund Berkeley, in his popular book *Giant Brains; or, Machines That Think*, described a near future in which computers radically transformed a broad range of human cognitive and occupational activities, including business, law, education, and medicine.[3] Despite the fact that electronic computers were in this period little more than glorified calculating machines, the provocative image of the computer as a "giant" or "mechanical brain" quickly became established in the popular imagination. Within just a few years of the introduction of the first commercial electronic computers, even mass-market publications like *Time* and *Newsweek* were predicting the use of computers in wide variety of commercial and scientific applications. Indeed, as Stephen Schnaars and Sergio Carvalho have recently suggested, far from underestimating its potential, during the 1950s the press in the United States "fell in lov tne" with computer technology.[4]

In the business literature in particular, the coming computer revolution was declared boldly, widely, and repeatedly.[5] The expectation was that electronic computers would soon become an integral part of the already large and thriving business machines industry. As *Fortune* magazine confidently predicted in a 1952 survey of the computer industry, "office robots" were poised to "eliminate the human element" in many clerical operations, enabling massive gains in productivity.[6] While these wild predictions might have been unsettling to U.S. office workers, they did suggest a rapidly growing market for computer technology. At the very least, the computer manufacturers were convinced that computers were the wave of the future; in the early 1950s, dozens of firms—among them such major players as IBM, GE, Burroughs, RCA, and NCR—invested heavily in this potential new growth market.

And grow the market did. In 1950 there were only 2 electronic computers in use in the United States. By 1955 there were 240. Five years later, there were 5,400. By 1965, the grand total had grown to almost 25,000, and by 1970, 75,000.[7] By the end of the 1960s, electronic computers and their associated peripherals formed the basis of a $20 billion industry—an industry growing at an average rate of more than 27 percent annually. Within two decades of the development of the first electronic digital computer, the computer industry in the United States had emerged from nothing to become one of the largest and fastest-growing sectors of the U.S. economy—a position that it would hold for the next several decades.[8]

Coevolving with this flourishing new information industry was a novel species of technical professional: the computer programmer. In 1945 there were no computer programmers, professional or otherwise; by 1967 industry observers were warning that although there were at least a hundred thousand programmers working in the United States, there was an immediate need for at least fifty thousand more.[9] "Competition for programmers," declared a contemporary article in *Fortune* magazine, "has driven salaries up so fast that programming has become probably the country's highest paid technological occupation. . . . Even so, some companies can't find experienced programmers at any price."[10]

Of all the unanticipated consequences of the invention of the electronic computer in the mid-1940s, the most surprising was the sudden rise to prominence of the computer programmer. While the computer revolution itself might not have been unforeseen, the role of the computer programmer in bringing about that revolution certainly was. In all of the pioneering computer projects of this period, for example, programming was considered, at best, an afterthought. It was generally assumed that coding the computer would be a relatively simple process of translation that could be assigned to low-level clerical personnel. It quickly became apparent that computer programming, as it came to be known, was anything but straightforward and simple. Skilled programmers developed a reputation for creativity and ingenuity, and programming was considered by many to be a uniquely intellectual activity, a black art that relied on individual ability and idiosyncratic style. By the beginning of the 1950s, however, programming had been identified as a key component of any successful computer installation. By the early 1960s, the "problem of programming" had eclipsed all other aspects of commercial computer development. As the electronic computer increasingly moved out of the laboratory and into the marketplace, the centrality of programming—and programmers—became even more apparent.

Originally envisioned as little more than glorified clerical workers, programmers quickly assumed a position of power within many organizations that was vastly disproportionate to their official position in the organizational hierarchy. Defined by their mastery of the highest of high technology, they were often derided for their adherence to artisanal practices. Although associated with the emerging academic discipline of computer science, they were never widely considered to be either scientists or engineers. Neither laborers nor professionals, they defy traditional occupational categorizations. The ranks of the elite programmers included both high school dropouts and ex-PhD physicists. Even to this day, their occupational expertise remains difficult to clearly define or delineate. For example, the term programmer, which was widely used as a generic catchall description of a computing specialist in the 1960s, encompasses such a wide range of occupational categories—from the narrow and highly technical coder to the elite and influential "systems man"—that it is more useful as a rhetorical device than as an analytic category.

The questions of what programming was—as an intellectual and occupational activity—and where it fit into traditional social, academic, and professional hierarchies, were actively negotiated during the decades of the 1950s and 1960s. Programmers were well aware of their tenuous professional position, and they struggled to prove that they possessed a unique set of skills and training that allowed them to lay claim to professional autonomy. This chapter traces the history of computer programming from its origins as low-status clerical work (often performed by women) into one of the highest-paid technical occupations of the late 1950s and early 1960s. The focus is on the emergence of the computer programmer as a highly valued, well-compensated, and largely autonomous technical expert.

The Origins of Computer Programming

In the eyes of a computer scientist, all computers are created equal. That is to say, any true computing machine can, by definition, compute anything that is computable. Or to state the case a little more clearly, any device worthy of the name computer can be programmed to perform any task that can be performed by any other computer. This means that in theory at least, all computers are functionally equivalent: any given computer is but a specific implementation of a more general abstraction known as a Universal Turing Machine.

It is the Platonic ideal of the Universal Turing Machine, and not the messy reality of actual physical computers, that is the true subject of modern theoretical computer science; it is only by treating the computer as an abstraction, a mathematical construct, that theoretical computer scientists lay claim to their field being a legitimate *scientific*, rather than merely a technical or engineering, discipline. The story of this remarkable self-construction and its consequences is the subject of chapter 5.

The idealized Universal Turing Machine is, of course, only a conceptual device, a convenient fiction concocted by the mathematician Alan

Turing in the late 1930s as a means of exploring a long-standing puzzle in theoretical mathematics known as the *Entscheidungsproblem*. In order to facilitate his exploration, Turing invented a new tool, an imaginary device capable of performing simple mechanical computations. Each Turing Machine, which consisted of only a long paper tape along with a mechanism for reading from and writing to that tape, contained a table of instructions that allowed it to perform a single computation. As a computing device, the Turing Machine is deceptively simple; as a conceptual abstraction, it is extraordinarily powerful. As it turns out, the table of instructions for any Turing Machine can be rewritten to contain the instructions for building any other Turing Machine. The implication, as articulated in the Church-Turing thesis, is that every Turing Machine is a Universal Turing Machine, and by extension, every computing machine is essentially equivalent.

In the real world, the appealingly egalitarian abstractions of the Church-Turing thesis quickly break down in the face of the temporal and spatial constraints of the physical universe. To implement even the simplest computations on an archetypal paper tape–based Turing Machine, for example, would require an enormous and prohibitive amount of resources. In fact, the figures involved quickly become absurdly Saganesque: the number of miles of paper tape required would be more than the total number of atoms in the universe, and the amount of time required would be more than all of known cosmological history. To the emerging discipline of theoretical computer scientists, perhaps, none of these practical realities were particularly significant. But to working computer engineers and programmers, such constraints were a daily reality, even in the era of electronic computing. Extracting acceptable performance and reliability out of the early electronic computers required an enormous degree of messy tinkering, local knowledge, and idiosyncratic technique. The developing tension between the messy tinkering of real-world computing and the clean abstractions of academically minded computer scientists would come to define one of the sharp divides within the ranks of the larger computing community. The struggle between theory and practice would become a major challenge for academics and practitioners alike, and would reflect itself in the structure of programming languages, professional societies, and academic curricula.

Conventional histories of computer programming tend to conflate programming as a vocational activity with computer science as an academic discipline. In many of these accounts, programming is represented as a subdiscipline of formal logic and mathematics, and its origins are identified in the writings of early computer theorists Alan Turing and John von Neumann. The development of the discipline is evaluated in terms of advances in programming languages, formal methods, and generally applicable theoretical research. This purely intellectual approach to the history of programming, however, conceals the essentially craftlike nature of early programming practice. The first computer programmers were not scientists or mathematicians; they were low-status, female clerical workers and desktop calculator operators. The origins of programming as a profession lie in the commercial traditions of machine-assisted, manual computation, not in the mainstream of theoretical mathematics.

The history of vocational computer programming begins, in the United States at least, with the construction of the ENIAC in summer 1945. Many historians have identified the ENIAC as the first true electronic computer. The question of "which was the first computer" is surprisingly difficult to answer. As Michael Williams suggests in a recent volume edited by Raul Rojas and Ulf Hashagen called *The First Computers* (note the crucial use of the plural), any particular claim to the priority of invention must necessarily be heavily qualified: if you add enough adjectives you can always claim your own favorite.[11] And indeed, the ENIAC has a strong claim to this title: not only was it digital, electronic, and programmable (and therefore looked a lot like a modern computer) but the ENIAC designers—John Mauchly and J. Presper Eckert—went on to form the first commercial computer company in the United States. The ENIAC and its commercial successor, the UNIVersal Automatic Computer (UNIVAC), were widely publicized as the first of the "giant brains" that presaged the coming computer age. But even the ENIAC had its precursors and competitors. For example, in the 1930s, a physicist at Iowa State University, John Atanasoff, had worked on an electronic computing device and had even described it to Mauchly. Others were working on similar devices. During the Second World War in particular, a number of government and military agencies, both in the United States and abroad, had developed electronic computing devices, many of which also have a plausible claim to being if not *the* first computer, then at least *a* first computer.

There are two major innovations in computing that the ENIAC embodied. The first was that it was electronic. Earlier computing devices, including tabulating machines, were either mechanical or electromechanical, meaning that they contained numerous moving parts. These moving parts were complicated to manufacture, difficult to maintain, and above all relatively slow. By replacing them with completely electronic components, Eckert and Mauchly were able to dramatically speed up the process of computation. Whereas the electromechanical Harvard Mark I (completed in 1943), which was of similar complexity to the ENIAC, could perform 2 or 3 additions per second, and a multiplication every six seconds, the ENIAC (completed just three years later) could perform 5,000 additions per second, or 333 multiplications. Although this extraordinary improvement in performance came at the price of increased cost and complexity—when completed the ENIAC weighed nearly thirty tons, occupied an entire room, and required more than eighteen thousand expensive and unreliable vacuum tubes—by the end of the 1940s it was clear that electronic computing was the wave of the future.

The second revolutionary feature of the ENIAC was its ability to be programmed. This meant that the machine could be reconfigured to perform different types of computation. In the case of the ENIAC the machine had to be physically wired, or "set up," as the process was called at the time, to compute specific functions—a complicated process that could take as long as two days.[12] Within a short time, however, the ENIAC was modified to allow it to be "programmed" automatically using punch cards.[13] In the meantime, the physicist and mathematician von Neumann had published his now-infamous *First Draft of a Report on the EDVAC*, which provided a description of the computer that was to be heir to the ENIAC.[14] This successor machine, which was called the Electronic Discrete Variable Automatic Computer (EDVAC), was the world's first stored-program computer. Unlike previous programmable machines, the EDVAC stored-program computer did not distinguish between data and instructions. This allowed it to modify its own instructions, which effectively allowed the computer to program itself. This not only allowed for greater flexibility in programming but also paved the way for the development of assemblers, compilers, and other programming tools. The concept of the stored-program computer was so significant that it has come to define the essence of the modern computer; today a device is only considered to be a true computer if it is a stored-program machine.

And this is what brings us back to the centrality of software to the history of computing: it was not so much the original invention of the electronic computer that launched the computer revolution but the later discovery that such computers could be made programmable. To be sure, prior to the electronic computer there were machines that could be controlled automatically. A Jacquard loom, for instance, used a series of steel cards, as many as twenty thousand at a time, to control the weaving of patterns on fabric.[15] Tabulating machines could also be programmed to a certain degree by rewiring their components. But the combination of speed and flexibility provided by the combination of an electronic digital computer and well-designed software was unprecedented. The electronic digital computer would eventually become a universal machine whose potential applications were limited only by the imagination of its programmers.

Therein lies the rub: the very aspect of electronic computing that made it so powerful and appealing was the aspect of least interest to its original designers. Computer programming began as little more than an afterthought in most of the pioneering wartime electronic computing projects, an offhand postscript to what was universally regarded as the much more pressing challenge of hardware development.

There were certainly legitimate reasons for privileging hardware over software; simply managing to keep the early electronic computers running without failure for more than a few minutes was an engineering challenge of heroic proportions. As was mentioned earlier, the core computational units of the ENIAC machine relied on more than eighteen thousand vacuum tubes, each of which had an average lifespan of just three thousand hours. This meant that statistically speaking, six of these tubes would fail every hour; or in other words, at least one tube failed every ten minutes. Figuring out how to control the rate of failure of vacuum tubes was one of the great contributions of the ENIAC's brilliant chief engineer, J. Presper Eckert. Similarly, the construction of mercury delay lines, which were an early form of short-term memory used in the Cambridge University EDSAC, the world's first working stored-program computer, required the precise coordination of acoustical waves moving at 1,450 meters per second. There is no question that overcoming the engineering challenges posed by the electronics of electronic computing was essential to the further development of computer technology.

But solving the programming hurdles was equally vital. Although in the decades after the ENIAC we have come to regard the electronic computer as an almost infinitely protean and useful machine, this is largely a reflection of the successes of software. In the immediate postwar period even programmable computers like the ENIAC were considered impressive but limited. It was not hard to imagine that the military and the government might have a need for a small number of such devices, yet few would have predicted how rapidly the commercial market for computers would expand over the course of the next decade.

"Glorified Clerical Workers"

The low priority given to programming was reflected in who was assigned to the task. Although the ENIAC was developed by academic researchers at the University of Pennsylvania's Moore School of Electrical Engineering, it was commissioned and funded by the Ballistics Research Laboratory (BRL) of the U.S. Army. Located at the nearby Aberdeen Proving Grounds, the BRL was responsible for the development of the complex firing tables required to accurately target long-range ballistic weaponry. Hundreds of these tables were required to account for the influence of highly variable atmospheric conditions (air density, temperature, etc.) on the trajectory of shells and bombs. Prior to the arrival of electronic computers, these tables were calculated and compiled by teams of human "computers" working eight-hour shifts, six days a week. From 1943 onward, essentially all of these computers were women, as were their immediate supervisors. The more senior women (those with college-level mathematical training) were responsible for developing the elaborate "plans of computation" that were carried out by their fellow computers.

In June 1945, six of the best human computers at Aberdeen were hired by the leaders of the top secret "Project X"—the U.S. Army's code name for the ENIAC project—to set up the ENIAC machine to produce ballistics tables. Their names were Kathleen McNulty, Frances Bilas, Betty Jean Jennings, Elizabeth Snyder Holberton, Ruth Lichterman, and Marlyn Wescoff. Collectively they were known as "the ENIAC girls."[16] Today the ENIAC girls are often considered the first computer programmers. In the 1940s, they were simply called coders.

The use of the word coder in this context is significant. At this point in time the concept of a program, or of a programmer, had not yet been introduced into computing. Since electronic computing was then envisioned by the ENIAC developers as "nothing more than an automated form of hand computation," it seemed natural to assume that the primary role of the women of the ENIAC would be to develop the plans of computation that the electronic version of the human computer would follow.[17] In other words, they would code into machine language the higher-level mathematics developed by male scientists and engineers. Coding implied manual labor, and mechanical translation or rote transcription; coders were obviously low on the intellectual and professional status hierarchy. It was not until later that the now-commonplace title of programmer was widely adopted. The verb "to program," with its military connotations of "to assemble" or "to organize," suggested a more thoughtful and system-oriented activity.[18] Although by the mid-1950s the word programmer had become the preferred designation, for the next several decades programmers would struggle to distance themselves from the status (and gender) connotations suggested by coder.

The first clear articulation of what a programmer was and should be was provided in the late 1940s by Goldstine and von Neumann in a series of volumes titled *Planning and Coding of Problems for an Electronic Computing Instrument*. These volumes, which served as the principal (and perhaps only) textbooks available on the programming process at least until the early 1950s, outlined a clear division of labor in the programming process that seems to have been based on the practices used in programming the ENIAC. Goldstine and von Neumann spelled out a six-step programming process: (1) conceptualize the problem mathematically and physically, (2) select a numerical algorithm, (3) do a numerical analysis to determine the precision requirements and evaluate potential problems with approximation errors, (4) determine scale factors so that the mathematical expressions stay within the fixed range of the computer throughout the computation, (5) do the dynamic analysis to understand how the machine will execute jumps and substitutions during the course of a computation, and (6) do the static coding. The first five of these tasks were to be done by the "planner," who was typically the scientific user and overwhelmingly was male; the sixth task was to be carried out by coders. Coding was regarded as a "static" process by Goldstine and von Neumann—one that involved writing out the steps of a computation in a form that could be read by the machine, such as punching cards, or in the case of the ENIAC, plugging in cables and setting up switches. Thus, there was a division of labor envisioned that gave the highest-skilled work to the high-status male scientists and the lowest-skilled work to the low-status female coders.

As the ENIAC managers and coders soon realized, however, controlling the operation of an automatic computer was nothing like the process of hand computation, and the Moore School women were therefore responsible for defining the first state-of-the-art methods of programming practice. Programming was an imperfectly understood activity in these early days, and much more of the work devolved on the coders than anticipated. To complete their coding, the coders would often have to revisit the underlying numerical analysis, and with their growing skills, some scientific users left many or all six of the programming stages to the coders. In order to debug their programs and distinguish hardware glitches from software errors, they developed an intimate knowledge of the ENIAC machinery. "Since we knew both the application and the machine," claimed ENIAC programmer Betty Jean Jennings, "as a result we could diagnose troubles almost down to the individual vacuum tube. Since we knew both the application and the machine, we learned to diagnose troubles as well as, if not better than, the engineers."[19] In a few cases, the local craft knowledge that these female programmers accumulated significantly affected the design of the ENIAC and subsequent computers. ENIAC programmer Betty Holberton recalled one particularly significant episode:

> In the fall of '46 when the new idea of wiring up the ENIAC with sort of semi-permanent wiring with instruction codes [emerged] . . . a number of us worked with Dr. von Neumann in setting up this code. . . . We felt we wouldn't need that many settings for all of the instructions. We sort of worked along for a while. But to my astonishment, he never mentioned a stop instruction. So I did coyly say, "Don't we need a stop instruction in this machine?" He said, "No we don't need a stop instruction. We have all these empty sockets here that just let it go to bed." And I went back home and I was really alarmed. After all, we had debugged the machine day and night for months just trying to get jobs on it.
>
> So the next week when I came up with some alterations in the code, I approached him again with the same question. He gave me the same answer. Well I really got red in the face. I was so excited and I really wanted to tell him off. And I said, "But Dr. von Neumann, we are programmers and we sometimes make mistakes." He nodded his head and the stop order went in.[20]

The deference with which Holberton proposes her tentative suggestion and von Neumann's initial patronizing dismissal are indicative of the status of the programmers relative to that of their scientific and engineering colleagues. Von Neumann's eventual acceptance reflects his recognition of the importance of local craft knowledge and an increasing acceptance of the value of programming expertise. Given that the programmers "were often able to point out to a technician which individual vacuum tube needed to be changed," they were able to interact much more with the computer engineers and technicians than was probably originally intended. This had the positive effect of convincing the ENIAC managers that programmers were essential to the success of the overall project and that well-informed, technically proficient, high-quality programmers were especially indispensable.

Thus, what was supposed to have been a low-level skill, a static activity, prepared these women coders well for careers as programmers, and indeed, those who did pursue professional careers in computing often became programmers and thrived at it. A few women, Grace Hopper and Betty Holberton of UNIVAC as well as Ida Rhodes and Gertrude Blanche of the National Bureau of Standards in particular, continued to serve as leaders in the programming profession. But despite the success of the ENIAC women in establishing a unique occupational niche for the programmer within the ENIAC community, programming continued to be perceived as marginal to the central business of computer development. By nature of their gender (female) and education (nonscientific and nonengineering), the early programmers remained isolated from their engineering and scientific managers. If software was admitted to be important, hardware was considered to be essential.

The conflation of programming and coding, and the association of both with low-status clerical labor, indicated the ways in which early software workers were gendered female. In the ENIAC project, of course, the programmers actually were women. In this respect programming inherited the gender identity of the human computing projects in which it originated. But the suggestion that coding was low-status clerical work also implied an additional association with female labor. As Margery Davies, Sharon Strom, and Elyce Rotella have described, clerical work had, by the second decade of the twentieth century, become largely feminized.[21] This was particularly true of clerical occupations that were characterized by the rigid division of labor and the introduction of new technologies. Some of these occupations carried over directly into the computer era: the job of keypunch operator, for example, had been thoroughly feminized long before it became associated with electronic data processing.[22] And although today we do not associate the work of keypunchers with the work of the computer programmer, in the 1950s and 1960s the differentiation between keypunch operators and other forms of computer work was not always clear. In any case, the historical pattern of the nineteenth and twentieth centuries has been that low-status occupations, with the exception of those requiring certain forms of physical strength, have often become feminized. In terms of the ENIAC, for example, the telephone switchboardlike appearance of the ENIAC programming cable-and-plug panels reinforced the notion that programmers were mere machine operators, that programming was more handicraft than science, more feminine than masculine, more mechanical than intellectual. The programmer/coder continued to occupy an uncertain position within the nascent association of computer professionals.

Throughout the next several decades programmers struggled to distance themselves from the status (and gender) connotations suggested by coder. An early manuscript version of the UNIVAC *Introduction to Programming* manual, for instance, highlighted the distinction between the managerial programmer and the technical coder: "In problem preparation, the detailed work may be accomplished by two individuals. The first, who may be called the 'programmer,' studies the problem, determines the appropriate method of solution, and prepares the flow chart. This person must be well versed in the particular field in which the problem lies, and should also be able to fully exploit the flexibility and versatility of the UNIVAC system. The second person, referred to as the 'coder,' need only be familiar with the technique of reducing the flow chart to the specific instructions, or coding, required by the UNIVAC to solve the problem."[23] By differentiating between these two tasks, one clerical and the other analytic, the manual reinforced the Goldstine and von Neumann model of the programmer. In this model the real business of programming was analysis: the actual coding aspect of programming was trivial and mechanical. "Problems must be thoroughly analyzed to determine the many factors that must be taken into consideration," suggested the same preliminary UNIVAC manual, but once this analysis had been completed, the "pattern of the [programming] solution would be readily apparent." Although this division of the programming process into two distinct and unequal phases did not survive into the published version of the UNIVAC documentation, its early inclusion highlighted the persistence of the programmer/coder distinction.

The Art of Programming

Although they continued to struggle with questions of status and identity, by the end of the 1950s computer programmers were generally considered to be anything but routine clerical workers. A Price Waterhouse report from 1959 titled *Business Experience with Electronic Computers* argued that "high quality individuals are the key to top grade programming. Why? Purely and simply because much of the work involved is exacting and difficult enough to require real intellectual ability and above average personal characteristics."[24] In fact, the study's authors observed that "the term 'programmer' is . . . unfortunate since it seems to indicate that the work is largely machine oriented when this is not at all the case. . . . [T]raining in systems analysis and design is as important to a programmer as training in machine coding techniques; it may well become increasingly important as systems get more complex and coding becomes more automatic."[25] Although Goldstine and von Neumann had envisioned a clear division of labor between planners and coders, in reality this boundary became increasingly indistinct. The clear implication of recent experience, in both scientific computation and business data processing, was that programmers should be given more responsibility for design and analysis, the idea that coding could be left to less-experienced or lower-grade personnel was "erroneous," and "the human element is crucial in programming."[26] Indeed, by the mid-1950s, a new model for programming had emerged that emphasized individual expertise and creativity. During this period computers remained a primarily scientific and military technology, and computer programming as a discipline retained a close association with the practice of mathematics. The limitations of early hardware devices usually meant that a simple programming problem could quickly turn into a research excursion into algorithm theory and numerical analysis. Computer programmers developed a reputation for creativity and ingenuity. Contemporary storage devices were so slow and had such little capacity that programmers had to develop great skill and craft knowledge to fit their programs into the available memory space. As John Backus (the IBM researcher best known as the inventor of the FORTRAN programming language) would later describe the situation, "Programming in the 1950s was a black art, a private arcane matter. . . . [E]ach problem required a unique beginning at square one, and the success of a program depended primarily on the programmer's private techniques and inventions."[27]

The notion that programming was a black art pervades the literature from this period. There are several reasons why programming was so difficult. To begin with, the programmer had to develop an algorithm suitable to the problem at hand. Since the primary purpose of the earliest computers was to produce solutions to complex mathematical functions that could not be solved analytically, these programs necessarily required skill in numerical analysis. Numerical analysis is the set of tools that mathematicians have developed to provide approximate solutions to otherwise-insoluble equations. This process of analysis was itself something of an art form: numerical solutions always involved a compromise between speed and accuracy—even when using the fastest computers. Choosing the right approximation required the programmer to balance acceptable error against the specific limitations of a given machine.

**If you're the kind
of systems
programmer who
has a mind that's
deep enough
for Kant,**

**and sufficiently
precise to enjoy
the esoteric
language of the
computer,**

**broad enough for
science fiction,**

look into RCA. You're our kind of person.

You probably think far ahead
of your time.

You want to take software out
of its infancy. Into the 4th, 5th
and 6th generations.

You want a chance to
influence hardware design,
instead of the other way around.

You want a variety of projects
with definite objectives, instead
of an endless task.

You want challenging work
and inspiring rewards.

If this is what you're looking
for, find it at RCA.

Write to us if you've had
experience in language
processors, operating
systems, utility systems or
communications systems.

We also have openings in
Sales, Field Systems Support,

and Product Planning and
Engineering.

Contact Mr. J. C. Riener,
Dept. D-11, RCA Information
Systems Division, Bldg. 202-1,
Cherry Hill, New Jersey 08101.
We are an equal opportunity
employer.

Figure 2.1
RCA advertisement, 1962.

For problems that were not mathematical in nature, developing an appropriate algorithm could be even more challenging. This was a particular problem for the corporate users of computers. Even the simplest business activities can be difficult, if not impossible, to describe in terms of the limited instruction set understood by a computer. Programmers first had to thoroughly understand the activity in question, including all of its exceptional cases, imprecise terms, and potential errors. Not only was this process inherently difficult but it also frequently involved social and analytic skills foreign to the average programmer. "Because the background of the early programmers was acquired mainly in mathematics or other scientific fields, they were used to dealing with well-formulated problems and they delighted in a sophisticated approach to coding their solutions," noted the Price Waterhouse report. "When they applied their talents to the more sprawling problems of business, they often tended to underestimate the complexities and many of their solutions turned out to be oversimplifications. Most people connected with electronic computers in the early days will remember the one- or two-page flow charts which were supposed to cover the intricacies of the accounting aspects of a company's operations."[28] Most companies attempted to differentiate the more social and organizational processes essential to algorithm development, often referred to as system analysis, from the more technical procedures associated with programming. Inevitably the two would bleed into one another, however.[29]

Even after a suitable algorithm had been selected, the process of transforming that algorithm into a form that could be understood by a computer was challenging. Most electronic computers represented numbers internally in binary form, and so conversion routines from decimal to binary (and back) had to be developed. If the machine was a fixed-point machine, all of the numbers also scaled to stay within the bounds of the fixed-point arithmetic units. Since in a stored-program computer both programs and data were stored in the same memory, it was possible to confuse the two and create strange errors that were almost impossible to trace. Most of these machines had limited debugging capabilities (if any) and complicated mechanisms for accessing subroutine libraries. Programmers had to use obscure techniques to optimize for size rather than for legibility or ease of maintenance due to the limited amount of available memory. In order to coax every bit of speed out of a relatively slow storage device such as a rotating memory drum, programmers would carefully organize their coded instructions in such a way as to assure that each instruction passed by the magnetic read head in just the right order and at just the right execution time.[30] Only the best programmers could hope to develop applications that worked at acceptable levels of usability and performance. They had to cultivate a series of idiosyncratic and highly individual craft techniques designed to overcome the limitations of primitive hardware.[31]

In his memoir describing "Programming in America in the 1950s," John Backus offered an especially detailed example of the many ways in which a programmer project could run into problems:

Some idea of the machine difficulties facing early programmers can be had by a brief survey of a few of the bizarre characteristics of the Selective Sequence Electronic Calculator (SSEC).

This vast machine (circa 1948–1952) had a store of 150 words; instructions, constants, and tables of data were read from punched tapes the width of a punched card; the ends of an instruction tape were glued together to form a paper loop, which was then placed on one of 66 tape-reading stations. The SSEC could also punch intermediate data into tapes that could subsequently be read by a tape-reading station.

One early problem strained the SSEC's capacity to the limit. The computation was divided into three phases; in the first phase a tape of many yards of intermediate results was punched out; during the second phase this tape was glued into a loop and mounted on a tape-reading station so that in the third phase it could be read many times.

The problem ran successfully through many cycles of these three phases, but then a mysterious error began to appear and disappear regularly in the third phase. For a long time no one could account for it.

Finally, the large pile of intermediate data tape was pulled from the bin below its reading station and a careful inspection revealed that it had been glued to form a Mobius strip rather than a simple loop. The result was that on every second revolution of the tape each number would be read in reverse order.[32]

As this anecdote suggests, writing programs under these constraints was a time-consuming and error-prone process. One the oldest-surviving computer programmers, a 126-line debugging tool developed for the Cambridge EDSAC machine (notable as being the first working stored-program computer in the world) was recently discovered to have contained more than twenty errors.[33] Because the author of the program, the mathematical physicist Maurice Wilkes, literally wrote the book on computer programming in the early 1950s (his 1951 *Preparation of Programs for an Electronic Digital Computer* is considered the first widely available textbook on programming), we can assume that this was not an unrepresentative example.[34] As Wilkes later recalled in his memoirs, early on in the life of the EDSAC, its programmers had "begun to realize that it was not so easy to get a program right as had at one time appeared." It was with some shock and dismay that he himself realized that "a good part of the remainder of my life was going to be spent in finding errors in my own programs."[35] The tedious process of identifying and removing these errors, known as "debugging," was time-consuming, difficult, and intellectually unfulfilling. As much as one-half of the budget of a large programming project could be spent on testing and debugging—activities that were perceived as being low-status and unpleasant.[36]

As will be described in subsequent chapters, improvements in computer hardware along with the development of compilers and other programming utilities would help alleviate some of the challenges associated with coding. But as many FORTRAN and COBOL programmers would soon realize, the dull and mechanical aspects of software development did not disappear with the advent of compilers and automatic programming languages. Nor did the intellectual challenges associated with analysis and design. Mistakes were inevitable, even from the most proficient of programmers. In one widely recited and tragic (and possibly apocryphal) example, a minor transcription error in control software for the Mariner I probe to Venus caused the spacecraft to veer off-course four minutes after takeoff, forcing NASA to destroy it remotely. The mistake that the programmer allegedly made was to replace the FORTRAN statement

DO 3 I = 1,3

with

DO 3 I = 1.3

Instead of looping through a series of statements, as the code in the first version would have required, the latter form was interpreted by the FORTRAN compiler as the assignment of a variable. That the loss of the Mariner I could be caused by such a seemingly trivial error highlighted for many observers the central importance of employing only the most skilled programmers.[37] This perception holds true regardless of whether or not the Mariner I anecdote is factually accurate. During the late 1950s and 1960s such stories of software-related disaster were a staple of the popular press, and helped set the stage for the emergence of a full-blown software crisis in the late 1960s.

Building Castles in the Air

In describing his experiences as the project manager of the single-largest and most expensive software development effort ever undertaken in the history of the IBM Corporation, the noted computer scientist Frederick Brooks provided a curiously literary portrayal of the computer programmer: "The programmer, like the poet, works only slightly removed from pure-thought stuff. He builds his castles in the air, from air, creating by exertion of the imagination."[38]

That a technical manager in a conservative corporation should use such lofty language in reference to such a seemingly prosaic occupation like programming is striking yet not unusual. But Brooks meant his literary metaphors to be taken seriously. Even more so than the poet, he argued, the programmer worked in the medium of the imagination, using words to bring to life grand conceptual structures. In fact, in the case of the programmers the relationship between words and reality was almost magical: "One types the correct incantation on a keyboard, and a display screen comes to life, showing things that never were nor could be." And like the magical incantation, the computer program demanded perfection: "If one character, one pause, of the incantation is not strictly in proper form, the magic doesn't work." This is what made programming so difficult, he suggested: "Human beings are not accustomed to being perfect, and few areas of human activity demand it. Adjusting to the requirement for perfection is, I think, the most difficult part of learning to program."[39]

Like many of his contemporaries, Brooks was struggling to understand why software development projects seemed almost impossible to manage using conventional management techniques. In the late 1960s, Brooks had been the manager of the IBM OS/360 development project. The OS/360 operating system was the cornerstone of IBM's larger System/360 strategy, which consolidated IBM's computer product lines into a single range of hardware- and software-compatible machines. Although the System/360 turned out to be a tremendous success for IBM, it had almost been derailed by problems with the development of OS/360. In the years between 1963 and 1966, over five thousand staff years of effort went into the design, construction, and documentation of OS/360. When it was finally delivered in 1967, nine months late and riddled with errors, it had cost the IBM Corporation half a billion dollars—four times the original budget, and the single-largest expenditure in company history. And according to Brooks, the personal

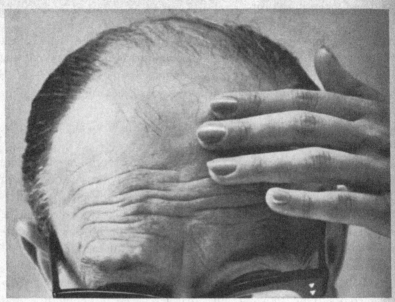

Do you know what it means to find and care for a good programmer, and keep him happy?
Or maybe a couple of him (or her)?

They don't grow in labs.

They're an unusual breed.

Practically speaking, a profession.

It's not easy to tell who'll be a good programmer. Or who won't. Genius or plodder, once they're in the business, something within them comes out.

We bring it out.

Good programmers often come to us because we give them the company of so many others from whom they will learn.

And place them in one of our centers where they'll be happiest. And give them lots of training and experience.

And give them IBM computers to work with. The 1620, the 1401, the 7094, and soon the System/360. The latest. The small ones for small problems. The big ones for big problems.

And a team of technicians who can run them. And seldom waste a second.

They love to tackle matters like numerical control, multicomponent distillation, Type II structural steel frame specification, refinery operations forecasting, urban transportation planning, piping flexibility, rocket fuel evaluation, hydraulic network analysis, thermochemical equilibrium, supermarket chain and department store operations, high-rise apartment and industrial plant construction.

They get a thrill from Linear Programming and critical path scheduling (PERT) and generalized interrelated flow simulation (GIFS).

They get their triumphs from giving the computer a program with fewer steps.

So it solves problems faster. Cheaper. In the data processing business, it's a *coup* when one company gets such a programmer.

Over 12,000 SBC customers know what we mean.

They know that the difference between computer services in this day and age of data processing machines is people.

Can SBC help you? How much does it cost? There's a way to find out quickly. Your Yellow Pages. "Data Processing Services." There we are.

SBC®   Service Bureau Corporation
Computing Sciences Division
425 Park Avenue
New York, N.Y., 10022

Figure 2.2
Service Bureau Corporation advertisement, 1964.

toll that OS/360 took on IBM's software personnel was perhaps even more significant.

The highly publicized failure of the OS/360 project served as a dramatic illustration of the shortcomings of the traditional management methods in software development. It was in *The Mythical Man-Month*, his postmortem analysis of the OS/360 disaster, that Brooks first compared programming to poetry. His larger point was that computer programming, as an inherently artistic activity, was resistant to most forms of industrial production. Take, for example, his own experience with OS/360: when faced with serious schedule slippages, quality problems, and unanticipated changes in scope, he and the other project leaders had done what traditional manufacturing managers were accustomed to doing, which was to add more resources. The only noticeable result was that the project fell more and more behind schedule.

After diagnosing the disease, Brooks proposed its cure. If skilled programmers were the sine qua non of quality software development, they must be elevated to the center of the production process. The remainder of *The Mythical Man-Month* is an attempt to figure out how to harness the power of highly artistic programmer/poets to the demands of industrial-strength software development. The development methodology that Brooks outlined was never widely adopted in industry, but his larger argument about the inherently creative nature of programming was. *The Mythical Man-Month* quickly became one of the most widely read and oft-quoted references on the practice of software development.

There is no doubt that in the formative years of commercial computing, there was widespread dissension within the programming community over the goals and direction of the programming profession. Computer scientists, corporate employers, and vocational programmers disagreed about the proper relationship between formal and idiosyncratic technique, local knowledge and generally applicable theory. What was largely agreed on, however, was that in the early 1960s, programming was "not yet a science, but an art that lacks standards, definitions, agreement on theories and approaches."[40] This popular perception of computer programming as a poorly understood, idiosyncratic, and creative process defined the discipline as it emerged in the 1950s, and continues to influence the culture and practice of programming even today. The notion that programming was an art served as both a resource and a source of much anxiety and discomfort for programmers.

For all of these reasons and more, programming in the 1950s acquired a reputation for being incomprehensible to all but a small set of extremely talented insiders. As John Backus would later describe it, "Each [programming] problem required a unique beginning at square one, and the success of a program depended primarily on the programmer's private techniques and invention."[41] Techniques developed for one application or installation could not be easily adapted for other purposes. There were few useful or widely applicable tools available to programmers, and certainly no science of programming. Programmers often worked in relative isolation, and had few opportunities for formal or even informal education. They generally perceived little value in the work going on at other firms or laboratories, as it was equally haphazard and idiosyncratic. They placed great emphasis on local knowledge and individual ability.

The widespread perception that programming was a black art pervades the industry and technical literature of the 1950s and 1960s.[42] Even today, more than a half century after the invention of the first electronic computers, the notion that computer programming still retains an essentially artistic character is still widely accepted.[43] Whether or not this is desirable is an entirely different question—one that remains a subject of considerable and contentious debate. What is important for the purposes of this book is the various ways in which the language of art, aesthetics, and craft is used throughout the history of computing to elevate, denigrate, or castigate programmers and other software specialists. By characterizing the work that they did as artistic, programmers could lay claim to the autonomy and authority that came with being an artist. If it were true, as one industry observer suggested in the late 1960s, that "generating software is 'brain business,' often an agonizingly difficult intellectual effort," then talented programmers were effectively irreplaceable, and should be treated and compensated accordingly.[44]

On the other hand, being artistic might also imply that one was not scientific or professional. One common usage of the word art, of course, is in reference to the visual, literary, or performing arts. In this context, describing programmers as artists implied that they were might be nonconformist, unreliable, or eccentric—not traits likely to endear them to straitlaced corporate managers. Although some programmers (and managers) did apply this meaning of the word art to programming—Brooks used a "programmers as poets" metaphor—for the most part the word was used in its more traditional association with craft technique and preindustrial forms of production.[45] When participants at the NATO

Conference on Software Engineering in 1968 portrayed computer programming as being "too artistic," they was using the word in this latter sense, as a rhetorical device for contrasting its "backward" craft sensibilities with "the types of theoretical foundations and practical disciplines" that they believed characterized "the established branches of engineering."[46] Note that the appeal here is to the tradition of the artisan or craftsperson, which is a masculine identity, rather than to the potentially effeminate artsy type.

For those computer programmers who also had academic aspirations, the word art was always used in opposition to science. For them the word suggested an undesirable lack of theoretical or mathematical rigor. They needed to distance the more artistic practices of programming from the more respectable discipline of computer science. This often brought these academically minded proto–computer scientists into conflict with working programmers, who had different professional and occupational agendas. The differences between these agendas would come to light in subsequent debates about programmer recruitment practices, programming language adoption, and academic curriculum.

3

Chess Players, Music Lovers, and Mathematicians

In one inquiry it was found that a successful team of computer specialists included an ex-farmer, a former tabulating machine operator, an ex-key punch operator, a girl who had done secretarial work, a musician and a graduate in mathematics. The last was considered the least competent.
—Hans Albert Rhee, *Office Automation in a Social Perspective*, 1968

In Search of "Clever Fellows"

The "Talk of the Town" column in the *New Yorker* magazine is not generally known for its coverage of science and technology. But in January 1957, the highbrow gossip column provided for its readers an unusual but remarkably prescient glimpse into the future of electronic computing. Already there were more than fifteen hundred of the electronic "giants" scattered around the United States, noted the column editors, with many more expected to be installed in the near future. Each of these computers required between thirty and fifty programmers, the "clever fellows" whose job it was to "figure out the proper form for stating whatever problem a machine is expected to solve." And as there were currently only fifteen thousand professional computer programmers available worldwide, many more would have to be trained or recruited immediately. After expressing "modest astonishment" over the size of this strange new "profession we'd never heard of," the "Talk of the Town" went on, in its inimitable breezy style, to accurately describe a problem that industry observers were only just beginning to recognize: namely, that the looming shortage of computer programmers threatened to strangle in its cradle the nascent commercial computer industry.[1]

The impetus for the "Talk of the Town" vignette was a series of advertisements that the IBM Corporation had recently placed in the *New York Times*. At first glance the ads read as rather conventional help-wanted fare. Promising the usual "exciting new jobs" in a "new and dynamic field," they sought out candidates for a series of positions in programming research. That particularly promising candidates might be those who "enjoy algebra, geometry and other logical operations" was also not remarkable, given the context. What caught the eye of the "Talk of the Town" columnists, however, was the curious addition of an appeal to candidates who enjoyed "musical composition and arrangement," liked "chess, bridge or anagrams," or simply possessed "a lively imagination."[2] Struck by the incongruity between these seemingly different pools of potential applicants, one technical and the other artistic, the columnists themselves "made bold to apply" to the IBM manager in charge of programmer recruitment. "Not that we wanted a programming job, we told him; we just wondered if anyone else did."[3]

The IBM manager they spoke to was Robert W. Bemer, a "fast-talking, sandy-haired man of about thirty-five," who by virtue of his eight-years experience was already considered, in the fast-paced world of electronic computing, "an old man with a long beard." It was from Bemer that they learned of the fifteen thousand existing computer programmers. An experienced programmer himself, Bemer nevertheless confessed astonishment at the unforeseen explosion into being of a programming profession, which even to him seemed to have "happened overnight." And for the immediate future, at least, it appeared inevitable

Are **YOU** the man

to command electronic giants?

From the recent advance of electronic digital computers has emerged an exciting new job—creating instructions that enable these giant computers to perform logical operations for a variety of tasks in business, science and government.

You could be eligible for a position in computer programming. Because it is a new and dynamic field, there are no rigid qualifications. Do you enjoy algebra, geometry or other logical operations? Can you do musical composition or arrangement? Do you have an orderly mind that enjoys such games as chess, bridge or anagrams . . . finally, do you have a lively imagination?

If you do, you can qualify. You will receive training (at full pay) and work at IBM's Engineering Laboratories—among the most modern in the world. For more information, write to: G. W. Woodsum, Dept. 203, International Business Machines Corp., Research Laboratory, Poughkeepsie, N. Y.

DATA PROCESSING
ELECTRIC TYPEWRITERS
TIME EQUIPMENT
MILITARY PRODUCTS

INTERNATIONAL
BUSINESS MACHINES
CORPORATION

Figure 3.1
IBM Advertisement, *New York Times*, May 31, 1969.

that the demand for programmers would only increase. With obvious enthusiasm, Bemer described a near future in which computers were much more than just scientific instruments, where "every major city in the country will have its community computer," and where citizens and businesspeople of all sorts—"grocers, doctors, lawyers"— would "all throw problems to the computer and will all have their problems solved." The key to achieving such a vision, of course, was the availability of diverse and well-written computer programs. Therein lay the rub for recruiters like Bemer: in response to the calls for computer programmers he had circulated in the *New York Times*, *Scientific American*, and the *Los Angeles Times*, he had received exactly seven replies. That IBM considered this an excellent return on its investment highlights the peculiar nature of the emerging programming profession.

Of the seven respondents to IBM's advertisements, five were experienced programmers lured away from competitors. This kind of poaching occurred regularly in the computer industry, and although this was no doubt a good thing from the point of view of these well-paid and highly mobile employees, it only exacerbated the recruitment and retention challenges faced by their employers. The other two were new trainees, only one of whom proved suitable in the long-term. The first was a chess player who was really "interested only in playing chess," and IBM soon "let him go back to his board." The second "knew almost nothing about computing," but allegedly had an IQ of 172, and according to Bemer, "he had the kind of mind we like. . . . [He] taught himself to play the piano when he was ten, working on the assumption that the note F was E. Claims he played that way for years. God knows what his neighbors went through, but you can see that it shows a nice independent talent for the systematic translation of values."[4]

Eventually the ad campaign and subsequent *New Yorker* coverage did net IBM additional promising programmer trainees, including an Oxford-trained crystallographer, an English PhD candidate from Columbia University, an ex-fashion model, a "proto-hippie," and numerous chess players, including Arthur Bisguier, the U.S. Open Chess champion, Alex Bernstein, a U.S. Collegiate champion, and Sid Noble, the self-proclaimed "chess champion of the French Riviera."[5] The only characteristics that these aspiring programmers appeared to have in common were their top scores on a series of standard puzzle-based aptitude tests, the ability to impress Bemer as being clever, and the chutzpah to respond to vague but intriguing help-wanted ads.

The haphazard manner in which IBM recruited its own top programmers, and the diverse character and backgrounds of them, reveals much
about the state of computer programming at the end of its first decade
of existence. On the one hand, computer programming had successfully
emerged from the obscurity of its origins as low-status, feminized clerical
work to become the nation's fastest-growing and highest-paid technological occupation.[6] The availability of strong programming talent was
increasingly recognized as essential to the success of any corporate computerization effort, and individual programmers were able to exert an
inordinate amount of control over the course of such attempts.

But at the same time, the "long-haired programming priesthood"—the
motley crew of chess players, music lovers, and mathematicians who
comprised the programming profession in this period—fit uncomfortably
into the traditional power structures of the modern corporate organization.[7] The same arcane and idiosyncratic abilities that made them well-
paid and highly sought-after individuals also made them slightly suspect.
How could the artistic sensibilities and artisanal practices of programmers be reconciled with the rigid demands of corporate rationality? How
could corporate managers predict and control the course of computerization efforts when they were so dependent on specific individuals? If good
programmers "were born, not made," as was widely believed, then how
could the industry ensure an adequate supply?[8]

The tension between art and science inherent in contemporary programming practices, unwittingly but ably captured by the "Talk of the
Town" gossip columnists, would drive many of the most significant
organizational, technological, and professional developments in the
history of computing over the course of the next few decades. This
chapter will deal with early attempts to use aptitude tests and personality
profiles to manage the growing "crisis" of programmer training and
recruitment.

The Persistent Personnel Problem

The commercial computer industry came of age in the 1960s. At the
beginning of that decade the electronic computer was still a scientific
curiosity, its use largely confined to government agencies as well as a few
adventurous and technically sophisticated corporations; by the decade's
end, the computer had been successfully reinvented as a mainstream
business technology, and companies such as IBM, Remington Rand, and
Honeywell were selling them by the thousands.

But each of these new computers, if we are to take Bemer's reckoning seriously, would require a support staff of at least thirty programmers. Since almost all computer programs in this period were effectively custom developed—the packaged software industry would only begin to emerge in the late 1960s—every purchase of a computer required the corresponding hire of new programming personnel. Even if we were to halve Bemer's estimates, the predicted industry demand for computer programmers in 1960 would top eighty thousand.

In truth, no one really knew for certain exactly how many programmers would be required. Contemporary estimates ranged from fifty thousand to five hundred thousand.[9] What was abundantly clear, however, was that whatever the total demand for programmers might eventually turn out to be, it would be impossible to satisfy using existing training and hiring practices. By the mid-1960s the lack of availability of trained computer programmers threatened to stifle the adoption of computer technology—a grave concern for manufacturers and employers alike. Warnings of a "gap in programming support" caused by the ever-worsening "population problem" pervade the industry literature in this period.[10] In 1966, the personnel situation had degraded so badly that *Business Week* magazine declared it a "software crisis"—the first appearance of the crisis mentality that would soon come to dominate and define the entire industry.[11]

Wayne State Conference

It did not take long after the invention of the first electronic computers for employers and manufacturers to become aware of the "many educational and manpower problems" associated with computerization. In 1954, leaders in industry, government, and education gathered at Wayne State University for the Conference on Training Personnel for the Computing Machine Field. The goal was to discuss what Elbert Little, of the Wayne State Computational Laboratory, suggested was a "universal feeling" among industry leaders that there was "a definite shortage" of technically trained people in the computer field.[12] This shortage, variously described by an all-star cast of scientists and executives from General Motors, IBM, the RAND Corporation, Bell Telephone, Harvard University, MIT, the Census Bureau, and the Office of Naval Research, as "acute," "unprecedented," "multiplying dramatically," and "astounding compared to the [available] facilities," represented a grave threat to the future of electronic computing. Already it was serious enough to demand a "cooperative effort" on the part of industry, government, and educational institutions to resolve.[13]

The proceedings of the Conference on Training Personnel for the Computing Machine Field provide the best data available on the state of the labor market in the electronic computer industry during its first decade. Representatives from almost every major computer user or manufacturer were in attendance; those who could not be present were surveyed in advance about their computational requirements and personnel practices.

The most obvious conclusion to be drawn from these data are that the computer industry in this period was growing rapidly, not just in size, but also in scope. The survey of the five hundred largest manufacturing companies in United States, compiled by Milton Mengel of the Burroughs Corporation, revealed that almost one-fifth were already using electronic computers by 1954, with another fifth engaged in studying their feasibility. The extent of this early and widespread adoption of the computer by large corporations is confirmed by other sources, and is a reflection of the increased availability of low(er)-cost and more reliable technology. By 1954, for example, IBM had already released its first mass-produced computer, the IBM 650, which sold so many units that it became known as the "Model T" of electronic computing. The IBM 650 and successors were in many ways evolutionary developments, designed specifically to integrate smoothly into already-existing systems and departments of computation.

This increase in the number of installed computers was, in and of itself, enough to cause a serious shortage of experienced computer personnel. Truman Hunter, of the IBM Applied Sciences Division (an entirely separate group from that headed by Bemer), anticipated doubling his programming staff (from fifty to a hundred) by the end of the year.[14] Similar rates of growth were reported in the aircraft, automobile, and petroleum industries, with one survey respondent expected to triple its number of programmers.[15] Charles Gregg, of the Air Force Materiel Command, declined to even estimate the demand for trained computer personnel in the U.S. government, suggesting only that "we sure need them badly," and that as far as training was concerned, "we have a rough row to hoe."[16] If we include in our understanding of computer personnel not just programmers but also keypunch and machine operators, technicians, and supervisory staff, the personnel shortage appears even more dramatic.

"Since you've had an introductory course in programming,
we'll just fill out those employment forms later."

© DATAMATION

Figure 3.2
Cartoon from *Datamation* magazine, 1968.

In the face of this looming crisis, the existing methods for training programmers and other computer personnel were revealed as ludicrously insufficient. At this point, there were no formal academic programs in computer science in existence, and those few courses in computer programming that were offered in universities were at the master's or PhD level. Computer manufacturers, who had a clear stake in ensuring that their customers could actually use their new machines, provided some training services. But in the fifteen months prior to the 1954 conference, confessed M. Paul Chinitz of Remington Rand UNIVAC (at that point the largest manufacturer of computers in the world), the company had only managed to train a total of 162 programmers.[17] He estimated that the total training capacity of all of the manufacturers combined at a mere 260 programmers annually. And so the majority of computer users were left to train their own personnel.[18] This in-house training was expensive, time-consuming, and generally inadequate.[19]

Part of the problem, of course, was that computer programming was inherently difficult. As was described in the previous chapter, programming in the 1950s—particularly in the early 1950s—was an inchoate discipline, a jumble of skills and techniques drawn from electrical engineering, mathematics, and symbolic logic. It was also intrinsically local and idiosyncratic: each individual computer installation had its own unique software, practices, tools, and standards. There were no programming languages, no operating systems, no best-practice guidelines, and no textbooks. The problem with the so-called electronic brains, as Truman Hunter of IBM noted, is that they were anything but: computers might be powerful tools, yet they were "completely dependent slaves" to the human mind. The development of these machines was resulting in "even greater recognition of, and paying a greater premium for," the skilled programmers who transformed their latent potential into real-world applications.[20]

It was one thing to identify, as Truman Hunter did, the increasing need for "men [programmers] . . . who were above average in training and ability" to accomplish this transformation, but what kind of training, and what kind of abilities?[21] Although government laboratories and engineering firms remained the primary consumers of computer technology through the early 1950s, a growing number were being sold to insurance companies, accounting firms, and other, even less technically oriented customers. Not only were these users less technically proficient and less likely to have their own in-house technical specialists but they also used their computers for different and in many ways more complicated types of applications. The Burroughs study, for example, suggested an interesting shift in the way in which computers were being used in this period, and by whom. While the majority of computers (95 percent) currently in service were being used for engineering or scientific purposes, the data on anticipated future purchases indicated a shift toward business applications.[22] The next generation of computers, the survey suggested, would be used increasingly (16 percent) for business data processing rather than scientific computation.[23]

These new business users saw the electronic computer as more than mere number crunchers; they saw them as payroll processing devices, data processing machines, and management information systems. This broader vision of an integrated "information machine" demanded of the computer new features and capabilities, many of them software rather than hardware oriented.[24]

As the computer became more of a tool for business than a scientific instrument, the nature of its use—and its primary user, the computer programmer—changed dramatically. The projects that these business programmers worked on tended to be larger, more highly structured (while at the same time less well defined), less mathematical, and more tightly coupled with other social and technological systems than were their scientific counterparts. Were the programmers who worked on heterogeneous business data processing systems technologists, managers, or accountants? As Charles Gregg of the Air Force Materiel Command jokingly suggested, the people who made the best programmers were "electronics engineers with an advanced degree in business administration." Such multitalented individuals were obviously in short supply. "If anyone can energize an educational program to produce such people in quantity," he quickly added, "we would certainly like to be put on their mailing list." His fellow conference participants no doubt agreed with this assessment: the needs of business demanded a whole new breed of programmers, and plenty of them.[25]

The 1954 Conference on Training Personnel for the Computing Machine Field was to be the first of many. The "persistent personnel problem," as it soon became known in the computing community, would only get worse over the course of the next decade.[26] It was clear that recruiting programmers a half dozen at the time with cute advertisements in the *New York Times* was not a sustainable strategy. But what was the alternative? If employers truly believed, as was argued in the previous chapter, that computer programmers formed a unique category of technical specialists—more creative than scientific, artisanal rather than industrial, born and not made—then how could they possibly hope to ensure an adequate supply to meet a burgeoning demand? How did they reconcile contemporary beliefs about the idiosyncratic nature of individual programming ability with the rigid demands of corporate management and control?

Aptitude Tests and Psychological Profiles

So how did companies deal with the need to train and recruit programmers on a large scale? Here the case of the System Development Corporation (SDC) is particularly instructive.

SDC was the RAND Corporation spin-off responsible for developing the software for the U.S. Air Force's Semi-Automated Ground Environment (SAGE) air-defense system. SAGE was perhaps the most ambitious and expensive of early cold war technological boondoggles. Comprised of a series of computerized tracking and communications centers, SAGE cost approximately $8 billion to develop and operate, and required the services of over two hundred thousand private contractors and military operators.

A major component of the SAGE project was the real-time computers required to coordinate its vast, geographically dispersed network of observation and response centers. IBM was hired to develop the computers themselves but considered programming them to be too difficult. In 1955 the RAND Corporation took over software development. It was estimated that the software for the SAGE system would require more than one million lines of code to be written. At a time when the largest programming projects had involved at most fifty thousand lines of code, this was a singularly ambitious undertaking.[27]

Within a year, there were more programmers at RAND than all other employees combined. Overwhelmed, RAND spun-off SDC to take over the project. By 1956, SDC employed seven hundred programmers, which at the time represented three-fifths of the available programmers in the entire United States.[28] Over the next five years, SDC would hire and train seven thousand more.[29] In the space of a few short years the personnel department at SDC had effectively doubled the number of trained programmers in the country. "We trained the industry," SDC executives were later fond of saying, and in many respects they were correct; for the next decade, at the very least, any programming department of any size was likely to contain at least two or three SDC alumni.[30]

In order to effectively recruit, train, and manage an unprecedented number of programmers, SDC pursued three interrelated strategies. The first involved the construction of an organizational and managerial structure that reduced its reliance on highly skilled, *experienced* programmers. The second focused on the development and use of aptitude tests and personality profiles to filter out the most promising potential programmers. And finally, SDC invested heavily in internal training and development programs. In a period when the computer manufacturers combined could only provide twenty-five hundred student weeks of instruction annually, SDC devoted more than ten thousand student weeks to instructing its own personnel to program.[31]

The engineers who founded SDC explicitly rejected what they called the "nostalgic" notion, common in the industry at that time, that programmers were "different," and "could not work and would not prosper" under the rigid structures of engineering management.[32] They organized SDC along the lines of a "software factory" that relied less on skilled workers, and more on centralized planning and control. The principles behind this approach were essentially those that had proven so successful in traditional industrial manufacturing: replaceable parts, simple and repetitive tasks, and a strict division of labor. The assumption was that a complex computer program like the SAGE control system could be neatly broken down into simple, modular components that could be easily understood by any programmer with the appropriate training and experience. Programmers in the software factory were mere machine operators; they had to be trained, but only in the basic mechanisms of implementing someone else's design. In the SDC hierarchy, managers made all of the important decisions.[33]

The hierarchical approach to software development was attractive to SDC executives for a number of reasons. To begin with, it was a familiar model for managing government and military subcontractors. Engineering management promised scientific control over the often-unpredictable processes of research and development. It allowed for the orderly production of cutting-edge science and technology.[34] In the language used by the managers themselves, it was a solution that "scaled" well, meaning that it could accommodate the rapid and unanticipated growth typical of cold war–era military research. Scientific management techniques and production technologies could be substituted for human resources. It was not a system dependent on individual genius or chance insight. It replaced skilled personnel with superior process. For these and other reasons, it seemed the perfect solution to the problem posed by the mass production of computer programs. (Coincidentally, it was easier to justify billing the government for a large number of mediocre low-wage employees than a smaller number of excellent but expensive contractors.)

It is important to note that the SDC approach did not attempt to solve its programmer personnel problem by reducing the number of programmers it required. On the contrary, the SDC software factory strategy (or as detractors dismissively referred to it, the "Mongolian Horde" approach to software development) probably demanded more programmers than was otherwise necessary. But the programmers that SDC was interested in were not the idiosyncratic "black artists" that most employers were desperately in search of. SDC still expected to hire and train large numbers of programmers, yet it hoped that these programmers would be much easier to identify and recruit. Most of its trainees had little or no experience with computers; in fact, many managers at SDC preferred it that way.[35]

The solution that SDC ultimately employed to identify and recruit potential programmers was to become standard practice in the industry. Building on techniques pioneered at RAND and MIT's Lincoln Laboratory in the early 1950s, SDC developed a suite of aptitude tests and psychological profiles that were used to screen large numbers of potential trainees.[36] Candidates who scored well on the tests were then interviewed, tested a second time—this time for desirable psychological characteristics—and then assuming that all went well, offered a position. The aptitude tests were meant to filter for traits thought essential to good programming, such as the ability to think logically and do abstract reasoning. The psychological profiles were meant to identify individuals with the appropriate personality for programming work.[37]

The use of psychometric tools such as aptitude tests and psychological profiles was not unique to computing. Such tests had long been used by the U.S. military in the recruitment of soldiers. The SDC exams, for example, were based on the Thurstone Primary Mental Abilities Test and the Thurstone Temperament Schedule, which had both been in wide use since the 1930s.[38] In the period following the end of the Second World War, similar metrics had been enthusiastically adopted by the advocates of scientific personnel research.[39] SDC was able to choose from more than thirty available tests when it established its test battery in the late 1950s.[40]

Could you answer these test questions?

Sample these questions given to applicants for computer-programer training by Honeywell Inc. for a hint as to whether you have the aptitude to be an electronic-brain feeder.

1 An electronic-parts distributor has some transformers in one of his stockrooms. They all look alike but he knows that a mistake has been made and that there are two types of transformers (types A & B) in the room, and that there are four of each type for a total of eight. He receives a rush order from a customer for either two type-A transformers, or two type-B transformers. The customer has the equipment to tell the difference between the transformers, but the parts distributor does not. Since the transformers are very expensive to ship, the distributor ships the minimum number necessary. How many does he ship?

2 If the statement, "There are more dogs in the U.S. than there are hairs on any one dog in the U.S.," is true, then is the statement, "There are at least two dogs in the U.S. with exactly the same number of hairs," true or false? And why?

3 If a brick balances evenly with three-quarters of a pound weight plus three-quarters of a brick, what is the weight of the whole brick?

4 A light flashes once every five minutes; another light flashes once every 14 minutes. If they both flash together at 1:00 p.m., what time will they next flash together?

5 Alice is as old as Betty and Christine together. Last year Betty was twice as old as Christine. Two years hence Alice will be twice as old as Christine. Their ages?

6 A man and his wife live on the fifth floor of an apartment building and have no phone. Frequently, when he comes home from work at night, his wife asks him to run an errand before dinner, but of course not the same errand every night. So, in order to save himself a trip up the stairs every evening, she puts a light in each of the four windows that can be viewed from the street. What is the most number of errand messages his wife can choose from, at any one time?

Answers: (1) 3. (2) True. The number of dogs exceeds the possible variations in the number of hairs they have. (3) 3 pounds. (4) 2:10 p.m. (5) 8, 5, and 3. (6) 15, assuming that dark windows are not a signal for an errand.

Figure 3.3
Honeywell Corporation Aptitude Test, 1965.

The central assumption of all such aptitude tests was that there was a particular innate characteristic, or set of characteristics, that could be positively correlated with occupational performance. These traits were necessarily innate—otherwise they could simply be taught, rather then only identified—and tended to be cognitive, personality related, or some combination of both. The Thurstone Primary Mental Abilities Test, for example, claimed to evaluate specific skills, such as "verbal meaning" and "reasoning," as well as more general qualities such as "emotional stability." The verbal meaning section presented a series of words for which the test taker would have to identify the closest synonym. The reasoning section involved the completion of number series using rules implicit in the given portion of the series. The emotional stability questions purported to measure an amalgam of desirable personality traits, including patience and a willingness to pay close attention to detail.

The scientific validity of aptitude testing was at best equivocal. At an Association for Computing Machinery conference in 1957, the company's own psychometrician, Thomas Rowan, presented a paper concluding that "in every case," the correlation between test scores and subsequent performance reviews "was not significantly different from zero."[41] The best he could say was that scores on the aptitude test did correlate somewhat with grades in the programming course. Nevertheless, SDC continued to use aptitude tests, including those tests that Rowan had identified as unsatisfactory, as the primary basis for its selection procedures at least until the late 1960s.

Why persist in using aptitude testing when it was so obviously inadequate? The simple answer seems to be that SDC had no other option. Having accepted a $20 million contract from the Air Defense Command to develop the SAGE software, SDC necessarily had to expand rapidly. Even had SDC managed to hire away *all* of the computer programmers then working in the United States, it could still not have adequately staffed its growing programming division. The entire SDC development strategy had been constructed around the notion that complex software systems could be readily broken down into simpler modules that even relatively novice programmers—properly managed—could adequately develop. The SDC software factory was a deliberate attempt to industrialize the programming process, to impose on it the lessons learned from traditional industrial manufacturing. Like all industrial systems, the software factory required not only new organizational forms and production technologies (in this case, automated development and testing utilities) but also new forms of workers. As with the replacement of skilled machinists with unskilled machine operators in the automobile factories of the early twentieth century, these new software workers would require less experience and training than their predecessors, but the availability of large numbers of them was essential. The mass production of computer programs necessitated the mass production of programmers.

As will be discussed further below, it is questionable whether the SDC vision of the software factory was ever truly realized—by SDC itself or any of its many imitators. But for the time being it is enough to say that the aptitude testing methods that SDC originated and then disseminated throughout the industry assumed programming to be a well-defined, largely mechanical process. In the words of Thomas Rowan, the person primarily responsible for the SDC personnel selection process, programming was only "that activity occurring after an explicit statement of the problem had been obtained."[42] Specifically excluded from programming were any of the creative activities of planning or design. In other words, SDC had redefined computer programming as exactly the type of skill that aptitude tests were meant to accurately identify: straightforward, mechanical, and easily isolated. The SDC aptitude tests were not so much an attempt to identify programmer skill and ability as to embody it.

IBM PAT

Despite the seeming inability of the SDC aptitude testing regime to accurately capture the essence of programming ability, similar tests continued to be widely developed and adopted, not only by SDC, but also increasingly by other large employers. Of these second-generation tests, the most significant was the IBM Programmer Aptitude Test (PAT). In 1955, IBM contracted with two psychologists, Walter McNamara and John Hughes, to develop an aptitude test to identify programming talent. The programmer test was based on an earlier exam for card punch operators. Originally called the Aptitude Test for EDPM (Electronic Data Processing Machine) Programmers, it was renamed PAT in 1959.[43]

Over the next few decades, IBM PAT would become the industry standard instrument for evaluating programming ability. By 1962 an estimated 80 percent of all businesses used some form of aptitude test when hiring programmers, and half of these used IBM PAT.[44] Most of the many vocational schools that emerged in this period to train programmers used PAT as a preliminary screening device. In 1967 alone, PAT was administered to more than seven hundred thousand individuals.[45] Well into the 1970s, IBM PAT served as the de facto gateway into the programming occupation.

Like the SDC exams, IBM PAT focused primarily on mathematical aptitude, with most of the questions dealing with number series, figure analogies, and arithmetic reasoning. Although several minor variations of PAT were introduced over the course of the next several decades, the overall structure of the exam remained surprisingly consistent. The first section required examinees to identify the underlying rule defining the pattern of a series of numbers. The second section was similar to the first, but involved geometric forms rather than number series. The third and final section posed word problems that could be reduced to algebraic forms, such as "How many apples can you buy for sixty cents at the rate of three for ten cents?"[46] Examinees had fifty minutes to answer roughly one hundred questions, and so speed as well as accuracy was required.

Critics of PAT argued that its emphasis on mathematics made it increasingly irrelevant to contemporary programming practices. It might once have been the case, as Gerald Weinberg acknowledged in his acerbic critique of IBM PAT in 1971, that programmers would have to add two or three hexadecimal numbers in order to find an address in a dump of a machine or assembly language program. But even then the arithmetic involved was relatively trivial, and the development of high-level programming languages had largely eliminated the need for such mental mathematics. And as for an aptitude for understanding geometric relationships, Weinberg noted sarcastically, "I've never met a programmer who was asked to tell whether two programs were the same if one was rotated 90 degrees."[47] At best such measures of basic mathematical ability were a proxy for more general intelligence; more likely, however, they were worse than useless, a deliberate form of self-deception practiced by desperate employers and the "personnel experts" who preyed on them.[48]

Weinberg was not alone in his critique of the mathematical focus of PAT and other exams. As early as the late 1950s, a Bureau of Labor report had identified the growing sense of corporate disillusionment with the mathematical approach to computing, contending that "many employers no longer stress a strong background in mathematics for programming of business or other mass data if candidates can demonstrate an aptitude for the work."[49] As more and more computers were used for business data processing rather than scientific computation, the types of problems that programmers were required to solve changed accordingly. The mathematical tricks that were so crucial in trimming valuable processor cycles in scientific and engineering applications had no place in the corporate environment, which privileged legibility and ease of maintenance over performance.[50] Not surprisingly, scientific programmers scored better on PAT than business programmers.[51]

The relevance of mathematical aptitude to programming ability remained, and still does, a perennial question in the industry. At least one study of programmers identified no significant difference in performance between those with a background in science or engineering and those who studied humanities or the social sciences.[52] Even the authors of IBM PAT concluded that at best, mathematical ability was associated with particular applications and not programming ability in general.[53]

Some observers went so far as to suggest that by privileging mathematical aptitude, PAT was downright pathological, selecting for "a type of logical mind which . . . is not very often supported by maturity or reasoned thinking ability."[54] As a result, these selection processes tended to segregate individuals whose personality traits made it difficult to cooperate with management and fellow employees. At the very least, the mathematical mind-set frequently precluded the kinds of complex solutions typical of business programming applications.

As will be described in more detail in chapter 5, the emerging discipline of computer science, in its own quest for academic respectability, continued to emphasize mathematics, while industry leaders regularly dismissed it as irrelevant.[55] For the time being, it is enough to note that the continuing controversy over mathematics reflected deeper disagreement, or at least ambiguity, about the true nature of programming ability.

The larger question, of course, was whether or not scores on PAT corresponded with real-world programming performance. On this question the data are ambiguous. Most employers did not even attempt to correlate test scores with objective measures of performance such as supervisor ratings.[56] The small percentage that did concluded that there was no relationship between PAT scores and programming performance at all, at least in the context of business programming.[57] At best, these studies identified a small correlation between PAT scores and *academic success in training programs*. Few argued that such correlations translated into accurate indicators of future success in the workplace.[58] Even IBM recommended that PAT be used only in the context of a larger personnel screening process.

Over the course of the next decade, there were several attempts to recalibrate the tests to make them more directly relevant to real-world programming. IBM itself created several modifications to its original PAT, including the Revised Programmer Aptitude Test (1959) and the Data Processing Aptitude Test (1964), although neither successfully replaced the popular PAT.[59] The Computer Usage Company's version of a programmer aptitude test required examinees to solve logical problems using the console lights on an IBM 1401 computer.[60] The Aptitude Assessment Battery: Programming, developed in 1967 by Jack Wolfe, a prominent critic of IBM PAT, eliminated mathematics and concentrated on an applicant's ability to focus intensively on complex, multiple-step problems.[61] The Programmer Aptitude and Competence System required examinees to develop actual programs using a simplified programming language.[62] The Basic Programmer Knowledge Test (1966) tested everything from design and coding to testing and documentation.[63]

Personality Profiles

Since even their most enthusiastic advocates recognized the limitations of aptitude testing, most particularly their narrow focus on mathematics and logic, many employers also developed personality profiles that they hoped would help isolate the less tangible characteristics that made for a good programmer trainee. Some of these characteristics, such as being task oriented or detail minded, overlapped with the skills measured by more conventional aptitude tests. Many simply reinforced the conventional wisdom captured by the "Talk of the Town" column almost a decade earlier. "Creativity is a major attribute of technically oriented people," suggested one representative profile. "Look for those who like intellectual challenge rather than interpersonal relations or managerial decision-making. Look for the chess player, the solver of mathematical puzzles."[64] But other profiles emphasized different, less obvious personality traits such as imagination, ingenuity, strong verbal abilities, and a desire to express oneself.[65] Still others tested for even more elusive qualities, such as emotional stability.[66] Such traits were obviously difficult to capture in a standard, skills-oriented aptitude test. Personality profiles relied instead on a combination of psychological testing, vocational interest surveys, and personal histories to provide a richer, more nuanced set of criteria on which to evaluate programmers.

The idea that particular personality traits might be useful indicators of programming ability was clearly a legacy of the origins of programming in the early 1950s. The central assumption was that programming ability was an innate rather than a learned ability, something to be identified rather than instilled. Good programming was believed to be dependent on uniquely qualified individuals, and that what defined these people was some indescribable, impalpable quality—a "twinkle in the eye," an "indefinable enthusiasm," or what one interviewer depicted as "the programming bug that meant . . . we're going to take a chance on him despite his background."[67] The development of programmer personality profiles seemed to offer empirical evidence for what anecdote had already determined: the best programmers appeared to have been born, not made.

The use of personality profiles to identify programmers began, as with other industry-standard recruiting practices, at SDC. Applicants at SDC were first tested for aptitude, then interviewed in person, and only then profiled for desirable personality characteristics. Like other psychological profiles from this period, the SDC screens identified as valuable only those skills and characteristics that would have been assets in any white-collar occupation: the ability to think logically, work under pressure, and get along with people; a retentive memory and the desire to see a problem through to completion; and careful attention to detail.

By the start of the 1960s, however, SDC psychologists had developed more sophisticated models based on the extensive employment data that the company had collected over the previous decade as well as surveys of members of the Association for Computer Machinery and the Data Processing Management Association. In a series of papers published in serious academic journals such as the *Journal of Applied Psychology* and *Personnel Psychology*, SDC psychologists Dallis Perry and William Cannon provided a detailed profile of the "vocational interests of computer programmers."[68] The scientific basis for their profile was the Strong Vocational Interest Bank (SVIB), which had been widely used in vocational testing since the late 1920s.

The basic SVIB in this period consisted of four hundred questions aimed at eliciting an emotional response ("like," "dislike," or "indifferent") to specific occupations, work and recreational activities, types of people, and personality types. By the 1960s, more than fifty statistically significant collections of preferences ("keys") had been developed for such occupations as artist, mathematician, police officer, and airplane pilot. Perry and Cannon were attempting to develop a similar interest key for programmer. They hoped to use this key to correlate a unique programmer personality profile with self-reported levels of job satisfaction. In the absence of direct measures of job performance, such as supervisors' evaluations, it was assumed that satisfaction tracked closely with performance. The larger assumption behind the use of the SVIB profiles was that candidates who had interests in common with those individuals who were successful in a given occupation were themselves also likely to achieve similar success.

Many of the traits that Perry and Cannon attributed to successful programmers were unremarkable: for the most part programmers enjoyed their work, disliked routine and regimentation, and were especially interested in problem and puzzle-solving activities.[69] The programmer key that they developed bore some resemblance to the existing keys for engineering and chemistry, but not to those of physics or mathematics, which Perry and Cannon saw as contradicting the traditional focus on mathematics training in programmer recruitment. A slight correlation with the musician key offered "some, but not very strong," support for "the prevalent belief in a relationship between programming and musical ability."[70] Otherwise, programmers resembled other white-collar professionals in such diverse fields as optometry, public administration, accounting, and personnel management.

In fact, there was only one really "striking characteristic" about programmers that the Perry and Cannon study identified. This was "their disinterest in people." Compared with other professional men, "programmers dislike activities involving close personal interaction. They prefer to work with things rather than people."[71] In a subsequent study, Perry and Cannon demonstrated this to be true of female programmers as well.[72]

The idea that computer programmers lacked people skills quickly became part of the lore of the computer industry. The influential industry analyst Richard Brandon suggested that this was in part a reflection of the selection process itself, with its emphasis on mathematics and logic. The "Darwinian selection" mechanism of personnel profiling, Brandon maintained, selected for personality traits that performed well in the artificial isolation of the testing environment, but that proved dysfunctional in the more complex social environment of a corporate development project. Programmers were "excessively independent," argued Brandon, to the point of mild paranoia. The programmer type is "often egocentric, slightly neurotic, and he borders upon a limited schizophrenia. The incidence of beards, sandals, and other symptoms of rugged individualism or nonconformity are notably greater among this demographic group. Stories about programmers and their attitudes and peculiarities are legion, and do not bear repeating here."[73]

Although Brandon's evidence was strictly anecdotal, his portrayal of the neurotic programmers was convincing enough that the psychologist Theodore Willoughby felt compelled to refute it on scientific grounds in his 1972 article "Are Programmers Paranoid."[74] But whether or not Brandon's paranoia was, from a strictly medical perspective, an accurate diagnosis is irrelevant. The idea that "detached" individuals made good programmers was embodied, in the form of the psychological profile, into the hiring practices of the industry.[75] Possibly this was a legacy of the murky origins of programming as a fringe discipline in the early 1950s; perhaps it was self-fulfilling prophecy. Nevertheless, the idea of the programmer as being particularly ill equipped for or uninterested in social interaction did become part of the conventional wisdom of the industry. Although the short-term effect of this particular occupational stereotype was negligible, it would later come back to haunt the programming community as it attempted to professionalize later in the decade. As we will see in later chapters, the stereotype of the computer programmer as a machine obsessed and antisocial was used to great effect by those who wished to undermine the professional authority of the computer boys.

For the most part, however, the personality profiles that Perry and Cannon as well as others developed simply became one component of a larger set of tools used by employers to evaluate potential programmers.[76] According to one survey of Canadian employers, more than two-thirds used a combination of aptitude and general intelligence tests, personality profiles, and interest surveys in their selection processes.[77]

The Situation Can Only Get Worse

Despite the massive amount of effort that went into developing the science of programmer personnel selection, the labor market in computing only seemed to deteriorate. Many of the technological and demographic trends identified at the Wayne State Conference in 1954 continued to accelerate. By 1961, industry analysts were fretting publicly about a "gap in programming support" that "will get worse in the next several years before it gets better."[78] In 1962, the editors of the powerful industry journal *Datamation* declared that "first on anyone's checklist of professional problems is the manpower shortage of both trained and even untrained programmers, operators, logical designers and engineers in a variety of flavors."[79] At a conference held that year at the MIT School of Industrial Management, the "programming bottleneck" was identified as the central dilemma in computer management.[80] In 1966, the labor situation had gotten so bad that *Business Week* declared it a "software crisis."[81] An informal survey in 1967 of management information systems (MIS) managers identified as the primary hurdle "handicapping the progress of MIS" to be "the shortage of good, experienced people."[82] By the late 1960s, the demand for programmers was increasing by more than 50 percent annually, and it was predicted that "the software man will be in even greater demand in 1970 than he is today."[83] Indeed, estimates of the number of programmers that would be required by 1970 ranged as high as 650,000.[84]

It would be difficult to overstate the degree to which concern about the software labor crisis dominated the industry in this period. The popular and professional literature during this time was obsessed with the possible effects of the personnel crisis on the future of the industry. "Competition for programmers has driven salaries up so fast," warned a contemporary article in *Fortune* magazine, "that programming has become probably the country's highest paid technological occupation. . . . Even so, some companies can't find experienced programmers at any price."[85] A study in 1965 by Automatic Data Processing, Inc., then one of the largest employers of programmers, predicted that average salaries in the industry would increase 40 to 50 percent over the next five years.[86] The ongoing "shortage of capable programmers," argued *Datamation* in 1967, "had profound implications, not only for the computer industry as it is now, but for how it can be in the future."[87] These potentially profound implications included everything from financial collapse to software-related injury or death to the emergence of a packaged software application industry.

Faced with a growing shortage of skilled programmers, employers were forced to expand their recruitment efforts and lower their hiring standards. Although by 1967 IBM alone was training ten thousand programmers annually (at a cost of $90 to $100 million), it was becoming increasingly clear that computer manufacturers alone could not produce trained programmers fast enough.[88] As a result, many companies reluctantly assumed the costs of expensive internal training programs, "not because they want to do it, but because they have found it to be an absolute necessary adjunct to the operation of their business."[89] It is difficult to find accurate data on the size of such programs, as many organizations refused to disclose details about them to outsiders, "on the theory that to do so would only invite raiding" from other employers.[90] The job market was so competitive in this period that as many as half of all programmer trainees would leave within a year to pursue more lucrative opportunities.[91] And since the cost of training or recruiting a new programmer was estimated at almost an entire year's salary, such high levels of turnover were expensive.[92] Many employers were thus extremely secretive about their training and recruitment practices; some even refused to allow their computer personnel to attend professional conferences because of the rampant headhunting that occurred at such gatherings.[93] Because of the low salaries that it paid relative to the industry, the U.S. government had a particular problem retaining skilled employees, and so in 1963, Congress passed the Vocational Education Act, which made permanent the provisions of Title VIII of the National Defense Education Act of 1959 for training highly skilled technicians. By 1966, the act had paid for the training of thirty-three thousand computer personnel—requiring in exchange only that they work for a certain time in government agencies.[94]

In numerous cases, the aptitude tests that many corporations hoped would alleviate their personnel problems had entirely the opposite effect. Whatever small amount of predictive validity the tests had was soon compromised by applicants who cheated or took them multiple times. Since many employers relied on the same basic suite of tests, would-be programmers simply applied for positions at less-desirable firms, mastered the aptitude tests and application process, and then transferred their newfound testing skills to the companies they were truly interested in. Taking the same test repeatedly virtually assured top scores.[95] Copies of IBM PAT were also stolen and placed in fraternity files.[96] By the late 1960s it appeared that all of the major aptitude tests had been thoroughly compromised. One widely circulated book contained versions of the IBM, UNIVAC, and NCR exams. Updated versions were published almost annually.[97]

Paradoxically, even as the value of the aptitude tests diminished, their use began to increase. All of the major hardware vendors developed their own versions, such as the National Cash Register Programmer Aptitude Test and the Burroughs Corporation Computer Programmer Aptitude Battery.[98] Aptitude testing became the "Hail Mary pass" of the computer industry. Some companies tested all of their employees, including the secretaries, in the hope that hidden talent could be identified.[99] A group called the Computer Personnel Development Association was formed to scour local community centers for promising programmer candidates.[100] Local YMCAs offered the test for a nominal fee, as did local community colleges.[101] In 1968 computer service bureaus in New York City, desper-

Figure 3.4
Cartoon from *Datamation* magazine, 1962.

ate to fill the demand for more programmers, began testing inmates at the nearby Sing-Sing Prison, promising them permanent positions pending their release.[102] That same year, *Cosmopolitan Magazine* urged "Cosmo Girls" to go out and become "computer girls" making "$15,000 a year" as programmers. Not only did the widespread personnel problem in computing make it possible for women to break into the industry but the field was also currently "overrun with males," making it easy to find desirable dating prospects. Programming was "just like planning a dinner," the article quoted software pioneer Admiral Grace Hopper as saying. "Women are 'naturals' at computer programming." And in true *Cosmopolitan* fashion, the article was also accompanied by a quiz: in this case, a mini programmer aptitude test adapted from an exam developed at NCR.[103] The influx of new programmer trainees and vocational school graduates into the software labor market only exacerbated an already-dire labor situation. The market was flooded with aspiring programmers with little training and no practical experience. As one study by the Association for Computing Machinery's (ACM) SIGCPR warned, by 1968 there was a growing *oversupply* of a certain undesirable species of software specialist. "The ranks of the computer world are being swelled by growing hordes of programmers, systems analysts and related personnel," the SIGCPR argued. "Educational, performance and professional standards are virtually nonexistent and confusion grows rampant in selecting, training, and assigning people to do jobs."[104]

It was not just employers who were frustrated by the confused state of the labor market. "As long as I have been programming, I have heard about this 'extreme shortage of programmers,'" wrote one *Datamation* reader, whose husband had unsuccessfully tried to break into the computer business. "How does a person . . . get into programming?"[105] "Could you answer for me the question as to what in the eyes of industry constitutes a 'qualified' programmer?" pleaded another aspiring job candidate. "What education, experience, etc. are considered to satisfy the 'qualified' status?"[106] A background in mathematics seemed increasingly irrelevant to programming, particularly in the business world, and even the emerging discipline of computer science appeared to offer no practical solution to the problem of training programmers en masse. In the absence of clear educational standards or functional aptitude exams, would-be programmers and employers alike were preyed on by a growing number of vocational schools that promised to supply both programmer training and trained programmers. During the mid-1960s these schools sprang up all over the country, promising high salaries and dazzling career opportunities, and flooding the market with candidates who were prepared to pass programming aptitude tests but nothing more. Advertisements for these vocational schools, which appeared everywhere from the classified section of newspapers to the back of paper matchbooks, emphasized the desperate demand for programmers and the low barriers of entry to the discipline: "There's room for everyone. The industry needs people. You've got what it takes."[107]

The typical vocational school offered between three and nine months of training, and cost between $1,000 and $2,500. Students at these schools would receive four to five hours a day of training in various aspects of electronic data processing, including programming but also more basic tasks such as keypunch and tabulating machine operation. What programming training they did receive focused on the memoriza-

"But I don't want to be a computer programmer!"

Figure 3.5
Cartoon from *New Yorker* magazine, May 31, 1969. © Vahan Shirvanian/The
New Yorker Collection/www.cartoonbank.com.

tion of syntax rather than hands-on problem solving. Because of the high
costs associated with renting computer time, the curriculum was often
padded with material only tangentially related to computing—such as
several days' worth of review of basic arithmetic. A few schools did lease
their own computers, but these were typically the low-end IBM/360
Model 20, which did not possess its own disk or tape mechanism. At
some schools students could expect to only receive as little as one hour
total of machine time, which had to be shared among a class of up to
fifteen students.[108]

These schools were generally profit-oriented enterprises more interested in quantity than quality. The entrance examinations, curriculum,
and fee structure of these programs were carefully constructed to comply
with the requirements of the GI Bill. Aggressive salespeople promised
guaranteed placement and starting salaries of up to $700 per week—at
a time when the industry average weekly salary for junior programmers
was closer to $400 to $500. Since these salespeople were paid on commission, and could earn as much as $150 for every student who enrolled
in a $1,000 course of study, they encouraged almost anyone to apply;
for many of the vocational schools, the "only meaningful entrance
requirements are a high school diploma, 18 years of age . . . and the

ability to pay."[109] Instructors were also compensated on a pay-as-you-go basis, which encouraged them to retain even the least competent of their students. Some of these instructors were working programmers moonlighting for additional cash, but given the overall shortage of experienced programmers in this period, most had little, if any, industry experience. Some had only the training that they had received as students in the very programs in which they were now serving as instructors.

Since these schools had an interest in recruiting as many students as possible, they made wide use of aptitude testing. Most included watered-down versions of IBM PAT in their marketing brochures, although a few offered coupons for independent testing bureaus. The version of PAT that many schools relied on was graded differently from the standardized test. A student could receive a passing grade after answering as few as 50 percent of the questions correctly, and a grade of A required only a score of 70 percent. The scores on these entrance examinations was basically irrelevant, with C and D students frequently receiving admission, but graduating students were required take the full version of PAT. Only the top-scoring students were passed on to employment agencies, thereby boosting the school's claims about placement records.[110]

There were some vocational training programs that were legitimate. The Chicago-based Automation Institute, for example—sponsored by the Council for Economic and Industrial Research (itself largely sponsored by the computer manufacturer Control Data Corporation)—maintained relatively strict standards in its nationwide chain of franchises. In 1967, the Automation Institute became the first EDP school to be accredited by the Accrediting Commission for Business Schools. There were also programs offered by community colleges and junior colleges (and even some high schools) that at least attempted to provide substantial EDP training. The more legitimate schools oriented their curricula toward the requirements of industry. But the requirements of the industry were poorly understood or articulated, and vocational schools suffered from many of the same problems that plagued industry personnel managers: a shortage of experienced instructors, the lack of established standards and curricula, and general uncertainty about what skills and aptitudes made for a qualified programmer. For the most part, the conditions at most vocational EDP schools was so scandalous that by the end of the decade many companies imposed strict "no EDP school graduate" policies.[111] A 1970 report by an ACM ad-hoc committee on private EDP schools confirmed this reluctance on the part of employers and concluded that fewer than 60 percent of EDP school graduates were able to land jobs in the EDP field.[112]

Making Programming Masculine

One unintended consequence of the uncertainty in the labor market for programming personnel reflected in—and in part created by—the widespread use of aptitude tests and personality profiles by corporate employers and vocational schools was the continued masculinization of the computing professions. We have already seen how the successful (re)construction of programming in the 1950s as a black art depended, in part, on particularly male notions of mastery, creativity, and autonomy. The increasingly male subculture of computer hacking (an anachronistic term in this period, but appropriately descriptive nevertheless) was reinforced and institutionalized by the hiring practices of the industry.

At first glance, the representation of programming ability as innate, rather than an acquired skill or the product of a particular form of technical education, might be seen as gender neutral or even female friendly. The aptitude tests for programming ability were, after all, widely distributed among female employees, including clerical workers and secretaries. And according to one 1968 study, it was found that a successful team of computer specialists included an "ex-farmer, a former tabulating machine operator, an ex-key punch operator, a girl who had done secretarial work, a musician and a graduate in mathematics." The last, the mathematician, "was considered the least competent."[113] As hiring practices went, aptitude testing at least had the virtue of being impersonal and seemingly objective. Being a member of the old boys' club does not do much for one's scores on a standardized exam (Except to the extent that fraternities and other male social organizations served as clearinghouses for stolen copies of popular aptitude tests such as IBM PAT. Such theft and other forms of cheating were rampant in the industry, and taking the test more than once was almost certain to lead to a passing grade.)

Yet aptitude tests and personality profiles did embody and privilege masculine characteristics. For instance, despite the growing consensus within the industry (especially in business data processing) that mathematical training was irrelevant to the performance of most commercial programming tasks, popular aptitude tests such as IBM PAT still emphasized mathematical ability.[114] Some of the mathematical questions tested

Figure 3.6
According to the original caption for this cartoon, "Programmers are crazy about puzzles, tend to like research applications and risk-taking, and don't like people." William M. Cannon and Dallis K. Perry, "A Vocational Interest Scale for Computer Programmers," *Proceedings of the Fourth SIGCPR Conference on Computer Personnel Research* (Los Angeles: ACM, 1966), 61–82.

only logical thinking and pattern recognition, but others required formal training in mathematics—a fact that even *Cosmopolitan* recognized as discriminating against women. Still, the kinds of questions that could be easily tested using multiple-choice aptitude tests and mass-administered personality profiles necessarily focused on mathematical trivia, logic puzzles, and word games. The test format simply did not allow for any more nuanced, meaningful, or context-specific problem solving. And in the 1950s and 1960s at least, such questions did privilege the typical male educational experience.

Even more obviously gendered were the personality profiles that reinforced the ideal of the "detached" (read male) programmer. It is almost certainly the case that these profiles represented, at best, deeply flawed scientific methodology. But they almost equally certainly created a gender-biased feedback cycle that ultimately selected for programmers with stereotypically masculine characteristics. The primary selection mechanism used by the industry selected for antisocial, mathematically inclined males, and therefore antisocial, mathematically inclined males were overrepresented in the programmer population; this in turn reinforced the popular perception that programmers *ought* to be antisocial and mathematically inclined (and therefore male), and so on ad infinitum. Combined with the often-explicit association of programming personnel with beards, sandals, and scruffiness, it is no wonder that women felt increasingly excluded from the center of the computing community.

Finally, the explosion of unscrupulous vocational schools in this period may also have contributed to the marginalization of women in computing. Not only were these schools constructed deliberately on the model of the older—and female-oriented—typing academies and business colleges, but they also preyed specifically on those aspirants to the programming professions who most lacked access to traditional occupational and financial assets, such as those without technical educations, college degrees, personal connections, or business experience. It was frequently women who fell into this category. At the very least, by sowing confusion in the programmer labor market through encouraging false expectations, inflating standards, and rigging aptitude tests, the schools made it even more difficult for women and other unconventional candidates to enter the profession.

This bias toward male programmers was not so much deliberate as it was convenient—a combination of laziness, ambiguity, and traditional male privilege. The fact that the use of lazy screening practices inadvertently excluded large numbers of potential *female* trainees was simply never considered. But the increasing assumption that the average programmer was also male did play a key role in the establishment of a highly masculine programming subculture.

The Search for Solutions

Given that aptitude tests were perceived by many within the industry to be inaccurate, irrelevant, and susceptible to widespread cheating, why did so many employers continue to make extensive use of them well into the 1980s? The most obvious reason is that they had few other options. The rapid expansion of the commercial computer industry in the early 1960s demanded the recruitment of large armies of new professional programmers. At the same time, the increasing diversity and complexity of software systems in this period—driven in large part by the shift in focus from scientific to business computing—meant that traditional measures of programming ability, most specifically formal training in mathematics or logic, were becoming ever less relevant to the quotidian practice of programming. The general lack of consensus about what constituted relevant knowledge or experience in the computer fields undermined attempts to systematize the production of programmers. Vocational EDP schools were seen as being too lax in their standards, and the emerging academic discipline of computer science was viewed as too stringent. Neither was believed to be a reliable short-term solution to the burgeoning labor shortage in programming.

In the face of such uncertainty and ambiguity, aptitude testing and personality profiling promised at least the illusion of managerial control. While many of the methods used by employers at this time appear hopelessly naive to modern observers, they represented the cutting edge of personnel research. Since at least the 1920s, personnel managers had been attempting to professionalize along the lines of a scientific discipline.[115] The large-scale use of psychometric technologies for personnel selection during the first and second world wars had seemed to many to validate their claims to scientific legitimacy.[116] In the immediate postwar period, personnel researchers established new academic journals, professional societies, and academic programs. It is no coincidence that the heyday of aptitude testing in the software industry corresponded with this period of intense professionalization in the fields that would eventually come to be known collectively as human resources management. The programmer labor crisis of the 1950s provided the perfect opportunity for these emerging experts to practice their craft.

On an even more pragmatic level, however, aptitude testing offered a significant advantage over the available alternatives. To borrow a phrase from contemporary computer industry parlance, aptitude testing was a solution that *scaled efficiently*. That is to say, the costs of aptitude testing grew only linearly (as opposed to exponentially) with the number of applicants. It was possible, in short, to administer aptitude tests quickly and inexpensively to thousands of aspiring programmers. Compared to such time-consuming and expensive alternatives such as individual interviews or formal educational requirements, aptitude testing was a cheap and easy solution. And since the contemporary emphasis on individual genius over experience or education meant that a star programmer was as likely to come from the secretarial pool as the engineering department, the ability to screen large numbers of potential trainees was preeminent.

Finally, in addition to its practical economic advantages, large-scale aptitude testing programs represented for many corporate employers a small but important step toward the eventual goal of mass-producing programmer trainees. Such tests were obviously not intended to evaluate the skills and abilities of experienced programmers; they were clearly tools for identifying the lowest common denominator among programmer talent. The explicit goal of testing programs at large employers like SDC was to reduce the overall level of skill among the programming workforce. By identifying the minimum level of aptitude required to be a competent programmer, SDC could reduce its dependence on individual programmers. It could construct a software factory out of the interchangeable parts produced by the impersonal and industrial processes of its aptitude test regimes.

It is this last consequence of aptitude testing that is the most interesting and perplexing. Like all of the proposed solutions to the labor shortage in programming, aptitude testing also embodied certain assumptions about the nature of the underlying problem. At first glance, the continued emphasis that aptitude tests and personality profiles placed on innate ability and creativity appeared to have served the interests of programming professionals. By reinforcing the contemporary belief that good programmers were born, not made, they provided individual programmers with substantial leverage in the job market. Experienced programmers made good money, had numerous opportunities for horizontal mobility within the industry, and were relatively immune from managerial imperatives. On the other hand, aptitude tests and personality profiles also emphasized the negative perception of programmers as idiosyncratic, antisocial, and potentially unreliable. Many computer specialists were keenly aware of the crisis of labor and the tension it was producing in their industry and profession as well as in their own individual careers. Although many appreciated the short-term benefits of the ongoing programmer shortage, many believed that the continued crisis threatened the long-term stability and reputation of their industry and profession.

As aptitude tests were increasingly used in a haphazard and irresponsible fashion, their value to both employers and computer specialists degraded considerably. Over the course of the late 1960s, new approaches to solving the personnel crisis emerged, each of which embodied different attitudes toward the nature of programming expertise. Beginning in the early 1960s aspiring professional societies, such as the Data Processing

Management Association, developed certification programs for specific fields in computer programming, systems analysis, and software design.[117] These were really certification exams, intended to validate the credentials of society members, not aptitude tests. But they suggested that a new approach to personnel management—the cultivation of professional norms and institutions—might be the solution to the personnel crisis. At the same time, academically minded researchers worked to elaborate a theory of computer science that would place the discipline of programming on a firm scientific foundation. For the time being, however, the preferred solution was technological rather than professional or theoretical: drawing from traditional industrial approaches to increasing productivity and eliminating human labor, computer manufacturers worked to automate the programming process. For managers and employers in the late 1950s and early 1960s, the development of "automatic programming systems" seemed to offer the perfect solution to the labor crisis in programming.

4

Tower of Babel

Is a language really going to solve this problem? Do we really design languages for use by what we might call professional programmers or are we designing them for use by some sub-human species in order to get around training and having good programmers? Is a language ever going to get around the training and having good programmers?
—RAND Symposium on Programming Languages, 1962

Automatic Programmers

The first commercial electronic digital computers became available in the early 1950s. For a short period, the focus of most manufacturers was on the development of innovative hardware. Most of the users of these early computers were large and technically sophisticated corporations and government agencies. In the middle of the decade, however, users and manufacturers alike became increasingly concerned with the rising cost of software development. By the beginning of the 1960s, the origins of "software turmoil" that would soon become a full-blown software crisis were readily apparent.[1]

As larger and more ambitious software projects were attempted, and the shortage of experienced programmers became more pronounced, industry managers began to look for ways to reduce costs by simplifying the programming process. A number of potential solutions were proposed: the use of aptitude tests and personnel profiles to identify the truly gifted superprogrammers; updated training standards and computer science curricula; and new management methods that would allow for the use of less-skilled laborers. The most popular and widely adopted solution, however, was the development of automatic programming technologies. These new tools promised to "eliminate the middle-man" by allowing users to program their computers directly, without the need for expensive programming talent.[2] The computer would program itself.

Despite their associations with deskilling and routinization, automatic programming systems could also work to the benefit of occupational programmers and academic computer scientists. High-level programming promised to reduce the tedium associated with machine coding, and allowed programmers to focus on more system-oriented—and high-status—tasks such as analysis and design. Language design and development served as a focus for productive theoretical research, and helped establish computer science as a legitimate academic discipline. And automatic programming systems never did succeed in eliminating the need for skilled programmers. In many ways, they contributed to the elevation of the profession, rather than the reverse, as was originally intended by some and feared by others.

In order to understand why automatic programming languages were such an appealing solution to the software crisis as well as why they apparently had so little effect on the outcome or severity of the crisis, it is essential to consider these languages as parts of larger social and technological systems. This chapter will describe the emergence of programming languages as a means of managing the complexity of the programming process. It will trace the development of several of the most prominent automatic programming languages, particularly FORTRAN and COBOL, and situate these technologies in their appropriate historical context. Finally, it will explore the significance of these technologies as potential solutions to the ongoing software crisis of the late 1950s and early 1960s.

Assemblers, Compilers, and the Origins of the Subroutine

At the heart of every automatic programming system was the notion that a computer could be used, at least in certain limited situations, to generate the machine code required to run itself or other computers. This was an idea with great practical appeal: although programming was increasingly seen as a legitimate and challenging intellectual activity, the actual coding of a program still involved tedious and painstaking clerical work. For example, the single instruction to "add the short number in memory location 25," when written out in the machine code understood by most computers, was stored as a binary number such as 111000000000110010. This binary notation was obviously difficult for humans to remember and manipulate. As early as 1948, researchers at Cambridge University began working on a system to represent the same instruction in a more comprehensible format. The same instruction to "add the short number in memory location 25" could be written out as A 25 S, where A stood for "add," 25 was the decimal address of the memory location, and S indicated that a "short" number was to be used.[3] A Cambridge PhD student named David Wheeler wrote a small program called Initial Orders that automatically translated this symbolic notation into the binary machine code required by the computer.

The focus of early attempts to develop automatic programming utilities was on eliminating the more unpleasant aspects of computer coding. Although in theory the actual process of programming was relatively straightforward, in practice it was quite difficult and time-consuming. A single error in any one of a thousand instructions could cause an entire program to fail. It often took hours or days of laborious effort simply to get a program to work properly. The lack of tools made finding errors next to impossible. As Maurice Wilkes, another Cambridge researcher, would later vividly recall, "It had not occurred to me that there was going to be any difficulty about getting programs working. And it was with somewhat of a shock that I realized that for the rest of my life I was going to spend a good deal of my time finding mistakes that I had made in my programs."[4]

These errors, or bugs as they soon came to be known, were often introduced in the process of transcribing or reusing code fragments. Wilkes and others quickly realized that there was a great deal of code that was common to different programs—a set of instructions to calculate the sine function, for example. In addition to assigning his student Wheeler to the development of the Initial Orders program, Wilkes set him to the task of assembling a library of such common subroutines. This method of reusing previously existing code became one of the most powerful techniques available for increasing programmer efficiency. The publication in 1951 of the first textbook on the *Preparation of Programs for an Electronic Digital Computer* by Wilkes, Wheeler, and Cambridge colleague Stanley Gill helped disseminate these ideas throughout the nascent programming community.[5]

While Wilkes, Wheeler, and Gill were refining their notions of a subroutine library, programmers in the United States were developing their own techniques for eliminating some of the tedium associated with coding. In 1949, John Mauchly of UNIVAC created his Short Order Code for the BINAC computer. The Short Order Code allowed Mauchly to directly enter equations into the BINAC using a fairly conventional algebraic notation. The system did not actually produce program code, however: it was an interpretative system that merely called up predefined subroutines and displayed the result. Nevertheless, the Short Order Code represented a considerable improvement over the standard binary instruction set.

In 1951 Grace Hopper, another UNIVAC employee, wrote the first automatic program compiler. Although Hopper, like many other programmers, had benefited from the development of a subroutine library, she also perceived the limitations connected with its use. In order to be widely applicable, subroutines had to be written as generically as possible. They all started at line 0 and were numbered sequentially from there. They also used a standard set of register addresses. In order to make use of a subroutine, a programmer had to both copy the routine code exactly and make the necessary adjustments to the register addresses by adding an offset appropriate to the particular program at hand. And as Hopper was later fond of asserting, programmers were both "lousy adders" and "lousy copyists."[6] The process of utilizing the subroutine code almost inevitably added to the number of errors that eventually had to be debugged.

To avoid the problems associated with manually copying and manipulating subroutine libraries, Hopper developed a system to automatically gather subroutine code and make the appropriate address adjustments. The system then compiled the subroutines into a complete machine program. Her A-0 compiler dramatically reduced the time required to put together a working application. In 1952 she extended the language to include a simpler mnemonic interface. For example, the mathematical statement $X + Y = Z$ could be written as ADD 00X 00Y 00Z. Multiplying Z by T to give W was MUL 00Z 00T 00W. The combination of an algebraic-language interface and a subroutine compiler became the basis for almost all modern programming languages. By the end of 1953 the A-2 compiler, as it was then known, was in use at the Army Map Service, Lawrence Livermore Laboratories, New York University, the Bureau of Ships, and the David Taylor Model Basin. Although it would take some time before automatic programming systems were universally adopted, by the mid-1950s the technology was well on its way to becoming an essential element of programming practice.

Over the course of the next several decades, more than a thousand code assemblers, programming languages, and other automatic programming systems were developed in the United States alone. Understanding how these systems were used, how and to whom they were marketed, and why there were so many of them is a crucial aspect of the history of the programming professions. Automatic programming languages were the first and perhaps the most popular response to the burgeoning software crisis of the late 1950s and early 1960s. In many ways the entire history of computer programming—both social and technical—has been defined by the search for a silver bullet capable of slaying what Frederick Brooks famously referred to as the werewolf of "missed schedules, blown budgets, and flawed products."[7] The most obvious solution to what was often perceived to be a technical problem was, not surprisingly, the development of better technology.

Automatic programming languages were an appealing solution to the software crisis for a number of reasons. Computer manufacturers were interested in making software development as straightforward and inexpensive as possible. After all, as an early introduction to programming on the UNIVAC pointedly reminded its readers, "The sale and acceptance of these machines is, to some extent, related to the ease with which they can be programmed. As a result, a great deal of research has been done, or is being done, to make programming simpler and more understandable."[8] Advertisements for early automatic programming systems made outrageous and unsubstantiated claims about the ability of their systems to simplify the programming process.[9] In many cases, they were specifically marketed as a replacement for human programmers. Fred Gruenberger noted this tendency as early as 1962 in a widely disseminated transcript of a RAND Symposium on Programming Languages: "You know, I've never seen a hot dog language come out yet in the last 14 years—beginning with Mrs. Hopper's A-0 compiler . . . that didn't have tied to it the claim in its brochure that this one will eliminate all programmers. The last one we got was just three days ago from General Electric (making the same claim for the G-WIZ compiler) that this one will eliminate programmers. Managers can now do their own programming; engineers can do their own programming, etc. As always, the claim seems to be made that programmers are not needed anymore."[10]

Advertisements for these new automatic programming technologies, which appeared in management-oriented publications such as *Business Week* and the *Wall Street Journal* rather than *Datamation* or the *Communications of the ACM*, were clearly aimed at a pressing concern: the rising costs associated with finding and recruiting talented programming personnel. This perceived shortage of programmers was an issue that loomed large in the minds of many industry observers. "First on anyone's checklist of professional problems," declared a *Datamation*

Susie Meyer meets PL/I

The story of how a single language answers the question, "Can a young girl with no previous programming experience find happiness handling both commercial and scientific applications, without resorting to an assembler language?"
Let's face it. The cost of programming just keeps going up. So for some time to come, how well you do your job depends on how programmers like Susie Meyer do theirs.

That's the reason for PL/I, the high-level language for both scientific and commercial applications.

With PL/I, programmers don't have to learn other high-level languages. They can concentrate more on the job, less on the language.

So think about PL/I. Not just in terms of training, but in terms of the total impact it can have on your operation.

Figure 4.1
"Susie Meyers Meets PL/1" advertisement, IBM Corporation, 1968.

editorial in 1962, "is the manpower shortage of both trained and even untrained programmers, operators, logical designers and engineers in a variety of flavors."[11] The so-called programmer problem became an increasingly important feature of contemporary crisis rhetoric. "The number of computers in use in the U.S. is expected to leap from the present 35,000 to 60,000 by 1970 and to 85,000 in 1975," *Fortune* magazine ominously predicted in 1967; "The software man will be in even greater demand in 1970 than he is today."[12] Automatic programming systems held an obvious appeal for managers concerned with the rising costs of software development.

Figure 4.1 shows one of a series of advertisements that presented an unambiguous appeal to gender associations: machines could not only replace their human female equivalents but also were an improvement on them. In its "Meet Susie Meyers" advertisements for its PL/1 programming language, the IBM Corporation asked its users an obviously rhetorical question: "Can a young girl with no previous programming experience find happiness handling both commercial and scientific applications, without resorting to an assembler language?" The answer, of course, was an enthusiastic "yes!" Although the advertisement promised a "brighter future for your programmers" (who would be free to "concentrate more on the job, less on the language"), it also implied a low-cost solution to the labor crisis in software. The subtext of appeals like this was none too subtle: if pretty little Susie Meyers, with her spunky miniskirt and utter lack of programming experience, could develop software effectively in PL/1, so could just about anyone.

It should be noted that use of women as proxies for low-cost or low-skill labor was not confined to the computer industry. One of the time-honored strategies for dealing with labor "problems" in the United States has been the use of female workers. There is a vast historical literature on this topic; from the origins of the U.S. industrial system, women have been seen as a source of cheap, compliant, and undemanding labor.[13] The same dynamic was at work in computer programming. In a 1963 *Datamation* article lauding the virtues of the female computer programmer, for example, Valerie Rockmael focused specifically on her stability, reliability, and relative docility: "Women are less aggressive and more content in one position. . . . Women consider fringe benefits of more importance than their male peers and are more prone to stay on the job if they are content, regardless of a lack of advancement. They also maintain their original geographic roots and are less willing to travel or change job locations, particularly if they are married or engaged." In an era in which turnover rates for programmers *averaged* 20 percent annually, this was a compelling argument for employers, since their substantial initial expenditures on training "pays a greater dividend" when invested in female employees. Note that this was something of a backhanded compliment, aimed more at the needs of employers than female programmers. In fact, the "most undesirable category of programmers," Rockmael contended, was "the female about 21 years old and unmarried," because "when she would start thinking about her social commitments for the weekend, her work suffered proportionately."[14]

Whatever the motivation behind the development and adoption of any particular automatic programming system, by the mid-1950s, a number of these systems were being proposed by various manufacturers. Two of the most popular and significant were FORTRAN and COBOL, each developed by different groups and intended for different purposes.

FORTRAN

Although Hopper's A-2 compiler was arguably the first modern automatic programming system, the first widely used and disseminated programming language was FORTRAN, developed in 1954–1957 by a team of researchers at the IBM Corporation. As early as 1953, the mathematician and programmer John Backus had proposed to his IBM employers the development of a new, scientifically oriented programming language. This new system for mathematical FORmula TRANslation would be designed specifically for use with the soon-to-be-released IBM 704 scientific computer. It would "enable the IBM 704 to accept a concise formulation of a problem in terms of a mathematical notation and [would] produce automatically a high-speed 704 program for the solution of the problem."[15] The result would be faster, more reliable, and less expensive software development. FORTRAN would not only "virtually eliminate programming and debugging" but also reduce operation time, double machine output, and provide a means of feasibly investigating complex mathematical models. In January 1954 Backus was given the go-ahead by his IBM superiors, and a completed FORTRAN compiler was released to all 704 installations in April 1957.

From the beginning, development of the FORTRAN language was focused around a single overarching design objective: the creation of efficient machine code. Project leader Backus was highly critical of existing automatic programming systems, which he saw as little more than mnemonic code assemblers or collections of subroutines. He also felt little regard for most contemporary human programmers, who he often derisively insisted on referring to as coders. When asked about the transformation of the coder into the programmer, for instance, Backus dismissively suggested that "it's the same reason that janitors are now called 'custodians.' 'Programmer' was considered a higher class enterprise than 'coder,' and things have a tendency to move in that direction."[16]

A truly automatic programming language, believed Backus, would allow scientists and engineers to communicate directly with the computer, thus eliminating the need for inefficient and unreliable programmers.[17] The only way that such a system would be widely adopted, however, was to ensure that the code it produced would be at least as efficient, in terms of size and performance, as that produced by its human counterparts.[18] Indeed, one of the primary objections raised against automatic programming languages in this period was their relative inefficiency: one of the higher-level languages used by SAGE developers produced programs that ran an order of magnitude slower than those hand coded by a top-notch programmer.[19] In an era when programming skill was considered to be a uniquely creative and innate ability, and when the state of contemporary hardware made performance considerations paramount, users were understandably skeptical of the value of automatically generated machine code.[20]

The focus of the FORTRAN developers was therefore on the construction of an efficient compiler, rather than on the design of the language.

In order to ensure that the object code produced by the FORTRAN compiler was as efficient as possible, several design compromises had to be made. FORTRAN was originally intended primarily for use on the IBM 704, and contained several device-specific instructions. Little thought was given to making FORTRAN machine independent, and early implementations varied greatly from computer to computer, even those developed by the same manufacturer. The language was also designed solely for use in numerical computations, and was therefore difficult to use for applications requiring the manipulation of alphanumeric data. The first FORTRAN manual made this focus on mathematical problem solving clear: "The FORTRAN language is intended to be capable of expressing any problem of numerical computation. In particular, it deals easily with problems containing large sets of formulae and many variables and it permits any variable to have up to three independent subscripts." For problems in which machine words have a logical rather than numerical meaning, however, FORTRAN is less satisfactory, and it may fail entirely to express some such problems. Nevertheless many logical operations not directly expressible in the FORTRAN language can be obtained by making use of provisions for incorporating library routines.[21]

The power of the FORTRAN language for scientific computation can be clearly demonstrated by a simple real-world example. The mathematical expression described by the function $Z(i) = \sqrt{A_i X_i^2 + B_i Y_i}$ could be written in FORTRAN using the following syntax:

Z(I) = SQRTF(A(I)*X(I)**2 + B(I)*Y(I))

Using such straightforward algorithmic expressions, a programmer could write extremely sophisticated programs with relatively little training and experience.[22]

Although greeted initially with skepticism, the FORTRAN project was enormously successful in the long term. A report on FORTRAN usage written just one year after the first release of the language indicated that "over half [of the 26 installations of the 704] used FORTRAN for more than half of their problems."[23] By the end of 1958, IBM produced FORTRAN systems for its 709 and 650 machines. As early as January 1961 Remington Rand UNIVAC became the first non-IBM manufacturer to provide FORTRAN, and by 1963 a version of the FORTRAN compiler was available for almost every computer then in existence.[24] The language was updated substantially in 1958 and again in 1962. In 1962, FORTRAN became the first programming language to be standardized through the American Standards Association, which further established FORTRAN as an industrywide standard.[25]

The academic community was an early and crucial supporter of FORTRAN, contributing directly to its growing popularity. The FORTRAN designers in general, and Backus in particular, were regular participants in academic forums and conferences. Backus himself had delivered a paper at the seminal Symposium on Automatic Programming for Digital Computers hosted by the Office of Naval Research in 1954. One of his top priorities, after the compilation of the FORTRAN *Programmer's Reference Manual* (itself a model of scholarly elegance and simplicity), was to publish an academically oriented article that would introduce the new language to the scientific community.[26] Backus would later become widely known throughout the academic community as the codeveloper of the Backus-Naur Form, the notational system used to describe most modern programming languages.

FORTRAN was appealing to scientists and other academics for a number of reasons. First of all, it was designed and developed by one of their own. Backus spoke their language, published in their journals, and shared their disdain for coders and other "technicians." Second, FORTRAN was designed specifically to solve the kinds of problems that interested academics. Its use of algebraic expressions greatly simplified the process of defining mathematical problems in machine-readable syntax. Finally, and perhaps most significantly, FORTRAN provided them more direct access to the computer. Its introduction "caused a partial revolution in the way in which computer installations were run because it became not only possible but quite practical to have engineers, scientists, and other people actually programming their own problems without the intermediary of a professional programmer."[27] The use of FORTRAN actually became the centerpiece of an ongoing debate about "open" versus "closed" programming "shops." The closed shops allowed only professional programmers to have access to the computers; open shops made these machines directly available to their users.

The association of FORTRAN with scientific computing was a self-replicating phenomenon. Academics preferred FORTRAN to other languages because they believed it allowed them to do their work more effectively and they therefore made FORTRAN the foundation of their computing curricula. Students learned the language in university courses and were thus more effective at getting their work done in FORTRAN. A positive feedback loop was established between FORTRAN and academia. A survey in 1973 of more than thirty-five thousand students taking college-level computing courses revealed that 70 percent were learning to program using FORTRAN. The next most widely used alternative, BASIC, was used by only 13 percent, and less than 3 percent were exposed to business-oriented languages such as COBOL.[28] Throughout the 1960s and 1970s, FORTRAN was clearly the dominant language of scientific computation.

COBOL

On April 8, 1959, a group of computer manufacturers, users, and academics met at the University of Pennsylvania's Computing Center to discuss a proposal to develop "the specifications for a common business language [CBL] for automatic digital computers."[29] The goal was to develop a programming language specifically aimed at the needs of the business data processing community. This new language would rely on simple Englishlike commands, would be easier to use and understand than existing scientific languages, and would provide machine-independent compatibility: that is, the same program could be run on a wide variety of hardware with little modification.

Although this proposal originated in the ElectroData Division of the Burroughs Corporation, from the beginning it had broad industrial and governmental support. The director of data systems for the U.S. Department of Defense readily agreed to sponsor a formal meeting on the proposal, and his enthusiastic support indicates a widespread contemporary interest in business-oriented programming: "The Department of Defense was pleased to undertake this project: in fact, we were embarrassed that the idea for such a common language had not had its origin in Defense since we would benefit so greatly from such a project."[30]

The first meeting to discuss a CBL was held at the Pentagon on May 28–29, 1959. Attending the meeting were fifteen officials from seven government organizations; fifteen representatives of the major computer manufacturers (including Burroughs, GE, Honeywell, IBM, NCR, Phillips, RCA, Remington Rand UNIVAC, Sylvania, and ICT); and eleven users and consultants (significantly, only one member of this last group was from a university). Despite the diversity of the participants, the meeting produced both consensus and a tangible plan of action. The group not only decided that CBL was necessary and desirable but also agreed on its basic characteristics: a problem-oriented, Englishlike syntax; a focus on the ease of use rather than power or performance; and a machine-independent design. Three committees were established, under the auspices of a single Executive Committee of the Conference on Data Systems Languages (CODASYL), to suggest short-term, intermediate, and long-range solutions, respectively. As it turned out, it was the short-term committee that produced the most lasting and influential proposals.

The original purpose of the Short-Range Committee was to evaluate the strengths and weaknesses of existing automatic compilers, and recommend a "short term composite approach (good for the next year or two) to a common business language for programming digital computers."[31] There were three existing compiler systems that the committee was particularly interested in considering: FLOW-MATIC, which had been developed for Remington Rand UNIVAC by Grace Hopper (as an outgrowth of her A-series algebraic and B-series business compilers), and which was actually in use by customers at the time; AIMACO, developed for the Air Force Air Materiel Command; and COMTRAN (soon to be

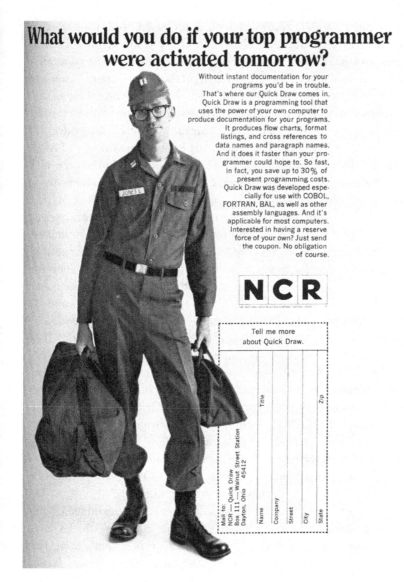

What would you do if your top programmer were activated tomorrow?

Without instant documentation for your programs you'd be in trouble. That's where our Quick Draw comes in. Quick Draw is a programming tool that uses the power of your own computer to produce documentation for your programs. It produces flow charts, format listings, and cross references to data names and paragraph names. And it does it faster than your programmer could hope to. So fast, in fact, you save up to 30% of present programming costs. Quick Draw was developed especially for use with COBOL, FORTRAN, BAL, as well as other assembly languages. And it's applicable for most computers. Interested in having a reserve force of your own? Just send the coupon. No obligation of course.

NCR

Tell me more about Quick Draw.

Mail to:
NCR — Quick Draw
Box 111 — Walnut Street Station
Dayton, Ohio   45412

Name
Title
Company
Street
City
State
Zip

Figure 4.2
NCR, Quickdraw programming language, 1968.

renamed the Commercial Translator), a proposed IBM product that existed only as a specification document. Other manufacturers such as Sylvania and RCA were also working on the development of similar languages. Indeed, one of the primary goals of the Short-Range Committee was to "nip these projects in the bud" and provide incentives for manufacturers to standardize on the CBL rather than pursue their own independent agendas. Other languages considered were Autocoder III, SURGE, FORTRAN, RCA 501 Assembler, Report Generator, and APG-1.[32] At the first meeting of one of the Short-Range Committee task groups, for example, most of the time was spent getting statements of commitment from the various manufacturers.[33]

From the start, the process of designing the CBL was characterized by a spirit of pragmatism and compromise. The Short-Range Committee, referred to by insiders as the PDQ ("pretty darn quick") Committee, took seriously its charge to work quickly to produce an interim solution. Remarkably enough, less than three months later the committee had produced a nearly complete draft of a proposed CBL specification. In doing so, the CBL designers borrowed freely from models provided by Remington Rand UNIVAC's FLOW-MATIC language and the IBM Commercial Translator. In a September report to the Executive Committee of CODASYL, the Short-Range Committee requested permission to continue development on the CBL specification, to be completed by December 1, 1959. The name COBOL (Common Business Oriented Language) was formally adopted shortly thereafter. Working around the clock for the next several months, the PDQ group was able to produce its finished report just in time for its December deadline. The report was approved by CODASYL, and in January 1960 the official COBOL-60 specification was released by the U.S. Government Printing Office.

The structure of the COBOL-60 specification reveals its mixed origins and commercial orientation. Although from the beginning the COBOL designers were concerned with "business data processing," there was never any attempt to provide a real definition of that phrase.[34] It was clearly intended that the language could be used by novice programmers and read by managers. For example, an instruction to compute an employee's overtime pay might be written as follows:

MULTIPLY NUMBER-OVTIME-HRS BY OVTIME-PAY-RATE

GIVING OVTIME-PAY-TOTAL

It was felt that this readability would result from the use of English-language instructions, although no formal criteria or tests for readability were provided. In many cases, compromises were made that allowed for conflicting interpretations of what made for "readable" computer code. Arithmetic formulas, for instance, could either be written using a combination of arithmetic verbs—that is, ADD, SUBTRACT, MULTIPLY, or DIVIDE—or as symbolic formulas. The use of arithmetic verbs was adapted directly from the FLOW-MATIC language, and reflected the belief that business data processing users could not—and should not—be forced to use formulas. The capability to write symbolic formulas was included (after much contentious debate) as a means of providing power and flexibility to more mathematically sophisticated programmers. Such traditional mathematical functions such as SINE and COSINE, however, were deliberately excluded as being unnecessary to business data processing applications.

Another concession to the objective of readability was the inclusion of extraneous "noise words." These were words or phrases that were allowable but not necessary: for example, in the statement

READ *file1* RECORD INTO *variable1* AT END *goto procedure2*

the words RECORD and AT are syntactically superfluous. The statement would be equally valid written as

READ *file1* INTO *variable1* END *goto procedure2*.

The inclusion of the noise words RECORD and AT was perceived by the designers to enhance readability. Users had the option of including or excluding them according to individual preference or corporate policy.

In addition to designing COBOL to be Englishlike and readable, the committee was careful to make it as machine-independent as possible. Most contemporary programming systems were tied to a specific processor or product line. If the user wanted to replace or upgrade their computer, or switch to machines from a different manufacturer, they had to completely rewrite their software from scratch, typically an expensive, risky, and time-consuming operation. Users often became bound to outdated and inefficient hardware systems simply because of the enormous costs associated with upgrading their software applications. This was especially true for commercial data processing operations, where computers were generally embedded in large, complex systems of people, procedures, and technology. A truly machine-independent language would allow corporations to reuse application code, thereby reducing the programming and maintenance costs. It would also allow manufacturers to sell or lease more of their most recent (and profitable) computers.

The COBOL language was deliberately organized in such a way as to encourage portability from one machine to another. Every element of a COBOL application was assigned to one of four functional divisions: IDENTIFICATION, ENVIRONMENT, DATA, and PROCEDURE. The IDENTIFICATION division offered a high-level description of the program, including its name, author, and creation date. The ENVIRONMENT division contained information about the specific hardware on which the program was to be compiled and run. The DATA division described the file and record layout of the data used or created by the rest of application. The PROCEDURE division included the algorithms and procedures that the user wished the computer to follow. Ideally, this rigid separation of functional divisions would allow a user to take a deck of cards from one machine to another without making significant alterations to anything but the ENVIRONMENT description. In reality, this degree of portability was almost impossible to achieve in real-world applications in which performance was a primary consideration. For example, the most efficient method of laying out a file for a twenty-four-bit computer was not necessarily optimal for a thirty-six-bit machine. Nevertheless, machine independence "was a major, if not *the* major," design objective of the Short-Range Committee.[35] Achieving this objective proved difficult both technically and politically, and greatly influenced both the design of the COBOL specification and its subsequent reception within the computing community.

One of the greatest obstacles to achieving machine independence was the computer manufacturers themselves. Each manufacturer wanted to make sure that COBOL included only features that would run efficiently on their devices. For instance, a number of users wanted the language to include the ability to read a file in reverse order. For those machines that had a basic machine command to read a tape backward this was an easy feature to implement. Even those computers without this explicit capability could achieve the same functionality by backing the tape up two records and then reading forward one. Although this potential READ REVERSE command could therefore be logically implemented by everyone, it significantly penalized those devices without the basic machine capability. It was therefore not included in the final specification.

There were other compromises that were made for the sake of machine independence. In order to maintain compatibility among different machines with different arithmetic capabilities, eighteen decimal digits were chosen as the maximum degree of precision supported. This particular degree of precision was chosen "for the simple reason that it was *dis*advantageous to every computer thought to be a potential candidate for having a COBOL compiler."[36] No particular manufacturer would thus have an inherent advantage in terms of performance. In a similar manner, provisions were made for the use of binary computers, despite the fact that such machines were generally not considered appropriate for business data processing. The decision to allow only a limited character set in statement definitions—using only those characters that were physically available on almost all data-entry machines—was a self-imposed constraint that had "an enormous influence on the syntax of the language," but was nevertheless considered essential to widespread industry adoption. The use of such a minimal character set also prevented the designers from using the sophisticated reference language techniques that had so enamored theoretical computer scientists of the ALGOL 58 specification.

This dedication to the ideal of portability set the Short-Term Committee at odds with some of its fellow members of CODASYL. In October 1959, the Intermediate-Range Committee passed a motion declaring that the FACT programming language—recently released by the Honeywell Corporation—was a better language than that produced by the Short-Range Committee and hence should form the basis of the CBL.[37] Although many members of the Short-Range Committee agreed that FACT was indeed a technically advanced and superior language, they rejected any solution that was tied to any particular manufacturer. In order to ensure that the CBL would be a truly *common* business language, elegance and efficiency had to be compromised for the sake of readability and machine independence. Despite the opposition of the Intermediate-Range Committee (and the Honeywell representatives), the Executive Committee of CODASYL eventually agreed with the design priorities advocated by the PDQ group.

The first COBOL compilers were developed in 1960 by Remington Rand UNIVAC and RCA. In December of that year, the two companies hosted a dramatic demonstration of the cross-platform compatibility of their individual compilers: the same COBOL program, with only the ENVIRONMENT division needing to be modified, was run successfully on machines from both manufacturers. Although this was a compelling demonstration of COBOL's potential, other manufacturers were slow to develop their own COBOL compilers. Honeywell and IBM, for example, were loath to abandon their own independent business languages. Honeywell's FACT had been widely praised for its technical excellence, and the IBM Commercial Translator already had an established customer base.[38] By the end of 1960, however, the U.S. military had put the full weight of its prestige and purchasing power behind COBOL. The Department of Defense announced that it would not lease or purchase any new computer without a COBOL compiler unless its manufacturer could demonstrate that its performance would not be enhanced by the availability of COBOL.[39] No manufacturer ever attempted such a demonstration, and within a year COBOL was well on its way toward becoming an industry standard.

It is difficult to establish empirically how widely COBOL was adopted, but anecdotal evidence suggests that it is by far the most popular and widely used computer language *ever*.[40] A recent study undertaken in response to the perceived Y2K crisis suggests that there are seventy billion lines of COBOL code currently in operation in the United States alone. Despite its obvious popularity, though, from the beginning COBOL has faced severe criticism and opposition, especially from within the computer science community. One programming language textbook from 1977 judged COBOL's programming features as fair, its implementation dependent features as poor, and its overall writing as fair to poor. It also noted its "tortuously poor compactness and poor uniformity."[41] The noted computer scientist Edsger Dijkstra wrote that "COBOL cripples the mind," and another of his colleagues called it "terrible" and "ugly."[42] Several notable textbooks on programming languages from the 1980s did not even include COBOL in the index.

There are a number of reasons why computer scientists have been so harsh in their evaluation of COBOL. Some of these objections are technical in nature, but most are aesthetic, historical, or political. Most of the technical criticisms have to do with COBOL's verbosity, its inclusion of superfluous noise words, and its lack of certain features (such as protected module variables). Although many of these shortcomings were addressed in subsequent versions of the COBOL specification, the academic world continued to vilify the language. In an article from 1985 titled "The Relationship between COBOL and Computer Science," the computer scientist Ben Schneiderman identified several explanations for this continued hostility. First of all, no academics were asked to participate on the initial design team. In fact, the COBOL developers apparently had little interest in the academic or scientific aspects of their work. All of the articles included in a May 1962 *Communications of the ACM* issue devoted to COBOL were written by industry or government practitioners. Only four of the thirteen included even the most basic references to previous and related work; the lack of academic sensibilities was immediately apparent. Also noticeably lacking was any reference to the recently developed Backus-Naur Form notation that had already become popular as a metalanguage for describing other programming languages. No attempt was made to produce a textbook explaining the conceptual foundations of COBOL until 1963. Most significant, however, was the sense that the problem domain addressed by the COBOL designers—that is, business data processing—was not theoretically sophisticated or interesting. One programming language textbook from 1974 portrayed COBOL as having "an orientation toward business data processing . . . in which the problems are . . . relatively simple algorithms coupled with high-volume input-output (e.g., computing the payroll for a large organization)." Although this dismissive account hardly captures the complexities of many large-scale business applications, it does appear to accurately represent a prevailing attitude among computer scientists. COBOL was considered a "trade-school" language rather than a serious intellectual accomplishment.[43]

Despite these objections, COBOL has proven remarkably successful. Certainly the support of the U.S. government had a great deal to do with its initial widespread adoption. But COBOL was attractive to users— business corporations in particular—for other reasons as well. The belief that Englishlike COBOL code could be read and understood by nonprogrammers was appealing to traditional managers who were worried about the dangers of "letting the 'computer boys' take over."[44] It was also hoped that COBOL would achieve true machine independence— arguably the holy grail of language designers—and of all its competitors, COBOL did perhaps come closest to achieving this ideal. Although critics have derided COBOL as the inelegant result of "design by committee," the broad inclusiveness of CODASYL helped ensure that no one manufacturer's hardware would be favored. Committee control over the language specification also prevented splintering: whereas numerous competing dialects of FORTRAN and ALGOL were developed, COBOL implementations remained relatively homogeneous. The CODASYL structure also provided a mechanism for ongoing language maintenance with periodic "official" updates and releases.

ALGOL, Pascal, ADA, and Beyond

Although FORTRAN and COBOL were by far the most popular programming languages developed in the United States during this period,
they were by no means the only ones to appear. Jean Sammet, editor of
one of the first comprehensive treatments of the history of programming
languages, has estimated that by 1981, there were a least one thousand
programming languages in use nationwide. It would be impossible to
even enumerate, much less describe, the history and development of each
of these languages. Figure 4.3 contains a "genealogical" listing of some
of the more widely used programming languages developed prior to
1970. This section will focus on a few of the more historically significant
alternatives to FORTRAN and COBOL.

More than a year before the Executive Committee of CODASYL
convened to discuss the need for a common business-oriented programming language, an ad hoc committee of users, academics, and federal
officials met to study the possibility of creating a universal programming
language. This committee, which was brought together under the
auspices of the ACM, could not have been more different from the
group organized by CODASYL. Whereas the fifteen-member Executive
Committee had contained only one university representative, the identi-
cally sized ACM-sponsored committee was dominated by academics. At
itsr first meeting, this committee decided to follow the model of
FORTRAN in designing an algebraic language. FORTRAN itself was
not acceptable because of its association with IBM.

The ACM "universal language" project soon expanded into an
international initiative. Europeans in particular were deeply interested
in a language that would both transcend political boundaries and
help avoid the domination of Europe by the IBM Corporation. During
an eight-day meeting in Zurich, a rough specification for the new
International Algebraic Language (IAL) was hashed out. Actually, three
distinct versions of the IAL were created: reference, publication, and
hardware. The reference language was the abstract representation of
the language as envisioned by the Zurich committee. The publication
and hardware languages would be isomorphic implementations of
the abstract reference language. Since these specific implementations
required careful attention to such messy details as character sets and
delimiters (decimal points being standard in the United States and
commas being standard in Europe), they were left for a later and unspeci-
fied date. The reference language was released in 1958 under the

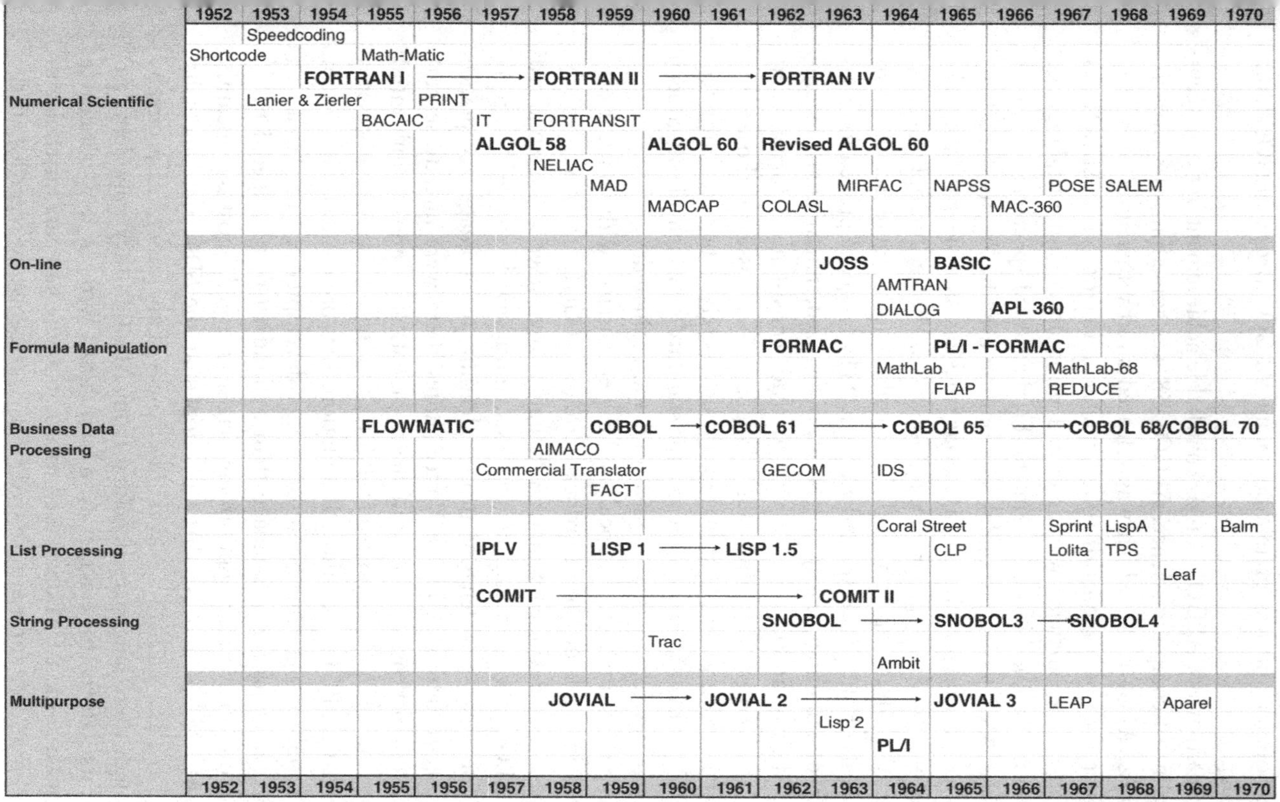

Numerical Scientific
Speedcoding · Shortcode · Math-Matic · FORTRAN I · Lanier & Zierler · BACAIC · PRINT · FORTRAN II · IT · FORTRANSIT · ALGOL 58 · NELIAC · MAD · ALGOL 60 · Revised ALGOL 60 · FORTRAN IV · MADCAP · COLASL · MIRFAC · NAPSS · MAC-360 · POSE · SALEM

On-line
JOSS · AMTRAN · DIALOG · BASIC · APL 360

Formula Manipulation
FORMAC · PL/I - FORMAC · MathLab · FLAP · MathLab-68 · REDUCE

Business Data Processing
FLOWMATIC · AIMACO · Commercial Translator · FACT · COBOL · COBOL 61 · GECOM · IDS · COBOL 65 · COBOL 68/COBOL 70

List Processing
IPLV · LISP 1 · LISP 1.5 · Coral Street · CLP · Sprint · Lolita · LispA · TPS · Leaf · Balm

String Processing
COMIT · COMIT II · SNOBOL · Trac · Ambit · SNOBOL3 · SNOBOL4

Multipurpose
JOVIAL · JOVIAL 2 · Lisp 2 · PL/I · JOVIAL 3 · LEAP · Aparel

1952 1953 1954 1955 1956 1957 1958 1959 1960 1961 1962 1963 1964 1965 1966 1967 1968 1969 1970

Figure 4.3
Programming languages, 1952–1970. Based on a chart first developed by Jean Sammet. Reproduced with the permission of the ACM.

more popular and less pretentious name ALGOL (from ALGOrithmic Language).

In many ways, ALGOL was a remarkable achievement in the nascent discipline of computer science. ALGOL 58 was something of a work in progress; ALGOL 60, which was released shortly thereafter, is widely considered to be a model of completeness and clarity. The ALGOL 60 version of the language was described using an elegant metalanguage known as Backus Normal Form (BNF), developed specifically for that purpose. BNF, which resembles the notation used by linguists and logicians to describe formal languages, has since become the standard technique for representing programming languages. The elegant sophistication of the ALGOL 60 report appealed particularly to computer scientists. In the words of one well-respected admirer, "The language proved to be an object of stunning beauty. . . . Nicely organized, tantalizingly incomplete, slightly ambiguous, difficult to read, consistent in format, and brief, it was a perfect canvas for a language that possessed those same properties. Like the Bible, it was meant not merely to be read, but interpreted."[45] ALGOL 60 soon became the standard by which all subsequent language developments were measured and evaluated.

Despite its intellectual appeal, and the enthusiasm with which it was greeted in academic and European circles, ALGOL was never widely adopted in the United States. Although many Americans recognized that ALGOL was an elegant synthesis, most saw language design as just one step in a lengthy process leading to language acceptance and use. In addition, in the United States there were already several strong competitors currently in development. IBM and its influential users group SHARE supported FORTRAN, and business data processors preferred COBOL. Even those installations that preferred ALGOL often used it only as a starting point for further development, more "as a rich set of guidelines for a language than a standard to be adhered to."[46] Numerous dialects or spin-off languages emerged, most significantly JOVIAL, MAD, and NELIAC, developed at the SDC, the University of Michigan, and the Naval Electronics Laboratory, respectively. Although these languages benefited from ALGOL, they only detracted from its efforts to emerge as a standard. With a few noticeable exceptions—the ACM continued to use it as the language of choice in its publications, for example—ALGOL was generally regarded in the United States as an intellectual curiosity rather than a functional programming language.

The real question of historical interest, of course, is not so much why specific individual programming languages were created but rather why *so many*. In the late 1940s and early 1950s there was no real programming community per se, only particular projects being developed at various institutions. Each project necessarily developed its own techniques for facilitating programming. By the mid-1950s, however, there were established mechanisms for communicating new research and development, and there were deliberate attempts to promote industrywide programming standards. Nevertheless, there were literally hundreds of languages developed in the decades of the 1950s and 1960s. FORTRAN and COBOL have emerged as important standards in the scientific and business communities, respectively, and yet new languages continued—and still do—to be created.[47] What can explain this curious Cambrian explosion in the evolutionary history of programming languages?

Some of the many divergent species of programming languages can be understood by looking at their functional characteristics. Although general-purpose languages such as FORTRAN and COBOL were suitable for a wide variety of problem domains, certain applications required more specialized functions to perform most efficiently. The General-Purpose Simulation System was designed specifically for the simulation of system elements in discrete numerical analysis, for example. APT was commissioned by the Aircraft Industries Association and the U.S. Air Force to be used primarily to control automatic milling machines. Other languages were designed not so much for specialized problem domains as for particular pedagogical purposes—in the case of BASIC, for instance, the teaching of basic computer literacy. Some languages were known for their fast compilation times, and others for the efficiency of their object code. Individual manufacturers produced languages that were optimized for their own hardware, or as part of a larger marketing strategy.

Different languages were also developed with different users in mind. In this sense, they embodied the organizational and professional politics of programming in this period. At the RAND Symposium on Programming Languages in 1962, for example, Jack Little, a RAND consultant, lamented the tendency of manufacturers to design languages "for use by some sub-human species in order to get around training and having good programmers."[48] Dick Talmadge and Barry Gordon of IBM admitted to thinking in terms of an imaginary "Joe Accountant" user; the problem that IBM faced, according to Bernard Galler, of the University of Michigan Computing Center, was that "if you can design a language

Volume 4 / Number 1 / January, 1961

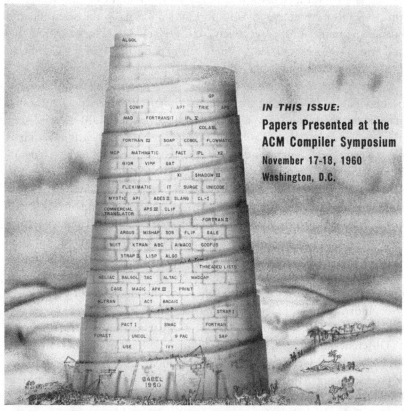

Figure 4.4
This now-famous "Tower of Babel" cover appeared first in the *Communications of the ACM*, January 1961. Reproduced with permission of the ACM.

that Joe Accountant can learn easily, then you're still going to have problems because you're probably going to have a lousy language."[49] Fred Gruenberger, a staff mathematician at RAND, later summed up the essence of the entire debate: "COBOL, in the hands of a master, is a beautiful tool—a very powerful tool. COBOL, as it's going to be handled by a low grade clerk somewhere, will be a miserable mess. . . . Some guys are just not as smart as others. They can distort anything."[50]

There were also less obviously utilitarian reasons for developing new programming languages, however. Many common objections raised against existing languages were more matters of style rather than substance. The rationale given for creating a new language often boiled down to a declaration that "this new language will be easier to use or better to read or write than any of its predecessors." Since there were generally no standards for what was meant by "easier to use or better to read or write," such declarations can only be considered statements of personal preference. As Jean Sammet has suggested, although lengthy arguments have been advanced on all sides of the major programming language controversies, "in the last analysis it almost always boils down to a question of personal style or taste."[51]

For the more academically oriented programmers, designing a new language was a relatively easy way to attract grant money and publish articles. There have been numerous languages that have been rigorously described but never implemented. They served only to prove a theoretical point or advance an individual's career. In addition, many in the academic community seemed to be afflicted with the NIH ("not invented here") syndrome: any language or technology that was designed by someone else could not possibly be as good as one that you invented yourself, and so a new version needed to be created to fill some ostensible personal or functional need. As Herbert Grosch lamented in 1961, filling these needs was personally satisfying yet ultimately self-serving and divisive: "Pride shades easily into purism, the sin of the mathematicians. To be the leading authority, indeed the only authority, on ALGOL 61B mod 12, the version that permits black letter as well as Hebrew subscripts, is a satisfying thing indeed, and many of us have constructed comfortable private universes to explore."[52]

One final and closely related reason for the proliferation of programming languages is that designing programming languages was (and is) fun. The adoption of metalanguages and the BNF allowed for the rapid development and implementation of creative new languages and dialects. If programming was enjoyable, even more so was language design.[53]

No Silver Bullet

In 1987, Frederick Brooks published an essay describing the major developments in automatic programming technologies that had occurred over the past several decades. As an accomplished academic and experienced industry manager, Brooks was a respected figure within the programming community. Using characteristically vivid language, his "No Silver Bullet: Essence and Accidents of Software Engineering," reflected on the inability of these technologies to bring an end to the ongoing software crisis:

Of all the monsters that fill the nightmares of our folklore, none terrify more than werewolves, because they transform unexpectedly from the familiar into horrors. For these, one seeks bullets of silver that can magically lay them to rest.

The familiar software project, at least as seen by the nontechnical manager, has something of this character; it is usually innocent and straightforward, but is capable of becoming a monster of missed schedules, blown budgets, and flawed products. So we hear desperate cries for a—silver bullet—something to make software costs drop as rapidly as computer hardware costs do.

But, as we look to the horizon of a decade hence, we see no silver bullet. There is no single development, in either technology or in management technique, that by itself promises even one order-of-magnitude improvement in productivity, in reliability, in simplicity.[54]

Brook's article provoked an immediate reaction, both positive and negative. The object-oriented programming (OOP) advocate Brad Cox insisted, for example, in his aptly titled "There Is a Silver Bullet," that new techniques in OOP promised to bring about "a software industrial revolution based on reusable and interchangeable parts that will alter the software universe as surely as the industrial revolution changed manufacturing."[55] Whatever they might have believed about the possibility of such a silver bullet being developed in the future, though, most programmers and managers agreed that none existed in the present. In the late 1980s, almost three decades after the first high-level automatic programming systems were introduced, concern about the software crisis was greater than ever. The same year that Brooks published his "No Silver Bullet," the Department of Defense warned against the real possibility of "software-induced catastrophic failure" disrupting its strategic weapons systems.[56] Two years later, Congress released a report titled "Bugs in the Program: Problems in Federal Government Computer Software Development and Regulation," initiating yet another full-blown attack on the fundamental causes of the software crisis.[57] Ironically, the

Department of Defense decided that what was needed to deal with this most recent outbreak of crisis was yet another new programming language—in this case ADA, which was trumpeted as a means of "replacing the idiosyncratic 'artistic' ethos that has long governed software writing with a more efficient, cost-effective engineering mind-set."[58]

Why have automatic programming languages and other technologies thus far failed to resolve—or apparently even mitigate—the seemingly perpetual software crisis? First of all, it is clear that many of these languages and systems were not able to live up to their marketing hype. Even those systems that were more than a "complex, exception-ridden performer of clerical tasks which was difficult to use and inefficient" (as John Backus characterized the programming tools of the early 1950s) could not eliminate the need for careful analysis and skilled programming.[59] As Willis Ware portrayed the situation in 1965, "We lament the cost of programming; we regret the time it takes. What we really are unhappy with is the total programming process, not programming (i.e., writing routines) per se. Nonetheless, people generally smear the details into one big blur; and the consequence is, we tend to conclude erroneously that all our problems will vanish if we can improve the language which stands between the machine and the programmer. T'aint necessarily so." All the programming language improvement in the world will not shorten the intellectual activity, thinking, and analysis that is inherent in the programming process. Another name for the programming process is "problem solving by machine; perhaps it suggests more pointedly the inherent intellectual content of preparing large problems for machine handling."[60]

Although programming languages could reduce the amount of clerical work associated with programming, and did help eliminate certain types of errors (mostly those associated with transcription errors or syntax mistakes), they also introduced new sources of error. In the late 1960s, a heated controversy broke out in the programming community over the use of the "GOTO statement."[61] At the heart of this debate was the question of professionalism: although high-level languages gave the impression that just about anyone could program, many programmers felt this was a misconception disastrous to both their profession and the industry in general.

The designers and advocates of various automatic programming systems never succeeded in addressing the larger issues posed by the difficulties inherent in the programming process. High-level languages were necessary but not sufficient: that is, the use of these languages became an essential component of software development, but could not in themselves ensure a successful development effort. Programming remained a highly skilled occupation, and programmers continued to defy traditional methods of job categorization and management. By the end of the 1960s the search for a silver bullet solution to the software crisis had turned away from programming languages and toward more comprehensive techniques for managing the programming process. Many of these new techniques involved the creation of new automatic programming technologies, but most revolved around more systemic solutions as well as new methods of programmer education, management, and professional development.

5

The Rise of Computer Science

At present there is a flavor of "game-playing" about many courses in computer science. I hear repeatedly from friends who want to hire good software people that they have found the specialist in computer science is someone they do not want. *Their experience is that graduates in our programs seem to be mainly interested in playing games, making fancy programs that really do not work, writing trick programs, etc.*
—Richard Hamming, "One Man's View of Computer Science," 1968

The Humble Programmer

The first computer programmers came from a wide variety of occupational and educational backgrounds. Some were recruited from the ranks of the female "human computers" who had participated in wartime manual computation projects. Others were former clerical workers or tabulating machine operators with experience in corporate data processing. A few were erstwhile scientists and engineers drawn into computing in pursuit of intellectual or professional opportunities.

For this last group of well-educated "converts" to computing, it was not always clear where their adopted discipline stood in relation to more traditional intellectual activities. Although the electronic computers were increasingly used in this period as *instruments* of scientific production, their status as legitimate *objects* of scientific and professional scrutiny had not yet been established. Scientists and engineers who drifted out of the "respectable" disciplines into the uncharted waters of electronic computing faced self-doubt, professional uncertainty, and even ridicule.

One such emigrant from the sciences was the physicist-turned-programmer Edsger Dijkstra. In the early 1950s, as a result of "a long series of coincidences" associated with his doctoral research in theoretical physics, Dijkstra became the first person in his native Holland to program a computer. The experience was life changing, and by 1955 he had decided to relinquish physics to take up computing full-time. His dissertation in 1959 on "communication with an automatic computer" described his development of an assembly code for the mathematical computation center at the University of Amsterdam.[1]

Like many of his fellow scientists, Dijkstra was not so much interested in the electronic computer as a technology as he was in computing as an intellectual activity. While the electronic computer itself would no doubt have an enormous impact on society, it would be "but a ripple on the surface of our culture" compared to the potential influence of the science of computing. The emergence of the computing sciences, Dijkstra declared, represented an intellectual opportunity "without precedent in the cultural history of mankind." To program a computer efficiently was to master complexity, and the mastery of complexity was the fundamental challenge of modern science and society.[2]

Despite his enthusiasm for the challenge and potential of computing, however, Dijkstra's decision to abandon physics for computing was fraught with doubt and uncertainty. As Dijkstra would later recall in his 1972 Turing Award Lecture (revealingly titled "The Humble Programmer"),

I had to make up my mind, either to stop programming and become a real, respectable theoretical physicist, or to carry my study of physics to formal completion only, with a minimum of effort, and to become . . . what? A programmer? But was that a respectable profession? After all what was programming? Where was the sound body of knowledge that could support it as an intellectually respectable discipline? I remember quite vividly how I envied my hardware colleagues, who, when asked about their professional competence, could at least point out that they knew everything about vacuum tubes, amplifiers and the rest, whereas I felt that, when faced with that question, I would stand empty-handed.

The principal problem with programming in this early period, according to Dijkstra, was the persistence of a black art mentality among many of its practitioners. Programmers too often saw their work as temporary solutions to local problems, rather than as an opportunity to develop a more permanent body of knowledge and technique. They reveled in the popular notion that programmers were idiosyncratic geniuses, and that "a really competent programmer should be puzzle-minded and very fond of clever tricks." To Dijkstra these were pernicious anachronisms that encouraged a provincial, "tinkering" approach to software development. Such "clumsy and expensive" processes might have been tolerated when computer software, like computer hardware, was still relatively primitive. But the increased power and reliability of contemporary computers "made solutions feasible that programmers had not dared to dream about a few years ago." What computing needed to realize its true revolutionary potential, Dijkstra argued, was a more rigorous approach to programming—one modeled after the science of applied mathematics.[3]

Dijkstra's lament about the deplorable lack of theoretical rigor in computing would have resonated with his audience. The ACM membership, to whom Dijkstra addressed his reminiscences, was dominated by those in the computing community who advocated a more scientific approach to computing. The majority of ACM members had college degrees (often in science, engineering, or mathematics) and the ACM as an organization worked for decades to draw distinct boundaries between computer science as an academic discipline and computer programming as an occupational activity. It was an ACM journal that first introduced the discipline of computer science, and an ACM committee that developed its first standardized curriculum. The Turing Award itself was an ACM invention, intended to recognize—and stimulate—theoretical work in the emerging discipline of computer science. By the beginning of the early 1970s, when Dijkstra received his Turing Award, computer science seemed well on its way to becoming just the sort of "sound body of knowledge" whose absence Dijkstra had so regretted when first he started to program.[4]

There were many reasons for Dijkstra and his fellows to aspire to academic legitimacy. To begin with, there seemed a compelling intellectual rationale for doing so. Beginning with John von Neumann's work on numerical meteorology in the late 1940s, computational models were increasingly being used to provide solutions—approximate solutions in many cases, but solutions nonetheless—to scientific problems that had previously been thought intractable.[5] Over the course of the 1950s, in fields as diverse as economics, linguistics, physics, biology, ecology, psychology, and cognitive science, techniques and concepts drawn from computing promised dramatic new insights and capabilities.[6] As was the case with Dijkstra, many of the most enthusiastic advocates of computer science had come from fields that had been transformed by the electronic computer. Computing was "as broad as our culture, as deep as interplanetary space," declared Herbert Grosch, a former astronomer (and future president of the ACM).[7] "Never before in the history of mankind" had there been a phenomenon of equal importance to "the pervasion of computers and computing into every other science field and discipline," argued Paul Armer, the head of computing at the RAND Corporation (and another future ACM president). "We've always thought of mathematics as the queen of the sciences pervading every other field, but computing is going to go much farther than that."[8] For many of these pioneering computer scientists, not only was theirs a "real" scientific discipline, it was perhaps *the* scientific discipline.

Even for those computer specialists whose professional aspirations were more commercial than academic, there were powerful incentives to encourage the establishment of an independent discipline of theoretical computer science. The late 1950s and 1960s was a period in which many white-collar occupations were actively working to "professionalize" their discipline.[9] And according to the growing body of sociological literature of this period, a necessary precondition to professional development was the control over an organized body of knowledge. Without a firm basis in science and theory, computer programming and data processing were doomed to remain low-status, technical occupations. The primary distinction between professionals and technicians, it was generally believed in this period, was that professionals underwent a "prolonged course of specialized, intellectual instruction and study," contended Malcolm Gotterer in letter to the editors of the industry journal *Datamation*.[10] Establishing computer science as a legitimate *theoretical* discipline was therefore an essential component in the professionalization agenda of all of its practitioners, whether or not they intended to pursue careers as research scientists. "A profession is under an obligation to develop and base itself on a body of knowledge rather than upon a body of applications," maintained C. M. Sidlo in a letter to the editors of the *Communications of the ACM* in 1961. "As a profession becomes mature it realizes that the science (not technology) needed by the profession must continually be extended to more basic content rather than restricted only to the obvious applied science."[11] Within the status hierarchy of the university, of course, theory ranked higher than practice, and was therefore desirable for its own sake. Outside of the academy, theoretical knowledge offered a potential key to professional advancement. It provided a means of distinguishing the competent professional from the mere technician.

Computer manufacturers and corporate employers also had a stake in the development of computer science. One popular explanation for the seemingly perpetual "personnel crisis" in computer programming was the "virtual nonexistence" of educational standards in the industry.[12] The establishment of formal academic programs and standardized curriculum would allow manufacturers and employers to off-load the work of training and certifying programmers on the universities. Just what this training would look like, and how it would balance theory with practice, would become a subject of much contention, but the need for some form of academic discipline devoted to computing must have seemed evident to almost everyone in the industry.

In retrospect, the emergence of an academic discipline devoted to computer science seems almost overdetermined. How could the defining technology of our modern information age, the device most widely associated in the popular mind with progress in contemporary science and technology, not have attracted the attention of a wide variety of academic scientists and engineers? One would imagine that any number of disciplines would be clamoring for control over the science of computing and information technology. And indeed, by all of the traditional measures of academic accomplishment, including papers published, students graduated, and funding controlled, computer science has proven itself a resounding success. Within a few years of the founding of the first computer science programs in the United States, thousands of computer scientists were being graduated nationwide. For almost two decades afterward, the number of degrees granted in computer science would grow on average more than 20 percent annually. At the height of its popularity, more than 5 percent of all U.S. male college undergraduates would graduate with a degree in the computer and information sciences.[13] The remarkable rise to dominance of computer science as an autonomous discipline represents one of the great success stories of academic entrepreneurship of the late twentieth century.

But the development of a new technology, no matter how powerful or influential, did not necessarily justify the creation of a new academic discipline. There are many examples of scientific or technological accomplishments that were interesting, useful, and productive, but that did not require or deserve the development of their own disciplines or departments. "The creation of computer science departments is analogous to creating new departments for the railroad, automobile, radio, airplane or television technologies," argued one letter to the editors of the *Communications of the ACM*.[14] "These industrial developments were all tremendous innovations embodied in machinery, as is the development of computers, but this is not enough for a discipline or a major academic field."[15] According to this line of reasoning, no matter how powerful or even revolutionary, in the end the electronic computer was simply another tool or instrument, similar to the microscope or telephone. No one denied that such tools and instruments were essential to the practice of modern science and technology, but neither did they call for the creation of departments of microscopy or telephony.

There were, in fact, many objections raised against the establishment of an independent discipline of computer science. In his "Presidential Letter to the ACM Membership" in 1966, Anthony Oettinger outlined what he called these "numerous misconceptions" about computer science:

The computer is just a tool, and not [a] proper intellectual discipline. . . . It is not the business of universities to train computer center managers or systems experts. . . . The training of faculty and students in computer usage can better be done by people in the various disciplines who have acquired computer experience, rather than by a separate cadre of computer scientists. . . . The [future potential] of computers has been overrated, and when the current fad subsides, many universities will have . . . badly overextended themselves with respect to both equipment and teaching/research commitments in computer science per se. . . . Computer science is not a coherent intellectual discipline but rather a heterogeneous collection of bits and pieces from other disciplines.[16]

Some of these objections must have seemed absurd even to contemporaries; the suggestion that the electronic computer was simply a passing "fad" was unreasonable even in the early 1960s. But other critiques, such as the characterization of computer science as a grab bag of theories and techniques drawn from other disciplines, were much more salient. Judging from the reaction that Oettinger's list provoked from the ACM membership, there was a real fear within the nascent computer science community that its discipline was not being taken seriously, that it was considered by many little more than a "momentary aberration in the fields of mathematics and electrical engineering."[17] Oettinger himself later confessed to having doubts about whether or not computing, with its mix of the "purest mathematics" and the "dirtiest of engineering," would ever truly be considered a science.[18]

In order to demonstrate that computer science was a real, respectable intellectual activity, computer scientists needed to clearly define the body of theory that was at the center of their discipline. But what exactly was computer science the science of? Computers were, after all, human-made objects. Could there be such a thing, as Herbert Simon would later come to argue, as a "science of the artificial?"[19] Or was the computer ultimately incidental to computer science, which would turn out to be the study of some more basic entity, such as information or algorithms? Even among those who called themselves computer scientists, there were disagreements about what the science should look like or where it would fit into the established hierarchy of the university.[20] Some pushed for a theoretical approach akin to philosophy or mathematics, and others for engineering-oriented programs emphasizing practical techniques. A few departments continued to view hardware development as relevant, while others dismissed it entirely. How much to stress programming training was a perennial question, with industrial sponsors encouraging one approach and the academic hierarchy encouraging another.

Throughout the 1960s, aspiring computer scientists struggled to define a compelling, coherent agenda for their discipline. The ultimate success that they achieved conceals the messy social and intellectual work that was required to carve out a niche for computer science in an already-crowded university hierarchy. As William Aspray has suggested, the nascent discipline of computer science crossed virtually every academic boundary then established within the university, drawing content and people from mathematics, electrical engineering, psychology, and business.[21] These are not boundaries to be transgressed casually; academic departments are notoriously fierce about protecting their intellectual and curricular territory.[22] For example, at many research universities computing activity had been traditionally located within departments of mathematics or electrical engineering. By the end of the 1950s, an even broader range of disciplines in the sciences, engineering, and business not only controlled their own computing resources but were also offering their own courses in practical computer programming. It was not clear at all to these established departments that specialists in computer science had anything to offer, intellectually or otherwise. Indeed, as computer science threatened to draw resources and students from these traditional disciplines, heated battles erupted over faculty slots, graduate admissions, and courses.

This chapter explores the rise to dominance of theoretical computer science as the representative science of modern computing. It suggests that this rise was anything but inevitable, and that the academic discipline of computer science as it emerged in the period between 1955 and 1975 reflects a series of messy compromises about what the academic study of computing should look like, what subjects it should address, and how it should relate to other, more established disciplines—as well as to the rapidly growing commercial computer industry. It argues that the advocates of theoretical computer science pursued a strategy that served them well within the university, but that increasingly alienated them from their colleagues in industry. As the software crisis heated up in the late 1960s, university computer science programs served as a resource for practitioners in their struggle for professional legitimacy, but they also represented a battleground in which various groups competed for control over occupational and intellectual territory.

Comptologist, Turingeer, or Applied Epistomologist?

The first rigorous description of the discipline that would eventually become known as computer science appeared in a September 1959 article in the newly founded *Communications of the ACM* journal. This new discipline, claimed its author, the physicist Louis Fein, would consolidate the many computing activities that were currently dispersed across the university in departments of mathematics, business and economics, library science, physics, and electrical engineering. It would serve as the conduit for basic research in computing, the link between computing and the larger scientific community, and the training ground for students and industrial programmers. It would rationalize the currently haphazard and dispersed efforts of industry, academia, and government. And by establishing a truly scientific approach to computing, it would unleash the "enormous potential" of the electronic computer to revolutionize society.[23] Fein proposed several possible names for this new discipline, including "information science," "intellitronics," "synnoetics" (the term that he himself would later come to prefer), and "computer science."[24] Others would add "datalogy," "hypology" (derived from the Greek root *hypologi*, meaning "to compute"), "applied epistemology," and "Turingineering" to this list.[25] Computer science was the name that stuck.

The idea that the various fields associated with computing deserved their own unifying discipline was not entirely original to Fein—a year earlier, a researcher at IBM's Applied Programming Division had suggested the umbrella term "comptology"—but Fein was the first to back up his proposal with specific recommendations for curriculum, departments, and research agendas.[26] Fein had been commissioned by Stanford University in 1957 to study computing education, and had emerged as an outspoken advocate of the formation of *autonomous* departments of computer science independent of existing programs in mathematics and electrical engineering.[27] In 1960 he was appointed the chair of the ACM Education Committee, and a year later published a fictionalized description (written from the perspective of a 1975 observer) of the program he had developed for Stanford. Interestingly enough, the name of his idealized department was synnoetics (from the Greek for the "science of the mind") rather than computer science. Synnoetics was Fein's term for "the cooperative interaction, or symbiosis of people, mechanisms, plant or animal organisms, and automata into a system that results in a mental power (power of knowing) greater than that of its individual components." In many ways, synnoetics was much more akin to the contemporary discipline of cybernetics that to the modern discipline of computer science.

Computer Bureaus and Computing Laboratories

Computing in the universities did not begin with the electronic computer. Small-scale computing projects organized around mechanical calculators and human computers had existed for decades in departments of physics and astronomy.[28] For the most part, however, these human computing projects had no identity independent of that of their host department. They were funded and staffed locally, and regarded computing as important only in the context of a larger scientific agenda.

By the 1930s a few research universities had established computing centers that did serve multiple faculties. Many of these were operated in collaboration with computing equipment manufacturers. IBM started donating tabulating equipment to Columbia University in the 1920s, for example, and in 1934 helped establish what would become the Thomas J. Watson Astronomical Computing Bureau, operated jointly by IBM, Columbia, and the American Astronomical Society. The bureau attracted researchers from mathematics and physics as well as astronomy, and in 1945 was transformed into the Watson Scientific Computing Laboratory, which provided computing services to a broad range of scientists at Columbia and beyond. In 1946 the laboratory began offering an introductory course in scientific computing that over the next two decades enrolled more than sixteen hundred researchers from twenty countries.[29]

At Harvard, a young graduate student in physics named Howard Aiken convinced the IBM Corporation to construct for him an electromechanical computer intended to help fulfill the pressing need "for more powerful calculating methods in the mathematical and physical sciences."[30] The Harvard Mark I, as it came to be known, was a truly massive machine: fifty feet long, weighing more than five tons, comprised of more than seven hundred thousand individual parts. During the war the Mark I served as the foundation for the Harvard Computational Laboratory (commanded by Aiken, who was a Naval Reserve officer).

After the war Aiken transformed the laboratory into a center for training and research in the emerging fields of computer science. By 1947, Harvard had established a one-year master's degree program in applied mathematics "with special reference to computing machinery."[31] The following year, with funding from the U.S. Air Force, the program began offering doctoral degrees. By 1954, it had graduated nineteen MA and eight PhD students. It was not until 1962 that an academic program in computer science was established outside the Computational Laboratory.[32]

MIT had a similarly long tradition of scientific computing that began in the 1920s with Vannevar Bush and his colleagues in the electrical engineering department. By this time MIT was already known for its close ties to business and government, and its influential electrical engineering department represented the cutting edge of scientific computing in this period. Bush's differential analyzer, which solved differential equations by mechanical integration, was only the most well-known of the analog computing devices developed at MIT during the interwar period. In the late 1930s, funding from the Carnegie Corporation helped found the MIT Center for Analysis, in which differential analyzers, network analyzers, and IBM punch card calculators were harnessed to serve the computational needs of a wide variety of faculty, industry, and government users. Although the Center for Analysis collapsed, somewhat inexplicably, shortly after the end of the war, other computing activities helped propel MIT to the forefront of computing research.[33] The real-time computing Project Whirlwind was not only transformed, in 1951, into the Digital Computing Laboratory but also spun off the influential Lincoln Laboratory (and ultimately, the System Development Corporation). Project MAC was an Advanced Research Project Agency–funded project that produced important innovations in time-sharing and networking, and in 1975 became the MIT Laboratory for Computer Science. Other projects and laboratories at MIT incorporated computing into programs in communications, library science, and operations research.[34]

Despite the central role that MIT played in postwar computing research, it was not until 1969 that the university offered an undergraduate major in computer science. Its graduate program in computer science would not be established for another decade. This is not to say that courses in computing were not offered at MIT prior to this period; indeed, as early as 1935 Samuel Caldwell was teaching a graduate seminar in machine computation. But prior to the late 1960s, instruction in computer science was distributed throughout various departments and laboratories. When computing did enter the formal MIT undergraduate curriculum, it did so under the auspices of the powerful electrical engineering department. The program that was established in 1969 was only an optional major within electrical engineering. And even then the curriculum was at best a combination of basic computer science and computer engineering.[35] Theory clearly took a backseat to practical circuit design and basic physics. It was not until 1975 that the students could receive a BS degree in computer science—rather than a BSE in electrical engineering—from the newly renamed Department of Electrical Engineering and Computer Science.

Other universities had similar arrangements. The Moore School of Electrical Engineering had long served as a computing center for both the University of Pennsylvania and the nearby Naval Ballistics Laboratory in Aberdeen, Maryland. In addition to its large staff of human computers, the Moore School had also acquired a copy of a Bush differential analyzer. In 1954, Princeton University acquired the computer that John von Neumann had built for the Princeton Institute for Advanced Study. The responsibility for operating the computer was given to the mathematics department, which despite having a strong tradition in just the types of mathematical logic that were becoming central to theoretical computer science, was not much interested in making use of it. The statistician John Tukey did have an interest in practical computing, as did the electrical engineering department, and in the early 1960s it was agreed that the statistics department would take over responsibility for computing science, while electrical engineering would provide training in computer science.[36] In the end it was the electrical engineering department, in part because of its control over the Princeton Computing Center, that incorporated both. It was not until 1984 that Princeton was to have a separate department of computer science.

Trading Zones

The adoption of the new technology of electronic computing seems to have followed, at most universities, the pattern established by the pre-existing computing centers: the cost of expensive equipment was justified by its ability to serve the needs of researchers in established disciplines such as physics, astronomy, mathematics, and electrical engineering.

In many ways this arrangement was advantageous for the emerging computer sciences. As Atsushi Akera has described in his study of early scientific computing activities, many of the pioneering academic computing scientists learned their trade in the centralized computing facilities that provided computational services to other researchers.[37] Akera compares such centers to the "trading zones" examined by the historian of physics Peter Galison in his work on bubble chambers. Like the bubble chamber, the electronic computer created around it an inter-disciplinary space in which researchers from a variety of backgrounds could productively interact. In such trading zones, researchers did not have to agree on the universal meaning or significance of the instrument but only on local protocols and practices. And so a physicist using the computer to perform Monte Carlo simulations could regard the com-puter as a simply another experimental apparatus, while the computer programmer that he or she was working with might imagine it as an object of study in and of itself.[38] In the computer that the theorists con-sidered only in terms of its logical architecture, the electrical engineers saw circuits and wiring diagrams. Both could be interested in the same machine for different reasons, and still have interactions in the trading zone that were productive and significant.

The trading zone did have its limits. For those who saw the computer as a tool of more universal interest and applicability, the confines of the computing centers could be limiting. The isolation of computing in com-puting centers was at once physical, professional, and intellectual. Early computers were large, power hungry, and because of the extensive cooling required to dissipate the heat they produced, noisy. They required constant maintenance. They generally never left the engineering labs in which they were constructed, reinforcing their status as experimental and highly specialized instruments. Each machine was unique, and the tech-nology was changing so rapidly that every new machine was essentially a prototype. It is hardly surprising that computing appeared to be a subset of electrical engineering.

Compared to the massive machinery of the computer engineers, the contributions of the computer theorists seemed intangible and insignifi-cant. This was a particular problem for programmers, whose work lacked even the subdued glamour of mathematical equations or the claim to fundamental scientific knowledge. Demonstrating a new machine to visitors was "orders of magnitude more spectacular" than showing them a few handwritten sheets of code.[39] The image of the blinking "giant electronic brain" captured both the public and scientific imagination in a way that mere concepts or procedures never could.[40] And of course at this point the word software, or even the concept it would come to embody, simply did not exist. Where the hardware engineers were able to demonstrate constant progress toward machines that were smaller, faster, and more reliable, their colleagues in software only seemed to discover new and more perplexing challenges and difficulties.

That computing itself was a curious amalgam of disciplinary techniques and traditions drawn from mathematics and engineering was both an asset and a liability. There is no question that nascent computer professionals benefited immensely from their ability to make themselves useful to a broad range of academic researchers. But having interdisciplinary appeal was not the same as owning your own discipline. Computer center personnel had difficulty shedding their image as service providers rather than legitimate researchers. In a report to the ACM Curriculum Committee in 1966, the noted computer scientist David Parnas warned that computer science was "viewed by other disciplines as a rather easily mastered tool." "It is easy, in any field, to confuse the work of a technician with the work of a professional," suggested Parnas, "but this is easier in computer science because a worker in another discipline will consider himself an 'expert' after learning to use a computer to process his data."[41]

The development of high-level programming languages exacerbated this situation. For example, by 1958 the majority of users of IBM's line of scientific computers were using FORTRAN to develop their software. FORTRAN had been developed specifically for scientists, with its syntax deliberately mirroring conventional arithmetic notation.[42] There was no reason why a department of mathematics or physics could not offer a FORTRAN programming course sufficient for the needs of its faculty and graduate students.

In fact, this is just what happened. Departments of mathematics, engineering, and business were able to develop what they saw as perfectly serviceable courses of instruction in computer programming. Anticipating a debate that would soon develop in the commercial computing industry, they considered disciplinary-specific training as being *more* relevant than that provided by computer specialists. It was not computing per se that was important or interesting; what mattered was the application of computing to a particular problem domain, and who was better qualified to teach scientific programming than a specialist in that domain. A good physicist could easily pick up enough programming to get by on, but even the best programmers could never learn enough physics to become truly useful. If the physicist's code was not quite as optimal as the professional programmer's, it was always possible to buy a more powerful computer.

As we have seen in the case of all the early academic centers of electronic computing—Columbia, Harvard, MIT, and the University of Pennsylvania—computing activity itself was confined to the computing laboratories, while theoretical work and practical instruction in computing tended to be distributed throughout the university, with departments of mathematics and electrical engineering serving as de facto administrators of computer-related education. This was certainly the situation as Fein described it in his 1959 report. It was not inevitable, at least through the end of the 1960s, that computer science would be able to distance itself from its origins in other disciplines. As long as courses in computing theory or at least practical programming were being offered by individual departments, it was not obvious that it needed to. Some of the traditional disciplines clearly felt threatened by the newcomer. At Harvard and Princeton, for example, undergraduate enrollments grew rapidly in computer science while they stagnated in other areas of applied science and engineering. At Penn and MIT, an increasing number of electrical engineering students chose to focus on computer-related subjects rather than on other areas of electrical engineering. As computer-related subfields began drawing resources and students from traditional disciplines, heated battles erupted over faculty slots, graduate admissions, and courses. Its early success at attracting students and resources notwithstanding, computer science was repeatedly forced to defend its academic legitimacy. And so the real historical question seems to be not why it took so long for an autonomous discipline of computer science to be established but why it ever got established in the first place.

Is Computer Science Science?

The most obvious answer is that computer science exists because the computer scientists wanted it to. The community of computing researchers that emerged out of the digital computing laboratories of the 1950s represented a definitive break from the earlier tradition of the scientific computing bureau. These were not the female human computers or tabulating machine operators of the previous generation; they were men with MAs or PhDs in fields like physics, mathematics, and astronomy. They had been attracted to computing because they found the work challenging and rewarding, not because they had no other options. A few already had positions as university faculty; most had academic aspirations; all believed computing, as a generalized phenomenon, was a subject worthy of sustained and concentrated scientific attention. It seemed both essential and inevitable that their professional identity as computer scientists would be constructed around a solid foundation of theoretical knowledge.

Such academically minded individuals were naturally drawn to the ACM. The ACM had been founded in 1947 by MIT professor Samuel Caldwell. Although as its name implies the ACM had been established with computing machinery in mind, by the early 1950s it had distanced itself from the more engineering-oriented aspects of computing in favor of the "other phases" of computing, including numerical analysis, logical design, and programming.[43] As will be discussed further in chapter 7, the ACM deliberately styled itself an as academic organization; its annual meetings resembled academic conferences, with published proceedings, and the articles in its journals, the first of which appeared in 1953, were peer reviewed, highly technical, and generally theoretically oriented. Many of the original members either were or had been associated with a major university computation project, and most were university educated. The ACM was the first computing association to impose educational standards on its members, develop standardized computer science curricula, and join national scientific organizations such as the American Association for the Advancement of Science and the National Academy of Sciences. Almost half of the institutional members of the ACM were educational organizations, and after 1962 a thriving student membership program was developed. In 1966, the ACM established the prestigious Turing Award, which remains to this day the highest academic honor awarded in computer science. The ACM clearly attracted those computing specialists most invested in a particular vision of computer science in which the "sole abstract purpose of advancing truth and knowledge" remained primary.[44]

Of course, it was not enough for computer scientists to call themselves scientists. Although by the early 1960s the term computer science was being used widely within both academia and industry to describe the formal study of computing, the broader recognition of computer science as a legitimate science had yet to be established.[45] The elevation of university computing centers to departments of computer science did not necessarily change the widespread perception that computing was still essentially a service activity. "Any field that has the word science in its name," argued the mathematician Frank Harary, "is guaranteed thereby not to be a science."[46] The historical association of computing with low-skilled, feminized labor did nothing to improve this perception, nor did the more recent dominance by the technology of the electronic computer.

In order to gain real academic respectability, computer scientists had to convince others not only that having such a discipline was desirable and necessary but also that it addressed some fundamental scientific objective.

On this first point computer scientists were greatly assisted by the contemporary boom in commercial electronic computing. As has been discussed previously, this was more than just a function of the increasing availability of fast, reliable, and (relatively) low-cost computing power. The growing realization that software could be used to transform the general-purpose electronic computer into a broad range of information- and decision-related devices greatly expanded the range of applications to which this computing power could be productively applied. By the early 1960s, the electronic computer had become a significant presence not only in the research laboratory and the military but in the corporate and government sectors as well. It was no great rhetorical leap to argue, as did the computer scientist Peter Wegner in a 1966 essay, that society was on the verge "of a computer revolution that will be as profound in its effects as the industrial revolution of the eighteenth and nineteenth centuries."[47] Similar assertions were being made by numerous business leaders and government officials in this period. The real question was not whether or not, as Wegner went on to contend, there was "a growing organized body of knowledge and theory relating to computers," but whether "this body of knowledge and theory is called computer science."[48]

The general excitement generated by the rapid expansion of the commercial computer industry lent support to the claims of computer scientists that their discipline was of central economic and social significance. The burgeoning personnel crisis in the computing fields described in previous chapters was just one sign of a larger interest in computer-related training and education. But although computer scientists clearly benefited from the growing demand for practical training in computer programming, their relationship with commercial computing was from the beginning ambivalent. On the one hand, the practical and commercial potential of the electronic computer is what attracted attention and funding from industry as well as the government. On the other hand, in order to differentiate themselves from mathematics or electrical engineering, and establish computing as more than just a service industry, they had to distance themselves from the more technical activities associated with computing.

There were attempts in this period to define computer science in terms of computer technology. In a letter to the editors of *Science* in 1967, the noted computer scientists Herbert Simon, Allen Newell, and Alan Perlis maintained that the answer to the perennial question of "Is there such a thing as computer science, and if there is, what is it?" was really quite simple: just as biology was the study of life, and astronomy the study of stars, computer science was the study of computers. That the former were natural phenomenon and the latter was artificial was irrelevant (an argument that the Nobel Prize–winning Simon would make more thoroughly in 1967 in his *The Sciences of the Artificial*).[49] Yes, computers involved technology as well as science. Yes, computing represented a dirty mix of mathematics, electronics, psychology, and many other already-established disciplines. But computers produced interesting, novel, and complex phenomenon, and that was justification enough for a science of computing.

For most aspiring computer scientists, however, this was not a satisfactory definition. It smacked too much of the physicality of engineering. "Computer science is no more about the computer than astronomy is about telescopes," Edsger Dijkstra famously declared.[50] "We were blinded by the huge success of computers as practical tools," Louis Fein argued, and therefore "overemphasized the importance of computer design and programming."[51] A first-rate program in the computer sciences "should be possible without any computing equipment at all, just as a first-rate program in certain areas of physics can exist without a cyclotron."[52] It was a "widespread misconception" that computer science was "simply concerned with the design of computing devices," echoed a report by the ACM Curriculum Committee in 1965.[53] Even the choice to include machinery in the title of their association seemed increasingly improvident to many ACM members. Over the course of the next several decades, regular attempts would be made to change the name of the ACM to something more science oriented.[54]

For a growing number of computer scientists, the computer itself was increasingly just an abstraction, a "universal machine" that could be transformed into whatever particular solution happened to be required. It was the process of transformation, and its possibilities and constraints, that was of central theoretical importance; the physical characteristics of the underlying object of that transformation were immaterial.

The first important step toward the establishment of a science of computing independent of the computer had originated with John von

Neumann, the peripatetic physicist, mathematician, and economist who, during the Second World War and its immediate aftermath, was intimately involved with the development of both the electronic computer and the hydrogen bomb. In the course of his work at Los Alamos on the modeling of thermonuclear reactions, von Neumann became aware of the ENIAC project at the University of Pennsylvania. There he began working with the ENIAC designers on a successor machine called the EDVAC, which was in concept the first modern, stored-program electronic computer. In 1945–1946, von Neumann circulated an informal "First Draft of a Report on the EDVAC," which described the EDVAC in terms of its logical structure, using notation borrowed from neurophysiology. Ignoring most of the physical details of the EDVAC design, such as its vacuum tube circuitry, von Neumann focused instead on the main functional units of the computer: its arithmetic unit, memory, and input and output. The "von Neumann architecture," as it came to be known, served as the logical basis for almost all computers designed in subsequent decades.

By abstracting the logical design of the digital computer from any particular physical implementation, von Neumann took a crucial first step in the development of a modern theory of computation.[55] His was not the only contribution; in 1937, for example, Turing had described, for the purposes of demonstrating the *limits* of computation, what would become known as the Universal Turing Machine. Eventually, the Universal Turing Machine would become an even more fundamental construct of modern computer science. According to the Church-Turing thesis, first articulated in 1943 by the mathematician Stephen Kleene, any function that can be physically computed can be computed by a Universal Turing Machine.

The abstraction of the technology of computing in the theoretical construct of the Turing Machine mirrored the shift toward software that was occurring in the larger commercial computing industry. Independent of the work of theoretical computer scientists, working programmers—and their corporate employers—were discovering to their chagrin that computer software was even more complicated and expensive to develop than computer hardware. It was the growing number of data processing departments and commercial programming houses that provided the majority of employment opportunities for the graduates of fledgling programs in computer science. Establishing computer science as a discipline substantially different from computer engineering had been relatively easy given the growing (and visible) distinction between software and hardware. Clearly defining the relationship between computer science and computer programming was much more difficult and problematic.

On the surface, the relationship between the two seems obvious: computer science was the theoretical basis underlying the practical occupation of computer programming. Dijkstra had implied as much in his "Humble Programmer" lecture, and most of his contemporaries would have agreed that there was at least some relationship between the two. But what exactly was the nature of this relationship? As we have seen, computer programming in the 1950s was generally regarded as an inherently undisciplined and unscientific activity. Computer programmers prided themselves on their clever and idiosyncratic solutions to problems. Most working programmers in this period had no formal education in computing, and many did not even possess a college degree. By the end of the 1950s, as discussed earlier, many employers had started questioning the value of mathematics to most commercial programming. Indeed, the only firm conclusion one review of the literature on the selection of computer programmers at this time identified was that "majoring in mathematics was not found to be significantly related to performance as a programmer!"[56] Computer scientists expressed disdain for professional programmers, and professional programmers responded by accusing computer science of being overly abstract or irrelevant.[57] Much more will be said about this conflict between theory and practice in this and subsequent chapters. For the time being, it is important only to note that the professionalization strategies pursued by academic computer scientists were distinct from those of professional business programmers. The skills and abilities that were rewarded within the university hierarchy were not necessarily valued within the corporate environment.

The struggle to define a unique intellectual identity for computer science played itself out over the course of the 1960s in the development of specific programs, departments, and curriculum. The first of these reflected the origins of computing research in computing centers and mathematics departments. They included a mix of courses in numerical analysis, Boolean algebra, and statistics, combined with more practical training in programming.[58] Over the next decade, the more research-oriented programs expanded to include offerings in artificial intelligence, automata theory, and computational complexity. As the historian Michael Mahoney has argued, this conglomeration of concepts and techniques did represent a convergence on a shared intellectual agenda for theoretical computer science.[59] But to a certain degree, computer science in the early 1960s did also appear, at least from the outside, as just the kind of conceptual grab bag that its opponents accused it of being.

In 1965, the ACM Curriculum Committee attempted to bring unity to computer science by defining it in terms of a single fundamental unit of analysis: computer science "is concerned with *information* in much the same sense that physics is concerned with energy; it is devoted to the *representation, storage, manipulation,* and *presentation* of information."[60] This redefinition of computer science around the study of information offered several immediate benefits. Not only did it lay claim to the valuable intellectual territory suggested by the commonsense understanding of information as knowledge or data but it also linked the discipline to the specific formulation of information developed in the late 1940s by the mathematician Claude Shannon. In his seminal book with Warren Weaver from 1949, *A Mathematical Theory of Communication,* Shannon had defined information in terms of the physical concept of negative entropy.[61] His information theory appealed to scientists in a wide variety of disciplines, and for a time it appeared as if information might serve as a broadly unifying concept in the sciences.[62] But despite its intellectual appeal, Shannon's mathematical definition of information was never widely applicable outside of communications engineering. And as for more commonsense notions of information, there already seemed to be claimants to that problem domain. Librarians were already experts at classification, storage, and data retrieval. Statisticians specialized in numerical data. Most academic disciplines, to a certain degree, were devoted to the management and analysis of information. In Europe, various versions of the German word *informatik* (including the French *informatique,* the Spanish *informatica,* and the English informatics) had been successfully mobilized to organize the emerging "computing sciences" (a minor but significant difference in terminology) around the study of information, rather than computers per se, but in the United States such efforts achieved much traction.[63]

In the end, though, it would not be information that emerged as the foundational concept of modern computer science but rather the algorithm.

Fundamental Algorithms

A revolution in science can only be considered complete, according to the influential philosopher of science Thomas Kuhn, when it has written its own textbook history. Textbook histories are the short, celebratory narratives that accompany most textbook introductions to a scientific discipline. Their purpose is to provide aspiring practitioners with a sense of participation in a heroic and coherent disciplinary tradition. They do so not by celebrating revolutionary developments but instead by concealing them. By emphasizing only those details of past discoveries that contribute directly to present-day understandings, highly selective histories situate contemporary theories and practices in a larger tradition of continuity and cumulative discovery. In doing so, they allow practitioners to locate themselves within a disciplinary tradition more mythical than realistic. The construction of such inherently selective histories is an essential move toward the development of what Kuhn called "normal science." The practice of normal science is what defines and perpetuates a discipline. Without normal science, there is no discipline.[64]

Computer science became normal science in the late 1960s. In the same year that the ACM defined the first standard curriculum in computer science, one of its most noted practitioners published its first official history. In 1968, the Stanford University computer scientist Donald Knuth opened the first volume of his canonical *The Art of Computer Programming* with a survey overview of the history of computing. As Kuhn would have anticipated, Knuth's history closely mirrored his theory. It located the origins of the discipline in a treatise by the ninth-century Persian mathematician Muhammad ibn Mūsā al-Khwārizmī. It is from al-Khwārizmī that we derive the modern word algorithm, and for Knuth it was the study of the algorithm that defined the modern discipline of computer science. A history of computing in which the algorithm was fundamental was the ideal companion to a volume subtitled *Fundamental Algorithms*.[65]

As Paul Ceruzzi has convincingly demonstrated, by the beginning of the 1970s Knuth and his colleagues had successfully established the algorithm as the fundamental unit of analysis of computer science.[66] In his compelling interweaving of history and mathematics, Knuth not only defined for computer science an intellectual lineage worthy of the most basic and fundamental of sciences but also skillfully distanced electronic computing from its origins in mechanical computation and electrical engineering. One of the most common objections raised against computer science was that it was a technical rather than a scientific enterprise, the study of local particularities rather than fundamental entities. Despite what Herbert Simon might suggest about the legitimacy of the sciences of the artificial, computing still seemed to many to be the domain of the engineer and accountant rather than the theoretician or scientist.

But the algorithm was by definition an abstraction, that aspect of computing that most lent itself to isolation and formalization. Algorithms were the mechanical procedures followed by a computer, but they were not limited to the computer itself. In theory, algorithms lay at the heart of all self-directed activity, whether mechanical, electrical, or biological. Algorithms were the essence of intelligence, isolated and refined into a precisely defined series of instructions for completing a task. One did not even need a computer to study algorithms; in fact, actual computers were more often than not simply a distraction. Where computers were clearly human-made and particular, algorithms were conceptual and therefore universal. "The notion of a mechanical process and of an algorithm," Peter Wegner would declare, "are as fundamental and general as the concepts that underlie the empirical and mathematical sciences."[67] By suggesting that the algorithm was as fundamental to the technical activity of computing as Sir Isaac Newton's laws of motion were to physics, Knuth and his fellow computer scientists could claim full fellowship with the larger community of scientists.

In addition to its claims to fundamental metaphysical significance, the algorithm provided aspiring computer scientists with a practical agenda for advancing their discipline. Algorithms were amenable to mathematical analysis, which encouraged formalization and abstraction, but not so much that they could be subsumed under applied mathematics, which allowed the computer scientists to claim disciplinary autonomy. The development of efficient algorithms provided clear and well-defined problems (along with some exemplary solutions) for students of the discipline to study and pursue. To borrow once again from Kuhn, algorithms represent the ideal "puzzles" for normal scientists to solve: challenging but not insoluble, intellectually interesting and yet still technically familiar. As a disciplinary agenda, the study of the algorithm has proved enormously productive. Knuth's *The Art of Computer Programming* alone now spans three volumes and more than twenty-one hundred pages—with four more volumes anticipated before it is completed.

But while textbook histories are essential for the articulation of disciplinary identity, it is in the establishment of specific educational curricula that such identities become tangible. It was the publication of the ACM's "Curriculum '68" recommendations that firmly embedded the study of the algorithm in the fabric of computer science education and research. Curriculum '68 provided detailed guidelines for computer science programs at both the undergraduate and graduate levels. The curriculum it proposed was unabashedly theoretical: although it recognized that practical training in programming was "an important by-product" of an education in computer science, the development of programming skill was "by no means its main purpose." Numerical analysis figured heavily, as did computability theory, formal languages, and automata theory.

As Goshal Gupta has suggested, although Curriculum '68 did not end all debate about what computer science should look like or where it should fit into the university, it did represent a landmark moment in the history of the discipline.[68] Curriculum '68 "established computer science as an academic field of study and specified to a great extent its content," concluded a follow-up report from the late 1970s. Within two years of their publication the Curriculum '68 guidelines had been implemented in at least twenty-six universities.[69] The special committee assembled by the ACM to produce the Curriculum '68 report, the Curriculum Committee on Computer Science (C^3S), followed up with a series of articles in the *Communications of the ACM* highlighting specific topics from the recommendations, including computational linguistics, formal languages, automata, and abstract switching and computability. In collaboration with the National Science Foundation, the C^3S also hosted a series of conferences aimed at enabling smaller universities and teaching colleges to implement Curriculum '68.[70] Over the course of the next decade, the C^3S would continue to refine and monitor its recommendations.

"Cute Programming Tricks"

Not everyone agreed with the theoretical turn that computer science took in the late 1960s. For many occupational computer programmers, most of what was happening in theoretical computer science seemed irrelevant or even counterproductive, a "sort of holier than thou academic intellectual sort of enterprise" divorced from practical concerns of commercial computing.[71] Even as computer science succeeded in its quest to establish itself as an academic discipline, industry observers were noting that academic success did not necessarily translate into real-world accomplishments. In the keynote address at the Conference on Personnel Research in 1968, IBM researcher Hal Sackman acknowledged the need for "proper education" for programmers, yet then asked, "But who can we look to for such education? Not the new departments of computer science in the universities. . . . [T]hey are too busy teaching simon-pure courses in their struggle for academic recognition to pay serious time and attention to the applied work necessary to educate programmers and systems analysts for the real world."[72] Later that same year, in his Turing Award lecture titled "One Man's View of Computer Science," Bell Laboratories research scientist Richard Hamming criticized the ACM's recently released Curriculum '68 report for its overemphasis on theory:

At present there is a flavor of "game-playing" about many courses in computer science. I hear repeatedly from friends who want to hire good software people that they have found the specialist in computer science is someone they do not want. Their experience is that graduates in our programs seem to be mainly interested in playing games, making fancy programs that really do not work, writing trick programs, etc., and are unable to discipline their own efforts so that what they say they will do gets done on time and in practical form.

Although Hamming was a firm believer in the inclusion of advanced mathematics in the computer science curriculum, he held that if the discipline were going to turn out "responsible, effective people who meet the real needs of our society," it would need to abandon its love affair with pure mathematics and embrace a hands-on engineering approach to computer science education.[73]

Industrial employers in particular were becoming increasingly disgruntled with the products of the academic computer science departments. "Possibly the most blatant failure of our industry has been its ineffective efforts at communicating with the academic community," argued one article in 1970 on the so-called people problem: "Ours is the first major industry in modern history to develop with only limited support from colleges and universities. . . . [M]ost colleges and universities still have not initiated degree programs leading to data processing careers. Those who do offer computer training frequently give the curriculum a scientific orientation, thus ignoring the additional skills needed by our industry."[74] Abraham Kandel noted the "vicious circle" of intellectual introspection that followed the minimization of practical programming training in the Curriculum '68 guidelines. "Some computer science departments have done such a magnificent job of de-emphasizing the importance of the experimental laboratory in their program that their graduates emerge thoroughly unprepared to tackle the intricacies associated with design work in the real-life world."[75]

Given the perceived incompatibility between the needs of business and the output of the universities, the rise of computer science as an academic discipline contributed little to the professionalization of data processing. Corporate employers began turning to other sources of educated practitioners. A *Datamation* survey in 1972 of corporate data processing managers noticed "another attitude common to most of *Datamation*'s wise men: the relative uselessness of departments of computer sciences . . . and the people they are capable of turning out." For those people thinking about entering the field, the article recommended, "the consensus advice seems to be: stay out of computer sciences. Take a bachelor's degree in a technical subject, add a master's in business administration."[76] Fred Gruenberger, himself a computer science educator, suggested that "most programming managers in large corporations tell the same story repeatedly (although regrettably few people listen). Please, they say, give us well-educated MBAs, not Computer Science graduates." Why business training and not computer science? "It has been repeatedly proven in both scientific and commercial data processing that programming can be taught to bright, well-motivated and well-educated people, but that company identification and a general feeling for 'business' can almost never be taught."[77] Employers also began to look at mechanisms other than education for ensuring the quality of their workforce, especially professional certification exams. This will be the subject of chapter 7.

Science as Professional Identity

In his pathbreaking work on the intellectual history of theoretical computer science, Michael Mahoney has described the emergence of that discipline in terms of the setting of intellectual agendas. An agenda, in Mahoney's formulation, is "what practitioners of the discipline agree ought to be done, a consensus concerning the problems of the field, their order of importance or priority, the means of solving them, and perhaps most importantly, what constitute solutions."[78] It is the ability to set agendas and make progress toward achieving them that determines the intellectual standing of a discipline. In the years between 1955 and 1975, Mahoney argues, theoretical computer science did manage to converge on a set of agendas—automata theory, formal languages, computational complexity, and formal semantics—that provided it with a coherent disciplinary identity. By the end of this period, computer science had unquestionably established itself as a mathematically oriented discipline with real scientific credibility.

The desire to set an academic agenda was itself a form of agenda, or at least a strategy for pursuing a larger agenda. In this case the larger agenda was the professionalization of the computer industry. As will be argued more completely in the following chapter, the accomplishment of professional status for "computer people" was a goal shared by almost everyone in the computer industry: occupational programmers, aspiring computer scientists, computer manufacturers, software development firms, human resources departments, corporate managers, and regulatory agencies.[79] The real question was not whether the industry should professionalize but instead what form this professionalization should follow. The model of the research scientist or the scientifically informed software engineer were both powerful paradigms of professional development, but as we shall see, they were by no means the only models available; the certified public accountant was, for many data processing personnel, an even more compelling example of autonomous professional expertise. The point is that the emergence of computer science as an academic discipline can only be understood in terms of the larger pursuit of professional status.

6

The Cosa Nostra of the Data Processing Industry

We are at once the most unmanageable and the most poorly managed specialism in our society. Actors and artists pale by comparison. Only pure mathematicians are as cantankerous, and it's a calamity that so many of them get recruited by simplistic personnel men.

—Herbert Grosch, "Programmers: The Industry's Cosa Nostra," 1966

Unsettling the Desk Set

The 1957 film *Desk Set* is best known to movie buffs as a lightweight but enjoyable romantic comedy, the eighth of nine pictures in which Spencer Tracy and Katherine Hepburn acted together, and the first to be filmed in color. The film is generally considered frivolous yet enjoyable, not one of the famous pair's best, though still popular and durable. The plot is fairly straightforward: Tracy, as Richard Sumner, is an efficiency expert charged with introducing computer technology into the reference library at the fictional Federal Broadcasting Network. There he encounters Bunny Watson, the Hepburn character, and her spirited troop of female reference librarians. Watson and her fellow librarians, who spend their days researching the answers to such profound questions as "What kind of car does the king of the Watusis drive?" and "How much damage is caused annually to American forests by the spruce budworm?" immediately suspect Sumner of trying to put them all out of a job. After the usual course of conventional romantic comedy fare—mutual mistrust, false assumptions, sublimated sexual tension, and humorous misunderstandings—Watson comes to see Sumner as he truly is: a stand-up guy who was only seeking to make her work as a librarian easier and more enjoyable.

What is less widely remembered about *Desk Set* is that it was sponsored in part by the IBM Corporation. The film opens with a wide-angle view of an IBM showroom, which then closes to a tight shot of a single machine bearing the IBM logo. The equipment on the set was provided by IBM, and the credits at the end of the film—in which an acknowledgment of IBM's involvement and assistance features prominently—appear as if printed on an IBM machine. IBM also supplied equipment operators and training.

The IBM Corporation's involvement with *Desk Set* was more than an early example of opportunistic product placement. Underneath the trappings of a lighthearted comedy, *Desk Set* was the first film of its era to deal seriously with the organizational and professional implications of the electronic computer. In the midst of the general enthusiasm that characterized popular coverage of the computer in this period crept hints of unease about the possibility of electronic brains displacing humans in domains previously thought to have been free from the threat of mechanization. In 1949 the computer consultant Edmund Berkeley, in the first popular book devoted to the electronic computer, had dubbed them "Giant Brains; or, Machines That Think." The giant brain metaphor suggested a potential conflict between human and machine—a conflict that was picked up by the popular press. "Can Man Build a Superman?" *Time* magazine asked in a cover story in 1950 on the Harvard Mark III computer.[1] More pressingly, asked *Colliers* magazine a few years later, "Can a Mechanical Brain Replace You?"[2] Probably it could, concluded *Fortune* magazine, at least if you worked in an office, where "office robots" were poised to "eliminate the human element."[3] IBM's participation in production of *Desk Set* can only be understood in terms of its ongoing efforts, which started in the early 1950s, to reassure the public that despite rumors to the contrary, computers were not poised "to take over the world's affairs from the human inhabitants."[4]

Seen as a maneuver in this larger public relations campaign, *Desk Set* was an unalloyed triumph for IBM.[5] The film is unambiguously positive about the electronic computer. The idea that human beings might ever be replaced by machines is represented as amusingly naive. Sumner's Electronic-Magnetic Memory and Research Arithmetic Calculator (EMERAC) is clearly no threat to Watson's commanding personality and efficiency. In fact, "Emmy" turns out to be charmingly simpleminded. When a technician mistakenly asks the computer for information on the Island "Curfew" (as opposed to Corfu), Emmy goes amusingly haywire. Fortunately, she could easily be put right using only a bobby pin, judiciously applied. The reassuring message was that computers were useful but dimwitted servants, and unlikely masters. As one reviewer described the situation, "It simply does not seem very ominous when they threaten to put a mechanical brain in a broadcasting company's reference library, over which the efficient Miss Hepburn has sway. . . . The prospect of automation is plainly no menace to Kate."[6]

But if the computer held no dangers for Hepburn, it did for many of the real-life office workers watching the film. Like Watson and her librarians, most would have greeted the arrival of a computer-toting efficiency expert with fear and trepidation. Although Tracy imbued the character of Sumner with his trademark gruff-but-likable persona, such experts were generally seen as the harbingers of reorganization, mechanization, and what the economist Thorstein Veblen described as the "degradation of labor."[7] And as Thomas Haigh has suggested, it was no coincidence that Sumner was both an efficiency expert and a computer designer; many of the "systems men" of the early electronic computer era were efficiency experts turned computer consultants. In any case, the specter of computer-driven unemployment looms large over *Desk Set*, if only as the source of initial conflict between Sumner and Watson. But even the most casual viewers of *Desk Set* might have suspected that absent the feisty Hepburn, the librarians at the Federal Broadcasting Network might not have gotten off so easily. Although the film alluded to a second EMERAC that had been installed in the payroll department, no mention was made of the payroll workers having a Watson of their own. Even if the skilled reference librarians and accountants were immune from computerization, though, what about other, less specialized workers? Did anyone really expect the two Emmies to remain confined to the library and payroll departments? It seemed inevitable that at least some Federal Broadcasting Network employees would be reduced to the status of mere machine operators, or perhaps replaced altogether.

Insofar as the *Desk Set* has been interpreted critically, it is in the context of these larger concerns about the replacement of human beings with computers. The struggle of human versus machine (or more precise, woman versus machine) depicted in the film is often seen as a metaphor for worker resistance to computerization. Although the possibility that computers might supersede humans was much discussed in the popular press during the 1950s and early 1960s, with the exception of a small number of occupational categories the adoption of computer technology generally *did not* involve large-scale worker displacement. For the most part, what resistance to corporate computerization efforts did emerge came not from ordinary workers but rather from their managers. It was these managers who frequently saw their work most directly affected by the applications developed by computer programmers and systems analysts. Over the course of the 1950s corporations had discovered that the electronic computer was more than just an improved version of the mechanical calculator or Hollerith machine. What was originally envisioned as a "chromium-plated tabulator," as Haigh has portrayed it, was increasingly seen as a tool for managerial control and communication.[8] As the electronic computer was gradually reinterpreted in larger organizational terms, first as an "electronic data processing" device and then again as a "management information system," it was increasingly seen as a source of institutional and professional power.

Computers Can't Solve Everything

The 1960s were something of a golden age for the computer industry. The industry grew at an average annual rate of 27 percent during this period.[9] At the beginning of the decade there were roughly fifty-four hundred computers installed in the United States; by 1970 this number had grown to more than seventy-four thousand.[10] In 1969 alone U.S. firms purchased $7 billion worth of electronic computers and related equipment. An additional $14 billion was spent on computer personnel and materials. The corporate world's total investment in computing that year represented 10 percent of the nation's total annual expenditure on capital equipment.[11] These corporate investors were also getting increasingly more for their money. In the first half of the decade, innovations in transistor and integrated circuit technology had increased the memory size and processor speed of computers by a factor of ten, providing an effective performance improvement of almost a hundred. By the end of the decade, the inexorable march toward smaller, faster, and cheaper computing predicted by Gordon Moore in 1965 was clearly in evidence.[12]

It was during this period that the IBM Corporation rose to worldwide dominance, establishing in the process a series of institutional structures and technological standards that shaped developments in the industry for the next several decades. Under IBM's substantial umbrella a broad and diverse set of subsidiary industries flourished, including not just manufacturers of complementary (or even competing) hardware products but also programming services companies, time-sharing "computer utilities," and independent data processing service providers. When we consider such subsidiary industries, our estimate of the total size of the computer industry almost doubles.[13]

And yet by the late 1960s there were signs of trouble in paradise. Foreshadowing the "productivity paradox" debate of later decades, hints began to appear in the literature that a growing number of corporations were questioning the value of their investment in computing. As an article in 1969 in *Fortune* magazine entitled "Computers Can't Solve Everything" described the situation, "After buying or leasing some 60,000 computers during the past fifteen years, businessmen are less and less able to state with assurance that it's all worth it." The article recited a litany of overambitious and ultimately unsuccessful attempts to computerize planning and management processes at such firms as Pillsbury, Westinghouse, and the International Minerals and Chemical Corporation. The success that many companies experienced in computerizing their clerical operations in the 1950s, argued industry reporter Thomas Alexander, had generated unrealistic expectations about their ability to apply computing power to more sophisticated applications, such as controlling manufacturing operations, optimizing inventory and transportation flows, and improving the quality of managerial decision making. But perhaps one in ten businesses was "showing expertise in the management of the computer" to higher-order activities. The rest were slowly and uncomfortably "waking up to the fact that they were oversold" on computer technology—not just by self-interested manufacturers and computer consultants, but by their own data processing personnel.[14]

Fortune was not alone in its assessment of the apparent unprofitability of many corporate computerization efforts. Beginning in the mid-1960s, the noted Harvard Business School professor John Dearden published a series of articles in the *Harvard Business Review* dismissing as "myths" and "mirages" the alleged benefits of computerized corporate information systems.[15] Prominent industry analyst John Diebold complained, also in the pages of the *Harvard Business Review*, about the "naive standards" that many businesses used to evaluate the costs and benefits of computer technology. "Nowhere is this lack of [business] sophistication more apparent than in the way in which computers are applied in American industry today."[16] Management consultant David Hertz argued that computers were "oversold and underemployed."[17] A survey in 1968 by the Research Institute for America had determined that only half of all corporate computer users were convinced that their investment in computing had paid off. The inability of computerization projects to justify their own existence signaled "the fizzle in the 'computer revolution,'" suggested the accounting firm Touche Ross and Company.[18]

Perhaps the most devastating critique of corporate computing came from the venerable consulting firm McKinsey and Company. In 1968 McKinsey released a report titled "Unlocking the Computer's Profit Potential," in which it claimed that "computer efforts, in all but a few exceptional companies, are in real, if often unacknowledged, trouble." Despite years of investment in "sophisticated hardware," "larger and increasingly costly computer staffs," and "complex and ingenious applications," most of these companies were nowhere near realizing their anticipated returns on the investment in electronic computing. Instead, they were increasingly characterized by rising costs, lost opportunities, and diminishing returns. Although the computer had transformed the administrative and accounting operations of many U.S. businesses, "the computer has had little impact on most companies' key operating and management problems."[19]

The McKinsey report was widely cited within the business and technical literature. The editors of *Datamation* endorsed it almost immediately, declaring that it "lays waste to the cherished dream that computers create profits."[20] *Computers and Automation* reprinted it in its entirety several months later. References to the report appear in a diverse range of journals for at least two decades after its initial publication.[21]

The dissatisfaction with corporate computerization efforts expressed in the McKinsey report and elsewhere must be interpreted within the context of a larger critique of software that was percolating in this period. As mentioned earlier, the "gap in programming support" that emerged in 1950s had worsened to "software turmoil" in the early 1960s, and by the end of the decade was being referred to as a full-blown "software crisis."[22] And in 1968, the first NATO Conference on Software Engineering firmly established the language of the software crisis in the vernacular of the computer community. Large software development projects had acquired a reputation for being behind schedule, over budget, and bug ridden. Software had become "a scare item for management . . . an unprofitable morass, costly and unending."[23]

It is important to note that the use of the word software in this period was somewhat inconsistent. As Thomas Haigh has suggested, the meaning of the word software was changing rapidly during the 1960s, and could refer alternatively to something specific—the systems software and utilities that today we would describe as an operating system—or more generally to the applications, personnel, and processes associated with computing. He argues that the software crisis as it was understood by the NATO conference organizers referred only to the former definition.[24]

Substantial evidence shows that as early as 1962 the term "software" was being used much more broadly to refer to a broad range of computer-based applications.[25] But even if one were to insist on a narrow systems-oriented definition of the word "software," however, then the predicament described by the McKinsey report might simply be recharacterized as an "applications crisis."[26] From a more modern understanding of software as the heterogeneous collection of tools, applications, personnel, and procedures that together comprise the system of computing in action, the distinction is immaterial.

Whether we call them a software crisis or an applications crisis, the concerns of corporate managers were clearly about the "softer" elements of computer-based systems. The crucial distinction to be made between the applications crisis discussed in the business literature and the more technical literature on the software crisis lies not in its identification of symptoms but rather in its diagnosis of the underlying disease. Both communities were concerned with the apparent inability of existing software development methods to produce cost-effective and reliable commercial applications. But where the technical experts identified the root causes of the crisis in terms of production—in other words, as a function of the difficulties inherent in *building software right*—many corporate managers believed that the real challenge was in determining the *right software to build*. Faced with exponentially rising software costs, and threatened by the unprecedented degree of autonomy that top-level executives seemed to grant to computer people, many corporate managers began to reevaluate their largely hands-off policies toward programmer management. Whereas in the previous decade computer programming had been widely considered to be a uniquely creative activity—and therefore almost impossible to manage using conventional methods—by the end of the 1960s new perspectives on these problems began to appear in the industry literature. The real reason that most data processing installations were unprofitable, according to the McKinsey report, was that "many otherwise effective top managements . . . have abdicated control to staff specialists." These specialists might be "good technicians," but they had "neither the operation experience to know the jobs that need doing nor the authority to get them done right."[27] Or as another contemporary report summarized the situation, "many managers sat back and let the computer boys monkey around with systems that were doomed to failure or mediocrity."[28]

The dramatic shift in tone of the management literature during this time is striking. Prior to the late 1960s the conventional wisdom was that computer programming was a uniquely creative activity—genuine "'brain business,' often an agonizingly difficult intellectual effort"—and therefore almost impossible to manage using conventional methods.[29] But by the end of the decade, the same journals that had previously considered programming unmanageable were filled with exhortations toward better software development management: "Controlling Computer Programming"; *New Power for Management;* "Managing the Programming Effort"; and *The Management of Computer Programming Efforts.*[30] The same qualities that had previously been seen as essential indicators of programming ability, such as creativity and a mild degree of personal eccentricity, now began to be perceived as merely unprofessional. As part of their rhetorical construction of the applications crisis as a crisis of programmer management, corporate managers accused programmers of lacking professional standards and loyalties: "too frequently these people [programmers], while exhibiting excellent technical skills, are non-professional in every other aspect of their work."[31] A widely quoted psychological study that identified as a "striking characteristic of programmers . . . their disinterest in people," reinforced the managers' contention that programmers were insufficiently concerned with the larger interests of the company.[32] Computer specialists were increasingly cast as self-interested peddlers of whizbang technologies. "In all too many cases the data processing technician does not really understand the problems of management and is merely looking for the application of his specialty," wrote William Walker in a letter to the editor in the management-oriented journal *Business Automation.*[33] Calling programmers the "Cosa Nostra" of the industry, the colorful former-programmer-turned-technology-management-consultant Herbert Grosch declared that computer specialists "are at once the most unmanageable and the most poorly managed specialism in our society. Actors and artists pale by comparison. Only pure mathematicians are as cantankerous, and it's a calamity that so many of them get recruited by simplistic personnel men." He warned managers to "refuse to embark on grandiose or unworthy schemes, and refuse to let their recalcitrant charges waste skill, time and money on the fashionable idiocies of our [computer] racket."[34]

The most obvious explanation for the sudden reversal in management attitudes toward computer people is that just as corporate investment in computing assets escalated rapidly in this period, so did its economic interest in managing these assets effectively. And since the costs of computer software, broadly defined to include people, planning, and processes, were growing rapidly in relation to hardware—for every dollar spent on computer hardware, claimed the McKinsey report, two dollars were spent on staff and operations—it should be no surprise that personnel issues were the focus of particular attention. Computer programmers alone required at least 35 percent of the total operational budget. The size of the average computer department had doubled in the years between 1962 and 1968, and was expected to double again by 1975. A report in 1966 by the American Federation of Information Processing Societies (AFIPS) estimated that in 1960, there were already 60,000 systems analysts and as many as 120,000 computer programmers working in the industry. AFIPS expected this number to more than double by the end of the decade.[35]

There is no question that the rising costs of software development caused tension between computer personnel and their corporate managers. The continuous gap between the demand and supply of qualified computer personnel had in recent years pushed up their salary levels far faster (and in many cases higher) than those of other professionals and managers. In 1965 the ADP (Automatic Data Processing, Inc.) newsletter predicted average salary increases in data processing in the range of 40 to 50 percent over the next five years.[36] Programming professionals had a "personal monopoly" that "manifests itself in the market place," which provided them with considerable opportunities for horizontal mobility, either in pursuit of higher salaries or more challenging positions.[37] Simply maintaining existing programming staff levels proved a real trial for personnel managers.[38] One large employer experienced a sustained turnover rate of 10 percent *per month*.[39] For entry-level programmers whose marketability increased rapidly the turnover rate was a high as 100 percent, one personnel manager estimated, which further exacerbated the problem of training and recruitment.[40] Who was willing to train programmers only to see them leverage that investment into a higher salary elsewhere? The problem of "body snatching" of computer personnel by search firms and other personnel consultants became so bad that AFIPS banned recruiters from the annual Joint Computer Conferences.[41] This simply shifted the action to nearby bars and hotel rooms, where headhunters would slip blanket job offers under every door.

But although the rising cost of software and software personnel was certainly a factor in the perceived applications crisis of the late 1960s, this was more than simply a recapitulation of the personnel problems of the previous decade. Then it had been largely accepted that the work that the computer specialists did was valuable enough to deserve special consideration. It might be a problem for the industry that good computer programmers and systems analysts were hard to find and develop, but this was because software development was inherently difficult. The solutions proposed to this problem generally involved elevating the computer personnel: developing better tools for screening potential programmer trainees, establishing programs for computer science education and fundamental research, and encouraging programmers to professionalize. Even the development of new automatic programming systems such as FORTRAN and COBOL, although originally intended to eliminate the need for skilled programmers altogether, had the unintended effect of elevating their status. For those interested in advancing the academic status of computer science, the design of programming languages provided an ideal forum for exploring the theoretical aspects of their discipline. More practical-minded programmers saw programming languages as a means of eliminating the more onerous and error-prone aspects of software development. By eliminating much of the tedium associated with low-level machine coding, they allowed programmers to focus less on technical minutia and more on high-status activities such as design and analysis. In any case, the organizational conflicts that define the applications crisis of the late 1960s were rarely mentioned in the first decade or so of commercial computing. As late as 1963 a survey of programmers found that the majority (59 percent) reported that the general attitude toward them and their work was positive.[42]

What is novel and significant about the applications crisis of the late 1960s is that it marked a fundamental change in attitude toward computer personnel. This change was reflected in both the increasingly dismissive language used by corporate managers to refer to their computer personnel—not only did the formerly affectionate "computer boys" acquire a new, patronizing edge but even less flattering titles appeared, such as "the new theocracy," "prima donnas," and "industrial carpetbaggers"—and also the solutions that were proposed to the now seemingly perpetual crisis in software development.[43] It was in this period that the rhetoric of crisis became firmly established in the industry literature. But more important, it was during this time that the emerging crisis became defined as fundamentally managerial in nature. Many of the technological, managerial, and economic woes of the software industry became wrapped up in the problem of programmer management. Indeed, as will be described in a subsequent chapter, many of the most significant innovations in software engineering to be developed in the immediate NATO conference era were as much managerial innovations as they were technological or professional ones.

By reconstructing the emerging software crisis as a problem of management technique rather than technological innovation, advocates of these new management-oriented approaches also relocated the focus of its solution, removing it from the domain of the computer specialist and placing it firmly in the hands of traditional managers. Programmers and systems analysts, it was argued, "may be superbly equipped, technically speaking, to respond to management's expectations," but they are "seldom strategically placed (or managerially trained)—to fully assess the economics of operations or to judge operational feasibility."[44] By representing programmers as shortsighted, self-serving technicians, managers reinforced the notion that they were ill equipped to handle the big picture, mission-critical responsibilities. After all, according to the McKinsey report, "only managers can manage the computer in the best interests of the business."[45] And not just any managers would do: only those managers who had traditional business training and experience were acceptable, since "managers promoted from the programming and analysis ranks are singularly ill-adapted for management."[46] It would be this struggle for organizational authority and managerial control that would come to dominate later discussions about the nature and causes of the software crisis.

Seat-of-the-Pants Management

Computer specialists had always posed something of a conundrum for managers. The expectation that they would quietly occupy the same position in the organizational hierarchy as the earlier generation of data processing personnel was quickly proven unrealistic. Unlike a tabulating machine, the electronic computer was a large, expensive technology that required a high level of technical competence to operate effectively. The decision to purchase a computer had to be made at the highest levels of the organization. But although the high-tech character of electronic computing appealed to upper management, few executives had any idea how to integrate this novel technology effectively into their existing social, political, and technological networks. Many of them granted their computer specialists an unprecedented degree of independence and authority.

Even the lowest ranking of these specialists possessed an unusual degree of autonomy. To be sure, the occupations of machine technician and keypunch operators remained relatively unskilled and, to a certain degree, feminized. Yet the largest and fastest-growing segment of this population, the computer programmers, were increasingly being recognized as being valuable—perhaps even irreplaceable—corporate employees. This was certainly true of the first generation of programmers, whose idiosyncratic techniques for coaxing maximum performance out of primitive equipment were absolutely indispensable. The fact that the technology of computing was changing so rapidly in this period further complicated the ability of even data processing managers—who generally lacked practical programming experience—to understand and supervise the activities of programmers. The "best practice" guidelines that applied to one particular generation of equipment were quickly superseded by a different set of techniques and methodologies.[47] Even as the technology of computing stabilized over the course of the early 1950s, though, programmers maintained their position of central importance. Perhaps even more crucial, programming acquired a reputation for being a uniquely creative endeavor, one relatively immune from traditional managerial controls. The discovery (allegedly) of great disparities between programmers reinforced the conventional wisdom that good programmers were born, not made. One widely cited IBM study determined that code produced by a truly excellent programmer was twenty-six times more efficient than that produced by their merely average colleagues.[48] Despite the serious methodological flaws that compromised this particular study (including a sample population of only twelve individuals), the twenty-six to one performance ratio quickly became part of the standard lore of the industry. The implication was that talented programmers were effectively irreplaceable. "The vast range of programmer performance indicated earlier may mean that it is difficult to obtain better size-performance software using machine code written by an army of programmers of lesser than average caliber," argued Dr. Edward E. David of Bell Telephone Laboratories.[49] All of this suggested that "the major managerial task" was finding—and keeping—"the right people": "with the right people, all problems vanish."[50]

The idea that computer programmers possessed an innate and inarticulable skill was soon embodied in the hiring practices of the industry, which selected programmers on the basis of aptitude tests and personality profiles that emphasized mathematical ability and logical thinking over business knowledge or managerial savvy. In fact, many of these early selection mechanisms seemed to pick traits that were entirely opposed to traditional corporate virtues. "Look for those who like intellectual challenge rather than interpersonal relations or managerial decision-making. ... Do not consider the impulsive, the glad hander, or the 'operator.'"[51] The one personality characteristic of programmers that appeared to be universally recognized was their "disinterest in people." According to an influential study by the SDC personnel psychologists Dallis Perry and William Cannon, compared with other corporate employees, "programmers dislike activities involving close personal interaction. They prefer to work with things rather than people."[52] Whether this lack of sociability was an inherent trait of talented programmers, a reflection of self-selection within the profession, or an undeserved stereotype is largely irrelevant: the point is that the perception that programmers were "difficult" was widespread in the industry. As the management consultant Richard Brandon described it, the average programmer was "often egocentric, slightly neurotic, and he borders upon a limited schizophrenia." As a group, programmers could be singled out in any corporation by their higher incidence of "beards, sandals, and other symptoms of rugged individualism or nonconformity."[53] Programmers were hardly a group that seemed destined to get along well with traditional managers.

There is some truth to the perception that the "longest-haired computer theorists" were seen as corporate outsiders.[54] Leaving aside the fact that apparently enough working programmers took their artistic persona seriously enough to flaunt corporate conventions of dress and appearance, the need to keep expensive computers running as continuously as possible meant that many programmers worked nonstandard hours. During the day the machine operators had privileged access to the machines, so programmers frequently worked at night and were therefore not always available during traditional business hours. The need to work nights appeared to have a particular problem for female programmers, who were frequently barred by company policy from being on the premises during the off-hours.[55] Combined with their sometimes slovenly appearance, this practice of keeping odd hours suggested to more conventional employees that programmers considered themselves superior. The direct supervisors of computer personnel might have understood the underlying reasons for these apparent eccentricities, but the majority of managers did not. The fact that data processing was seen as a service department within the larger organization also did nothing to help ingratiate programmers to their colleagues. Whereas most other employees saw themselves as part of a collective endeavor to make things or provide services, service staffs were seen as a necessary though nonproductive

Figure 6.1
Datamation cartoon, 1963.

second-class citizens. They were essentially just an overhead cost, like heat or electricity.

But despite this latent, low-level corporate resentment of computer specialists, there were few overt expressions of outright hostility. The general consensus through the mid-1960s seemed to be that computer programming was somehow an "exceptional" activity, unconstrained by the standard organizational hierarchy and controls. "Generating software is 'brain business,' often an agonizingly difficult intellectual effort," argued one article in *Fortune* magazine in 1967. "It is not yet a science, but an art that lacks standards, definitions, agreement on theories and approaches."[56] The anecdotal evidence seemed to indicate that "the past management techniques so successful in other disciplines do not work in programming development. . . . Nothing works except a flying-by-the-seat-of-the-pants approach."[57] The general consensus was that computer programming was "the kind of work that is called creative [and] creative work just cannot be managed."[58]

The word creative and its various analogs have frequently been used to describe the work of computer specialists—and computer programmers in particular—most often in the context of discussions about their alleged unmanageability. But what did it mean to do creative work in the corporate context? Surely computer programming is not the only white-collar occupation that requires skill, ingenuity, and imagination? And why did the supposed creativity of programmers suddenly, in a relatively short period in the late 1960s, become a major professional liability rather than the asset it had been just a few years earlier?

The earliest and most obvious references to programmer creativity appear in discussions of the black art of programming in the 1950s. For the most part these references are disparaging, referring to the arcane and idiosyncratic techniques as well as mysterious—and quite possibly chimerical—genius of individual programmers. John Backus, for example, had no use for such expressions of programmer creativity.[59] Yet for many others the idea of the programmer as artist was compelling and captured useful truths. When Frederick Brooks described the programmer as a poet, building "castles in the air, from air, creating by exertion of the imagination," he meant the metaphor to be taken seriously.[60] The noted computer scientist Donald Knuth also frequently portrayed programming as a legitimate literary genre, and went so far as to suggest that it "is best regarded as the process of creating literature, which are meant to be read."[61] Although references to programming as an creative activity in this artistic sense pervade the technical and popular literature on computing, and play an important role in defining the programming community's self-identity from the 1950s to the present, this is not the sense in which programming was considered creative by most corporate managers.[62]

The meaning of creativity most often mobilized in the corporate context was intended to differentiate the mechanical tasks associated with programming—the coding of machine instructions, for example—from the more intellectual activities associated with design and analysis. As was described in chapter 2, early attempts to define programming in terms of coding did not long survive their infancy. Translating even the simplest and most well-defined algorithm into the limited set of instructions understood by a computer turned out to require a great deal of human ingenuity. This is one expression of programmer creativity. But more important, the process of constructing the algorithm in the first place turned out to be even more challenging. Even the most basic human cognitive processes are surprisingly difficult to reduce to a series of discrete and unambiguous activities. The skills required to do so were not just technical but also social and organizational. In order to computerize a payroll system, for instance, an applications developer had to interview everyone currently involved in the payroll process, comprehend and document their contributions to the process in explicit detail—not failing to account for exceptional cases and infrequent variations to normal procedures—and then translate these complex activities first into a form that other programmers could understand and eventually into the precise commands required by the computer. Since the payroll department did not operate in isolation, it had to work with other departments to coordinate activities, standardize the required inputs and outputs to the procedures, and negotiate points of conflict and contention. It also had to produce documentation, train users, arrange testing and verification procedures, and manage the logistics of implementation and rollout. All of this had to happen without a major interruption of service, since missing a payroll cycle would make everyone in the company extremely unhappy. These were all of the activities associated with the broad term software development. It is not hard to see why such development required creativity, or also why such expressions of creativity could be perceived as threatening. As Carl Reynolds of the Computer Usage Corporation described the situation, "There's a tremendous gap between what the programmers do and what the managers want, and they can't express these things to each other."[63]

In many companies, the various activities associated with software development were split among several categories of computer personnel. The primary division was between programmers and systems analysts. The systems analysts were charged with the more organizational and design-related activities, and programmers with the more technical elements. But although many companies maintained seemingly rigid hierarchies of occupational categories—junior programmer, senior programmer, systems analyst, and senior systems analyst—in practice these neat divisions of labor quickly broke down.[64] In any case, to the rest of the corporation, both groups were generally referred to as programmers. Computer programming, broadly defined to include the entire range of activities associated with designing, producing, and maintaining heterogeneous software systems, remained an activity with ambiguous boundaries, a combination of technical, intellectual, and organizational expertise that increasingly brought programmers into conflict with other white-collar employees.

The first glimpse of this potential can be seen in a Price Waterhouse report from 1959 called *Business Experience with Electronic Computers*. The report was the first book-length, comprehensive, publicly available study of corporate computing efforts, and appears to have been made widely available. In it, a group of Price Waterhouse consultants concludes that the secret to success in computing was the availability of high-quality programming, and confirmed the conventional wisdom that "high quality individuals" were the "key to top grade programming." Why? Because "to 'teach' the equipment, as is amply evident from experience to date, requires considerable skill, ingenuity, perseverance, organizing ability, etc. The human element is crucial in programming." In emphasizing the "considerable skill, ingenuity, perseverance, [and] organizing ability" required of programmers, the study deliberately conflated the roles of programmer and analyst. In fact, its authors suggested, "the term 'programmer' . . . is unfortunate since it seems to indicate that the work is largely machine oriented when this is not at all the case. . . . [T]raining in systems analysis and design is as important to a programmer as training in machine coding techniques; it may well become increasingly important as systems get more complex and coding becomes more automatic." Perhaps even more significantly, the study blurred the boundary between business experience and technical expertise. If anything, it privileged the technical, since "a knowledge of business operations can usually be obtained by an adequate expenditure of time and effort," whereas "innate ability . . . seems to have a great deal to do with a man's capacity to perform effectively in . . . systems design."[65]

Management, Information, and Systems

As software projects expanded in scope to encompass not only traditional data processing applications (payroll, for example) but also management and control, computer personnel began to encroach on the domains of operational managers. The changing role of the computer in corporate management and the rising power of EDP professionals did not go unnoticed by other midlevel managers. As early as 1959, observers were noting a sense of "disenchantment" on the part of many managers. Overambitious computerization efforts had "placed stresses on established organizational relationships," and demanded skills "not provided by the previous experience of people assigned to the task."[66] The increasing inclusion of computer personnel as active participants in all phases of software development, from design to implementation, brought them into increasing contact—and conflict—with other corporate employees.

The situation was complicated by the publication in 1958 of an article in the *Harvard Business Review* titled "Management in the 1980s," in which Howard Leavitt and Thomas Whisler predicted a coming revolution in U.S. business management. Driven by the emergence of what they called "information technology," this revolution would radically reshape the landscape of the modern corporation, completely reversing the recent trend toward participative management, recentralizing power in the hands of a few top executives, and utterly decimating the ranks of middle management. And although "major resistance" could be expected during the process of transforming "relatively autonomous and unprogrammed middle-management jobs" into "highly routinized programs," the benefits offered to top-level executives meant that an information technology revolution would be inevitable.[67]

The central premise of Leavitt and Whisler's vision was that information technology—which they described as a heterogeneous system comprised of the electronic computer, operations research techniques, and sophisticated decision-support software—would largely eliminate the need for autonomous middle managers. Jobs that had previously required the discernment and experience of skilled managers would be replaced by scientifically "programmed" systems and procedures. "Just as planning was taken from the hourly worker and given to the industrial engineer," so too would it be taken from the operational managers. Information technology allowed "the top to control the middle just as Taylorism allowed the middle to control the bottom." The top would increasingly include what Leavitt and Whisler called a "programmer elite." And although the *programmer* being referred to here was obviously a logistical or mathematical planner rather than a computer programmer, it was also clear that this new elite would be intimately familiar with computer technology and software design.[68]

Although "Management in the 1980s" is most generally cited for its role in introducing the term information technology, it is best understood in the context of a more general shift in management practices in the decades after the Second World War. The war had produced a series of "managerial sciences"—including operations research, game theory, and systems analysis—all of which promised a more mathematical and technologically oriented approach to business management. As Philip Mirowski and others have suggested, these nascent "cyborg" sciences were deeply connected to the emerging technology of electronic computing.[69] Not only did many of these new techniques require a significant amount of computing power in and of themselves but they relied on the electronic computer as a central metaphor for understanding the nature of the modern bureaucratic organization.[70] Many of the most visionary proposals for the use of the electronic computer in management frequently rode into the corporation on the back of this new breed of expert consultants.

Foremost among these new computer radicals was Herbert Simon, who in 1949 helped found the Carnegie-Mellon University's Graduate School of Industrial Administration (and who in 1978 was awarded a Nobel Prize for his work on the economics of rational decision making). In his book *The New Science of Management* in 1960, Simon outlined his version of a machine-aided system of organizational management. An early pioneer in the field of artificial intelligence, Simon had no doubts about the ability of the electronic computer to transform organizations; as a result of advances in decision-support software, Simon argued, technologically sophisticated firms were "acquiring the technical capacity to replace humans with computers in a rapidly widening range of 'thinking' and 'deciding' tasks." Within twenty-five years, he predicted, firms will "have the technical capability of substituting machines for any and all human functions in organizations." Interestingly enough, Simon did not believe that this radical new use of the computer would lead to the creation of a computing elite but rather that improvements in artificial intelligence would lead to the elimination of the computer specialist altogether.[71]

The idea that "thinking machines" would soon replace expert computer programmers was not widely shared outside the artificial intelligence community, however. More common was the notion that the need for such decision makers could be made redundant by the development of an integrated management system that would feed information directly to high-level executives, bypassing middle managers completely. John Diebold described one version of such a system in an article in the *Harvard Business Review* in 1964. When Diebold had introduced the concept of "automation" more than a decade earlier, he had confined the use of automatic control systems to traditional manufacturing and production processes. But his article proposed a "bolder, more innovative" approach to automatic data processing (ADP) that blurred the boundaries between factory floor and office space. Calling ADP the "still-sleeping giant" of modern corporate management, Diebold described, in vividly organic terms, a single information system that would "feed" an entire business. This system would be "the arteries through which will flow the life stream of the business: market intelligence, control information, strategy decisions, feedback for change." Gradually, the system would grow to encompass and absorb the entire organization. And after that, suggested Diebold, "management would never be the same."[72]

The monolithic information system portrayed by Diebold became the management enthusiasm of the 1960s, variously referred to in the literature as the "total systems concept," "management system," "totally integrated management information system," and most frequently, MIS. As Thomas Haigh has convincingly demonstrated, during the decade of the 1960s "a very broad definition of MIS spread rapidly and was endorsed by industrial corporations, consultants, academic researchers, management writers, and computer manufacturers."[73] Although important differences existed between the specific versions of MIS presented by these various champions, in general they shared several key characteristics: the assumption that information was a critical corporate and managerial asset; a general enthusiasm for the electronic computer and its ability to centralize managerial information; and the clear implication that such centralization would come at the expense of middle managers.

A New Theocracy—or Industrial Carpetbaggers?

Although the dream of the total management system never really came to fruition, the shift of power from operational managers to computer specialists did seem to occur in at least some organizations. In a follow-up to "Management in the 1980s" in 1967 titled "The Impact of Information Technology on Organizational Control," Thomas Whisler reiterated his view that information technology "tends to shift and scramble the power structure of organizations. . . . The decision to locate computer responsibility in a specific part of an organization has strong implications for the relative authority and control that segment will subsequently achieve." It seemed unlikely, he argued, that anyone "can continue to hold title to the computer without assuming and using the effective power it confers." He cited one insurance executive as saying that "there has actually been a lateral shift to the EDP manager of decision-making from other department managers whose departments have been computerized." Whisler also quoted another manager at length who was concerned about the relative decline of managerial competence in relation to computer expertise: "The supervisor . . . has been replaced as the person with superior technical knowledge to whom the subordinates can turn for help. This aspect of supervision has been transferred, at least temporarily, to the EDP manager and programmers or systems designers involved with the programming. . . . [U]nderneath, the forward planning function of almost all department managers has transferred to the EDP manager."[74]

Whisler was hardly alone in his assessment of the role of computing personnel in organizational power shifts.

In 1962 the *Harvard Business Review* warned against "computer people ... attempting to assume the role of high priests to the [electronic brain]," who would "ignore all the people with operating experience and concern themselves with looking for a place to apply some new trick technique."[75] A 1964 article in *U.S. News and World Report* asked if the computer was "running wild" within the corporation, and quoted one expert as saying that the "computer craze" would end as a "nightmare" for executives.[76] In 1965, Robert McFarland warned of an "electronic power grab" in which computer specialists were "stealing" decision-making authority from top executives: "Control of data processing activities can mean control of the firm—without the knowledge of top management."[77] A textbook for managers from 1969 complained that "all too often management adopts an attitude of blind faith (or at least hope) toward decisions of programmers."[78] In her book *How Computers Affect Management* from 1971, Rosemary Stewart described how computer specialists mobilized the mystery of their technology to "impinge directly on a manager's job and be a threat to his security or status."[79] The adoption of computer technology threatened to bring about a revolution in organizational structure that carried with it tangible implications for the authority of managers: "What has not been predicted, to any large degree, is the extent to which political power would be obtained by this EDP group. Top management has helped . . . by not doing their job and controlling computer systems."[80] The frequent association of computer boys with external consultants only compounded the resentment of regular employees.

There is no doubt that by the end of the decade, traditional corporate managers were extremely aware of the potential threat to their occupational territory posed by the rise of computer professionals. Thomas Alexander, in his *Fortune* article in 1969, noted a growing cultural clash between programmers and managers: "Managers . . . are typically older and tend to regard computer people either as mere technicians or as threats to their position and status—in either case they resist their presence in the halls of power."[81] In that same year, Michael Rose, in his *Computers, Managers, and Society*, suggested that local departmental managers

obviously tend to resist the change. For a start, it threatens to transform the concern as they know and like it. . . . At the same time the local's unfamiliarity with and suspicion of theoretical notions leave him ill-equipped to appreciate the rationale and benefits of computerization. It all sounds like dangerously far-fetched nonsense divorced from the working world as he understands it. He is hardly likely to hit it off with the computer experts who arrive to procure the organizational transformation. Genuine skepticism of the relevance of the machine, reinforced by emotional factors, will drive him towards non-cooperation.[82]

It is not difficult to understand why many managers came to fear and dislike computer programmers and other software specialists. In addition to the usual suspicion with which established professionals generally regarded unsolicited changes in the status quo, managers had particular reasons to resent EDP departments. The unprecedented degree of autonomy that corporate executives granted to computer people seemed a deliberate affront to the local authority of departmental managers. The "inability or unwillingness of top management to clearly define the objectives of the computer department and how it will be utilized to the benefit of the rest of the organization" lead many operational managers to "expect the worst and, therefore, begin to react defensively to the possibility of change"[83] In the eyes of many nontechnical managers, the personnel most closely identified with the digital computer "have been the most arrogant in their willful disregard of the nature of the manager's job. These technicians have clothed themselves in the garb of the arcane wherever they could do so, thus alienating those whom they would serve."[84]

The Revolt of the Managers

In response to this perceived challenge to their authority, managers developed a number of interrelated responses intended to restore them to their proper role in the organizational hierarchy.

The first was to define programming as an activity, and by definition programmers as professionals, in such a way as to assign it and them a subordinate role as mere technicians or service staff workers. As the sociologists Haroun Jamous and Bernard Peloille argued in their groundbreaking study of the organizational politics of professional development, this technique of reducing the contributions of competing groups to the merely technical is a time-honored strategy for defending occupational and professional boundaries.[85] We have already seen some of the ways in which the rhetoric of management literature reinforced the notion that computer specialists were self-interested, narrow technicians rather than future-minded, bottom-line-oriented good corporate citizens. "People close to the machine can also lose perspective," maintained one computer programming "textbook" for managers. "Some of the most enthusiastic have an unfortunate knack of behaving as if the computer were a toy. The term 'addictive' comes to mind."[86] Managers emphasized the youthfulness and inexperience of most programmers. The results of early aptitude tests and personality profiles—those that emphasized their "dislike for people" and "preference for . . . risky activities"—were widely cited as examples of the "immaturity" of the computer professions. In fact, one of the earliest and most widely cited psychological profiles of programmers suggested that there was a negative correlation between programming ability and interpersonal skills.[87]

The perception that computer programmers were particularly antisocial, that they "preferred to work with things rather than people," reinforced the notion that programming was an inherently solitary activity, ill suited to traditional forms of corporate organization and management. The same qualities that had previously been thought essential indicators of programming ability, such as creativity and a mild degree of personal eccentricity, now began to be perceived as being merely unprofessional. As part of their rhetorical construction of the applications crisis as a problem of programmer management, corporate managers accused programmers of lacking professional standards and loyalties: "Too frequently these people [programmers], while exhibiting excellent technical skills, are non-professional in every other aspect of their work."[88]

Another common strategy for deprecating computer professionals was to challenge their technical monopoly directly. If working with computers was in fact not all that difficult, then dedicated programming staffs were superfluous. One of the alleged advantages of the COBOL programming language usually touted in the literature was its ability to be read and understood—and perhaps even written—by informed managers.[89] The combination of new programming technology and stricter administrative controls promised to eliminate management's dangerous dependency on individual programmers: "The problems of finding personnel at a reasonable price, and the problem of control, are both solved by good standards. If you have a set of well-defined standards you do not need clever programmers, nor must you find yourself depending on them."[90] At the very least, managers could learn enough about computers to avoid being duped by the "garb of the arcane" in which many programmers frequently clothed themselves.[91] At West Point, cadets were taught enough about computers to prevent them from "being at the mercy of computers and computer specialists. . . . [W]e want them to be confident that they can properly control and supervise these potent new tools and evaluate the significance of results produced by them."[92]

In much of the management literature of this period, computer specialists were cast as self-interested peddlers of whizbang technologies. "In all too many cases the data processing technician does not really understand the problems of management and is merely looking for the application of his specialty."[93] In the words of one Fortune 500 data processing executive, "They [EDP personnel] don't exercise enough initiative in identifying problems and designing solutions for them. . . . They are impatient with my lack of knowledge of their tools, techniques, and methodology—their mystique; and sometimes their impatience settles into arrogance. . . . In sum, these technologists just don't seem to understand what I need to make decisions."[94] The book *New Power for Management* emphasized the myopic perspective of programmers: "For instance, a technician's dream may be a sophisticated computerized accounting system; but in practice such a system may well make no major contribution to profit."[95] Others attributed to them even more Machiavellian motives: "More often than not the systems designer approaches the user with a predisposition to utilize the latest equipment or software technology—for his resume—rather than the real benefit for the user."[96]

Experienced managers stressed the critical differences between "real-world problems" and "EDP's version of real-world problem."[97] The assumptions about programmers embedded in many of these accounts—that they were narrowly technical, inexperienced, and "poorly qualified to set the course of corporate computer effort"—resonated with many corporate managers.[98] The accounts provided a convenient explanation for the burgeoning software crisis. Managers had in effect "abdicated their responsibility and let the 'computer boys' take over."[99] The fault was not entirely the manager's own, though. Calling electronic data processing "the biggest rip-off that has been perpetrated on business, industry, and government over the past 20 years," one author suggested that business executives have been actively prevented "from really bearing down on this situation by the self-proclaimed cloak of sophistication and mystique which falsely claims immunity from normal management methods. They are still being held at bay by the computer people's major weapon—the snow job."[100] Computer department staffs, although "they may be superbly equipped, technically speaking, to respond to management's expectations," are "seldom strategically placed (or managerially trained)—to fully assess the economics of operations or to judge operational feasibility."[101] Only the restorations of the proper balance between computer personnel and managers could save the software projects from a descent into "unprogrammed and devastating chaos."[102]

The Road to Garmisch

In the late 1960s, new perspectives on the problem of programmer management began to appear in the industry literature. "There is a vast amount of evidence to indicate that writing—a large part of programming is writing after all, albeit in a special language for a very restricted audience—can be planned, scheduled and controlled, nearly all of which has been flagrantly ignored by both programmers and their managers," argued Robert Gordon in 1968 in a review of contemporary software development practices.[103] Although it was admittedly true "that programming a computer is more an art than a science, that in some of its aspects it is a creative process," this new perspective on software management suggested that "as a matter of fact, a modicum of intelligent effort can provide a very satisfactory degree of control."[104]

It was the NATO Conference on Software Engineering in 1968 that irrevocably established software management as one of the central rhetorical cornerstones of all future debates about the nature and causes of the software crisis. In the fall of that year, as mentioned earlier, a diverse group of influential computer scientists, corporate managers, and military officials gathered in Garmisch, Germany, to discuss their growing concern that the production of software had become "a scare item for management . . . an unprofitable morass, costly and unending." The solution to the budding software crisis, the conference organizers claimed, was for computer programmers to embrace an industrialized software engineering approach to development. By defining the software crisis in terms of the discipline of software engineering, the NATO conference set an agenda that influenced many of the technological, managerial, and professional developments in commercial computing for the next several decades.

7

The Professionalization of Programming

In the development of professional standards, the computer field must be unrelenting in advocating stringent requirements for professional status, whether these include education, experience, examination, character tests, or what not.
—Charles M. Sidlo, "The Making of a Profession," 1961

Too frequently these people [programmers], while exhibiting excellent technical skills, are non-professional in every other aspect of their work.
—Malcolm Gotterer, "The Impact of Professionalization Efforts on the Computer Manager," 1971

The Certified Public Programmer

In 1962, the editors of the electronic data processing journal *Datamation* proposed what they believed would be the solution to the "many problems" that were "embarrassingly prominent" in the nascent commercial computing industry. The majority of these problems, they argued, were caused by the lack of "professional competency" among programming personnel. The recent explosive growth in commercial computing had brought with it a "mounting tide of inexperienced programmers, newborn consultants, and the untutored outer circle of controllers and accountants all assuming greater technical responsibility." Few of these so-called computer experts were well qualified or experienced, and the result was the crisis of confidence that was plaguing the industry. The solution to this crisis, contended the *Datamation* editors, was the establishment of a new breed of technical professional: the certified public programmer.[1]

By defining clear standards of professional competency, an industry-wide certification program would serve several important purposes for the programming profession. First, it would establish a shared body of abstract occupational knowledge—a "hard core of mutual understanding"—common across the entire professional community. Second, it would help elevate the public reputation of computer personnel from its current stature of "cautious bewilderment and misinterpretation," to "at least, confused respect." Finally, and perhaps most significantly, it would enable computer professionals to erect entry barriers to their increasingly contested occupational territory: the flood of amateur programmers—"the industry's widely publicized upcoming incompetents"as the *Datamation* editorial dismissively referred to them—"would find their accession to financial stardom impeded by the need for specific qualification such as the passing of a reasonable test of competency."[2] In fact, in 1963 the DPMA's executive director Calvin Elliott named stamping out "bogus" data-processing schools as one of his organization's primary objectives.[3]

The *Datamation* call for the professionalization of programming coincided neatly with the announcement by the National Machine Accountants Association (NMAA) of its new CDP examination. The NMAA, which would later that year rename itself the Data Processing Management Association (DPMA), represented almost sixteen thousand data processing workers in the United States and Canada.[4] The NMAA had been working since 1960 to develop the CDP exam, which represented the first attempt by a professional association to establish rigorous standards of professional accomplishment in the data processing field. According to the NMAA's 1962 press release, the exam was intended to "emphasize a broad educational background as well as knowledge of the field of data processing," and represent "a standard of knowledge for organizing, analyzing and solving problems for which data processing equipment is especially suitable." It was open to anyone, NMAA member or not, who had completed a prescribed course of academic study, had at least three years of direct work experience in punched card and/or computer installations, and had "high character qualifications." The first year that the exam was offered, 1,048 applications took it—687 successfully.[5]

Despite being widely criticized for being superficial and irrelevant to real-world software development, the CDP clearly met a perceived need within the computing community. In 1965, 6,951 individuals took the CDP examination, and another 4,000 completed CDP refresher courses conducted by local DPMA chapters.[6] A number of large employers, including State Farm Insurance, the Prudential Insurance Company of America, and the U.S. Army Corps of Engineers, extended official recognition to the CDP program, and the city of Milwaukee used the CDP as a means to assign pay grades to data processing personnel.[7] By the end of 1975, 31,351 candidates had taken the CDP and 15,115 had been awarded the certificate.[8] Although it is difficult to find accurate employment information for software workers in this period, estimates from the Bureau of Labor indicate these 15,115 CDP recipients constituted approximately 10 percent of the overall computing community.

The CDP examinations represented just one step in the DPMA's ambitious "Six Measures of Professionalism Program," which included not only the development of standards of competence and codes of ethics but also programs for public service, continuing education, and fundamental research. Of these six measures, only the CDP program achieved even moderate industry acceptance. Nevertheless, simply by articulating a clear professional agenda the DPMA claimed for itself a leadership role in the computing community. Given the general lack of agreement about what skills and educational background were appropriate for computing personnel, the CDP program promised to guarantee at least a basic level of competence. Employers viewed certification as a tool for screening potential employees, evaluating performance, and assuring uniform product and quality.[9] Programmers saw it as an indication of professional status, a means of assuring job security and achieving promotions, and an aid to finding and obtaining new positions.[10] The certification of practitioners was generally considered to be one of the characteristic functions of any legitimate profession, and the professionalization of programming was seen by many at this time as the solution to a growing sense of crisis within the computing community.[11] The "question of professionalism," as it came to be known in the literature, would come to form the basis for explicit discussions of the software crisis in the late 1960s.

The growing discontent with a perceived lack of professionalism among computing personnel was in part a legacy of the massive expansion of the commercial computer industry over the course of the previous decade. As the *Datamation* editorial suggests, one response to the personnel crisis of the 1950s had been an influx of new programmer trainees and vocational school graduates into the software labor market. "The ranks of the computer world are being swelled by growing hordes of programmers, systems analysts and related personnel," warned a report in 1968 by the SIGCPR, and as a result "educational, performance and professional standards are virtually nonexistent."[12] And although computer specialists in general were appreciative of the short-term benefits of the ongoing personnel shortage in the computer industry—among them, above-average salaries and plentiful opportunities for occupational mobility—many believed that a continued crisis threatened the long-term stability and reputation of their industry and profession. "There is a tendency," observed a report by the SIGCPR, "for programming to be a 'dead-end' profession for many individuals, who, no matter how good they are as programmers, will never make the transition into a supervisory slot. And, in too many instances this is the only road to advancement."[13] Many programmers worried about becoming obsolete and felt pressure to constantly upgrade their technical skills.[14] Although starting salaries were high and individual programmers were able to move with relative ease horizontally throughout the industry, there were precious few opportunities for vertical advancement.[15] Whereas technical specialists in traditional engineering disciplines were often able (and in fact expected) to climb the corporate ladder into management positions, the computer boys were usually denied this opportunity.[16]

Many of the job advertisements for programmers reflected these concerns about a lack of professional status and longevity. Employers promised new hires a potential career path that involved more than just mere technical labor: "Is your programming career in a closed loop? Create a loop exit for yourself at [the Bendix Corporation]."[17] "Working your way toward obsolescence? At MITRE professional growth is limited only by your ability."[18] "At Xerox, we look at programmers . . . and see managers."[19] But as contemporary studies of such "dual ladder" programs for technical workers in the computer fields revealed, programmers rarely had many opportunities for professional development.[20] It was just not clear to many corporate employers how the skills—and personality types—possessed by programmers would map onto the skills required for management.

Given their growing uncertainty about the future of their occupation, it is not difficult to understand why programmers in the early 1960s were so concerned with establishing themselves as recognized professionals. Belonging to a profession provided an individual with a "monopoly of competence," or the control over a valuable skill that was readily transferable from organization to organization.[21] In more practical terms, professionalism offered a means of excluding undesirables and competitors from the labor market, thereby assuring at least basic standards of quality and reliability as well providing a certain degree of protection from the fluctuations of the labor market. Programmers in particular saw professionalism as means of distinguishing themselves from coders or other "mere technicians." Professionalism offered increased social

Figure 7.1
Bendix Corporation advertisement, 1962.

status, greater autonomy, improved opportunities for advancement, and better pay.[22]

The professionalization efforts of programmers were generally encouraged by their corporate employers. An increasing number of corporate managers were beginning to blame their growing dissatisfaction with the rising costs of software development on the lack of professionalism on the part of programmers. Professionalism, or at least a certain form of corporate-friendly professionalism, was represented by managers as a means of reducing corporate dependence on the whims of individual programmers.[23] It was also thought that professionalism might solve a number of other pressing management problems: it might motivate staff members to improve their capabilities; it could bring about more commonality of approaches; it could be used for hiring, promotions, and raises; and it could help solve the perennial question, Who is qualified?[24] "The concept of professionalism," argued one personnel research journal from the early 1970s, "affords a business-like answer to the existing and future computer skills market" by making computer personnel responsible for policing their own disciplinary identity.[25] Professionalism appeared to provide a familiar solution to the increasingly complex problems of managing the relationship between business and technological expertise.

In response to these various motivations to professionalize, programmers in the late 1950s and early 1960s worked to establish the institutional structures traditionally associated with the professions. These included the development of an academic infrastructure for supporting theoretical computer science research; support for industry-based certification and licensing programs; the establishment of professional societies and journals; the introduction of performance standards; and professional codes of ethics. Many of these institutional structures developed rapidly and were established on a provisional basis by the end of the 1950s.

But the existence of professional institutions did not necessarily translate readily into widely recognized professional status.[26] The early adoption of the structures of professionalism, however, obscured the deep intellectual and ideological schisms that existed within the programming community. Although many practitioners agreed on the need for a programming profession, they disagreed sharply about what such a profession should look like. What was the purpose of the profession? Who should be allowed to participate? Who would control entry into the profession, and how? What body of abstract knowledge would be used to support its claims to legitimacy? By the beginning of the 1960s, clearly discernible factions had emerged within the fledgling programming profession. Science- and engineering-oriented programmers worked to develop a theoretical basis for their discipline. They joined associations like the ACM that published academic-style journals, imposed strict educational requirements for membership, and resisted certification and licensing programs. Business data processing personnel, on the other hand, pursued a more practice-centered professional agenda. If they joined any professional associations at all, it was the DPMA. They read journals like *Datamation*, which emphasized plain speech and practical relevance over theoretical rigor. The tension that existed between these two groups of aspiring professionals—the academic computer scientists and the business data processors—greatly influenced the character and fortunes of the various professional institutions that each faction supported. Academic computer scientists struggled to establish a legitimate and autonomous intellectual discipline based on a sound body of theoretical research. Systems analysts and business programmers worked to improve their standing within the organizational hierarchy by distancing themselves from computer operators and other so-called technicians. Neither group was entirely successful.

This chapter will focus on the attempts of programmers to establish the institutional structures associated with professionalism, including professional societies, certification programs, educational standards, and codes of ethics. It argues that the professionalization of computer programming represented a potential solution to the looming software crisis that appealed to programmers and employers alike. But it also suggests that the controversy that surrounded the various professional institutions that were established in this period reveals the deep divisions that existed within the programming community about the nature of programming skill and the future of the programming professions. Many of the themes developed in previous chapters—the development of new programming technologies or more "efficient" management methodologies—are closely tied to questions of professional status. If skilled programmers could be replaced by automated development tools, for example, or by more "scientific" management methodologies, then they could hardly have much claim to professional legitimacy. The question of what programming was—as an intellectual and occupational activity—and where it fit into traditional social, academic and professional hierarchies, was actively negotiated during the decades of the 1950s and 1960s. Programmers were well aware of their tenuous professional position, and they struggled to prove that they possessed a unique set of skills and training that allowed them to lay claim to professional autonomy.

The Association for Computing Machinery

On January 10, 1947, at the Symposium on Large-Scale Digital Calculating Machinery at the Harvard Computation Laboratory, Professor Samuel Caldwell of MIT proposed to a crowd of more than three hundred the formation of a new association of those interested in computing machinery. His proposal obviously landed on fertile soil: within six months a "Notice on the Organization of an Eastern Association for Computing Machinery" was circulating within the computing community, and in September the first meeting of the Eastern Association for Computing Machinery was held at Columbia University. Seventy-eight individuals attended. Officers were elected, and the Executive Council was appointed. A second meeting, held in December at the Aberdeen Proving Grounds in Aberdeen, Maryland, attracted three hundred participants. The next year the organization dropped the word Eastern from its title, and was thereafter known simply as the Association for Computing Machinery (ACM).

During the 1950s the ACM grew steadily but not spectacularly. By 1951 there were 1,113 members, including 43 in other countries; in 1956 the total had risen to 2,305, and by 1959 it had reached 5,254. In the 1960s, the membership grew somewhat more slowly, and there were a few periods during which the total number of members actually decreased. Overall, though, the ACM continued to expand at a rate of about 16 percent annually. By the end of 1969 there were 22,761 regular members. Figure 7.2 shows the annual membership statistics for the years 1947 to 1972.

From its inception, the ACM styled itself as an academically oriented organization. Many of the original members either were or had been associated with a major university computation project, and most were university educated, including a number at the graduate level. The focus of the organization's early activities was a series of national conferences, the first of which was cosponsored by the Institute for Numerical Analysis at the University of California at Los Angeles. These meetings represented an outgrowth of an earlier series of university-sponsored conferences, and they retained an academic flavor. Many were low-budget affairs held at universities or research institutions, and they frequently

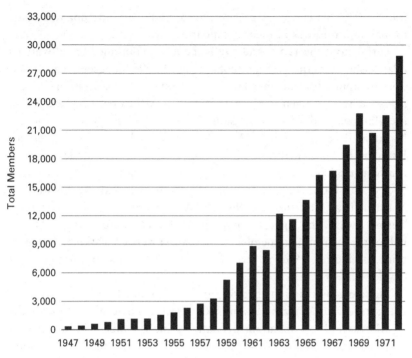

Figure 7.2
ACM members, 1947–1971.

made use of dormitory facilities. The papers presented were usually technical, and the proceedings were published. The ACM conferences never acquired the trade show atmosphere that characterized other national meetings. The National Computer Conference, which became almost entirely commercial, for instance, resembled a trade show much more than an academic conference. In fact, deliberate efforts were made to distance the ACM from the influence of the commercial vendors, particularly IBM. For many years the ACM resisted publishing its own journal, possibly because "some early ACM leaders saw the society as a declaration of independence from IBM, and, by extension, from all commercial considerations like the sale of publications and the solicitation of advertising."[27] Until 1953, when it began publishing the *Journal of the ACM*, the ACM exclusively supported the National Research Council's highly technical journal *Mathematical Tables and Other Aids to Computation*. Even then, the primary contents of the *Journal of the ACM* were theoretical papers, and the emphasis was on the dissemination of "information about computing machinery in the best scientific tradition."[28] Articles were peer-reviewed, and every attempt was made to maintain rigorous academic standards.

Throughout the 1950s and 1960s the ACM continued to cultivate its relationship with the academic community. In 1954 it accepted an invitation to apply for membership in the American Association for the Advancement of Science. Since 1958 the ACM has been represented in the Mathematical Sciences Division of the National Academy of Sciences National Research Council. In 1962 it affiliated with the Conference Board of the Mathematical Sciences, which also consisted of the American Mathematical Society, the Mathematical Association of America, the Society for Industrial and Applied Mathematics, and the Institute of Mathematical Statistics. In 1966 the ACM established the prestigious Turing Award, the highest honor awarded in computer science. Almost half of the institutional members of the ACM were educational organizations, and after 1962 a thriving student membership program was developed.[29]

The close association that the ACM maintained with the academic computer scientist proved a mixed blessing, however. Although the ACM was able to maintain a relatively high profile within scientific and mathematical circles, it was often castigated by the business community. Many business programmers looked on the ACM as "a sort of holier than thou academic intellectual sort of enterprise—not inclined to be messing around with the garbage that comptrollers worry about," and the ACM leadership was characterized as "a bunch of guys with their heads in the clouds worrying about Tchebysheff polynomials and things like that."[30] "These four-year computer science wonders are infinitely better equipped to design a new compiler than they are to manage a software development project. We don't need new compilers. We need on-time, on-budget, software development."[31] A *Datamation* article from 1963 titled "The Cost of Professionalism" warned that the members of the ACM had to "decide whether it's worth that much to belong to an organization which many feel has been dominated by—and catered pretty much to—Ph.D. mathematicians. . . . [T]he Association tends to look down its nose at business data processing types while claiming to represent the whole, wide wonderful world of computing."[32] A Diebold Group publication from 1966 characterized the ACM as a group "whose interests are primarily academic and which is helpful to those with scholastic backgrounds, theoreticians of methodology, scientific programmers and software people." Although the ACM president immediately denied this depiction, calling it "too narrow," the popular perception that the ACM catered solely to academics was difficult to counter.[33]

The ACM leadership was not entirely unaware of or unsympathetic to the needs of the business programmers. In his unsuccessful bid in 1959 for the ACM presidency, Paul Armer urged the ACM membership to "THINK BIG," to "visualize ACM as the professional society unifying *all* computer users."[34] That same year, Herbert Grosch, an outspoken proponent of a strong, American Medical Association–style professional society (and later ACM president), roundly criticized the ACM for its academic parochialism: "Information processing is as broad as our culture and as deep as interplanetary space. To allow narrow interests, pioneering though they might have been, to preempt the name, to relegate ninety percent of the field to 'an exercise left to the reader,' would be disastrous to the underlying unity of the new information sciences."[35] Several attempts were made during the next decade to make the ACM more relevant to the business community. In response to widespread criticism of the theoretical orientation of the *Journal of the ACM*, a new publication, *Communications of the ACM*, was introduced in 1958. The main contents of *Communications* were short articles, mostly unrefereed, on technical subjects such as applications, techniques, and standards.[36] In 1966 the Executive Council announced a $45,000 professional development program aimed at business data processing personnel. The program included short "skill upgrade" seminars offered at the national computer conferences, a traveling course series, and self-study materials.[37] There was even talk, in the mid-1960s, of a potential merger with the DPMA. In 1969, ACM president Bernard Galler announced a move toward "less formality, less science, and less academia."[38]

Despite these short-lived efforts to reconcile with the business community, however, the conservative ACM leadership continued to pursue a largely academic agenda. As early as 1959 it was suggested that the ACM should impose stringent academic standards on its members, and in 1965 a four-year degree became a prerequisite for receiving full membership. Frequent battles arose over repeated attempts to change the name of the association to something more broadly relevant. In 1965 a proposal to change it to the Association for Computing and Information Science was rejected; a decade later the same issue was still being debated.[39] When Louis Fein suggested in 1967 that the ACM faced a "crisis of identity," ACM president Anthony Oettinger insisted vehemently that the ACM had no such crisis. In doing so, he reaffirmed the association's commitment to a theoretical approach to computing: "Our science must, indeed, 'maintain as its sole abstract purpose of advancing truth and knowledge.'"[40]

This commitment to abstract science was further reinforced the following year when the ACM's C³S announced its Curriculum '68 guidelines for university computer science programs. Curriculum '68 advocated a rigorously theoretically approach to computer science that included little of interest to business practitioners.[41] Even when the ACM did recognize the growing importance of business data processing to the future of its discipline, the emphasis was always placed on research and education:

All of us, I am sure, have read non-ACM articles on business data processing and found them lacking. They suffer, I believe, from one basic fault: They fail to report fundamental research in the data processing field. The question of 'fundamentalness' is all-important. . . . In summary, this letter is intended to urge new emphasis on FUNDAMENTALISM in business data processing. This objective seems not only feasible but essential to me. It provides not only a technique for getting ACM into the business data processing business, but a technique (the same one) for getting the field of business data processing on a firm theoretical footing.[42]

There is little question that throughout the 1960s, the ACM pursued a professionalization strategy that was heavily dependent on the authority and legitimacy of its academic accomplishments.

It was not until the 1970s that the ACM began to seriously reconsider its policy toward business-oriented practitioners. In 1974 the ACM Executive Council commissioned a series of studies on business programming as part of its long-range planning report. In doing so, the ACM was responding both to long-standing criticism and a recent spate of anti-ACM editorials that had appeared in the industry newsletter *Computerworld*. "ACM had become not so much an industry professional group," declared one of these editorials, "as it was a home for members of educational institutions around the country to overwhelm us with their erudition on topics of vaguely moderate interest."[43] The author noted that while most business data processing installations had standardized on the COBOL and FORTRAN programming languages, the ACM still supported ALGOL. He quoted ACM president Anthony Ralston to the effect that although only 25 percent of the ACM membership were academics, ten out of twenty-five council members were academics.[44]

The long-range report noted that of the 320,000 software personnel then working in the United States, 85 percent dealt with business data processing. It admitted that while the ACM had a reputation for professionalism, "BDP [business data processing] people tend to be turned off by ACM's academically oriented leadership. . . . BDP professionals feel that academics don't understand what BDP needs, and they're right."[45] It concluded that any new ACM members were likely to come from business data processing, and recommended the development of a new publication aimed at that audience. The report signaled to many in the ACM that the organization needed to broaden its membership and become more accommodating. The next few years witnessed a bitterly contested presidential election (the cornerstone of which was a debate over business data processing), yet another attempt to change the name of the ACM to something more broadly relevant, and efforts to reconcile with its business-oriented competitor, the DPMA.

The Data Processing Management Association

The DPMA originated in 1949 as the NMAA. The NMAA was founded as an association of accountants and tabulating machine managers. It held its first convention in 1952, and grew rapidly over the next decade. By 1957 it represented more than ten thousand data processing workers in the United States and Canada, and by 1962 more than sixteen thousand.

In 1962 the NMAA changed its name to the DPMA. This was in part an attempt to expand its membership beyond finance and accounting professionals, and in part a reflection of the changing status of its discipline within the corporate hierarchy. As Thomas Haigh has suggested, punch card divisions at many large corporations had, by the beginning of the 1950s, acquired new status as the providers of strategic business information and other forms of valuable corporate data. The replacement of tabulating machine technology with electronic computers created a new role for data processors within the corporation; in fact, it was as part of a shift toward electronic data processing that most corporations invested in their first electronic computing equipment. From its inception, therefore, the DPMA represented the largest professional association of computing personnel.

The establishment of the CDP program later that year was part of a larger strategy of professional development. It was announced in conjunction with the DPMA's "Six Measures of Professionalism" program, which included as the "marks of professionalism" self-education, standard measures of knowledge, continuing research, a code of ethics, and mechanisms for self-policing and disciplining practitioners.[46] The DPMA's many national conferences, local chapter programs and seminars, and DPMA publications and home-study courses were all directed toward the self-education of individual members. The CDP program was obviously its provision for establishing a means of "measuring a minimum level of knowledge in the field." DPMA graduate research grants encouraged contributions to the "knowledge of the field." The DPMA code of ethics was part of its original charter, and was the first of such codes to be established for the computer-related professions. Finally, although the DPMA had no existing mechanisms for determining and punishing misconduct, it promised that the association would take a leading role in the development of an industry policing program. Although the DPMA's original focus was on data processing supervisors, more than those of any other aspiring professional organization its programs were aimed at the broad computing community. Programmers and systems analysts were clearly part of its imagined community of practitioners.

Unlike the ACM, the DPMA made every effort to reach a broad spectrum of data processing personnel. Although originally open only to data processing supervisors, by 1964 the national leadership was making determined attempts to cultivate programmers within its membership.[47] The structure of the organization, which included strong regional chapters, allowed for diversity, local control, and rapid expansion. Each region had its own representative on the Executive Council who served with several executive officers and implemented policy decisions from the International Board of Directors. In addition, the DPMA's official publication, the *Data Management Journal*, encouraged submissions on a much wider range of subjects than did the ACM's *Journal* or *Communications*. The DPMA also maintained a close association with the editors of *Datamation*, another widely read industry journal that focused on issues of timely concern and practical relevance.

The DPMA's inclusive approach to professional development brought it into conflict with competing societies, particularly the ACM. The differences between the two organizations mirrored the larger tensions that existed within the computing community: academic computer scientists versus the business data processors; theory versus practice. I have already shown how this tension affected the adoption of the DPMA's CDP program: the ACM's obvious lack of support helped to undermine the program's legitimacy and prevented its widespread adoption. This opposition was based on both philosophical grounds—many in the ACM believed that the CDP examinations were superficial and irrelevant—and institutional ones, since control over an industry-wide certification program would have granted the DPMA considerable political authority.[48] The two group also sparred over trivial issues, such as unauthorized use of member-address databases.[49] Despite several halfhearted attempts to explore an ACM/DPMA merger, or at least to establish an interassociation liaison, the two groups rarely communicated.[50] When AFIPS was established in the early 1960s, the NMAA and other industry-oriented groups were treated with dismissive contempt, and the DPMA resisted AFIPS affiliation until the mid-1970s. At a meeting arranged by AFIPS officials, for example, DPMA representatives were kept waiting, without explanation or apology, for over an hour.[51]

In the year that it was introduced, the CDP examination attracted 1,048 applicants, 687 of whom passed successfully. The exam itself included 150 multiple-choice questions on programming, numerical analysis, Boolean algebra, applications, elementary cost accounting, English, and basic mathematics (not including calculus). In response to criticism from the many otherwise-qualified programmers who did not have formal mathematical training or college-level degrees, the educational requirements for the CDP were suspended until 1965. The other prerequisites—three years' experience and "high character qualifications"—were so vague as to be almost meaningless, and appear to have been only selectively enforced.

By the end of 1965, almost seven thousand programmers and data processing supervisors had taken the exam. Figure 7.3 shows for the years between 1962 and 1973 the total number of candidates taking the exam, the total number of candidates who passed the exam, and the cumulative number of CDP holders.

The data in figure 7.3 reveal the mixed fortunes and troubled history of the CDP examination. The striking early success of the program, which more than quintupled in size in its first three years, suggests that many data processing personnel saw certification as an attractive professional strategy. This corresponds well with evidence from industry journals and other documentary sources. A survey of the candidates in 1963 reveals a remarkable range of background, experience, and education.[52] For the examination session in 1966, however, the education requirements outlined in the original program announcement from 1962 were finally put in place. These requirements included specific courses in math, English, managerial accounting, statistics, and data processing systems.

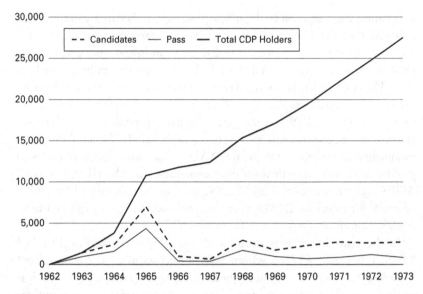

Figure 7.3
CDP recipients, 1961–1973.

Whereas participation in the exam in 1965 had jumped by more than 300 percent from the previous year (possibly in anticipation of the impo- sition of these requirements), applications for the session in 1966 dropped by almost 85 percent. Of the eighty-eight scheduled examination sites, twelve were dropped for lack of attendance. A major controversy erupted within the data processing community, particularly in DPMA-oriented publications such as *Datamation* and *Computerworld*.

Advocates of the academic requirements argued that such require- ments not only elevated the status and legitimacy of the CDP but also were standard for most other professions, including law, medicine, engi- neering, and accounting. Opponents claimed that the specific course requirements were ambiguous, meaningless, and irrelevant. The DPMA Committee for Certification, which administered the CDP program, was flooded with letters from disgruntled applicants requesting special dis- pensation. Each case had to be individually evaluated.[53] In 1966 only 1,005 candidates were approved to sit for the exam. In 1967, this number dropped to 646. This posed not only financial difficulties for the DPMA but presented a grave threat to the perceived legitimacy of the entire CDP program as well. Faced with the imminent collapse of their membership support, the DPMA admitted that "the established eligibility requirements had unintentionally excluded some of the people for whom the CDP program was originally designed."[54] The committee dropped the specific course requirements, providing a grandfather clause for those with three years' experience prior to 1965, and requiring others to have only two years of postsecondary education. Applications for the exam session in 1968 jumped back to almost three thousand.

Over the next several years, the CDP program struggled to regain its initial momentum. Annual enrollments dropped again briefly in 1969, then leveled off for the next several years at about twenty-seven hundred. In an industry characterized by rapid expansion, this noticeable lack of growth represented a clear failure of the CDP program. With each year CDP holders came to represent a smaller and smaller percentage of the programming community. In 1970 the program faced yet another crisis: the announcement that a bachelor's degree would be required of all CDP candidates, beginning with the examination in 1972. Once again a firestorm of debate broke out. The DPMA claimed that this new requirement merely reflected the changing realities of the labor market: since a college degree had already become a de facto requirement within the industry, requiring anything less for the CDP would severely undermine its legitimacy. The resulting controversy highlighted already-existing tensions within the data processing community, and further divided the already-fragmented DPMA Certification Council (many of whose own members could not satisfy the new degree requirement). Numerous observers called for the DPMA to relinquish control of the CDP examination to an independent certification authority. By the mid-1970s it became increasingly clear that the CDP program faced imminent dissolution.

In an attempt to restore momentum to their flagging certification initiative, the DPMA joined forces with seven other computing societies—the ACM, the IEEE (Institute of Electrical and Electronics Engineers) Computer Science Society, the Association for Computer Programmers and Analysts, the Association for Education Data Systems, the Automation One Association, the Canadian Information Processing Society, and the Society of Certified Data Processors (SCDP)—to form the Institute for Certification of Computer Professionals (ICCP). The DPMA had always been extremely possessive of its certification program, and its decision to relinquish control to an independent foundation reflects a growing sense of desperation about the future of the CDP.[55] The ICCP was charged with upgrading and expanding the CDP program, introducing new specialized examinations, and promoting professional development. In 1973 the ICCP took over responsibility for the CDP examinations. It also worked to develop a code of professional ethics to be adopted by its member organizations.

The ICCP failed to revive the CDP or institute a meaningful certification program of its own. Because it represented such a wide variety of constituents, the ICCP was hindered by the same internal divisions that plagued the larger programming community. Rivalries among the constituent member societies, many of whom were only superficially committed to the concept of certification, doomed the organization to internal conflict and inactivity.[56] The failure of the various competing professional associations to cooperate crippled the ability of the ICCP to develop meaningful certification standards. No single program was able to reflect the diverse needs of the collective software community. Furthermore, a series of highly critical assessments of the validity of the CDP examinations weakened popular and industry support.[57] The ICCP failed to present appealing alternative programs or examinations, and the organization languished during the 1970s.

In response to the inability of the professional associations to establish rigorous certification programs, the SCDP adopted an approach to professional standards that circumvented the ICCP altogether: state licensing of computer professionals. The SCDP was a grassroots organization of CDP holders dedicated to improving the status and legitimacy of the CDP program. Founded by the self-professed gadfly Kenniston W. Lord, the SCDP frequently challenged the wisdom and authority of associations such as the DPMA and the ICCP. For many years, Lord and his fellow SCDP member Alan Taylor carried out a vituperative verbal campaign against the DPMA (and later the ICCP) in the pages of the weekly newspaper *Computerworld*.[58] Taylor, a popular columnist for *Computerworld*, accused the DPMA of running the CDP examinations as a profit-making enterprise rather than an independent professional development program.[59] When the SCDP was denied formal representation in the ICCP in 1973, Lord proposed what was effectively a government takeover of responsibility for programmer certification. Unlike the certification programs voluntarily adopted by individuals and associations, however, government licensing would be mandatory. Since it is illegal to practice a licensed profession without the prior approval of the state, entry into that profession could be tightly controlled and monitored. Licensing would provide both control and protection as well as a certain degree of public recognition and legitimacy.

In 1974, the SCDP developed a model licensing bill and submitted it to a number of state legislatures. According to its model legislation, no person in a state that passes the SCDP bill could "practice, continue to practice, offer or attempt to practice data processing or any branch thereof" without either achieving a four-year degree in data processing and gaining three years of related experience, or successfully completing a certification examination and five years of experience. The bill also provided a five-year window in which those with twelve years of experience could be "grandfathered" into the profession. Practitioners were granted a twenty-four-month grace period in which to acquire the necessary qualifications. The legislation covered a wide variety of occupational activities and titles, including any that made use of the terms "data processing," "data processing professional," "computer professional," or any of their derivatives. The state was given the power to revoke the certification of any registrant who committed fraud, was proved guilty of negligence, or who violated the professional code of ethics.[60]

The proposed SCDP legislation is notable as the only concerted attempt in this period to encourage government involvement in the programming labor market. In fact, the specter of externally imposed state regulation had been raised as a primary justification for establishing certification programs in the first place: since self-regulation was considered to be one of the defining characteristics of a profession, surrendering control over this function to the state was essentially an admission of defeat. Observers warned that the lack of a solution from within the science would result in a solution imposed from without: "In several fields, the lack of professional and industrial standards has prompted the government to establish standards."[61] Ironically enough, even the defeat of the SCDP legislation proved humiliating to some practitioners; the state's unwillingness to legislate data processing activities was perceived as a slight to the entire industry's importance and reputation.[62]

Although the model SCDP legislation was adopted by none of the states to which it was submitted, the fact that it was proposed at all reveals one of the primary shortcomings of voluntary certification programs such as the CDP: the lack of effective methods of enforcement. The inability, or unwillingness, of associations like the ACM and the DPMA to self-regulate was widely criticized by industry observers. Neither group had ever taken action against one of their members accused of fraud or negligence, and both had reputations for being unwilling to take strong positions on issues of public interest or safety. Indeed, the DPMA was unable even to enforce the proper use of the CDP trademark. Individuals and organizations that abused the CDP designation, either by claiming to have received a CDP when in reality they had not or instituting their own CDP programs, received only ineffective warning letters. No legal action appears to have been taken.[63] According to SCDP president Kenniston Lord, the inability of the profession to regulate its own activities justified drastic action in regard to state licensing: "One does not truly have a profession until one has the ability, legally, to challenge a practitioner and when proven guilty, to see that he is separated from the practice. . . . This is one problem that the SCDP bill will solve."[64]

The lack of ability and willingness of the DPMA to equip its certification program with teeth was not the only reason why the CDP failed to achieve widespread industry acceptance, however. The program had other shortcomings as well. From almost the beginning, the examinations had been tainted by accusations of fraud and incompetent administration. In 1966 several individuals reported receiving offers from an existing CDP holder to take their examinations for them for a fee.[65] A copy of the 1965 exam was stolen from a locked storage cabinet at California State College, and its disappearance was covered up by the DPMA Committee for Certification.[66] Complaints about testing conditions and locations were frequent and vociferous. For example, at one examination site at the University of Minnesota, the noise caused by a nearby drama club rehearsal of a sword fight scene "was so severe as to shower the room with particles of plaster."[67] Other examinees suggested that poorly trained proctors ("the little old lady who passed out the papers") were not only unable to answer even basic questions about content and procedure but also in some cases switched rooms without notice, started sessions early for personal convenience, and misplaced completed examination booklets.[68] Although such administrative snafus were hardly unique to the CDP program, they undermined public confidence in the ability of the DPMA to adequately represent the profession.

Another reason why the DPMA was unable to push through its certification initiative was a lack of support from other professional associations. An article in 1968 on certification and accreditation in the *Communications of the ACM* failed to mention the CDP program. This conspicuous neglect of the most successful certification program then available reflects a growing tension between the two competing professional associations. The ACM recognized that a successful certification program required a strong controlling organization. The organization that controlled certification would effectively control the profession.

Indeed, the proposal that launched the CDP program in 1959 suggested that "the first association to undertake a Data Processor's Certificate is going to be the leading association in the data processing field."[69] Opposed to the idea that this controlling organization could be anything but the ACM, the Executive Council of the ACM worked to undermine the efforts of the DPMA at every occasion. In 1966 the council considered a resolution, clearly aimed at the CDP, to "warn employers against relying on examinations designed for subprofessionals or professionals as providing an index of professional competence."[70] An early draft of this document referred specifically throughout to the "DPMA certification program." Although the final published version referred only to unspecific "certification programs," the target of its attacks was obviously the CDP. Later that year the Executive Council established a Committee to Investigate the Implications of the CDP. The first order of business for the committee was the drafting of a strongly worded objection to the use of the word professional in association with the DPMA exam, and the wording of subsequent exam and program literature eliminated all references to such language: CDP therefore came to stand for "Certified Data Processor," rather than "Certified Data Professional."[71] Even this modest acronym was offensive to some professional groups. A member of a SHARE (an influential IBM users group) panel on certification was "disturbed to read [the] statement that many DPMA certificate holders are beginning to use the initials 'CDP' in their titles." Such pretentious behavior, he suggested, "will quickly bring down upon DPMA the wrath of other professions. It is probably illegal in some states. I fail to see how it can conceivably benefit the cause of professionalism which DPMA and others of us are working toward."[72] Although the DPMA insisted that "many persons who use the CDP initials do so more to publicize the certification program" than to promote their own personal interests, pressure from competing associations forced it to abandon many of its more ambitious claims for the CDP program.[73] A statement in 1966 conceded that "it would be presumptuous at this early stage in the program to suggest that CDP represents the assurance of competence, or that the Certificate should be considered as a requirement for employment or promotion in the field."[74] It is no wonder that so many employers and practitioners lost confidence in the ability of the DPMA to successfully administer an industry-wide certification program.

An even more troublesome problem for the DPMA was resistance from its primary constituency to its proposed educational requirements. The original CDP announcement included a list of specific academic prerequisites, including college-level courses in math, English, managerial accounting, statistics, and data processing systems as well as eight out of seventeen possible electives.[75] Many of the practicing EDP specialists who formed the core of the DPMA membership saw such requirements as being irrelevant, unattainable, or both. When the educational requirements were first enforced in 1966, applications dropped by more than 85 percent, never to recover.

The problem was not only that the new educational requirements were overly stringent for many aspiring EDP professionals; they were also entirely too specific. What exactly counted as a math, English, or managerial accounting course? Course titles and descriptions varied greatly by institution. Each application had to be evaluated individually to determine which courses legitimately counted toward the requirement. The Committee for Certification was immediately overwhelmed with paperwork: complaints, transcripts, notes from faculty, requests for exemptions, and so on. This was in addition to the massive efforts required to assure that each candidate had the requisite three years' work experience and high character qualifications. It is unclear exactly what was meant by this requirement. It does appear that certain candidates were eliminated on the basis of having misrepresented their qualifications, or having committed fraud or other crimes, but no written standards for the high character qualification seem to have existed. The situation quickly turned into an administrative nightmare for DPMA officials. The specific course prerequisites were soon replaced with a more straightforward, although no less controversial, two-year college requirement. When this prerequisite was modified to a four-year degree in 1972, opposition became even more vociferous. The head of the West Tennessee chapter of the DPMA wrote to complain that he, along with about one-third of his chapter's membership, had suddenly become ineligible to receive the CDP.[76] A *Computerworld* survey in 1970 indicated that many practitioners felt the new requirement "unduly harsh" and "ludicrous," believing that it would decimate the data processing staffs of many smaller departments.[77] The always-outspoken Herbert Grosch (himself a PhD astronomer and president of the ACM from 1976 to 1978) declared that "this policy is very ill-advised. What the hell is so hot about college—it turns out a bunch of knuckleheads—and a knucklehead PhD is no better that a knucklehead CDP."[78]

Despite the strong negative reaction generated by these educational requirements, the DPMA leadership continued to insist on their necessity. Such requirements had always been considered an essential component of the DPMA's professionalization program: only by defining a "standard of knowledge for organizing, analyzing, and solving problems for which data processing equipment is especially suitable" could programmers ever hope to distinguish themselves from mere technicians or other "sub-professionals."[79] Like the academic computer scientists, business programmers recognized the need for a foundational body of abstract knowledge on which to construct their profession; they differed only about what that relevant foundation of knowledge should include. In insisting on strong educational standards, the DPMA was in complete accord with the conventional wisdom of the contemporary professionalization literature.[80] And by the end of the 1960s, it was true that many employers did prefer to hire college graduates—although not necessarily computer science or data processing graduates—for entry-level programming positions.[81] According to a study published in September 1968 by the Office of Education, U.S. Department of Health, Education, and Welfare, 61 percent of the 353 business data processing managers surveyed preferred that programmers have a college degree. Over 60 percent indicated that educational background was a substantial factor in determining a programmer's chances for promotion.[82] As a recession hit the industry in the early part of the 1970s, this trend became even more pronounced.[83] An aspiring EDP school graduate, even with a CDP certificate, had little chance of breaking into data processing without a college degree. As one of these individuals lamented, "They told me 80% of all programmers don't have a college degree. Now everywhere I go I'm told they're sorry but they only want college people."[84] Although the DPMA's decision to raise the educational requirements for the CDP was highly controversial, it was also probably justified.

Ultimately, however, the DPMA never managed to convince employers and practitioners of the relevance of its educational standards, nor for that matter its certification exams. Neither group was convinced that a CDP meant much in terms of future performance. The DPMA Certification Council was not even able to pass a resolution requiring its own officials to possess the CDP.[85] In 1971, the Certification Council decided to drop the baccalaureate degree requirement. Although this decision was a response to pressure from within the data processing community, it was widely regarded as a sign of weakness rather than judicious concession.[86] As the director of the computing center at Virginia Tech wrote to the president of the local DPMA chapter, "The removal of the degree requirement has forced all of us to consider the attainment of the CDP not as an extension of our normal academic and work experience, but, as a matter of fact, something quite inferior to either one."[87] His letter provides a stinging but accurate indictment of the failure of the CDP program to achieve widespread acceptance and legitimacy:

My experience indicates that people seek certification from their professional peer group for only two reasons. Either it is required by law or the individual feels that the mark of acceptance stamped upon him by his peer group is sufficiently important to be worthy of the extra effort to achieve that certification. Unfortunately, in the data processing profession, many, certainly most, of the people we recognize as outstanding professional achievers and accomplishers, do not hold the CDP.[88]

One of the major criticisms leveled against the CDP examination by employers and data processing managers was that it tested "familiarity" rather than competence.[89] It was not clear to what skills and abilities the CDP was actually intended to certify: "The present DPMA examination measures breadth of data processing experience but does not measure depth. . . . It certainly does not measure or qualify programming ability. It makes no pretense of being any measure of management skills."[90] The problem was a familiar one for the industry: although most employers in this period believed that only "competent" programmers could develop quality software, no one agreed on what knowledge and abilities constituted that "competence."[91] As Fred Gruenberger suggested at a RAND symposium in 1975 on certification issues, "I have the fear that someone who has passed the certifying exams has either been certified in the wrong things (wrong to me, to be sure) or he has been tuned to pass the diagnostics, and in either case I distrust the whole affair."[92] His attitude reflects the ambivalence that many observers in this period felt about contemporary data processing training and educational practices. If data processing was simply a "miscellaneous collection of techniques applied to business, technology and science," rather than a unique discipline requiring special knowledge and experience, then no certification exam could possibly test for the broad range of skills associated with "general business knowledge." "Given the choice between two people from the same school, one of whom has the CDP, but the other appears brighter," Gruenberger argued, "I'll take the brighter guy."[93]

Although the DPMA revised and updated its examinations annually, and eventually introduced a Registered Business Programmers exam intended specifically for programmers, it was never able to convince the industry of the relevance of its certification programs. One data processing manager suggested that the CDP was at best "a minor plus for the person who can measure up to other standards," but that it would never be considered a "real" qualification for employment.[94] Another warned of a "lack of confidence" in the validity of the CDP exam: "I do not expect to apply for a CDP or to use the possession of a CDP as a criterion for employment."[95] Still another resented a perceived attempt on the part of the DPMA to foster a "closed shop" mentality, promising to "continue to regard the CDP holder with suspicion as to motive and qualification, the level of suspicion being in inverse proportion to the date of the certificate."[96] In the absence of a strong commitment to the CDP on the part of employers, many programmers saw little benefit in participating in the program. Those who did were increasingly self-selected from the lowest ranks of the labor pool—individuals for whom the CDP was a perceived substitute for experience and education.

Professional Societies or Technician Associations?

In spring 1975, on the eve of the annual National Computer Conference, a small group of the elite leaders of the computing community met in a nondescript conference room at a Quality Inn in Anaheim, California, to discuss the future of the computing profession. Similar meetings had been convened every year for the previous two decades, always with the intent to address the most pressing issues facing the computing community. Although the specific composition of the group changed from year to year, the attendees always represented the highest levels of leadership in the discipline: award-winning computer scientists, successful business entrepreneurs, association presidents, and prolific authors. The cumulative list of participants reads like a who's who of the computing industry: Gene Amdahl, Paul Armer, Herbert Bright, Howard Bromberg, Richard Canning, Herbert Grosch, Fred Gruenberger, Richard Hamming, J.C.R. Licklider, Daniel McCracken, Anthony Oettinger, Seymour Papert, and Joseph Weizenbaum, among many others. This particular meeting included high-ranking representatives from all of the major professional societies: the ACM, the DPMA, the IEEE Computer Society, and the ICCP. These societies represented the largest and most influential constituent members of the umbrella organization, AFIPS. On the agenda was a discussion of the role of AFIPS in the professional development of the discipline.

AFIPS had been founded in 1961 as a society of societies. The immediate goal had been to provide a U.S. representative to the upcoming International Federation of Information Processing (IFIP) conference.

IFIP had been established several years earlier under the aegis of the United Nations Educational, Scientific, and Cultural Organization (UNESCO). Beginning in 1959, IFIP hosted an annual international conference on computing. Each member nation was allowed to send representatives from a *single* organization. Since the United States had no single organization that spoke for its computing community, AFIPS was created to represent three of the largest computer-related societies: the ACM, the American Institute of Electrical Engineers (AIEE), and the Institute of Radio Engineers (IRE). (The AIEE and the IRE later merged into the IEEE.) It was hoped that AFIPS would eventually come to serve as the single national voice for computer interests in the United States.[97]

From the start, AFIPS proved a disappointment. AFIPS did represent the United States at the annual IFIP meeting. It was given control over the lucrative Joint Computer Conferences, but beyond that, it proved incapable of serving as "the voice of the computing profession in America."[98] It was crippled by a weak charter and a lack of tangible support from its founding societies. AFIPS was a society of societies, not a society of members, and it was therefore dependent on and subservient to the interests of its constituent societies, rather than to the larger computing community. In addition, several obvious candidates for membership, including the DPMA, had been conspicuously excluded from participation, and the AFIPS voting structure made it obvious that additional members would be unwelcome.[99] Even more limiting was a clause in the constitution, insisted on by the ACM as an essential precondition for its support, prohibiting AFIPS from placing itself "in direct competition with the activities of its member societies."[100] Although the constitution was revised in 1969 to provide for stronger leadership and a more inclusive atmosphere, AFIPS continued to struggle for support and recognition. The DPMA did not join until 1974, for example, and even then without much enthusiasm. The gathering in 1975 of the computing elite at the Quality Inn in Anaheim represented one of the many attempts to reinvigorate interest in this ailing association. In 1989, just two years after celebrating its twenty-fifth anniversary, AFIPS voted itself out of existence. The loss of control over the lucrative National Computing Conferences left it financially unstable and without any clear means of support. Few in the community mourned its passing.

The transcripts of the meeting are revealing. The existence of a powerful professional association was obviously considered by the many influential members of the computing community to be the cornerstone of a strong professional identity. And yet rivalries between the member societies, particularly the ACM and the DPMA, proved to be an endemic and ultimately insoluble barrier to the establishment of this identity. Participants in the various associations disagreed over membership qualifications, dues, voting privileges, and certification and licensing proposals. More important, however, was the lack of widespread popular support for these associations. One *Datamation* study indicated that less than 40 percent of all programmers belonged to any professional association, and "probably less than 1% do anything in connection with an association that requires an extra effort on the individual's part."[101] And even these low figures were probably inflated: a *Wall Street Journal* report from the same year revealed only that 13 percent of the data processing personnel surveyed belonged to any professional society.[102] These numbers correspond well with the low level of interest in the CDP certification program. Although it is difficult to compile exact figures on association membership, it is clear that at best only a small percentage of the eligible population chose to participate in any professional society.

If strong professional associations were widely perceived to be an important element of professional identity, why did groups like the ACM, the DPMA, and AFIPS have such difficulty attracting and keeping members? AFIPS had some obvious structural problems that almost assured its ineffectiveness. Individuals could not directly join AFIPS; it was merely an umbrella organization for other associations, and possessed little real authority. But what about the ACM and the DPMA, the two largest relevant member societies? Both of these groups were established early, were relatively high profile, and published their own widely distributed journals. Both were frequently mentioned as candidates for the position of *the* professional computing association. Yet neither was able to consolidate its control over any significant portion of the discipline's practitioners. The reasons behind their failure suggest the limitations of professional associations as an institutional solution to the software crisis.

The persistent conflict between the ACM and the DPMA revealed a much larger tension that existed within the computing community. As early as 1959, the outlines of a battle between academically oriented computer scientists and business programmers had taken shape around the issue of professionalism.[103] Although both groups agreed on the desirability of establishing institutional and occupational boundaries around the nascent computer-related professions, they disagreed sharply about what form these professional structures should take. Observers noted a deepening "programming schism" developing within the industry, a "growing breach between the scientific and engineering computation boys who talk ALGOL and FORTRAN . . . and the business data processing boys who talk English and write programs in COBOL."[104] Individuals who believed that the key to professional status was the development of formal theories of computer science resisted subprofessional certification programs and tended to join the ACM; business data processors who were skeptical of "cute mathematical tricks," either supported the DPMA or ignored the professional societies altogether.

It is obvious that the turf battles that raged between the ACM and the DPMA during the 1950s and 1960s helped undermine popular support for both organizations. In response to extensive *Datamation* coverage of a RAND symposium in 1959 on "the perennial professional society question," one reader commented that he "hadn't laughed so hard in a decade. Are these guys kidding? You won't solve this problem by self-interested conversation about it, nor is it solved by founding another organization."[105] In a retrospective in 1985 on the troubled history of AFIPS, Harry Tropp suggested that "the question of turf seems to have been there from the beginning. It shows up in the [1950s'] Rand Symposium. . . . There were the hardware and software types and then there were the users. We had the east coast/west coast turf problems. What I am hearing today is a whole new evolution of different turfs as this information processing society explodes."[106] The fact that the DPMA refused affiliation with AFIPS until the mid-1970s—largely because of the perception that the latter organization was dominated by the ACM—was a major factor in its perpetual ineffectiveness and eventual dissolution (in 1987, just two years after it celebrated its twenty-fifth anniversary). Herbert Grosch in particular was dismayed by the pettiness of the ACM-DPMA debates, which he believed detracted from the overall goal of establishing a legitimate professional identity:

I couldn't care less who publishes some abstract scientific paper! What I want to know is how do we pull together a hundred thousand warm bodies that are working on the outskirts of the computer business, give them a high-priced executive director, lots of advertising, a whole series of technical journals; in other words, organize a real rip-snorting profession? Whenever somebody starts worrying about which journal what paper should be published in, we get bogged down in an academic cross-fire we've been in for ten years."[107]

As damaging as these interassociation rivalries were to the influence and reputation of the ACM and the DPMA, what really hurt them was the lack of support that they received from industry practitioners. Neither organization was able to clearly establish its relevance to the needs of either workers or their managers. "Neither organization . . . has done much for the industry or for society as a whole," argued one *Datamation* editorial from 1965. "We think the time is ripe to more clearly define larger, more important long-range goals which distinguish a professional society from a technician's association."[108] Employers looked to the professional associations to provide a supply of reliable, capable programmers. As was apparent from the impassioned debates about the structure and relevance of computer science curricula, however, it was far from obvious to many managers that formal educational programs contributed much to the production of professional programmers. The ACM's continued devotion to theoretical computer science made it seem out of touch with the practical demands of business. The DPMA's CDP program, although it was much more oriented to business data processing, failed to achieve widespread industry acceptance. As a result, it also was not able to guarantee the kind of standardized labor force in which corporations were interested. Employers saw little value in either organization.

The Limits of Professionalism

In his monograph on *Office Automation in Social Perspective* from 1968, Oxford sociologist Hans Rhee observed that "the computer elite are beginning to erect collective defenses against the lay world. They are beginning to develop a sense of professional identity and values." But the process of establishing professional attitudes and controls, and a professional conscience and solidarity, Rhee suggested, had "not yet advanced very far."[109] He could just have easily been describing the computing professions as they existed a decade earlier or a decade afterward. By 1968 computing had acquired many of the trappings of professionalism: academic computer science departments, certification programs, and professional associations. And yet most computing practitioners were not widely regarded as professionals, at least not in the eyes of the general public. In 1967, for example, the U.S. Civil Service Commission declared data processing personnel to be nonexempt employees, officially categorizing programmers as technicians rather than professionals. Although this decision did not affect the lives or practices of programmers, it represented a symbolic defeat for professional associations such as the ACM, which lobbied hard to have it overturned.[110]

The inability of programmers and other data processing personnel to successfully professionalize raises a perplexing question for the historian: Given the apparent interest in professionalization on the part of both employers and practitioners, why were these efforts so ineffective? As was described earlier, industrial employers in the 1960s complained not so much about technical incompetence as a general lack of professionalism among programmers. "It was his distressing lack of professional attributes that most often undermines his work and destroys his management's confidence," declared Malcolm Gotterer. "Too frequently these people, while exhibiting excellent technical skills, are nonprofessional in every other aspect of their work."[111] Increased professionalism would presumably address the most frequent complaints leveled against data processing personnel: an overreliance on idiosyncratic craft techniques; an arrogant disregard for proper lines of authority; shoddy production quality; and a lack of commitment to the best interests of the organization. On the surface, the professionalization of programming appeared to be an ideal solution to many of the most deleterious symptoms of the burgeoning software crisis.

There are a number of explanations for the failure of most professionalization programs. Internal rivalries within the computing community undermined the effectiveness of groups such as the ACM and the DPMA. No single organization could meet the needs of a diverse community of computer people that included everyone from PhD mathematicians to high school dropout keypunch operators. As Louis Fein pointed out in his discussion of the ACM's crisis of identity, "It is not clear . . . that an organization can play simultaneously the role of a profession, of an industry, and of a science. . . . I cannot see that ACM members, or IEEE Computer Group members, or DPMA members, or Simulations Councils, Inc. members, are members of a profession. They are practitioners or scientists or engineers or programmers—members of a technical society."[112] The attempts of the computer scientists to rationalize the practice of programming and produce a body of generally applicable programming theory set them at odds with vocational programmers. The seemingly inconsistent and idiosyncratic practices of working programmers were used as foils for the elegant constructions of the academic computer scientists. The attempts of the vocational programmers to appeal to the language and ideals of science and engineering were ridiculed. When asked to explain the linguistic transition from coder to programmer, the prominent computer scientist John Backus dismissed it as purely rhetorical: "It's the same reason that janitors are now called 'custodians.' 'Programmer' was considered a higher-class enterprise than 'coder,' and things have a tendency to move in that direction."[113] As the programming community broke down into competing factions—such as theoretical versus practical, certified versus uncertified, and the ACM versus the DPMA—its members lost the leverage necessary to push through any particular professionalization agenda.

In addition to internal rivalries, the aspiring computing professions also faced external opposition. For many corporate managers, professionalism was a potentially dangerous double-edged sword. On the one hand, "professionalism might motivate staff members to improve their capabilities, it could bring about more commonality of approaches, it could be used for hiring, promotions and raises, and it could help determine 'who is qualified.'" On the other hand, "professionalism might well increase staff mobility and hence turnover, and it probably would lead to higher salaries for the 'professionals.'"[114] Computer personnel were seen as dangerously disruptive to the traditional corporate establishment. The last thing that traditional managers wanted was to provide data processing personnel with additional occupational authority. Professionalism was therefore encouraged only to the extent that it provided a standardized, tractable workforce; professionalization efforts that encouraged elitism, protectionism, or anything that smacked of unionism were seen as counterproductive.

Perhaps the most important reason that programmers and other data processing personnel failed to professionalize, however, was that the professional institutions that were set up in the 1950s and 1960s failed to convince employers of their relevance to the needs of business. A *Computerworld* survey in 1974 indicated that "no technical society has ever captured and held the attention of professionals in BDP."[115] Employers looked to professional institutions as a means of supplying their demand for competent, trustworthy employees. As we have seen, although computer science programs in the 1960s thrived in the universities, in the business world they were usually seen as overly theoretical and irrelevant. Likewise, the DPMA's CDP program failed to establish itself as a reliable mechanism for predicting programmer performance or ability. Neither the ACM nor the DPMA offered much to employers in terms of improving the supply or quality of the programming workforce.

Given this lack of active support from employers, the professional associations had little to offer most data processing practitioners. Neither a computer science education nor professional certification could ensure employment or advancement. In response to a *Computerworld* article in 1974 titled "Why Business Users Are Turned Off by ACM," AFIPS president George Glaser remarked that "the general lack of success of ACM in attracting business data processing professionals to its membership has relatively little to do with the nature and extent of the services it offers them. It is, rather, more attributable to a lack of interest on the part of these 'professionals' in any professional society."[116] Glaser's comment can be read either as an indictment of the apathy of the average computing practitioner or the policies of the ACM; either way, it suggests the strained relationship that existed between the two communities. Many working programmers saw little value in belonging to either the ACM or the DPMA, and support for both organizations as well as professional institutions in general languished during the late 1960s and early 1970s.

8

Engineering a Solution

We build software like the Wright brothers built airplanes: build the whole thing, push it off a cliff, and start over again.
—Ronald Graham, NATO Conference on Software Engineering[1]

Industrializing Software Development

In the collective memory of the programming community, the years between 1968 and 1972 mark a major turning point in the history of its industry and profession. It is during this period that the rhetoric of the crisis became firmly entrenched in the vernacular of commercial computing. Although there had been earlier concerns expressed about "software turmoil" and the "software gap," it was not until 1968 that the word "crisis" began to be applied to the challenges facing the software industry. Within a few short years, the existence of a looming software crisis had been widely and enthusiastically embraced within the popular and industry literature. The discourse of crisis became one of the defining features of the software industry; since the late 1960s, almost every new computer-science curriculum proposal, programming technology, or development methodology has positioned itself relative to this perception of widespread crisis. Even those who deny the very existence of the crisis are continually forced to engage with its pervasive discursive legacy.[2]

To a certain degree the emergence of the software crisis of the late 1960s represents the culmination of a long series of concerns about software: the seemingly perpetual shortage of programming personnel; the burgeoning complexity of both application and systems software; the apparent failure of automatic programming technologies to make the process of programming less mysterious or more cost-effective; the professional and political tensions inherent in management information systems and other organizationally disruptive technologies; and a growing sense at all levels of society that the changes associated with the computer revolution were more fundamental and pervasive—and at times intrusive—than had previously been anticipated.[3]

What is novel and significant about the software crisis discourse, therefore, was not in its identification of a series of problems but rather in the nature of its proposed solutions. For most historians as well as most contemporary observers, the software crisis of the late 1960s was defined by the emergence of new software-engineering approaches to the problems of software development.

The phrase "software engineering" appears to have first been used by the hardware engineer J. Presper Eckert in an address to the Eastern Joint Computer Conference in 1965 in reference to the growing conflict between computer programmers and their corporate employers. Computer programming "would only be manageable," he claimed, "when we could refer to it as 'software engineering.'"[4] But it was the 1968 NATO Conference on Software Engineering that marks the moment that software engineering dramatically entered the public consciousness.

In October 1968, a diverse group of academic computer scientists, corporate managers, and military officials gathered in Garmisch, Germany, for the first-ever NATO Conference on Software Engineering. The conference was intended to address what many industry observers believed to be an impending crisis in software production. Large software development projects had acquired a reputation for being behind schedule, over budget, and bug ridden. The solution to the so-called software crisis, suggested the conference organizers, was for software developers to adopt a more methodical and industrial approach. The phrase "software engineering" was "deliberately chosen as being provocative," suggested the conference organizers, "in implying a need for software manufacturing to be based on the types of theoretical foundations and practical disciplines that are traditional in the established branches of engineering."[5] In the interest of efficient software manufacturing, the black art of programming had to make way for the science of software engineering.

By defining the software crisis in terms of the discipline of software engineering, the conference set an agenda that influenced many of the technological, managerial, and professional developments in commercial computing for the next several decades. The general consensus among historians and practitioners alike is that the Garmisch meeting marked a major cultural shift in the perception of programming. In the aftermath of Garmisch, "software writing started to make the transition from being a craft for a long-haired programming priesthood to becoming a real engineering discipline. It was the transformation from an art to a science."[6] The call to integrate "good engineering principles" into the software development process has been the rallying cry of software developers from the late 1960s to the present.[7]

The fundamental problem with software, according to the NATO conference organizers, was not personnel or technology but rather technique. Software development was difficult because computer programmers had failed to follow an appropriate methodology. They persisted in their craft-based mentality when what was demanded was clearly an industrial system of manufacturing. "We undoubtedly produce software by backward techniques, argued M. Douglas McIlroy of Bell Telephone Laboratories: "We undoubtedly get the short end of the stick in confrontations with hardware people because they are the industrialists and we are the crofters."[8] Like many of his fellow participants, McIlroy rejected the notion that large software projects were inherently unmanageable. The imposition of engineering management methods had enabled efficient manufacturing in myriad other industries, and would not fail to do the same for computer programming. Software engineering promised to bring control and predictability to the traditionally undisciplined practices of software development.

For a number of conference participants, the key word in the provocative NATO manifesto was "discipline." For example, in his widely quoted paper on "mass-produced software components," McIlroy proposed applying mass-production techniques to software.[9] His vision of a software "components factory" invokes familiar images of industrialization and proletariatization. According to his proposal, an elite corps of "software engineers" would serve as the Frederick Taylors of the software industry, carefully orchestrating every action of a highly stratified programmer labor force. And like the engineers in more traditional manufacturing organizations, these software engineers would identify themselves more as corporate citizens than as independent professionals.[10]

Not every proposed solution to the software crisis suggested at Garmisch was as blatantly management oriented as McIlroy's. Nevertheless, the theme of transformation from a craft-based black art of programming to the industrial discipline of software engineering dominated many of the presentations and discussions. The focus on management solutions reflected—and reinforced—a larger groundswell of popular opinion that extended far beyond the confines of the actual conference. The industry literature of the period is replete with examples of this changing attitude toward software management. Even those proposals that seemed to be most explicitly technical, such as those advocating structured programming techniques or high-level language developments, contained a strong managerial component. Most required a rigid division of labor and the adoption of tight management controls over worker autonomy. When a prominent adherent of object-oriented programming techniques spoke of "transforming programming from a solitary cut-to-fit craft, like the cottage industries of colonial America, into an organizational enterprise like manufacturing is today," he was referring not so much to the adoption of a specific technology but rather to the imposition of established and traditional forms of labor organization and workplace relationships.[11] The solutions to the software crisis most frequently recommended by managers—among them the elimination of rule-of-thumb methods (i.e., the black art of programming), the scientific selection and training of programmers, the development of new forms of management, and the efficient division of labor—were not fundamentally different from the four principles of scientific management espoused by Frederick Taylor in an earlier era.[12]

Aristocracy, Democracy, and Systems Design

In practice, software engineering was more an expression of ideals than a well-defined agenda. At best it was a loose collection of techniques, technologies, institutions, and practices.[13] As Stuart Shapiro has suggested, the essence of the software-engineering movement was control: control over complexity, control over budgets and scheduling, and, perhaps most significantly, control over a recalcitrant workforce.[14] Although a number of technological or procedural innovations were developed to facilitate software engineering—structure programming techniques, the ADA programming language, Computer-Aided Software Engineering (CASE) environments—the focus of most software-engineering efforts were managerial. In this sense, software engineering represents the culmination of the turn toward managerial solutions to the software crisis that characterized the late 1960s.

Unhappy with the ballooning costs of software development, threatened by the growing power of the computer people, and frustrated by the apparent inability of either academic computer science or the professional societies to institute more formal methods for regulating the industry, corporate managers attempted to construct development methodologies that would eliminate the uncertainty and expense associated with computerization projects.

It would be impossible to describe all of the numerous approaches to programmer management that were developed in this and subsequent periods. The remainder of this chapter will focus on the defining characteristics of a few of the most prominent development methodologies that emerged in response to the declaration in 1968 of the software crisis: the hierarchical system, or software factory; the superprogrammer, or chief programmer team (CPT) approach; and the adaptive programmer team (or "egoless" programming) model. The hierarchical systems approach—originally developed for large, government-sponsored programming projects at the SDC and the IBM Federal Systems Division— resembles the highly stratified, top-down organizational structure familiar to most conventional corporate employees. The CPT, although it was also developed at the IBM Federal Systems Division, reflects an entirely different approach to programmer management oriented around the leadership of a single managerially minded superprogrammer. The adaptive team approach was popularized as egoless programming by the iconoclastic Gerald Weinberg in his classic *The Psychology of Computer Programming* from 1971.[15] Weinberg proposed an open, "democratic" style of management that emphasized teamwork and rotating leadership.

Although it is possible to arrange these approaches into a roughly chronological order, it is not my intention to suggest that they represent any simple evolution toward increasing managerial control or economic efficiency. Each of these management methodologies captures separate but interrelated visions about how computer programming as an economic activity, and computer programmers as aspiring professionals, could best be integrated into the established social and technological systems of the traditional corporation. Each of these approaches built on, and responded to, the innovations and shortcomings of the others. They also reflected the backgrounds and aspirations of their advocates and developers. By studying carefully the salient features of each of these three methodologies, we will be better able to situate them in their particular social and historical context, and hence to understand more fully their contribution to contemporary debates about the nature and causes of the software crisis.

Armies of Programmers

The first concerted attempts to manage software development projects using established management techniques occurred at the government- and military-sponsored SAGE air-defense project. The SAGE project was the heart of an ambitious early warning radar network intended to provide an immediate and centralized response to sneak attacks from enemy aircraft. The plan was to develop a series of computerized tracking and communications centers that would coordinate observation and response data from a widely dispersed system of interconnected perimeter warning stations. First authorized by Congress in 1954, by 1961 the SAGE system had cost more than $8 billion to develop and operate, and required the services of over two hundred thousand employees. The software that connected the specially designed, real-time SAGE computers was the largest programming development then under way. SDC, a RAND Corporation spin-off company responsible for developing this software, had to train and hire almost two thousand programmers. In the space of a few short years the personnel management department at SDC effectively doubled the number of trained programmers in the United States.

In order to effectively organize an unprecedented number of software developers, SDC experimented with a number of different techniques for managing the programming process. For the most part, however, SDC relied on a hierarchical structure that located most programmers at the lowest levels of a vast organizational pyramid built with layer on layer of managers.[16] The top of this hierarchy was occupied by nontechnical administrators. The middle layers were peopled by those EDP personnel who had exhibited a desire or aptitude for management. In other words, the managers in the SDC hierarchy were self-selected as being either uninterested or uncommitted to a long-term programming career. The management style in this hierarchical structure was generally autocratic. Managers made all of the important decisions. They assigned tasks, monitored the progress of subordinates, and determined when and what corrective actions needed to be taken.

This hierarchical approach to management was attractive to SDC executives for a number of reasons. First of all, it was a familiar model for government and military subcontractors. Second, it was often easier to justify billing for a large number of mediocre low-wage employees than a smaller number of excellent but expensive contractors. Finally, and perhaps most important, the "Mongolian horde" approach to software development corresponded nicely with contemporary constructions of the root causes of the burgeoning software turmoil. This was also known as the "Chinese Army" approach, at least until the phrase became unpopular in the early 1950s.

Faced with a shortage of experienced programmers, SDC embarked on an extensive programming of internal training and development. Most of its trainees had little or no experience with computers; in fact, many managers at SDC preferred it that way. Like many corporations in the 1950s, SDC believed that "it is much easier to teach our personnel to program than it is to teach outside experienced programmers the details of our business."[17] In any case, in the period between 1956 and 1961 the company trained seven thousand programmers and systems analysts. At a time when all the computer manufacturers combined could only provide twenty-five hundred student weeks of instruction annually, SDC devoted more than ten thousand student weeks to instructing its own personnel how to program.[18]

The apparent success that SDC achieved in mass-producing programming talent reinforced the notion that a hierarchical approach was the suitable model for large-scale software development. If large quantities of programmers could be produced on demand, then individual programmers were effectively anonymous and replaceable. A complex system like SAGE could be broken down into simple, modular components that could be easily understood by any programmer with the appropriate training and experience. The principles behind the approach were essentially those that had proven so successful in traditional manufacturing: replaceable parts, simple and repetitive tasks, and a strict division of labor.

The hierarchical model of software development was adopted by a number of other major software manufacturers, particularly those involved in similarly large military or government projects. It is not clear how direct the connection was between SDC and these other manufacturers. SDC certainly had a role in training a large number of programmers and EDP managers. "We trained the industry!" boasted SDC veterans: "Whatever company I visit, I meet two or three SDC alumni."[19] The labor historian Philip Kraft attributes much of what he refers to as the "routinization" of programming labor to the "degrading" influence of military-industrial organizations such as SDC. He describes the SDC so-called software factories as "the first systematic, large-scale effort on the part of EDP users to transform the highly idiosyncratic, artisan-like occupation" of computer programming into "one which more closely resembled conventional industrial work."[20] He argues that SDC played a significant role in diffusing and popularizing the hierarchical approach to software engineering management.

Whether the claim that SDC policies and SDC personnel played a direct role in diffusing the hierarchical system of management through-out the computer industry was valid, similar top-down methodologies were widely adopted. In the IBM Federal Systems Division, a multilevel organizational structure was used on all large government projects. IBM manager Philip Metzger provided a detailed description of the Federal Systems approach in his highly popular textbook *Managing a Programming Project*, which went through three editions in the period between 1973 and 1996.[21] An article titled "Issues in Programming Management" that appeared in 1974 in the respected industry newsletter *EDP Analyzer* listed the hierarchical systems approach as one of the most commonly implemented software management methodologies.[22] Joel Aron, another IBM Federal Systems veteran, used the hierarchical model as the basis for his series of books on the *Program Development Process*.[23] The hierarchical approach to software development was attractive to managers because it corresponded nicely with the contemporary management theories. In the first half of the twentieth century, corporate management became a professional activity dominated by specialists and experts. These professional managers developed a shared culture and value system reinforced by an increasingly formalized program of training and educa-tion. They exerted a high degree of control over the work practices of their subordinates, scientifically managing all aspects of the business and manufacturing process. EDP managers assumed that the techniques and structures that appeared to work so efficiently in traditional industries would translate naturally into the software development department. It was only a matter of identifying and implementing the one best way to develop software components.

Embedded in the hierarchical model of management were a series of assumptions about the essential character of programming as an occu-pational activity. Implied in the suggestion that the structures and pro-cedures of a traditional manufacturing organization could be seamlessly mapped onto the EDP department was a belief that the skills and experi-ence required to program a computer were, in effect, not all that different from those required to assemble an automobile. Managers could define, in the minutest detail, the specifications that the programmers would follow. In turn, the programmers need only be trained to perform a limited and specialized function. Individual programmers were looked on as interchangeable units.[24] They lacked a distinct professional identity. The path to advancement in the hierarchical system (if indeed there actually was one available to mere programmers) was through management. Certification programs were desirable in order to ensure a minimum level of competence, but only as a means for assuring a standard degree of performance and product.[25] Programmers were encouraged to be professionals only to the extent that being a professional meant self-discipline, a willingness to work long hours with no overtime pay, and loyalty to the corporation and obedience to supervisors.[26]

The notion that programmers could be treated as unskilled clerical workers was reinforced by a series of technical developments intended to allow managers to mechanically translate high-level systems designs into the low-level machine code required by a computer. For example, one of the alleged advantages of the COBOL programming language frequently touted in the literature was its ability to be read and understood—and perhaps even written—by informed managers.[27] More than a fashionable management technique, the hierarchical organizational model was a philosophy about what programming was and where programmers stood in relation to other corporate professionals. It embodied—in a complex of interrelated cultural, technical, and political systems—a particular social construction of the nature and causes of the software crisis.

Despite the obvious appeal that the theory of hierarchical systems held for conventional managers, it rarely worked as intended in actual practice. Although managers would have preferred to think of programming as routine clerical work and programmers as interchangeable laborers, experience suggested that in reality the situation was quite different. I have already described how, in the late 1950s and early 1960s, programming had acquired a reputation as being a uniquely creative activity requiring "real intellectual ability and above average personal characteristics."[28] "To 'teach' the equipment, as is amply evident from experience to date, requires considerable skill, ingenuity, perseverance, organizing ability, etc. The human element is crucial in programming."[29] The anecdotal evidence that suggested skilled programmers were essential elements of software development was supported by numerous empirical studies produced by industrial psychologists and personnel experts.

The realization that computer programming was a more intellectually challenging activity than was originally anticipated threw a monkey wrench into the elaborate hierarchical systems that managers had constructed. Whereas the software turmoil of the 1950s was attributed largely to numerical shortages of programmers, the "programmer quality" problems of the 1960s demanded a subtly different construction of the root causes of the software crisis. The problem could still be defined as a management problem requiring a management-driven solution. What had changed was the prevailing conception of what programmers were and what they did. "The massive attack on systems software poses difficult management problems," concluded Gene Bylinsky in the pages of *Fortune* magazine. "On the one hand, a good programmer, like a writer or composer, works best independently. But the pressure to turn out operating systems and other programs within a limited time make it necessary to deploy huge task forces whose coordination becomes a monstrous task." Echoing conventional wisdom about the creative nature of programming, Bylinsky maintained that the problem was "further complicated" by the fact that there is no "best way" to write computer programs. "Programming has nowhere near the discipline of physics, for example, so intuition plays a large part. Yet individual programmers differ in their creative and intuitive abilities."[30]

Companies that implemented hierarchical systems methodologies also discovered that programmers were not content with the professional identity that these systems imposed on them. Programmers voted with their feet by leaving for other firms, and salaries inflated dramatically.[31] One large employer experienced a sustained turnover rate of 10 percent *per month*.[32] The problem, according to one SDC survey of termination interviews, was that programmers working in hierarchical organizations "did not foresee for themselves the opportunities they want for professional growth and development . . . or for promotion and advancement."[33] The career aspirations of the programmers conflicted with the occupational role they had been assigned by the managers. Many preferred to pursue professional advancement *within* programming, rather than *away* from programming. In the hierarchical system, the higher that individuals advanced, the more they worked as administrators rather than technologists.

Superprogrammer to the Rescue

The IBM System/360 has been called "the computer that IBM made, that made IBM."[34] The System/360 systems solved a number of problems for IBM and its customers. It filled in the gaps in the IBM line of product offerings by providing an entire range of hardware- and software-compatible computers ranging from the low-end model 360/20 (intended to compete directly with the Honeywell H-200) to the model 360/90 supercomputer, which compared favorably to the CDC-6600. By making all of these machines software compatible (theoretically, at least), IBM supplied an inexpensive upgrade path for its customers. The client could purchase just the amount of computing power that they needed, knowing that if their needs changed in the future they could simply transfer their existing applications and data to the next level of System/360 hardware. They could also make use of their existing peripherals, such as tape readers and printers, without requiring an expensive upgrade.

The System/360 was an enormously risky and expensive undertaking. The *Fortune* journalist Tom Wise referred to it as "IBM's $5,000,000,000 Gamble." He quoted one senior IBM manager as calling it the "we bet the company" project.[35] The riskiest and most expensive component of System/360 development was the OS/360 operating system. As mentioned earlier, in the years between 1963 and 1966, over five thousand staff years of effort went into the design, construction, and documentation of OS/360. When OS/360 was finally delivered in 1967, nine months late and riddled with errors, it had cost the IBM Corporation half a billion dollars—four times the original budget, or "the single largest expenditure in company history."[36]

Although the System/360 project turned out to be a tremendous success for IBM, sealing its position of leadership in the commercial computer industry for the next several decades, the OS/360 project was generally considered to be a financial and technological disaster. The costs of the OS/360 debacle were human as well as material; according to Frederick Brooks, they were "best reckoned in terms of the toll it took on people: the managers who struggled to make and keep commitments to top management and to customers, and the programmers who worked long hours over a period of years, against obstacles of every sort, to deliver working programs of unprecedented complexity." Many in both groups left, victims of a variety of stresses ranging from technological to physical.[37]

The highly publicized failure of the OS/360 project served as a dramatic illustration of the shortcomings of the hierarchical management method. Techniques that had worked well on an application requiring ten thousand lines of code failed miserably when applied to a million lines of code project. Faced with serious schedule slippages, quality problems, and unanticipated changes in scope, the OS/360 managers did what traditional manufacturing managers were accustomed to doing:

they added more resources. The only noticeable result was that the project fell more and more behind schedule.

The Mythical Man-Month was OS/360 project leader Frederick Brooks's postmortem analysis of the failures of traditional hierarchical management. It is one of the most widely read and oft-quoted references on the practice of software engineering. The mythical man-month in the title refers to the commonly held notion that progress in software development projects occurs as a function of time spent times the number of workers allocated—the implication being that more workers equals faster production. Brooks dismissed this assumption with the now-famous Brooks's law, one of the most memorable aphorisms in the lore of software development: *adding personnel to a late software project makes it later*. Or to use one of Brooks's more earthy metaphors, "the bearing of a child takes nine months, no matter how many women are assigned."[38]

The highly quotable Brooks's law was neither the only nor even the most significant of the insights provided in *The Mythical Man-Month*. Brooks did more than criticize existing methodologies; he provided an entirely new model for understanding software development management. He was firmly convinced that there was a wide disparity in performance among individual programmers. Brooks believed that small teams of sharp programmers were substantially more productive than much larger groups of merely mediocre performers. But he also recognized that even the best small team could only accomplish so much in any given period of time. The small team approach simply did not scale well to larger projects. The problem of scalability was the heart of the "cruel dilemma" facing project managers: "For efficiency and conceptual integrity, one prefers a few good minds doing design and construction. Yet for large systems one wants a way to bring considerable manpower to bear, so that the product can make a timely appearance."[39] And yet the Mongolian horde model of throwing programming resources—so-called man-months—at projects was also obviously insufficient. What was needed was a way to apply the efficiency and elegance of the small team approach to the problems of large-project management.

Brooks proposed the adoption of what he called the "surgical team" model of software development. In doing so, he borrowed heavily from the work of IBM manager and researcher Harlan Mills, who had earlier developed the CPT concept. This notion was first introduced as one of two experimental superprogrammer projects by Aron in a paper given at a second NATO Software Engineering conference held in Rome in 1969. The first experiment involved a thirty-man-year project requiring fifty thousand instructions. Mills attempted to complete the project himself (using a prototype surgical team) in only six months. The project eventually required about six man-years of effort to complete, and was considered a moderate success. The second experiment mentioned by Aron at the Rome conference turned out to be the famous *New York Times* project, which established the reputation of the CPT approach when it was publicized by F. Terry Baker in 1971. In both versions of the CPT approach, a single, expert programmer was responsible for all major design and implementation decisions involved with system development. The chief programmer (or surgeon) defined the program specifications, designed the program, coded it, tested it, and wrote the documentation. The chief was assisted in their tasks by an operating team of support staff. Their immediate assistant (or copilot) was only slightly less expert than the chief programmer. The copilot was the chief programmer's mirror and alter ego, serving not only as an emergency backup or stand-in but also as an adviser, discussant, and evaluator. Although the assistant knew the program code intimately and may even have written some of it, it was the chief programmer who was ultimately responsible for it.

Other members of the Brooks's surgical team included an administrator, who handled schedules, money, personnel issues, and hardware resources; an editor, who provided the finishing touches to the chief programmer's documentation; two secretaries, who dealt with correspondence and filing; a program clerk, who maintained all the technical records for the project; a "toolsmith," who built, constructed, and maintained the interactive tools used by the rest of the team for programming, debugging, and testing; a tester, who served as the chief programmer's adversary and assistant, developed test plans to challenge the integrity of the program design, and devised test data for day-to-day debugging; and finally, the "language lawyer," who delighted in the mastery of the intricacies of a programming language. The language lawyer, unlike the chief programmer, was not involved in big-picture issues or system design; the lawyer's responsibility was finding "neat and efficient ways to use the language to do difficult, obscure, or tricky things." Language lawyers were usually called in only for special, short-term assignments.[40]

The advantage to the CPT approach, according to Mills and Brooks, was that it dramatically simplified communications between team members. Whereas a large, hierarchical organization of X number of employees could require as many as $(X^2 - X)/2$ independent paths of communication, in the CPT model all essential information passed through the person of the chief programmer. All team members reported to the chief directly and did not communicate with each other directly.

By centralizing all decision making in the person of the chief programmer, this approach assured the maintenance of the program's structural integrity. Brooks compared the conceptual architecture of the typical large software project to the haphazard design of many European cathedrals; the patchwork structure of these cathedrals revealed an unpleasant lack of continuity, reflecting the different styles and techniques of different builders in different generations. Brooks preferred the architectural unity of the cathedral at Reims, which derived "as much from the integrity of design as from any particular excellences." This integrity was achieved only through the "self-abnegation of eight generations of builders," each of whom "sacrificed some of his ideas so that the whole might be of pure design." Using wonderfully evocative biblical language, Brooks extolled the virtues of a unified conceptual design: "As the child delights in his mud pie, so the adult enjoys building things, especially things of his own design. I believe that this delight must be an image of God's delight in making things, a delight shown in the distinctiveness and newness of each leaf and each snowflake."[41] Only the CPT approach could guarantee such a degree of uncompromised architectural integrity.

The CPT approach differed from hierarchical systems methodologies in a number of essential characteristics. Whereas the hierarchical model allowed for (and in fact encouraged) the use of novice programmers, the CPT was built entirely around skilled, experienced professionals. This implied a radically different approach to professional development. Each member of the team was encouraged to develop within their own particular disciplinary competency; that is, it wasn't necessary to become a surgeon to advance one's career. For example, an aspiring language lawyer could continue to focus on their technical specialty without feeling pressure to transfer into management. The CPT approach embodied the belief that computer programming was a legitimate, respectable profession.

The CPT also reflected changing contemporary notions about the nature of programming ability. The primary justification for using small teams of experienced programmers rather than large hordes of novices was the belief that one good programmer was worth at least ten of their average colleagues. In the person of the chief programmer, the innate technical abilities of the superprogrammer were merged with the organizational authority of the traditional manager. The chief program-mer was both a technical genius and expert administrator. Programming aptitude could not be abstracted from its embodiment in particular indi-viduals; skilled programmers were anything but replaceable components of an automated software factory. In the elite surgical team model, the contributions of talented professionals far outweighed those provided by traditional management techniques or development methodologies.

Besides endowing computer programmers with considerable institu-tional power, *The Mythical Man-Month* reinforced the notion that pro-gramming was an exceptional activity, unlike any other engineering or manufacturing discipline. Brooks's suggestion that programming was akin to poetry strongly implied that programming was not an activity that could be readily systematized. What Brooks proposed was the adop-tion of useful tools and techniques, not some overarching methodology. As he later declared in a famous article titled "No Silver Bullet," although the management of large programming projects could be improved incre-mentally, there were no easy solutions to be derived from the lessons of traditional manufacturing.[42]

Like the hierarchical systems model, the CPT was intimately linked to specific techniques and technologies. Since all major decisions relating to both design and implementation had to be made by a single super-programmer, the CPT approach effectively demanded the adoption of top-down development techniques. Top-down programming was one of the foundational principles of the structured programming approach to software engineering advocated by many academic computer scientists in this period. The essence of top-down programming was the concept of abstraction: by proceeding step by step from general design goals to the specific implementation details, a systems architect could individually manage the otherwise-unmanageable complexity of a large software development project. The use of top-down programming techniques enabled the authoritarian chief programmer to maintain the architectural integrity that Brooks believed was so central to the design of useful and beautiful software programs. The heyday of the structured programming movement was coincident with the publication of *The Mythical Man-Month*, and the attractiveness of the surgical team approach to management was reinforced by, and helped to reinforce, the popularity of structured programming as a development technology.

In addition to borrowing heavily from the established techniques and technologies of structured programming, the CPT model also helped to define technological innovations of its own. The development support library (DSL) was a system of documents and procedures that provided for the "isolation and delegation" of secretarial, clerical, and machine operations.[43] In earlier accounts the DSL is referred to as the programming production library. Basically, the DSL was a set of technologies (including coding sheets, project notebooks, and computer control cards) that facilitated communications within the development team. It was envisioned as a means of further centralizing control in the hands of the chief programmer. "The DSL permits a chief programmer to exercise a wider span of control over the programming, resulting in fewer programmers doing the same job. This reduces communications requirements and allows still more control in the programming. With structured programming, this span of detailed control over code can be greatly expanded beyond present practice; the DSL plays a crucial role in this expansion."[44]

By providing a core set of public programs and documents that were highly visible to all members of the surgical team, the DSL was supposed to discourage the "traditional ad hoc mystique" associated with conventional craft-oriented programming.[45] The chief programmer could read, understand, and validate all of the work done by their subordinates. The technology of the DSL was clearly intended to reinforce a conventional management agenda: the transfer of control over the work practices of programmers into the hands of the managerial superprogrammer. In language remarkably reminiscent of the "head versus hand" dialectic emphasized by Karl Marx and his disciples, one proponent of the CPT approach described the DSL as having been "designed to separate the clerical and intellectual tasks of programming."[46]

Although the CPT received much attention in the industry literature, it does not seem to have been widely or successfully implemented.[47] The original concept had been popularized by Baker in a series of articles documenting the successful implementation of the approach by Mills. Mills had been the chief programmer in a team that developed a computerized information bank application for the *New York Times*. He claimed to accomplished in twenty-two months what a traditionally, hierarchically managed group would have required at least several more years of calendar time to develop. Baker's favorable reports on the *New York Times* project, which involved eighty-three thousand lines of code and eleven man-years of effort, convinced many computer professionals of the scalability of the CPT approach. The project was portrayed as having high productivity and low error rates, although questions later arose about the accuracy of Baker's assessment; Mills's system eventually proved unsatisfactory and was replaced with a less ambitious system.[48] For the time being, however, the *New York Times* system was considered to be proof positive of the efficiency of the CPT approach.

Several objections to the CPT approach were raised in the contemporary industry literature, though. The first is that it was difficult to find individuals with enough talent and energy to fulfill all of the functions required of the chief programmer.[49] The few who did exist were expensive, and were not interested in working on small computers and mundane applications. A second problem was a perceived overdependence on key individuals implied in the CPT approach: "What happens if [our super-programmer] snaps up a more lucrative offer elsewhere? He'll likely take our back-up programmer with him, leaving us high-and-dry."[50] A number of observers suggested that the surgical team model led to excessive specialization.[51] The computer scientist C.A.R. Hoare derided the small-team approach as a retreat "to the age of the master craftsman—more fashionably known as a chief programmer."[52] There were widespread doubts about the ability of the small-team approach to scale up to the needs of large development efforts.

The most revealing criticisms of the CPT system, however, had to do with the ways in which the presence of an elite administrator/programmer disrupted existing patterns of managerial authority: "The CPT perpetuates the prima donna image of the programmer. Instead of bringing the programmer into the organization's fold, it isolates and alienates him by encouraging the programmer to strive for a superhero image."[53] The CPT allowed for little participation by nontechnical administrators. A textbook, *Managing Software Development and Maintenance*, from 1981 corrected this perceived overdependence on technical personnel by proposing a revised chief programmer team (RCPT) in which "the project leader is viewed as a leader rather than a 'super-programmer.'" Whereas the chief programmer was clearly a technical specialist, the project leader was "an expert conceptualizer, designer, and project manager"—but not necessarily a superprogrammer. Because the project leader possessed both project management and technical skills, they were "able to direct, oversee, and review all technical functions."[54]

The RCPT approach was clearly intended to address a concern faced by many traditionally trained department-level managers—namely, that top executives had "abdicated their responsibility and let the 'computer boys' take over."[55] As was described in chapter 7, it was this fear of the loss of control over valuable occupational territory that most determined contemporary reactions to proposed managerial solutions to the software crisis.

Computer Programming as a Human Activity

The hierarchical model unapologetically attempted to make programmers' work as routine and mechanical as possible; the CPT provided a real creative outlet for a single superprogrammer only. For moderately skilled programmers attempting to establish for themselves a legitimate professional identity that would provide them with autonomy and status, both models were equally uninviting. What was needed was an alternative organizational model that could simultaneously support two seemingly contradictory agendas: increased managerial control over the "irrational" programming process, and ongoing support for the independent professional authority of programmers.

In 1969, the programmer and computing consultant Weinberg published *The Psychology of Computer Programming*. The book claimed to present the first detailed empirical study of computer programming as a complex human activity, and indeed, although Weinberg was neither a psychologist nor an ethnographer, his observations appear to be remarkably accurate and insightful. At the very least his work was well received by practitioners, whose personal experiences seem to have resonated with the anecdotes provided by Weinberg. *The Psychology of Computer Programming* has been widely cited as an accurate description of what really went on in actual programming projects.

Weinberg's book did more than simply portray existing attitudes and practices, though. It also proposed a new method for organizing and managing teams of software developers. The problem with existing hierarchical methods of software production, according to Weinberg, was that they encouraged programmers to become "detached" from the social environment—and overly possessive of their software. When programmers invest so much of themselves in their programs, Weinberg suggested, they lose the ability to evaluate their creations objectively. The immediate result was bad software—and ultimately a software crisis. "Programmers, if left to their own devices, will ignore the most glaring errors in their output—errors that anyone else can see in an instant." The solution to the crisis provoked by "property-oriented" programming, argued Weinberg, was the adoption of the "egoless programming team," in which every programmer is equal, and where all of the code is "attached" to the team rather than to the individual.[56] By opening up the programming process to self-reflection and criticism, the egoless (or adaptive) programming model would increase efficiency, eliminate errors, and enhance communication—all without inhibiting the creative abilities of programmers.

Although egoless programming represented a relatively radical departure from traditional software development methodologies, it was predicated on fairly conventional notions about the nature of programming ability. For Weinberg, there was little doubt that the majority of people in programming were detached personality types who preferred to be left to themselves. This tendency toward detachment was reinforced "both by personal choice and because hiring policies for programmers are often directed toward finding such people."[57] This detachment from people often led programmers to become excessively attached to their products. The "abominable practice" of attaching their names to their software (as in Jules' Own Version of the International Algebraic Language, better known as the JOVIAL programming language) offered evidence of the programmer's inability to disassociate themselves from their creations. The JOVIAL programming language was created for the U.S. Air Force in the late 1950s by the SDC. As it was to be a variant of the International Algebraic Language (eventually renamed ALGOL), it was suggested that it be called OVIAL (Our Own Version of the International Algebraic Language), but since OVIAL apparently had "a connotation relative to the birth process that did not seem acceptable to some people," the name was soon changed to JOVIAL. It was later decided that the J in JOVIAL would stand for Jules Schwartz, one of the programmers involved in the project. Hence, Jules' Own Version of the International Algebraic Language. This proprietary sense of ownership on the part of the creator was not necessarily an unusual or even undesirable tendency; after all, artists "owned" paintings, authors "owned books," and architects "owned" buildings. In many cases these attributions led to the admiration and emulation of good workers by lesser ones. What was different about computer programs, however, was that they were owned exclusively by their creators. Good programs, unlike good literature, were never read by anyone other than the author. Thus, according to Weinberg, "the admiration of individual programmers cannot lead to an emulation of their work, but only to an affectation of their mannerisms."[58] Junior programmers were unable to benefit from the wisdom and experience of their superiors. The only thing available to emulate was their mannerisms. The result was the perpetuation of bad work habits and personal eccentricities—"the same phenomenon we see in 'art colonies,' where everyone knows how to look like an artist, but few, if any, know how to paint like one."[59]

Weinberg believed that the use of small, unstructured programming teams and regular code reviews would alleviate the problem of programmer attachment. Each of the programmers in the group would be responsible for reading and reviewing all of the application code. Errors that were identified during the process were simply "facts to be exposed to investigation" with an eye toward future improvement, rather than personal attacks on an individual programmer.[60] By restructuring the social environment of the workplace and thereby restructuring the value system of the programmers, the ideal of egoless programming would be achieved. The result would be an academic style, peer-review system that would encourage high standards, open communication, and ongoing professional development. Junior programmers would be exposed to good examples of programming practice, and more senior developers could exchange subtle tricks and techniques. A piece of completed code would not be considered the product of an individual team member but rather of the team as a whole. The openness of this process would also encourage the development of proper documentation.

There were a number of other salient features of the egoless (or adaptive) programming team that differed from conventional team-oriented approaches. The most unusual and significant was that all major design and implementation decisions were to be determined by consensus instead of decree. There were no assigned team leaders, at least not in the conventional sense. Leadership shifted between team members based on the needs of the moment and the strength of the individual team members (hence the term adaptive). For example, if a particular phase of the project involved a lot of debugging, one of the team members especially skilled at debugging might assume the temporary role of team leader during that period. Even then, all of the important decisions would be made democratically. Work was assigned based on the strengths—and preferences—of the individual team members.

The democratic approach to software project management, in Weinberg's view, offered a number of advantages. It encouraged communication and flexibility. Schedule and design changes could be more readily accommodated, and resources could be allocated efficiently. Second, the lack of a formal hierarchy made the adaptive team significantly more robust than more structured alternatives. For instance, the adaptive team could readily adjust to the addition or removal of members.

The success of the project would no longer hinge on the presence of any one particular individual. In an era in which the performance of programmers was believed to vary dramatically from programmer to programmer, and when turnover in the software industry averaged upward of 25 percent annually, this was an appealing benefit. Last but not least, the social dynamics of the democratically managed adaptive team appeared to correspond well with the actual experiences and expectations of the average working programmer.[61] Weinberg provided a great deal of anecdotal evidence suggesting that programmers worked best in environments in which they participated in all aspects of project development, from design to implementation to testing. By eliminating the things that caused programmers to become dissatisfied, turnover could be reduced significantly. The adaptive team approach to programming, argued Weinberg, was not only cost-effective and efficient; it kept the programmers happy. And of course, happy programmers were productive programmers.

Like the CPT and the hierarchical system of management, egoless programming constituted a solution to a specific conception of the burgeoning software crisis. The advocates of the adaptive team approach shared with many of their contemporaries certain basic assumptions about the nature of programming as a skill and activity: that programming was an essentially creative undertaking; that individual programmers varied enormously in terms of style and productivity; and that current programming practices resembled craft more than they did science. They also believed that despite these exceptional characteristics, software development was an activity that could, to a certain extent, be managed and controlled. What was unusual about the adaptive team solution was the degree to which it offered computer programmers a legitimate career path and an attractive professional identity.

In the hierarchical system of management, programmers were generally regarded as technicians rather than professionals. The few programmers who rose through the hierarchy did so by abandoning their technical interests in favor of managerial careers. The CPT offered status and authority only to a small corps of elite superprogrammers. All but the most talented individuals served as much less privileged support personnel. As will be seen, many programmers were extremely concerned with issues of professional development, both as they related to themselves as individuals and to their larger disciplinary community. The journal articles, job advertisements, and letters to the editor from this period show that many programmers were worried about becoming dead-ended in purely technical positions. Hierarchical organizations and CPTs did not offer them an attractive model of professionalization.

The adaptive team approach, in comparison, offered promising career opportunities to a wide range of software workers. The goal of the adaptive team was to foster a family atmosphere in which every member's contributions were important. Team members were anything but interchangeable units. Programmers could cultivate their technical skills and advance their careers without feeling pressure to transfer into administration. As one knowledgeable observer suggested, in the adaptive team approach "a good programmer does not get further and further away from programmers, as occurs in a hierarchical structure when he moves up the management ladder. Instead, he stays with programming and gravitates toward what he does best."[62]

Judging from the response it received in the industry literature, *The Psychology of Computer Programming* appealed to a broad popular audience.[63] Weinberg's anecdotes about the real-life work habits of programmers rang true to many practitioners. His descriptions of the mischievous pranks that programmers played on their managers, for example, or the social significance of a strategically located Coca-Cola dispenser, captured for many of his readers the essential character of the programming profession. The book has remained in continuous publication since 1969, and was widely celebrated as one of the few classic texts in the programming literature.[64] Weinberg presented a romantic portrait of software development that emphasized the quiet professionalism of skilled, dedicated programmer-craftspeople. Of the many models for software engineering that were proposed in the late 1960s and early 1970s, the egoless programmer was by far the most attractive to the average practitioner.

Yet the popularity of egoless programming extended beyond the community of practitioners. Weinberg's theories about the efficiency of small family work groups and bottom-up, consensus decision making resonated with certain popular contemporary management theories. In 1971, Antony Jay's *Corporation Man* provided an ethological analysis of "tribal behavior" in modern corporations that reinforced Weinberg's conclusion that six- to ten-member teams were a "natural" organizational unit.[65] Douglas McGregor's *The Human Side of Enterprise* discriminated between the Theory X approach to management, which assumed that because of their innate distaste for regimented labor, most employees must be controlled and threatened before they would work hard enough, and the Theory Y belief that the expenditure of physical and mental effort in work is as natural as play or rest, and that the average person learns, under proper conditions, not only to accept but to seek responsibility.[66] For the supporters of Theory Y management, Weinberg's adaptive team represented an exemplary model of the participative problem-solving approach.[67]

The concept of egoless programming was rarely adopted in toto, though. In later descriptions of the chief programming team, Baker and Mills claimed that their system represented a form of egoless programming, in the sense that the code produced by the chief programmer was open for inspection by other members of the surgical team. By this point, egoless programming was interpreted by many managers in terms very favorable to management: it meant that programmers should not be defensive about code reviews, task assignments, and other management-imposed structures. The adaptive team terminology in this case seems to have been adopted for public relations purposes only. The whole point of the chief programming team was to consolidate all aspects of design and implementation into the hands of a single superprogrammer. It would have been impossible to maintain the level of architectural integrity desired by Brooks if the chief programmer were not heavily invested in their own individual conceptual structure.

Indeed, by the mid-1970s the language of egoless programming appears to have been almost entirely transformed and co-opted by conventional managers. These managers picked up on the idea that requiring programmers to develop open, nonpropriety code allowed for increased administrative oversight. To them, egoless programming meant that "all programmers were to adhere to rules that would make their products understandable to others and make the individual programmer replaceable."[68] Weinberg's original intention that egoless programming would enable programmers to develop as autonomous professionals appears to have gone entirely by the wayside. One management consultant reminded his audience that managers should "stress the non-punitive nature of the new approaches. Egoless programming is designed to help the programmer, not point out his faults."[69] The not-so-subtle subtext of this reminder is that by this period, egoless programming had acquired a reputation for being worker-hostile management jargon.

Although *The Psychology of Computer Programming* received a great deal of popular attention for its descriptive verisimilitude, it was less successful in its prescriptive capacity. Weinberg's recommendations do not appear to have been taken seriously by many academic or industry leaders. It may be that his adaptive teams did not scale well to large development efforts, and were used in nothing but small local projects. They may have proven inefficient or difficult to implement, although there is evidence that the use of informal, unstructured programming teams was standard practice in the industry. At least one author rejected the adaptive team approach because it failed to provide adequate mechanisms for formal managerial control.[70] It seems likely that this last objection was what ultimately proved fatal to Weinberg's proposal. The adaptive team approach reinforced the notion that programmers were independent professionals. It shifted organizational control and authority away from managers. It ceded valuable occupational territory to a group whose institutional power base had not yet been firmly established. Weinberg's adaptive teams were unappealing to everyone but programmers, and programmers did not have the leverage to push through such an unpopular agenda.

From Exhilaration to Disillusionment

The 1968 NATO Conference on Software Engineering was, according to contemporary accounts, an exhilarating experience for many participants. The public acknowledgment of a perceived software crisis was a cathartic moment for the industry. As one prominent computer scientist described it, "The general admission of the software failure in this group of responsible people is the most refreshing experience that I have had in a number of years, because the admission of shortcomings is the primary condition for improvement."[71] Despite the general recognition of impending crisis, the spirit of the conference was "positive, even liberatory."[72] Attendees rallied behind the organizers' call for "a switch from home-made software to manufactured software, from tinkering to engineering."[73] Software engineering emerged as the dominant rhetorical paradigm for discussing the future of software development. By adopting the "types of theoretical foundations and practical disciplines that are traditional in the established branches of engineering," computer programming could be successfully transformed from a black art into an industrial discipline. Software workers from a wide variety of disciplines and backgrounds adopted the rhetoric of software engineering as a shared discourse within which to discuss their mutual professional aspirations.

In order to capitalize on the enthusiasm generated in the wake of the Garmisch meeting, the NATO Science Committee quickly organized a second conference to be held the following year in Rome. The Rome conference in 1969 was intended to have an explicitly practical focus: the goal was to develop specific techniques of software engineering. As with the Garmisch meeting, a deliberate and successful attempt was made to attract a wide range of participants. The resulting conference, however, bore little resemblance to its predecessor. Whereas the Garmisch participants had coalesced around a shared sense of urgency, the Rome conference was characterized by conflict. According to the same observer who had referred glowingly to the Garmisch conference as a "most refreshing experience," the discussions at the Rome meeting were "sterile," the various groups of attendees "never clicked," and "most participants" left feeling "an enormous sense of disillusionment."[74] A prolonged debate about the establishment of an international software engineering institute proved so acrimonious and divisive that it was omitted from the conference proceedings: "All I remember is that it ended up being a lot of time wasted, and no argument ever turned up to make something happen—which is probably just as well."[75]

Why was the Rome conference considered to be such a disappointment relative to Garmisch? Many of the same participants had attended both meetings; there had been no significant changes in terms of demographic makeup or organizational structure. Neither were there any major new issues or technologies introduced or discussed. Many of the Rome presentations covered material that had previously been addressed, albeit at a less detailed and technical level, at Garmisch. And yet while the Garmisch conference is widely considered to have marked a pivotal moment in the history of software development—"a major cultural shift in the perception of programming"—the Rome one seems to have been deliberately forgotten.[76]

One obvious difference between the two events is that the earlier conference had encouraged participants to focus their attention on a commonly perceived but vaguely defined emergency, while the latter forced them to deal with specific controversial issues. Software engineering had emerged as a compelling solution to the software crisis in part because it was flexible enough to appeal to a wide variety of computing practitioners. The ambiguity of concepts such as professionalism, engineering discipline, and efficiency allowed competing interests to participate in a shared discourse that nevertheless enabled them to pursue vastly different personal and professional agendas. Industry managers adopted a definition of professionalism that provided for educational and certification standards, a tightly disciplined workforce, and increased corporate loyalty. Computer manufacturers looked to engineering discipline as a means of countering charges of incompetence and cost inefficiency. Academic computer scientists preferred a highly formalized approach to software engineering that was both intellectually respectable and theoretically rigorous. Working programmers tended to concentrate on the more personal aspects of professional accomplishment, including autonomy, status, and career longevity. The software engineering model seemed to offer something for everyone: standards, quality, academic respectability, status, and autonomy. As Michael Mahoney has suggested, software engineering "was not coined to characterize an ongoing activity but rather to express a desire for one. By 1967, when the computer industry was less than twenty years old, people felt the need for software engineering, even if they were not sure what it was."[77]

Yet the rhetorical flexibility that had served the consensus-seeking Garmisch participants proved unwieldy when it came to establishing specific standards and practices. The Rome conference illuminated in sharp relief the vast differences that existed between competing visions for the software engineering discipline. Unlike the conflict between workers and managers described in the previous chapter, these divisions were largely internal to the programming community. The primary split was between academic computer scientists and commercial software developers. The industry programmers resented being invited to Rome "like a lot of monkeys to be looked at by theoreticians"; the theoreticians complained of feeling isolated, of "not being allowed to say anything."[78] As the editors of the conference proceedings have pointed out, the "lack of communication between different sections of the participants" became the "dominant feature" of the meeting.[79] "The seriousness of this communications gap," and the realization that it "was but a reflection of the situation in the real world," caused the gap itself to become a major topic of discussion.[80] It was to remain an issue of central concern to the programming community for the next several decades.

Indeed, in the years after 1968 the rhetoric of the software crisis became even more heated. In 1987 the editors of *Computerworld* complained that "the average software project is often one year behind plan and 100% over budget."[81] In 1989 the House Committee on Science, Space, and Technology released a report highly critical of the "shoot-from-the-hip" practices of the software industry. Among other things, the report called for a professional certification program for programmers. The thirty-three-page report, "Bugs in the Program: Problems in Federal Government Computer Software Development and Regulation," was written by staff members James H. Paul and Gregory C. Simon of the Subcommittee on Investigations and Oversight of the House Committee on Science, Space, and Technology.[82] Later that same year the Pentagon launched a broad campaign to "lick its software problems" that included funds for a Software Engineering Institute and the widespread adoption of the ADA programming language. ADA was touted by Department of Defense officials as "a means of replacing the idiosyncratic 'artistic' ethos that has long governed software writing with a more efficient, cost-effective engineering mind-set."[83] The list of critical reports, denunciations of current practices, and proposed silver-bullet solutions goes on and on. In his 1996 summary of the legacy the first NATO Conference, W. Wayt Gibbs suggested that "a quarter of a century later software engineering remains a term of aspiration," rather than a real accomplishment: "The vast majority of computer code is still handcrafted from raw programming languages by artisans using techniques they neither measure nor are able to repeat consistently."[84]

9

Conclusions: Visible Technicians

Perhaps you've noticed that it's getting more and more difficult to locate and then hire the best people. This isn't an illusion; it's real, it's significant, and it's only going to get worse. It is, in fact, the heart of the real software crisis: There is more software to be developed than there are capable developers to do it. Demand will continue to outstrip supply for the foreseeable future. Hence, more and more software will be behind schedule, over budget, underpowered, and of poor quality—and there's nothing we can do about it.

—Bruce Webster, "The Real Software Crisis," 1988

Software's Chronic Crisis

In the closing minutes of the twentieth century, computer programmers around the world sat huddled around their computer screens, awaiting with bated breath the flip of a single digital bit. At stake was continued functioning of the millions of computerized systems that they and their fellow programmers had developed over the course of the previous half-century, many of them considered vitally important to the continued functioning of crucial infrastructure, both military and civilian. At midnight on December 31, 1999, it was widely believed, at least some of these systems would crash as a result of the inability of their internal clocks to distinguish properly between the years 2000 and 1900. The possible consequences of this seemingly trivial programming error included banks failing, airplanes falling out of the sky, possibly even an unintended nuclear war.[1] "The Y2K problem is the electronic equivalent of the El Niño," the United States Deputy Secretary of Defense John Hamre had warned a year earlier: "This is going to have implications in the world . . . that we can't even comprehend."[2] Over the course of the months leading up to the year 2000, computer programmers in the United States alone had invested more than $300 billion in last-minute attempts to remediate the possible consequences of the so-called Y2K

Bug; even still, the final minutes prior to midnight were tense with uncertainty.

Like most crises, the salience of the Y2K problem diminished almost immediately upon its failure to materialize. To the average citizen, the fuss that the computer people made about Y2K was just one of several apocalyptic scenarios that swirled around the turn of the millennium, all of which seem, in retrospect, self-evidently unfounded. It was difficult to remember, even just a few years later, how much time, energy, and effort were expended in addressing this latest iteration of the software crisis. For experienced observers of the computer industry, however, the shortcomings of contemporary software development practices revealed by Y2K were both very real and depressingly familiar. Once the proximate technical cause of the problem had been clearly identified (the shortsighted decision, intentional or otherwise, to code calendar year data with two digits instead of four; i.e., "72" rather than "1972"), the discussion quickly turned to the deeper, more endemic problems associated with software development: haphazard techniques, a lack of professionalism, and insufficient managerial controls.

In many respects, the Y2K problem was just another in long series of software crises which, as we have seen, have plagued the computer industry since its very inception. But Y2K in particular highlighted some of the lesser-known facets of the seemingly perpetual software crisis, the most interesting and surprising of which was the problem of software maintenance.

The problem of maintenance is a ubiquitous but neglected element of the history of technology. All complex technological systems eventually break down and require repair (some more than others); as David Edgerton has suggested, maintenance is probably the central activity of most technological societies.[3] But maintenance is also low-status, difficult, and risky. Engineers and inventors do not like, and generally do not perform maintenance, and therefore historians of technology have largely ignored it.

The problem of maintenance is particularly challenging for both practitioners and historians of computing. In theory, software should never need maintenance because software does not break down or wear out, at least in the conventional sense. Once a software-based system is working, it will work forever (or at least until the underlying hardware breaks down—but that is generally considered someone else's problem). Occasionally a stray cosmic ray might flip an unexpected bit in a software system and cause an error, but generally speaking software can never be broken.

Except that software does break—all the time, at great expense and inconvenience to its users. In fact, from the early 1960s on, software maintenance has represented between 50% and 70% of all total expenditures on software.[4] There is a strong argument to be made that the software crisis of the late 1960s was essentially a maintenance problem: what became increasingly expensive about software in this period was not so much development as ongoing maintenance.[5] In any case, from the 1960s to the present, it has continued to absorb between one half and two thirds of all software-related resources.[6]

But if software is a technology that can never be broken, what does it mean for software to stop working? The most obvious answer is that software can contain errors in implementation. Maurice Wilkes, one of the first people to program a modern, stored-program computer, famously recalled the moment in June 1949 when he suddenly realized that "a good part of the remainder of my life was going to be spent in finding errors in my own programs."[7] Wilkes was describing the process of debugging (the elimination of flaws in the original design or implementation, rather than the repair of accumulated errors), but the larger implication for the computing community is obvious: the delivery of a working application was only the beginning of the life-cycle of a software application. A programmer could (and many did) spend the majority of their career chasing down the bugs that gradually revealed themselves in the operation of a complex software-based system. In this respect, runs the well-worn joke, programming a computer is a little bit like having sex: "One mistake and you have to support it for the rest of your life."

But thinking about maintenance solely in terms of fixing bugs is misleading. Fixing such bugs in implementation accounts for only a minority of software maintenance. One exhaustive study from the early 1980s estimated such emergency fixes occupied at most one fifth of all software maintenance workers.[8] Even when the ongoing process of debugging software is excluded, maintenance still accounts for more than half of the overall cost of software development.

The majority of software maintenance involves what are euphemistically referred to in the literature as "enhancements." These enhancements sometimes involve strictly technical measures—such as implementing performance optimizations—but more commonly are what Richard Canning, one of the computer industry's most influential industry analysts, described as "responses to changes in the business environment."[9] This wonderfully flexible phrase included the introduction of new functionality, as dictated by market, organizational, or legislative developments and changes in the larger technological or organizational system in which the software is inextricably bound. Software maintenance also incorporated such apparently nontechnical tasks as "understanding and documenting existing systems; extending existing functions; adding new functions; finding and correcting bugs; answering questions for users and operations staff; training new systems staff; rewriting, restructuring, converting, and purging software; managing the software of an operational system; and many other activities that go into running a successful software system."[10] By the early 1980s, the industry and technical literature had settled on a shared taxonomy for talking about software maintenance: There was corrective maintenance (bug fixes), perfective maintenance (performance improvements), and adaptive maintenance (adaptations to the larger environment). Adaptive maintenance so dominated real-world maintenance that many observers pushed for an entirely new nomenclature; software maintenance was a misnomer, they argued: the process of adapting software to change would better be described as "software support," "software evolution," or "continuation engineering."[11]

The concept of adaptive maintenance captures neatly what has been referred to throughout this history as the "heterogeneous" nature of software. Despite their seemingly intangible nature, software applications are always inextricably linked to a network of social and technological systems. This means that although the material costs associated with building software are low (in comparison with traditional, physical systems), the degree to which software is embedded in larger, heterogeneous systems makes starting from scratch almost impossible. Consider Frederick Brooks's widely cited claim that "the programmer, like the poet, works only slightly removed from pure-thought stuff. He builds his castles in the air, from air, creating by exertion of the imagination."[12] To a certain degree, this is true—at least when the programmer is working on constructing a new system. But when charged with maintaining a "legacy" system, the programmer is working not with a blank slate but a palimpsest. The ease with which computer code can be written, modified, and deleted belies the durability of the underlying artifact. Because software is a tangible record, not only of the intentions of the original designer but of the social, technological, and organization context in which it was developed, it cannot be easily modified. "We [programmers] never have a clean slate," argued Barjne Stroudstroup, the creator of the widely used C++ programming language, "Whatever new we do must make it possible for people to make a transition from old tools and ideas to new."[13] In this sense, software is less like a poem and more like a contract, a constitution, or a covenant. Software is history, organization, and social relationships made tangible.

One of the remarkable implications of all of this surprising durability of software is that the software industry, which many consider to be one of the fastest-moving and most innovative industries in the world, is perhaps the industry most constrained by its own history. As one observer recently noted, today there are still more than 240 million lines of computer code written in the programming language COBOL, which was first introduced in 1959—and which was derided, even at its origins, as being backward looking and technically inferior. And yet 90% of the world's financial transactions are processed by applications written in COBOL, as is 75% of all business data processing. Five out of eight large corporations rely on COBOL code, many of them substantially. 70% of Merrill Lynch applications are coded in COBOL. The total value of active COBOL applications—many of them developed prior to the 1980s—is as high as $2 trillion.[14] All of this COBOL code needs to actively maintained, modified, and expanded. The vast majority of the code that had to be remediated prior to Y2K was written in COBOL.

That fact that so much of the $300 billion that was spent on Y2K involved the maintenance of existing code highlighted both the continued significance of, and dissatisfaction with, the work of computer programmers. Like all forms of maintenance, software maintenance is difficult, unpopular, and largely unrewarding. The maintenance requires programmers to work on live systems, where mistakes and failures have real and immediate consequences. Because maintenance does not generally involve design, it is considered boring and low-status. And because of the unique nature of software—its intangibility—software systems are often coded before they are completely specified. Many programmers find it easier to "just start coding" than to develop design documents. Most programs are poorly documented (if at all), and so most maintenance works involves intensive on-the-job learning. If ever a type of programming requires real skill, experience, and intelligence, it is software maintenance.

The trouble and expense associated with rewriting so much of the software that had been developed over the past several decades also raised uncomfortable questions about why the software had not been written properly in the first place. For some observers, at least, the Y2K fiasco was yet another indication that computer programmers were lazy and unprofessional. In the wake of Y2K, renewed criticisms were raised against the "artistic ethos" of many programmers, their continued neglect of the rigorous practices of software engineering, and their general failure to serve as solid corporate citizens.[15] Once again, programmers were castigated as outsiders, as "cowboys" and "hackers"; once again, a looming shortage of "good" and "experienced" programmers was predicted.

By the turn of the twenty-first century, of course, such indictments of the computer specialists had become almost conventional. By this point the rhetoric of crisis had become so commonplace in the computer industry literature that for many young programmers the software crisis was "less a turning point than a way of life."[16]

This comes back to some of the central questions of this book: How can we explain the continued existence of a seemingly perpetual crisis in what is generally considered to be one of the most successful and profitable industries of all time? How can we understand the role of computer specialists—in many respects the paradigmatic "knowledge workers" of post-industrial society—within this troubled framework of crisis, conflict, and contested identity? If, as Shoshona Zuboff has suggested, computer-based technologies are not simply neutral artifacts, but rather "embody essential characteristics that are bound to alter the nature of work within factories and offices, and among workers, professionals, and managers," then what are the "essential characteristics" of software and software development that shape our understanding of work, identity, and power in the information technology industry (and the many industries that rely on information technology)?[17] How can we understand the social and occupational history of the computer programmer in terms of a larger debate about the role of information technology in organizational transformation? How can we understand the social and occupational history of the computer programmer in terms of a larger debate about the role of information technology in organizational transformation?

Drawing Boundaries/Construction Disciplines

In his study of boundary work in Victorian science, sociologist Thomas Gieryn suggests that the process of disciplinary demarcation can be best understood through the study of rhetorical practice. Gieryn used the term boundary work to describe the ideological style used by nineteenth-century scientists in their attempts to create a public image favorable to science by contrasting it favorably to nonscientific intellectual or technical activities. Depending on what they thought would be most convincing to the audience that they were addressing, these scientists would represent their activities alternatively as being empirical or theoretical, pure or applied. In other word, scientists used rhetoric that was intrinsically flexible, that allowed them to use different, and sometimes even contradictory, definitions of what science was in an attempt to justify their claims to authority or resources.

This process of boundary work serves a number of practical purposes for practitioners: the expansion of intellectual authority and career opportunities; the denial of resources to deviants and nonprofessionals; and the protection of autonomy from external influences. Boundary work, according to Gieryn, functions as a "sociological parallel to the familiar literary device of a 'foil.' Just as readers come to know Holmes better through contrasts to his foil Watson, so does the public better learn about science through contrasts to non-science."[18]

The concept of boundary work is an indispensable tool for the historian of computing. Computer science as an academic discipline and computer programming as an occupation have struggled with various degrees of success to establish institutional boundaries. Programmers have struggled to distinguish themselves from mere technical craftspeople, on the one hand, and scientists and engineers, on the other. In doing so, they alternatively refer to the practice of programming as either an art or a science, depending on whom is being addressed and for what purpose. In the language of sociology, the "vocabularies" of the literary arts and scientific engineering are the "cultural repertoires" that programmers use in the construction of "ideological self-descriptions."[19]

The process of doing boundary work allowed programmers to mobilize the internal inconsistencies of their discipline as ideological resources with which to distinguish themselves from both craftspeople and scientists. When it helped them accomplish their particular individual or professional agenda, they talked about programming in artistic or artisanal terms; at other times they portrayed it as a scientific or engineering discipline. Although not every member of the computing community valued equally the craft tradition and artistic sensibilities of the "black art" of programming, enough did to make personal expressions of creativity an important aspect of the programming tradition. This concern for aesthetics functioned as a shared community value, unifying the otherwise-disparate traditions of vocational programming and academic computer science. As the Soviet computer scientist Andrei Ershov suggested in a 1972 address to the Joint Computer Conference of the ACM, "an understanding, a feeling for the aesthetic of programming, is needed, and not only as a driving force for the programmer: it is necessary for those who manage programmers, and especially for those who educate and train them." This artistic sensibility was not simply essential for cultivating creativity, Ershov argued, but also allowed computer experts to avoid being converted "what is simply a highly paid subgroup of the working class." "If such a tendency is to be resisted," Ershov suggested, "a programmer must find some system of inner values in his specialty, values which can help him both to assimilate industrial methods and, when necessary, to transcend them."[20]

At other points, of course, programmers were perfectly willing to lay claim to the epistemological status of a fundamental science. The point is that art and science were both rhetorical resources to be used in pursuit of professional development and institution-building strategies. Like Gieryn's Victorian scientists, programmers are able to endow their discipline with "just those characteristics needed to achieve professional and institutional goals, and to change those attributed characteristics as circumstances warrant."[21] Many of the apparent conflicts within programming should be reevaluated within the context of discipline formation and boundary work.

Despite the many differences in professional goals and theoretical orientation that existed between the vocational programmers and the academic computer scientists, the strength of their shared aesthetic values and craft traditions provided a basis for community solidarity. Even at the height of the software crisis, the average computer scientist had more in common with the vocational programmer than they did with the military and industrial managers. The software engineering movement failed to provide adequate incentives to either of these groups, and therefore failed to capture the full support of the majority of members of the programming community.

The goal of boundary work is the establishment of professional identity, and the sociology of professions literature provides another useful resource for interpreting the history of programming. During the 1950s and 1960s, many white-collar occupations attempted to professionalize, and computer programmers were no exception.[22] They established professional societies, codes of ethics, and certification and curriculum standards.[23] Belonging to a profession provided an individual with a "monopoly of competence," the control over a valuable skill that was readily transferable from organization to organization.[24] Professionalism provided a means of excluding undesirables and competitors; it assured basic standards of quality and reliability; it provided a certain degree of protection from the fluctuations of the labor market; and it was seen by many workers as a means of advancement into the middle class.[25] Programmers in particular saw professionalism as a means of distinguishing themselves from "coders" or other "mere technicians." Corporate managers generally embraced the concept of professionalism. It appeared to provide a familiar solution to the increasingly complex problems of programmer management: "The concept of professionalism," argued one personnel research journal from the early 1970s, "affords a business-like answer to the existing and future computer skills market."[26] The rhetoric of professionalism was ideologically neutral, and appealed to a wide variety of individuals and interest groups. Professionalization was one of several widely adopted strategies for dealing with the software crisis.

But did programmers ever truly professionalize? The historical evidence is ambiguous.[27] On one hand, as the historian William Aspray has suggested, it is remarkable how rapidly computing acquired the trappings of a profession: research laboratories and institutes, professional conferences, professional societies, and technical journals.[28] On the other hand, as we have seen, the existence of professional institutions did not necessarily translate readily into widely recognized professional status. Indeed, one of the most traditional interpretations of computer programmer has been as a failed profession.

The most prominent advocates of the "failed profession" interpretation are labor historians Philip Kraft and Joan Greenbaum. Building on the work of Harry Braverman and David Noble, Kraft and Greenbaum situate the history of programming in one of the grand conceptual structures of labor history: the ongoing struggle between labor and the forces of capital. In *Labor and Monopoly Capital: The Degradation of Work in the Twentieth Century*, Braverman argued that the basic social function of engineers and managers was to oversee the fragmentation, routinization, and mechanization of labor. Cloaked in the language of progress and efficiency, the process of routinization was characterized primarily as a means of disciplining and controlling a recalcitrant workforce. The ultimate result was the deskilling and degradation of the worker. In his 1977 book *Programmers and Managers: The Routinization of Computer Programming in the United States*, Kraft described a similar process at work in the computer industry. "Programmers, systems analysts, and other software workers are experiencing efforts to break down, simplify, routinize, and standardize their own work so that it, too, can be done by machines rather than people." The use of high-level programming technologies and structured development methodologies represented "elaborate efforts" to "develop ways of gradually eliminating programmers, or at least reduce their average skill levels, required training, [and] experience." The once-proud computer programmer, he contended, has been relegated largely to subsidiary and subordinate roles in the production process. "While a few of them sit at the side of managers, counseling and providing expert's advice, most simply carry out what someone else has assigned them."[29]

Kraft suggested that managers have generally been successful in imposing structures on programmers that have eliminated their creativity and autonomy. His analysis was remarkably comprehensive, covering such issues as training and education, structured programming techniques ("the software manager's answer to the conveyor belt"), the social organization of the workplace (aimed at reinforcing the fragmentation between "head" planning and "hand" labor), and careers, pay, and professionalism (encouraged by managers as a means of discouraging unions). Greenbaum followed Kraft's conclusions and methodology closely in her book *In the Name of Efficiency: Management Theory and Shopfloor Practice in Data-Processing Work* in 1979. More recently, she has defended their application of the Braverman deskilling hypothesis: "If we strip away the spin words used today like 'knowledge' worker, 'flexible' work, and 'high tech' work, and if we insert the word 'information system' for 'machinery,' we are still talking about management attempts to control and coordinate labor processes."[30]

There is validity to both interpretations of the changing attitude of managers toward programmers that occurred in the late 1960s. Certainly there were numerous technical innovations in both hardware and software that prompted managerial responses. It is true that many of the larger software development projects in this period did run over budget and fall behind schedule. The cost of software development relative to hardware purchases did continue to climb, and the labor cost of programming did become a serious burden to many manufacturers and users. It is also true that some managers were interested, as Kraft and Greenbaum maintain, in creating software factories where deskilled programmers cranked out mass-produced products that required little thought or creativity.[31] The SDC referred to its in-house programming methodology as the software factory. One guidebook from 1969 for managers captured the essence of this adversarial approach to programmer management by describing the successful computer manager as the "one whose grasp of the job is reflected in simple work units that are in the hand[s] of simple programmers; not one who, with control lost, is held in contempt by clever programmers dangerously maintaining control on his behalf."[32]

An uncritical reading of this and other similar management perspectives on the process of software development, with their confident claims about the value and efficacy of various performance metrics, development methodologies, and programming languages, might suggest that Kraft and Greenbaum are correct in their assessments. In fact, many of these methodologies do indeed represent "elaborate efforts" that "are being made to develop ways of gradually eliminating programmers, or at least reduce their average skill levels, required training, experience, and so on."[33] Their authors would be the first to admit it. A more critical reading of this literature, however, indicates that the claims of many management theorists represent imagined ideals more than current reality. Writing in 1971, the occupational sociologist Enid Mumford actually lauded data processing as an "area where the philosophy of job reducers and job simplifiers—the followers of Taylor—has not been accepted."[34]

The fact that the software crisis has survived a half century of supposed silver bullet solutions suggests that Kraft may have overlooked an essential component of this history. What is missing from his analysis is the perspective on the software labor process provided by the many companies that recognized that computer programming was, at least to a certain extent, a creative and intellectually demanding occupation, and that in their management of software personnel stressed "the importance of a judicious balance between control and individual freedom."[35] Kraft implied that most corporations adopted a hierarchical system of management aimed at eliminating worker autonomy. He ignored the many alternative methodologies that were proposed and adopted in this period. Like his mentors Braverman and Noble, he overemphasized the willingness and ability of the managerial "class," which he treats as a monolithic and homogeneous category, rather than as the diverse group of individuals operating in different social, political, and technical environments, to impose unilaterally their routinization agenda on the programming labor force. Many programmers were skilled workers who vigorously pursued their own professional advancement; it is clear that they were active participants in the struggle to develop the discipline of software engineering.[36]

A more nuanced reading of the contemporary industry literature suggests that the key to understanding the managerial response to the software crisis has less to do with economic imperatives or dialectical materialism than with what the sociologist Andrew Abbott has described as the "jurisdictional struggles" that occur among groups of professionals struggling for control over a particular occupational territory. In *The Systems of Professions: An Essay on the Division of Expert Labor*, Abbott provides an "ecological" model for understanding professional change and development. His model can be summarized briefly as follows: 1) professions grow when occupational niches become available to them, and they change when their particular territory becomes threatened; 2) the critical events in professional development are struggles over jurisdictions, and key environmental changes involve the creation or abolition of jurisdictions; and 3) professional struggle occurs at three levels: the workplace, culture and public opinion, and legal and administrative rules. These levels are loosely coupled. Most shifts in jurisdiction start in the workplace, move to public opinion, and may end up in the legal sphere. Hence, the most consequential struggles are over competence and theory—the core jurisdiction. Increasing abstraction allows for professional expansion, but overabstraction can dilute the core jurisdiction.[37]

My argument is that just one of these jurisdictional struggles occurred on commercial computing in the late 1960s. The continued persistence of a software crisis mentality among industrial and government managers as well as the seemingly unrelenting quest of these managers to develop a software development methodology that would finally eliminate corporate dependence on the craft knowledge of individual programmers can best be understood in light of a struggle over workplace authority that took shape in the early decades of computing. In the 1950s and 1960s, the electronic digital computer was introduced into the well-established technical and social systems of the modern business organization. As this technology became an increasingly important tool for corporate control and communication, existing networks of power and authority were uncomfortably disrupted. The conflicting needs and agendas of users, manufacturers, managers, and programmers all became wrapped up in a highly public struggle for control over the occupational territory opened up by the technology of computing.

Visible Technicians

Neither version of the professionalization narrative, whether they culminate in failure or success for programmers, are entirely satisfactory when applied to computer programmers. Despite their best efforts to establish the institutional structures of a profession, computer programmers were never able to achieve widespread professional recognition. They were unable, for example, to develop two of the most defining characteristics of a profession: control over entry into the profession, and the adoption of a shared body of abstract occupational knowledge—a "hard core of mutual understanding"—common across the entire occupational community. They failed to sufficiently convince employers of the value of professionalism, and were divided among themselves over issues involving academic standards and certification requirements. Complaints about the lack of professional standards among computer programmers continue to play a central role in discussions about the nature and causes of the software crisis. Despite the widespread adoption of the rhetoric of software engineering, most computer programmers are not engineers and would not identify themselves as such. Although the question of professionalism continues to be a live issue in the programming community, in general computer programmers are not considered to be professionals.[38]

So if they are not professionals, managers, or clerical support staff, what exactly are computer programmers? What does their unique history tell us about larger patterns in work practices and the organization of labor in the late twentieth century?

Perhaps the most useful way to think about the computer programmer is as a technician. As the organizational theorist Stephen Barley has pointed out, technicians are a relatively recent addition to the pantheon of occupations.[39] Although technicians do not fit easily into the interpretative framework of either labor history or the sociology of professions, they represent the fastest-growing sector of the U.S. labor force. They include such occupations as radiological technicians, science technicians, engineering technicians, and medical technicians. Their work transgresses traditional occupational boundaries; according to Barley, technicians "often wear white collars, carry briefcases, and conduct sophisticated scientific and mathematical analyses. Yet they use tools, work with their hands, make objects, repair equipment, and, from time to time, get dirty."[40] They are usually—albeit at times grudgingly—granted a great deal of autonomy by their employers.[41] Like computer programmers, technicians occupy an ambiguous occupational space that is difficult to categorize.

Also like computer programmers, technicians serve as mediators between the technological and social architectures of the organization. Technicians are frequently responsible for building, repairing, and monitoring the complex systems that keep a company running. Because they play a support role that is tangential to the core business of the organization and generally possess skills radically different from those of their colleagues, they are seen as foreigners to the work site.[42] Traditional employees generally resent their dependence on technicians and consider them insufficiently subservient.[43] Like the computer boys of the late 1960s, technicians regularly wield power disproportionate to their official position in the occupational hierarchy.

There are a number of other similarities between Barley's description of technicians and the history of the computer programmer. Although they are generally well educated and rely heavily on scientific or engineering training, technicians also value intuition and craft knowledge. They tend to learn on the job, rather than from formal academic or vocational training programs. They make extensive use of social networks and community-based systems of information exchange. Their expertise is typically local and idiosyncratic, and difficult to communicate or define as a set of abstract principles.[44]

It seems clear from these depictions that computer programmers can be considered as a type of technician. In fact, this seems to be the most useful way to make connections between software workers and other forms of technical labor. It captures the tension inherent in the practices of software development: the curious coexistence of high technology and artisanal sensibilities; the inability of programmers to conform to conventional professional, scientific, or engineering categories; the persistent attempts by corporate managers to restructure software development along the lines of traditional manufacturing; and the remarkable persistence of the forty-year-old software crisis.

Where Did All the Women Go?

In 1969 the Data Processing Management Association presented Rear Admiral Grace Hopper with its very first "man of the year" award. That a professional society in a technical field would, in this period, even consider awarding its very first major award to a woman seems astounding to modern sensibilities. In the decades since the "ENIAC girls" became the world's first computer programmers, the computer professions have become stereotypically masculine, and female enrollments in computer science programs have been declining since the mid-1980s. Participation rates for women in the computing fields are a perennial problem for the industry, and this has been the subject of much study and debate for the past several decades.

It was not always thus. As we have seen, women played an early and important role in the history of computing. Some of them became quite influential: in addition to Grace Hopper, Betty Snyder Holberton, Jean Sammet, and Beatrice Helen Worsley, among others, rose to positions of considerable prominence in the early computing industry.[45] In fact, as I have pointed out elsewhere, compared to most technical professions, computer programming remained unusually open to females throughout the 1950s and 1960s. However, during this same period the computer programming community was also actively pursuing a strategy of professional development that would eventually make it one of the most stereotypically male professions, inhospitable to most women.[46]

Contemporary estimates suggest that throughout the 1960s at least thirty percent of working computer programmers were women. One study puts the figure closer to fifty percent.[47] When the first official government statistics were calculated in 1970, twenty-three percent of programmers were identified as female—and this is during a period of intense contraction in the programmer labor market.[48] The term "programming" often encompassed a multitude of occupational categories, including high-status jobs such as systems analyst and lead programmer as well as low-status jobs like coder; women tended to (or were forced to) congregate in the lower end of the occupational pool. Nevertheless, there is ample evidence women were unusually welcome within the computing professions well into the late 1960s.

One explanation for the larger numbers of women in computing in this period was the intense shortage of available labor. In an employment market desperate for even moderately skilled computer workers, it would have been counterproductive to discriminate against women. The reliance on aptitude testing and internal promotion during this period meant that women were at least as likely to be selected as programmer trainees as men. Many firms tested all of their employees for programming aptitude, so even women working in such highly feminized (and low-status) occupations as stenography had a chance to become programmers.

Additionally, there is evidence that female programmers were not just acceptabled but preferred. In a 1963 *Datamation* article lauding the virtues of female computer programmers, for example, Valerie Rockmael focused specifically on women's stability, reliability, and relative docility: "Women are less aggressive and more content in one position . . . Women consider fringe benefits of more importance than their male peers and are more prone to stay on the job if they are content, regardless of a lack of advancement. They also maintain their original geographic roots and are less willing to travel or change job locations, particularly if they are married or engaged."[49] In an era in which turnover rates for programmers averaged twenty percent annually, this was a compelling argument for employers.

A 1968 article in *Cosmopolitan* magazine captured perfectly the promise of opportunity available to women in the early decades of computing. Entitled simply "The Computer Girls," the article noted that there were already more than 20,000 women working as computer programmers in the United States, and that there was an immediate demand for 20,000 more.[50] The author quotes Grace Hopper herself as saying that programming was "just like planning a dinner": "You have to plan ahead and schedule everything so it's ready when you need it. Programming requires patience and the ability to handle detail. Women are 'naturals' at computer programming."[51] The rapid expansion of the computer industry meant that "sex discrimination in hiring" was unheard of, the article's author confidently declared, and anyone with aptitude—male or female, college-educated or not—could succeed in the field. As one of the article's sources described it, computing was one of the few occupations in which a woman could be "fully accepted as a professional."[52]

The *Cosmo* article is full of seemingly silly details—such as a confession from Sally Brown, "a redhead from South Bend, Indiana," that "she doesn't mind working late" because there is often "a nice male programmer to take a girl home"—but for the most part it accurately reflects the contemporary sense of the opportunities available to women in computing. After all, "every company that makes or uses computers hires women to program them," the article noted matter-of-factly, "If a girl is qualified, she's got the job." And, in true *Cosmopolitan* style, the article concludes with a quiz; by answering a few simple questions, any *Cosmo* girl could see whether she too had what it took to be a professional computer programmer making "$15,000 after five years."[53] The questions on the quiz were drawn directly from an aptitude test used by the Honeywell Corporation, and so was more relevant to the real world than the magazine's usual fare.

In many ways, however, the idealized gender-neutral profession described in "The Computer Girls" was already becoming increasingly divorced from reality. Over the course of the 1960s, developments in the computing professions were creating new barriers to female participation. An activity originally intended to be performed by low-status, clerical—and more often than not, female—computer programming was gradually and deliberately transformed into a high-status, scientific, and masculine discipline.

Professionalization was crucial aspect of this masculinization process. As Margaret Rossiter and others have suggested, professionalization nearly always requires the exclusion of women.[54] Among other things, it requires segmentation and stratification. In order to elevate the overall status of their discipline, aspiring professionals had to distance themselves from those aspects of their work that were seen as low-status and routine, work that became increasingly feminized. In addition, the imposition of formal educational requirements on the part of the professional societies, such as a college degree, made it difficult for women—particularly women who had taken time off to raise children—to enter the profession. In 1965, for example, the Association for Computing Machinery imposed a four-year degree requirement for membership that, in an era when there were almost twice as many male as there were female college undergraduates, excluded significantly more women than men.[55] A survey from the late 1970s showed that fewer than 10% of ACM members were women.[56] Similarly, certification programs or licensing requirements erected barriers to entry that disproportionately affected women. Finally, professionalism also suggests a certain degree of managerial authority and competence—skills and characteristics that were often seen as being masculine rather than feminine. The CDP examinations, for example, explicitly required candidates to have at least three years of experience, and the majority of CDP holders worked in middle management.[57] In his 1971 book *The Psychology of Computer Programming*, Gerald Weinberg notes the commonly held belief that female programmers were incapable of leading a group or supervising their male colleagues.[58] The more programmers were seen as potential managers (a new development that came with professionalization), the more women were excluded.

All of this suggests that as computer programmers constructed a professional identity for themselves during the crucial decades of the

1950s and 1960s, that they also constructed a gender identity. Masculinity was just one of many resources that they drew on to distance their profession from its low-status origins in clerical data processing. The question of "who made for a good programmer" increasingly involved in its answer the qualifier "male." The stereotype of the antisocial programmer, wearing sandals and a beard, was not simply a product of the pseudoscientific personality profiles used for recruitment in this period; over time, it became a deliberate self-construction embraced by the community. Yesterday's "computer boys" are today's "IT guys." The moniker may have changed, but the gender (and status) connotations remain.

To suggest that a discipline has been made masculine, however, is not to claim that all of its practitioners are male but rather that the ideals of the discipline are seen as masculine ideals. It is entirely possible, for example, to talk about science being gendered male without arguing that there are no female scientists. To the degree that women succeed in masculinized disciplines, however, it is by suppressing their femininity: to act female in such contexts is to act "unprofessionally."[59] There is a large literature on the ways in which women in such fields are forced to accommodate themselves to the dominant gender dynamics of the discipline. The masculinization of a profession erects barriers to female participation, but it does not eliminate it altogether.[60]

From Crisis to Opportunity

The continued existence of a four-decades-long crisis in one of the largest and fastest-growing sectors of the U.S. economy suggests an interesting dichotomy: on the one hand, software is the technological success story of the past half century; on the other hand, its reputation and identity continue to be marked by perceptions of crisis and failure. What can we make of these strange contradictions and the remarkable persistence of a crisis mentality? More important, how can understanding this duality contribute to advancing the art and science of software development?

There seem to be at least three crucial lessons to be learned from the history of the software crisis:

The first is a simple and obvious observation: just as software is about more than just computer code, the software crisis is about more than just software. Software is what links the powerful technology of digital computing to larger human actions, agendas, and interactions. As such, it cannot be isolated from its social, economic, and political context. User dissatisfaction with software often has less to do with technical failure than it does with its failure to address the "real" problem (which was probably not technical in nature), or the implications that software has on larger patterns of work, power, and autonomy.

The second lesson follows naturally from the first: just as software itself is a heterogeneous system and the software crisis is a reflection of that heterogeneity, so too must the solution to the software crisis be heterogeneous. One of the appeals of software engineering as a solution to the crisis is that engineers have long experience in developing such complicated "systems of systems." And yet even more established branches of engineering struggle with the engineer's temptation to reduce everything to a technical problem. From the earliest days of electronic computing, users have been dissatisfied with the tendency of program-mers to oversimplify complex business problems. And although the context of software development has changed over time, laments about the inability of software designers to adequately comprehend and repre-sent the needs of users have not. Computer programmers in particular sat in the uncomfortable "interface between the world of ill-stated prob-lems and the computers."[61] Design in a heterogeneous environment is difficult; design is as much a social and political process as it is technical; cultivating skilled designers requires a comprehensive and balanced approach to education, training, and career development. As Frederick Brooks observed in his "No Silver Bullet," "The hardest single part of building a software system is deciding precisely what to build. No other part of the conceptual work is as difficult as establishing the detailed technical requirements, including all the interfaces to people, to machines, and to other software systems. No other part of the work so cripples the resulting system if done wrong. No other part is more difficult to rectify later."[62]

Finally, any proposed solution to the software crisis, whether it is technical, managerial, professional, or otherwise, has implications for individuals and organizations. The appeal of the software factory model might appear obvious to corporate managers; for skilled computer pro-fessionals, the idea of becoming a factory worker is understandably less desirable. Whether or not such a model would even be feasible depends a great deal on whether or not you believe software development as a process can be decomposed neatly into individual tasks. The history of software suggests that this is not at all an obvious or undisputed fact.

From this perspective, even the most seemingly technical debates cannot be isolated from this larger context of occupational identity and organizational power. As early as 1962, in a RAND Corporation

Symposium on Programming Languages, Jack Little lamented the tendency of manufacturers to design languages "for use by some sub-human species in order to get around training and having good programmers."[63] When the Department of Defense proposed ADA as a solution to yet another outbreak of the software crisis, it was trumpeted as a means of "replacing the idiosyncratic 'artistic' ethos that has long governed software writing with a more efficient, cost-effective engineering mind-set."[64] As was mentioned earlier, object-oriented programming enthusiasts advocate for "a software industrial revolution based on reusable and interchangeable parts that will alter the software universe as surely as the industrial revolution changed manufacturing."[65] Once again, the desirability of such a revolution, and its attendant implications for the character and quality of programming labor, is not universally recognized; witness the recent debate about outsourcing, which ties the history of the software crisis into a much larger and longer-running one about globalism, job protection, workers' rights, and national identity.

All of this is not to deny the remarkable success of the software industry or the accomplishments of aspiring software engineers. In fact, the success of software—in the face of a seemingly perpetual and unchanging rhetoric of crisis—is precisely what makes this history so interesting and relevant to contemporary practitioners. This is perhaps one of the few situations in which it actually is true that those who cannot learn from history are doomed to repeat it.

Historians of technology have long argued that all technologies are, at least to a certain degree, socially constructed. This is simply to say that the physical design of an artifact is inextricably influenced by its larger environment. In the 1950s and 1960s, the electronic digital computer was introduced into the well-established technical and social systems of the modern business organization. Like all new technologies, the computer took its shape from—and helped to shape—its social, cultural, and technological context. As the computer became an increasingly important part of the modern corporate organization, control over its use and identity became increasingly contested. The conflicting needs and agendas of users, manufacturers, managers, and programmers all became wrapped up in a highly public struggle for control over the professional territory opened up by the technology of computing. Thinking about the software crisis—and the invention of the discipline of software engineering—as a series of interconnected social and political negotiations, rather than an isolated technical decision about the one best way to develop software components, provides an essential link between internal developments in information technology and their larger social and historical context. It can help explain why, in an industry characterized by rapid change and innovation, the rhetoric of crisis has proven so remarkably persistent.

Despite the persistence of the software crisis mentality, programming continues to survive as an essentially craft-based occupation in the midst of a predominantly engineering-oriented corporate environment.[66] Although the rhetoric of software engineering has been generally adopted, the substance of software engineering has not. Military and industrial leaders continue to decry the lack of engineer standards in software development. "More and more software will be behind schedule, over budget, under powered, and of poor quality—and there's nothing we can do about it," complained an article in *Byte Magazine* in 1996. A 1998 study by the House Committee on Software Development and Regulation called software a shoot-from-the-hip industry, noting a "distinct vacuum in the treatment of ethics in computer science."[67] Almost thirty years after the first NATO Conference on Software Engineering, many programmers and project managers are still concluding that "excellent developers, like excellent musicians and artists, are born, not made."[68]

Notes

Chapter 1

1. Bureau of Labor Statistics, *U.S. Department of Labor, Occupational Outlook Handbook*, 2008–09 edition; *Aid to recovery: the economic impact of IT, software, and the Microsoft ecosystem on the global economy*. Springfield, MA: Interactive Data Corporation, 2009.

2. Stuart Shapiro and Steven Woolgar. "Balancing acts: reconciling competing visions of the way software technologists work," in *Proceedings of the Eighth IEEE International Workshop on Incorporating Computer Aided Software Engineering* (Los Alamitos, CA: IEEE Computer Society Press, 1997): 364–370; Stephen Barley and Gideon Kunda, *Gurus, Hired Guns, and Warm Bodies: Itinerant Experts in a Knowlege Economy* (Princeton, NJ: Princeton University Press, 2004).

3. Jackson Granholm, "How to Hire a Programmer," *Datamation* 8, no. 8 (1962): 31–32; Sherry Turkle, *The Second Self: Computers and the Human Spirit* (New York: Simon and Schuster, 1984); Ron Eglash, "Race, Sex, and Nerds: From Black Geeks to Asian American Hipsters," *Social Text* 2, no. 20 (2002): 49–64; Steve Lohr, *Go To: The Story of the Math Majors, Bridge Players, Engineers, Chess Wizards, Maverick Scientists, and Iconoclasts—The Programmers Who Created the Software Revolution* (New York: Basic Books, 2001).

4. Deborah Lupton, "The Embodied Computer User," *Body and Society* 1, no. 3–4 (1995): 97–112; Fergus Murray and David Knights, "Inter-managerial Competition and Capital Accumulation: IT Specialists, Accountants, and Executive Control," *Critical Perspectives on Accounting* 1, no. 2 (June 1990): 167–189.

5. Steve Silberman, "The Geek Syndrome," *Wired* 9, no. 12 (2001): 175–183; Majia Holmer Nadesan, *Constructing Autism: Unravelling the "Truth" and Understanding the Social* (London: Routledge, 2005), 199.

6. David Anderegg, *Nerds: Who They Are and Why We Need More of Them* (New York: Jeremy P. Tarcher, 2007); Benjamin Nugent, *American Nerd: The Story of My People* (New York: Scribner, 2008).

7. Joseph Weizenbaum, *Computer Power and Human Reason: From Judgment to Calculation* (New York: Penguin, 1976); Steven Levy, *Hackers: Heroes of the Computer Revolution* (Garden City, NY: Anchor Press, 1984); Katie Hafner, *CYBERPUNK: Outlaws and Hackers on the Computer Frontier, Revised* (New York: Simon and Schuster, 1995).

8. Philip Scranton, "None-too-Porous Boundaries: Labor History and the History of Technology," *Technology and Culture* 29, no. 744–778 (1988); Stephen Barley, "Technicians in the Workplace: Ethnographic Evidence for Bringing Work into Organization Studies," *Administrative Science Quarterly* 41, no. 3 (1996): 404–441; Nelly Oudshoorn and Trevor Pinch, eds., *How Users Matter: The Co-construction of Users and Technologies* (Cambridge, MA: MIT Press, 2003).

9. Michael S. Mahoney, "What Makes the History of Software Hard," *IEEE Annals of the History of Computing* 30, no. 3 (2008): 8–18.

10. Thomas Haigh, "Software in the 1960s as Concept, Service, and Product." *Annals of the History of Computing, IEEE* 24, no. 1 (2002): 5–13.

11. Andrew Friedman and Dominic Cornford, *Computer Systems Development: History, Organization, and Implementation* (Chichester, UK: Wiley, 1989), 10.

12. Martin Campbell-Kelly, *From Airline Reservations to Sonic the Hedgehog: A History of the Software Industry* (Cambridge, MA: MIT Press, 2003).

13. John Tukey, "The Teaching of Concrete Mathematics," *American Mathematical Monthly* 65, no. 1 (1958): 1–9.

14. Bernard Galler, "Definition of Software," *Communications of the ACM* 5, no. 1 (1961): 6.

15. Richard Christian, "The Computer and the Marketing Man," *Journal of Marketing* 26, no. 3 (1962): 79–82; "Hardware and Software," *British Medical Journal* 1, no. 5449 (1965): 1509; Robert Hayes, Ralph H. Parker, and Gilbert W. King. "Automation and the Library of Congress: Three Views," *Library Quarterly* 34, no. 3 (1964): 229–239; George Mitchell, "Exogenous Forces in the Development of Our Banking System," *Law and Contemporary Problems* 32, no. 1 (1967): 3–14.

16. J. H. Spigelman, "Implications of Recent Advances in Electronic Data Processing," *Financial Analysts Journal* 20, no. 5 (1964): 137–143; Arthur Nesse, "A User Looks at Software," *Datamation* 14, no. 10 (1968): 48–51; Allen Forte, "Review: Conference on the Use of Computers in Humanistic Research," *Computers and the Humanities* 1, no. 3 (1967): 110–112; "Abstracts of Papers for the Fourteenth Annual Meeting of the Radiation Research Society, Coronado, California February 13–16, 1966," *Radiation Research* 27, no. 3 (1966): 487–554; Maurice Ronayne, "'Leads' to Pertinent ADP Literature for the Public Administrator," *Public Administration Review* 24, no. 2 (1964): 119–125.

17. John Law, "Technology and Heterogeneous Engineering: The Case of the Portuguese Expansion," in *The Social Construction of Technical Systems: New Directions in the Sociology and History of Technology*, ed. Wiebe Bijker, Trevor Pinch, and Thomas Hughes (Cambridge, MA: MIT Press, 1987), 111–134; John

Law, "Notes on the Theory of Actor-Network: Ordering, Strategy, and Heterogeneity," *Systems Practice* 5, no. 4 (1992): 379–393.

18. Richard Canning, "The Maintenance 'Iceberg,'" *EDP Analyzer* 10, no. 10 (1972): 1–14.

19. J. H. Spigelman, "Implications of Recent Advances in Electronic Data Processing: Part II," *Financial Analysts Journal* 20, no. 6 (1964): 87–93; Richard Jones, "Practical Control of Preparatory Programming Time for a Computer Installation," *NAA Bulletin* 43, no. 8 (1962): 71; Ned Chapin, "Teaching Business Data Processing with the Aid of a Computer," *Accounting Review* 38, no. 4 (1963): 835–839.

20. Ralph Lewis, "Never Overestimate the Power of a Computer," *Harvard Business Review* 35, no. 5 (1957): 77–84.

21. Lewis, "Never Overestimate the Power of a Computer"; Felix Kaufman, "EDP and the Disenchanted," *California Management Review* 1, no. 41 (1959): 67; Arnold Keller, "Crisis in Machine Accounting," *Management and Business Automation* 5, no. 6 (1961): 30–31; Frederick P. Brooks, *The Mythical Man-Month: Essays on Software Engineering* (New York: Addison-Wesley, 1975).

22. Friedman and Cornford, *Computer Systems Development*, 162.

23. Donald Ervin Knuth, *The Art of Computer programming. Addison-Wesley Series in Computer Science and Information Processing* (Reading, MA: Addison-Wesley, 1968).

24. Kaufman, "EDP and the Disenchanted."

25. Thomas Whisler, "The Impact of Information Technology on Organizational Control." In *The Impact of Computers on Management*, ed. Charles A. Myers, 16–48 (Cambridge, MA: MIT Press, 1967).

26. John Golda, "The Effects of Computer Technology on the Traditional Role of Management" (master's thesis, Wharton School of Business, University of Pennsylvania, 1965), 34.

27. Kaufman, "EDP and the Disenchanted."

28. JoAnne Yates, *Structuring the Information Age: Life Insurance and Technology in the Twentieth Century* (Baltimore: Johns Hopkins University Press, 2005).

29. Thierry Bardini, *Bootstrapping: Douglas Englebart, Coevolution, and the Origins of Personal Computing* (Stanford, CA: Stanford University Press, 2000), 103.

30. John Dwyer, "Analysts Couched" (letter to the editor), *Datamation* 16, no. 1 (1970): 47; Gene Altshuler, "Programmers and Analysts" (letter to the editor), *Datamation* 16, no. 1(1970): 47.

31. Tukey, "The Teaching of Concrete Mathematics."

32. David Allan Grier, "The ENIAC, the Verb to Program, and the Emergence of Digital Computers," *Annals of the History of Computing* 18, no. 1 (1996): 53.

33. H. S. Tropp, "ACM's 20th Anniversary: 30 August 1967," *Annals of the History of Computing* 9, no. 3 (1988): 269.

34. John Backus, quoted in J. Howlett and Gian-Carlo Rota, eds., *A History of Computing in the Twentieth Century: A Collection of Essays* (New York: Academic Press, 1980), 126.

35. Thomas Haigh, "Technology, Information and Power: Managerial Technicians in Corporate America: 1917–2000" (PhD diss., University of Pennsylvania, 2002).

36. JoAnne Yates, *Control through Communication: The Rise of System in American Management* (Baltimore: Johns Hopkins University Press, 1989).

37. Arvid Jacobson, ed., *Proceedings of the First Conference on Training Personnel for the Computing Machine Field* (Detroit: Wayne State University Press, 1955).

38. Robert Patrick, "The Gap in Programming Support," *Datamation* 7, no. 5 (1961): 37.

39. Gene Bylinsky, "Help Wanted: 50,000 Programmers," *Fortune* 75, no. 3 (1967): 141.

40. Hal Sackman, "Conference on Personnel Research," *Datamation* 14, no. 7 (1968): 74–76, 81.

41. Hal Sackman, W. J. Erickson, and E. E. Grant, "Exploratory Experimental Studies Comparing Online and Offline Programming Performance," *Communications of the ACM* 11, no. 1 (1968): 3–11.

42. Dean Dauw, "Vocational Interests of Highly Creative Computer Personnel," *Personnel Journal* 46, no. 10 (1967): 653–659.

43. Stephen Barley and Julian Orr, eds., *Between Craft and Science: Technical Work in US Settings* (Ithaca, NY: ILR Press, 1997).

44. Richard Hamming, "One Man's View of Computer Science," in *ACM Turing Award Lectures: The First Twenty Years, 1966–1985* (Upper Saddle River, NJ: Pearson Education, 1987), 207–218.

45. Nathan Ensmenger, "The 'Question of Professionalism' in the Computer Fields," *IEEE Annals of the History of Computing* 4, no. 23 (2001): 56–73.

46. Daniel McCracken, "The Human Side of Computing," *Datamation* 7, no. 1 (1961): 9–11.

47. Willis Ware, "As I See It: A Guest Editorial," *Datamation* 11, no. 5 (1965): 27–28.

48. E. Burton Swanson and Cynthia Mathis Beath, "Departmentalization in software development and maintenance." *Communications of the ACM* 33, no. 6 (1990): 658–667; Raymond Berger, "Computer Personnel Selection and Criteria Development," in *Proceedings of the 2nd SIGCPR Conference on Computer Personnel Research* (New York: ACM Press, 1964), 65–77.

49. McCracken, "The Human Side of Computing," 9–10.

50. Nathan Ensmenger, "Letting the 'Computer Boys' Take Over: Technology and the Politics of Organizational Transformation," *International Review of Social History* 48, no. S11 (2003): 153–180.

51. Harold Leavitt and Thomas Whisler, "Management in the 1980's," *Harvard Management Review* 36, no. 6 (1958): 41–48.

52. Whisler, "The Impact of Information Technology on Organizational Control."

53. Golda, "The Effects of Computer Technology on the Traditional Role of Management," 34.

54. Rosemary Stewart, *How Computers Affect Management* (Cambridge, MA: MIT Press, 1971), 196.

55. Thomas Alexander, "Computers Can't Solve Everything," *Fortune* 80, no. 5 (1969): 169.

56. McKinsey and Company, "Unlocking the Computer's Profit Potential," *Computers and Automation* 16, no. 7 (1969): 33.

57. Ibid., 33.

58. Harry Larson, "EDP: A 20 Year Ripoff!" *Infosystems* (1974): 26.

59. Ensmenger, "Letting the 'Computer Boys' Take Over."

60. Barry Boehm, "Software and Its Impact: A Quantitative Assessment," *Datamation* 19, no. 5 (1973): 48–59; Michael Mahoney, "Software: The Self-Programming Machine," in *From 0 to 1: An Authoritative History of Modern Computing*, ed. Atsushi Akera and Frederik Nebeker (New York: Oxford University Press, 2002).

61. Edsger Dijkstra, "The Humble Programmer," *Communications of the ACM* 15, no. 10 (1972): 873.

62. Martin Campbell-Kelly and William Aspray, *Computer: A History of the Information Machine* (New York: Basic Books, 1996), 201.

63. W. Saba, "Letter to the Editor," *IEEE Computer* 29, no. 9 (1996): 10; Edward Nash Yourdon, ed., *Classics in Software Engineering* (New York: Yourdon Press, 1979); Herbert Freeman and Phillip Lewis, *Software Engineering* (New York: Academic Press, 1980).

64. Frank Wagner, "Letter to the Editors," *Communications of the ACM* 33, no. 6 (1990): 628–629.

65. Ann Dooley, "100% over Budget," *Computerworld* 21, no. 7 (1987): 5.

66. David Morrison, "Software Crisis," *Defense* 21, no. 2 (1989): 72.

67. John Shore, "Why I Never Met a Programmer I Could Trust," *Communications of the ACM* 31, no. 4 (1988): 372.

Chapter 2

1. I. Bernard Cohen, *Howard Aiken: Portrait of a Computer Pioneer* (Cambridge, MA: MIT Press, 1999).

2. Norbert Wiener, *Cybernetics, or, Control and Communication in the Animal and the Machine* (Cambridge, MA: Technology Press, 1948).

3. Edmund Callis Berkeley, *Giant Brains; or, Machines That Think* (New York: Wiley, 1949).

4. Steven P. Schnaars and Sergio Carvalho, "Predicting the Market Evolution of Computers: Was the Revolution Really Unforeseen," *Technology in Society* 26, no. 1 (2004): 1–16.

5. Roddy Osborn, "GE and UNIVAC: Harnessing the High-Speed Computer," *Harvard Business Review* 32, no. 4 (1954): 99–107; M. L. Hurni, "Some Implications of the Use of Computers in Industry," *Accounting Review*, 29, no. 3 (1954): 447; John S. Coleman, "Computers as Tools for Management," *Management Science* 2, no. 2 (1956): 107.

6. "Office Robots," *Fortune*, 1952, 82–87, 112, 114, 116, 118.

7. Kenneth Flamm, *Creating the Computer: Government, Industry, and High Technology* (Washington, DC: Brookings Institution Press, 1988).

8. James W. Cortada, "Commercial Applications of the Digital Computer in American Corporations, 1945–1995," *IEEE Annals of the History of Computing* 18, no. 2 (Summer 1996): 18–29.

9. Bruce Gilchrist and Richard Weber, eds., *The State of the Computer Industry in the United States* (New York: American Federation of Information Processing Societies, 1972).

10. Gene Bylinsky, "Help Wanted: 50,000 Programmers," *Fortune* 75, no. 3 (1967): 141.

11. See Raul Rojas and Ulf Hashagen, eds., *The First Computers: History and Architectures* (Cambridge, MA: MIT Press, 2000).

12. Adele Goldstine, *A Report on the ENIAC (Electronic Numerical Integrator and Computer)* (technical report, Moore School of Electrical Engineering, University of Pennsylvania, June 1, 1946).

13. Richard F. Clippinger, *A Logical Coding System Applied to the ENIAC (Electronic Numerical Integrator and Computer)* (technical report, Ballistic Research Laboratories, Ordnance Department, Aberdeen Proving Ground, 1948).

14. John von Neumann, *First Draft of a Report on the EDVAC* (Philadelphia: Moore School of Electrical Engineering, University of Pennsylvania, June 30, 1945).

15. B. Randell, "The Origins of Computer Programming," *IEEE Annals of the History of Computing* 16, no. 4 (1994): 6–14.

16. W. Barkley Fritz, "The Women of Eniac," *IEEE Annals of the History of Computing* 18, no. 3 (1996): 13–23.

17. David Allan Grier, "The ENIAC, the Verb to Program, and the Emergence of Digital Computers," *IEEE Annals of the History of Computing* 18, no. 1 (1996): 53.

18. Ibid., 52.

19. W. Barkley Fritz, "The Women of Eniac," *IEEE Annals of the History of Computing* 18, no. 3 (1996): 20.

20. Henry S. Tropp, "ACM's 20th Anniversary: 30 August 1967," *Annals of the History of Computing* 9, no. 3 (1988): 269.

21. Margery W. Davies, *Woman's Place Is at the Typewriter: Office Work and Office Workers, 1870–1930* (Philadelphia: Temple University Press, 1982); Sharon Hartman Strom, *Beyond the Typewriter: Gender, Class, and the Origins of Modern American Office Work, 1900–1930* (Urbana: University of Illinois Press, 1992); Elyce J. Rotella, *From Home to Office: U.S. Women at Work, 1870–1930. Volume No. 25* (Ann Arbor, MI: UMI Research Press, 1981).

22. Thomas Haigh, "The Chromium-Plated Tabulator: Institutionalizing an Electronic Revolution, 1954–1958," *IEEE Annals of the History of Computing* 4, no. 23 (2001), 75–104.

23. Remington Rand UNIVAC, *Introduction to Programming: Programming for the UNIVAC, Part 1*, (1949), Hagley Museum Archives, Accession 1825, Box 372.

24. B. Conway, J. Gibbons, and D. E. Watts, *Business Experience with Electronic Computers: A Synthesis of What Has Been Learned from Electronic Data Processing Installations* (New York: Price Waterhouse, 1959), 81.

25. Ibid., 89–90.

26. Ibid., 90.

27. John Backus, "Programming in America in the 1950s: Some Personal Impressions," in *A History of Computing in the Twentieth Century: A Collection of Essays*, ed. N. Metropolis, J. Howlett, and Gian-Carlo Rota (New York: Academic Press,1980), 126.

28. Conway, Gibbons, and Watts, *Business Experience with Electronic Computers*.

29. Willis Ware, "As I See It: A Guest Editorial," *Datamation* 11, no. 5 (1965): 27–28.

30. George Trimble and Elmer Kubie, "Principles of Optimum Programming of the IBM Type 650," *IBM Applied Science Division Technical Newsletter* 8 (1954), 5–16.

31. J. N. Patterson Hume, "Development of Systems Software for the Ferut Computer at the University of Toronto, 1952 to 1955," *IEEE Annals of the History of Computing* 16, no. 2 (1994): 13–19.

32. Backus, "Programming in the 1950s."

33. Martin Campbell-Kelly, "The Airy Tape: An Early Chapter in the History of Debugging," *IEEE Annals of the History of Computing* 14, no. 4 (1992): 16–26.

34. Maurice Wilkes, David Wheeler, and Stanley Gill, *Preparation of Programs for an Electronic Digital Computer* (Reading, MA: Addison-Wesley, 1951).

35. Campbell-Kelly, "The Airy Tape."

36. Frederick P. Brooks, *The Mythical Man-Month: Essays on Software Engineering* (New York: Addison-Wesley, 1975), 20.

37. G. J. Meyers, *Software Reliability: Principles and Practices* (John Wiley and Sons, 1976).

38. Brooks, *The Mythical Man-Month*, 7.

39. Ibid., 7.

40. Bylinsky, "Help Wanted: 50,000 Programmers," 141.

41. John Backus, "Programming in America in the 1950s: Some Personal Impressions," In *A History of Computing in the Twentieth Century: A Collection of Essays*, ed. N. Metropolis, J. Howlett, and Gian-Carlo Rota (New York: Academic Press, 1980), 126.

42. George F. Weinwurm, ed., *On the Management of Computer Programmers* (London: Auerbach Publishers, 1970).

43. P. Mody, "Is Programming an Art?" *Software Engineering Notes* 17, no. 4 (1992): 19–21; Maurice Black, "The Art of Code" (PhD diss., University of Pennsylvania, 2002).

44. Bylinsky, "Help Wanted: 50,000 Programmers," 141.

45. Frederick Brooks, The Mythical Man-Month: Essays on Software Engineering (New York: Addison-Wesley, 1975), 7.

46. Brian Randall and J. N. Buxton, *Software Engineering: Proceedings of the NATO Conferences* (New York: Petrocelli/Carter, 1976).

Chapter 3

1. Brendan Gill and Andy Logan, "Talk of the Town," *New Yorker* 5 (January 1957): 18–19.

2. IBM Corporation, "Are You the Man to Command Electronic Giants?" *New York Times*, May 13, 1956, 157.

3. Gill and Logan, "Talk of the Town."

4. Ibid.

5. Mark I. Halpern, "Memoirs (Part 1)," *IEEE Annals of the History of Computing* 13, no. 1 (1991): 101–111.

6. Gene Bylinsky, "Help Wanted: 50,000 Programmers," *Fortune* 75, no. 3 (1967): 445–556.

7. Martin Campbell-Kelly and William Aspray, *Computer: A History of the Information Machine* (New York: Basic Books, 1996).

8. Bruce Webster, "The Real Software Crisis," *Byte Magazine* 21, no. 1 (1996): 218.

9. Bylinsky, "Help Wanted: 50,000 Programmers"; Stanley Englebardt, "Wanted: 500,000 Men to Feed Computers," *Popular Science*, January 1965, 106–109.

10. Robert Patrick, "The Gap in Programming Support," *Datamation* 7, no. 5 (1961): 37; Don Madden, "The Population Problem: Inexperience Will Dominate," *Datamation* 8, no. 1 (1962): 26.

11. "Software Gap: A Growing Crisis for Computers," *Business Week*, November 5, 1966, 127.

12. Arvid Jacobson, ed., *Proceedings of the First Conference on Training Personnel for the Computing Machine Field* (Detroit: Wayne State University Press, 1955).

13. Ibid.

14. G. Truman Hunter, "Manpower Requirements by Computer Manufacturers," in *Proceedings of the First Conference on Training Personnel for the Computing Machine Field*, ed. Arvid Jacobson (Detroit: Wayne State University Press, 1955), 16.

15. Milton E. Mengel, "Present and Projected Computer Manpower Needs in Business and Industry," in *Proceedings of the First Conference on Training Personnel for the Computing Machine Field*, ed. Arvid Jacobson (Detroit: Wayne State University Press, 1955), 7.

16. Charles R. Gregg, "Personnel Requirements in Government Agencies in Machine Computation," in *Proceedings of the First Conference on Training Personnel for the Computing Machine Field*, ed. Arvid Jacobson (Detroit: Wayne State University Press, 1955), 14.

17. M. Paul Chinitz, "Contributions of Industrial Training Courses in Computers," in *Proceedings of the First Conference on Training Personnel for the Computing Machine Field*, ed. Arvid Jacobson (Detroit: Wayne State University Press, 1955).

18. Mengel, "Present and Projected Computer Manpower Needs in Business and Industry," 8.

19. Ibid., 8.

20. Hunter, "Manpower Requirements by Computer Manufacturers."

21. Ibid., 14–18.

22. Mengel, "Present and Projected Computer Manpower Needs in Business and Industry," 6.

23. Ibid., 6.

24. Campbell-Kelly and Aspray, *Computer.*

25. Gregg, "Personnel Requirements in Government Agencies in Machine Computation."

26. Richard Canning, "The Persistent Personnel Problem," *EDP Analyzer* 5, no. 5 (1967): 1–14.

27. Herbert Benington, "Production of Large Computer Programs" (reprint), *IEEE Annals of the History of Computing* 5, no. 4 (1983): 350–361.

28. Martin Campbell-Kelly, "Development and Structure of the International Software Industry, 1950–1990," *Business and Economic History* 24, no. 2 (1995): 73–110.

29. Claude Baum, *The Systems Builders: The Story of SDC* (Santa Monica, CA: System Development Corporation, 1981).

30. Ibid., 47.

31. Thomas C. Rowan, "The Recruiting and Training of Programmers," *Datamation* 4, no. 3 (1958): 16–18; Chinitz, "Contributions of Industrial Training Courses in Computers."

32. Benington, "Production of Large Computer Programs."

33. Baum, *The Systems Builders*, 52.

34. Thomas Hughes and Agatha Hughes, eds., *Systems, Experts, and Computers: The Systems Approach in Management and Engineering, World War II and After* (Cambridge, MA: MIT Press, 2000).

35. Baum, *The Systems Builders*, 48.

36. Rowan, "The Recruiting and Training of Programmers."

37. C. M. Sidlo, "The Making of a Profession" (letter to editor), *Communications of the ACM* 4, no. 8 (1961): 366–367.

38. L. L. Thurstone, *Primary Mental Abilities* (Chicago: University of Chicago Press, 1938).

39. Henry Eilbert, "The Development of Personnel Management in the United States," *Business History Review* 33 (1959): 345–364.

40. Thomas C. Rowan, "Psychological Tests and Selection of Computer Programmers," *Journal of the ACM* 4, no. 3 (1957): 350.

41. Ibid.

42. Ibid.

43. Walter L. McNamara and John L. Hughes, "A Review of Research on the Selection of Computer Programmers," *Personnel Psychology* 14, no. 1 (1961): 39–51.

44. Charles Lawson, "A Survey of Computer Facility Management," *Datamation* 8, no. 7 (1962): 29–32.

45. Walter J. McNamara, "The Selection of Computer Personnel: Past, Present, Future," in *SIGCPR '67: Proceedings of the Fifth SIGCPR Conference on Computer Personnel Research* (New York: ACM Press, 1967), 52–56.

46. Allan Bloom, "Advances in Use of Programmer Aptitude Tests," in *Advances in Computer Programming Management*, ed. Thomas Rullo (London: Heyden, 1980).

47. Gerald Weinberg, *The Psychology of Computer Programming* (New York: Van Nostrand Rheinhold, 1971), 174.

48. Ibid., 175.

49. William Paschell, *Automation and Employment Opportunities for Office Workers: A Report on the Effect of Electronic Computers on Employment of Clerical Workers* (Washington, DC: Bureau of Labor Statistics, 1958).

50. Joseph O'Shields, "Selection of EDP Personnel," *Personnel Journal* 44, no. 9 (1965): 472.

51. Jack Wolfe, "*Perspectives on Testing for Programming Aptitude,*" in *Proceedings of 1971 ACM Annual Conference* (New York: ACM Press, 1971), 268–277.

52. Raymond M. Berger and Robert C. Wilson, "Correlates of Programmer Proficiency," in *SIGCPR '66: Proceedings of the Fourth SIGCPR Conference on Computer Personnel Research* (New York: ACM Press, 1966), 83–95.

53. McNamara and Hughes, "A Review of Research on the Selection of Computer Programmers."

54. Richard Brandon, "The Problem in Perspective," in *Proceedings of the 1968 23rd ACM National Conference* (New York: ACM Press, 1968), 332–334.

55. Hal Sackman, "Conference on Personnel Research," *Datamation* 14, no. 7 (1968): 76.

56. Robert A. Dickmann and J. Lockwood, *1966 Survey of Test Use in Computer Personnel Selection. Technical Report* (Computer Personnel Research Group, Johns Hopkins University Applied Physics Lab, 1966).

57. Robert N. Reinstedt et al., *Computer Personnel Research Group Programmer Performance Prediction Study. Technical Report.* (Santa Monica, CA: RAND Corporation, 1964).

58. Report, "The Computer Personnel Research Group," *Datamation* 9, no. 1 (1963): 130; Markku Tukiainen and Eero Mönkkönen, "Programming Aptitude Testing as a Prediction of Learning to Program," in *Proceedings of the 14th Annual Workshop of the Psychology of Programming Interest Group*, eds. Jasna Kuljis and Lynne Baldwin and Rosa Scoble (Berlin: Springer, 2002), 130; Garland Y. DeNelsky and Michael G. McKee, "Prediction of Computer Programmer Training and Job Performance Using the AAPB Test," *Personnel Psychology* 27, no. 1 (1974): 130.

59. Ascher Opler, "Testing Programming Aptitude," *Datamation* 9, no. 10 (1963): 28–31.

60. George P. Hollenbeck and Walter J. McNamara, "Cucpat and Programming Aptitude," *Personnel Psychology* 18, no. 1 (1965): 101–106.

61. Bloom, "Advances in Use of Programmer Aptitude Tests."

62. "Programmer Aptitude and Competence Test Systems (PACTS)," in *Proceedings of the Ninth Annual SIGCPR* (New York: ACM Press, 1971), 3–25.

63. Berger and Wilson, "Correlates of Programmer Proficiency."

64. O'Shields, "Selection of EDP Personnel."

65. Terrence Polin, Robert Morse, and John Zenger, "Selecting Programmers from In-Plant Employees," *Personnel Journal* 41, no. 8 (1962): 398–400.

66. Enid Mumford and Thomas Ward, *Computers: Planning for People* (London: B. T. Batsford, 1968).

67. Report, "The Computer Personnel Research Group."

68. Dallis Perry and William Cannon, "Vocational Interests of Computer Programmers," *Journal of Applied Psychology* 51, no. 1 (1967): 28–34.

69. Ibid.

70. Ibid., 30.

71. Ibid.

72. Dallis Perry and William Cannon, "Vocational Interests of Female Computer Programmers," *Journal of Applied Psychology* 52, no. 1 (1968): 31.

73. Brandon, "The Problem in Perspective."

74. Theodore Willoughby, "Are Programmers Paranoid?" in *Proceedings of the Tenth Annual Conference on SIGCPR* (New York: ACM Press, 1972), 47–54.

75. Weinberg, *The Psychology of Computer Programming.*

76. Reinstedt et al., *Computer Personnel Research Group Programmer Performance Prediction Study.*

77. David Mayer and Ashford Stainaker, "Selection and Evaluation of Computer Personnel: The Research History of SIG/CPR," in *Proceedings of the 1968 23rd ACM National Conference* (New York: ACM Press, 1968), 657–670.

78. Patrick, "The Gap in Programming Support."

79. "Careers in Computers" (ad), *Datamation* 8, no. 1 (1962): 21.

80. G. W. Brown, cited in Martin Greenberger, *Management and the Computer of the Future* (Cambridge, MA: MIT Press, 1962), 278.

81. "Software Gap: A Growing Crisis for Computers," *Business Week*, November 5, 1966, 127.

82. "Not Quite All about MIS" (editorial), *Datamation* 13, no. 5 (1967): 21.

83. Edward Markham, "EDP Schools: An Inside View," *Datamation* 14, no. 4 (1968): 22–27.

84. Richard Tanaka, "Fee or Free Software," *Datamation* 13, no. 10 (1967): 205–206.

85. Bylinsky, "Help Wanted: 50,000 Programmers," 141.

86. Canning, "The Persistent Personnel Problem."

87. Tanaka, "Fee or Free Software," 205–206.

88. Canning, "The Persistent Personnel Problem"; John Johnsrud, "Computer Makers Set Up Own 'Universities,'" *New York Times* (September 24, 1961): F1.

89. James Saxon, "Programming Training: A Workable Approach," *Datamation* 9, no. 12 (1963): 48.

90. Canning, "The Persistent Personnel Problem," 9.

91. Gary Popkin, "The Junior College as a Source of Programming Personnel," in *Proceedings of the Ninth Annual SIGCPR Conference* (New York: ACM Press, 1971), 130.

92. Richard Canning, "Managing Staff Retention and Turnover," *EDP Analyzer* 15, no. 8 (1977): 1–13.

93. John Fike, "Vultures Indeed," *Datamation* 13, no. 5 (1967): 12.

94. Robert M. Knoebel, "The Federal Government's Role in the Education of Data Processing Personnel," in *SIGCPR '67: Proceedings of the Fifth SIGCPR Conference on Computer Personnel Research* (New York: ACM Press, 1967), 77–84.

95. Theodore Willoughby, "Staffing the MIS Function," *ACM Computing Surveys* 4, no. 4 (1972): 253.

96. Robert N. Reinstedt, "1966 Survey of Test Use in Computer Personnel Selection," in *Proceedings of the 4th Annual Computer Personnel Research Conference* (New York: ACM Press, 1966), 1–8.

97. Canning, "The Persistent Personnel Problem"; Willoughby, "Staffing the MIS Function."

98. McNamara, "The Selection of Computer Personnel."

99. Malcolm Gotterer and Ashford W. Stalnaker, "Predicting Programmer Performance among Non-Preselected Trainee Groups," in *SIGCPR '64: Proceedings of the Second SIGCPR Conference on Computer Personnel Research* (New York: ACM Press, 1964), 29–37.

100. Jean P. Gilbert and David B. Mayer, "Experiences in Self-selection of Disadvantaged People into a Computer Operator Training Program," in *SIGCPR '69: Proceedings of the Seventh Annual Conference on SIGCPR* (New York: ACM Press, 1969), 79–90.

101. George Heller, "Organizing a Local Program in Computing Education," *Datamation* 9, no. 1 (1963): 57–61.

102. "First Programmer Class at Sing-Sing Graduates," *Datamation* 14, no. 6 (1968): 97–98.

103. Lois Mandel, "The Computer Girls," *Cosmopolitan*, 1967, 52–56.

104. Sackman, "Conference on Personnel Research."

105. Peggy Randall, "Need for Warm Bodies," *Datamation* 9, no. 10 (1963): 14.

106. John Callahan, "Letter to the Editor," *Datamation* 7, no. 3 (1961): 7.

107. Edward Markham, "Selecting a Private EDP School," *Datamation* 14, no. 5 (1968): 33–40.

108. Ibid.

109. Markham, "EDP Schools: An Inside View."

110. Markham, "Selecting a Private EDP School."

111. "Roseman Takes Firm Position against Private EDP Schools," *Communications of the ACM* 11, no. 3 (April 1968): 206–207.

112. "Report from the ACM Ad-hoc Committee on Private EDP Schools," (January 20, 1970), CBI 88, "Data Processing Management Association records," Box 21, Folder 38, Archives of the Charles Babbage Institute, University of Minnesota, Minneapolis.

113. Hans A. Rhee, *Office Automation in Social Perspective: The Progress and Social Implications of Electronic Data Processing* (Oxford: Basil Blackwell, 1968).

114. Paschell, *Automation and Employment Opportunities for Office Workers*; Weinberg, *The Psychology of Computer Programming*.

115. Daniel Nelson, "A Newly Appreciated Art: The Development of Personnel Work at Leeds & Northrup, 1915–1923," *Business History Review* 94, no. 4 (1970), 520–535.

116. Daniel J. Kevles, "Testing the Army's Intelligence: Psychologists and the Military in World War I," *Journal of American History* 55, no. 3 (1968): 565–581; Donald S. Napoli, "The Mobilization of American Psychologists, 1938–1941," *Military Affairs* 42, no. 1 (1978): 32–36.

117. Theodore Willoughby, "Psychometric Characteristics of the CDP Examination," in *Proceedings of the Thirteenth Annual SIGCPR Conference* (New York: ACM Press, 1975), 152–160.

Chapter 4

1. Daniel McCracken, "The Software Turmoil: Nine Predictions for '62," *Datamation* 8, no. 1 (1962): 21–22; Robert Patrick, "The Gap in Programming Support," *Datamation* 7, no. 5 (1961): 37.

2. RAND Symposium, "On Programming Languages, Part II," *Datamation* 8, no. 11 (1962): 85.

3. Martin Campbell-Kelly and William Aspray, *Computer: A History of the Information Machine* (New York: Basic Books, 1996), 182.

4. H. S Tropp, "ACM's 20th Anniversary: 30 August 1967," *Annals of the History of Computing* 9, no. 3 (1988): 269.

5. Maurice Wilkes, David Wheeler, and Stanley Gill, *Preparation of Programs for an Electronic Digital Computer* (Reading, MA: Addison-Wesley, 1951).

6. Richard Wexelblat, ed., *History of Programming Languages* (New York: Academic Press, 1981), 10.

7. Frederick P. Brooks, "No Silver Bullet: Essence and Accidents of Software Engineering," *IEEE Computer* 20, no. 4 (1987), 10–19.

8. Remington Rand Univac. *An Introduction to Programming the UNIVAC 1103A and 1105 Computing Systems* (1958) Hagley Museum Archives, Accession 1825, Box 368.

9. John Backus, cited in Wexelblat, *History of Programming Languages*, 82.

10. RAND Symposium, "On Programming Languages, Part II," 25–26.

11. "Editor's Readout: A Long View of a Myopic Problem," *Datamation* 8, no. 5 (1962): 21–22.

12. Gene Bylinsky, "Help Wanted: 50,000 Programmers," *Fortune* 75, no. 3 (1967): 141.

13. See, for example, John Kasson, *Civilizing the Machine: Technology and Republican Values in America, 1776–1900* (Harmondsworth, UK: Penguin, 1976); Ruth Milkman, *Gender at Work: The Dynamics of Job Segregation by Sex during World War II. History E-Book Project* (Urbana: University of Illinois Press, 1987); Alice Kessler-Harris, *Out to Work: A History of Wage-Earning Women in the United States* (New York: Oxford University Press, 1982); and indeed, most of the rest of the history of labor and technology.

14. Valerie Rockmael, "The Woman Programmer," *Datamation* 9, no. 1 (1963): 41.

15. *Preliminary Report: Specifications for the IBM Mathematical Formula Translating System.* New York: Programming Research Group, Applied Science Division, IBM Corporation, November 10, 1954.

16. John Backus, "Programming in America in the 1950s: Some Personal Impressions," in *A History of Computing in the Twentieth Century: A Collection of Essays,* ed. Nicholas Metropolis, Jack Howlett, and Gian-Carlo Rota, 125–135. (New York: Academic Press, 1980).

17. Jean Sammet, *Programming Languages: History and Fundamentals* (Englewood Cliffs, NJ: Prentice-Hall, 1969), 148.

18. Wexelblat, *History of Programming Languages*, 28.

19. Sammet, *Programming Languages*, 144.

20. Herbert Grosch, "Magic Languages," *Datamation* 9, no. 2 (1963), 27.

21. Grace Mitchell, *The FORTRAN Automatic Coding System for the IBM 704 EDPM: Programmer's Primer* (IBM Corporation, 1956), cited in Sammet, *Programming Languages*, 150.

22. Grace Mitchell, *The 704 FORTRAN II Automatic Coding System* (Yorktown Heights, NY: IBM Research Center, 1959), 50.

23. "Automatic Programming: Properties and Performance of FORTRAN Systems I and II," in *Proceedings of Symposium on the Mechanization of the Thought Processes* (Middlesex, UK: National Physical Laboratory Press, 1958).

24. H. Oswald, "The Various FORTRANS," *Datamation* 10, no. 8 (1964): 25–29; "Survey of Programming Languages and Processors," *Communications of the ACM* 6, no. 3 (1965): 93–99.

25. USA Standard FORTRAN, United States of America Standards Institute, USAS X3.9–1966, New York, March 1966.

26. John Backus et al., "The FORTRAN Automatic Coding Language," in *Proceedings of the West Joint Computer Conference* (New York: ACM Press, 1957), 188–198.

27. Sammet, *Programming Languages*, 149.

28. Daniel McCracken, "Is There FORTRAN In Your Future?" *Datamation* 19, no. 5 (1973): 236–237.

29. I. Edward Block, "Report on Meeting Held at University of Pennsylvania Computing Center" (1959).

30. Charles Phillips, *Report from the Committee on Data Systems Languages* (presentation to the Association for Computing Machinery, Boston, September 1, 1959), cited in Wexelblat, *History of Programming Languages*, 200.

31. Charles Phillips, *Minutes, Meeting of the Executive Committee of the Conference on Data Systems Languages* (1959), cited in Wexelblat, *History of Programming Languages*, 202.

32. Wexelblat, *History of Programming Languages*, 204.

33. Jean Sammet, "Brief Summary of the Early History of COBOL." *Annals of the History of Computing* 7, no. 4 (1985): 288–203.

34. Jean Sammet, cited in Wexelblat, *History of Programming Languages*, 219.

35. Jean Sammet, cited in ibid., 234.

36. Wexelblat, *History of Programming Languages*, 231.

37. *Minutes of Meeting of the Intermediate-Range Task Force of the Committee for Data Systems Languages (CODASYL)* Dayton, Ohio. October 8–9, 1959. Reprinted in Annals of the History of Computing 7, no. 4 (1985): 329–341.

38. Robert Bemer, *Computers and Crisis: How Computers Are Shaping Our Future* (New York: ACM Press, 1971).

39. Campbell-Kelly and Aspray, *Computer: A History of the Information Machine*, 192.

40. Stanley Naftaly, "How to Pick a Programming Language," in *Data Processing, Practically Speaking*, ed. Stanley Naftaly and Fred Gruenberger (Los Angeles: Data Processing Digest, 1967): 79–90; "What's Happening with COBOL?" *Business Automation* 14, no. 4 (1966), 42–43.

41. Allan Tucker, *Programming Languages* (Reading, MA: Addison-Wesley, 1977).

42. Ben Shneiderman, "The Relationship between COBOL and Computer Science," *Annals of the History of Computing* 7, no. 4 (1985): 350.

43. Ibid., 351.

44. John Golda, "The Effects of Computer Technology on the Traditional Role of Management" (master's thesis, Wharton School of Business, University of Pennsylvania, 1965), 34, 85; Robert Gordon, "Personnel Selection," in *Data Processing, Practically Speaking* (1967), 34, 85.

45. Alan Perlis, cited in Wexelblat, *History of Programming Languages*, 60.

46. Alan Perlis, cited in ibid., 82.

47. "Angels, Pins, and Language Standards," *Datamation* 9, no. 4 (1963): 23–25.

48. Jack Little, cited in RAND Symposium, "On Programming Languages, Part II," 29–30.

49. Bernard Galler, cited in ibid., 27.

50. Fred Gruenberger, cited in ibid., 28.

51. Jean E. Sammet, "Programming Languages History," *Annals of the History of Computing* 13, no. 1 (1991): 49.

52. Herbert Grosch, "Software in Sickness and Health," *Datamation* 7, no. 7 (1961): 32–33.

53. Ibid., 33.

54. Brooks, "No Silver Bullet," 10.

55. Brad Cox, "There Is a Silver Bullet," *Byte Magazine* 15, no. 10 (1990): 209.

56. David Morrison, "Software Crisis," *Defense* 21, no. 2 (1989): 72.

57. The thirty-three-page report, titled "Bugs in the Program: Problems in Federal Government Computer Software Development and Regulation," was written by two staff members, James H. Paul and Gregory C. Simon, of the Subcommittee on Investigations and Oversight of the House Committee on Science, Space, and Technology. The content of the report was covered in the *Washington Post* (October 17, 1989), D1, and *Science* (November 10, 1989), 753, among many other publications. For example, see Gary Chapman, "Bugs in the Program," *Communications of the ACM* 33, no. 3 (1989): 251–252.

58. Ibid., 72.

59. John Backus, "Programming in America in the 1950s: Some Personal Impressions," in *A History of Computing in the Twentieth Century: A Collection of Essays*, ed. N. Metropolis, J. Howlett, and Gian-Carlo Rota (New York: Academic Press, 1980), 127.

60. Willis Ware, "As I See It: A Guest Editorial," *Datamation* 11, no. 5 (1965): 27.

61. Edsger Dijkstra, "Go to Statement Considered Harmful," *Communications of the ACM* 11, no. 3 (1968): 147–148.

Chapter 5

1. Edsger W. Dijkstra, "Communication with an Automatic Computer" (PhD diss., University of Amsterdam, 1959).

2. Edsger Dijkstra, "The Humble Programmer," *Communications of the ACM* 15, no. 10 (1972): 859–866.

3. Edsger Dijkstra, "Programming as a Discipline of Mathematical Nature," *American Mathematical Monthly* 81, no. 6 (1974): 608–612.

4. Dijkstra, "The Humble Programmer."

5. Michael Mahoney, "In Our Own Image: Creating the Computer," in *The Changing Image of the Sciences*, ed. Ida Stamhuis, Teun Koetsier, and Kees de Pater (Dordrecht: Kluwer Academic Publishers, 2002), 9–27.

6. Geoffrey Bowker, "How to Be Universal: Some Cybernetic Strategies, 1943–1970," *Social Studies of Science* 23, no. 1 (1993): 107–127.

7. RAND Symposium, "Is It Overhaul or Trade-in Time: Part I," *Datamation* 5, no. 4 (1959), 24–33.

8. Ibid.

9. Harold Wilensky, "The Professionalization of Everyone?" *American Journal of Sociology* 70, no. 2 (1964): 137–158.

10. Malcolm Gotterer, "The Impact of Professionalization Efforts on the Computer Manager," in *Proceedings of 1971 ACM Annual Conference* (New York: ACM Press, 1971), 371–372.

11. C. M. Sidlo, "The Making of a Profession" (letter to editor), *Communications of the ACM* 4, no. 8 (1961): 367.

12. Hal Sackman, "Conference on Personnel Research," *Datamation* 14, no. 7 (1968): 74–76, 81.

13. Susan B. Carter et al., *Historical Statistics of the United States Millennial Edition Online* (New York: Cambridge University Press, 2006).

14. Jack W. Carlson, "On Determining C. S. Education Programs," *Communications of the ACM* 9, no. 3 (1966): 135.

15. Ibid.

16. Anthony Oettinger, "President's Letter to the ACM Membership," *Communications of the ACM* 9, no. 12 (1966): 838–839.

17. Robert Rosin, "Relative to the President's December Remarks," *Communications of the ACM* 10, no. 6 (1967): 342.

18. Anthony Oettinger, "The Hardware-Software Complexity," *Communications of the ACM* 10, no. 10 (1967): 604.

19. Herbert A. Simon, *The Sciences of the Artificial*, vol. 1968 (Cambridge, MA: MIT Press, 1969).

20. George E. Forsythe, "What to Do Till the Computer Scientist Comes," *American Mathematical Monthly* 75, no. 5 (1968): 454–462.

21. William Aspray, "Was Early Entry a Competitive Advantage? US Universities That Entered Computing in the 1940s," *IEEE Annals of the History of Computing* 22, no. 3 (2000): 65.

22. Andrew Abbott, *The Systems of Professions: An Essay on the Division of Expert Labor* (Chicago: University of Chicago Press, 1988).

23. Louis Fein, "The Role of the University in Computers, Data Processing, and Related Fields," *Communications of the ACM* 2, no. 10 (1959): 7–14.

24. Ibid.

25. Quentin Correll, "Letters to the Editor," *Communications of the ACM* 1, no. 7 (1958): 2; Peter Naur, "The Science of Datalogy (Letter to Editor)," *Communications of the ACM* 9, no. 7 (1966): 485; P. A. Zaphyr, "The Science of Hypology" (letter to editor), *Communications of the ACM* 2, no. 1 (1959): 4; Editors of DATA-LINK, "What's in a Name? (Letter to Editor)," *Communications of the ACM* 1, no. 4 (1958): 6.

26. Correll, "Letters to the Editor."

27. Gopal Gupta, "Computer Science Curriculum Developments in the 1960s," *IEEE Annals of the History of Computing* 29, no. 2 (2007): 40–54.

28. David Allan Grier, *When Computers Were Human* (Princeton, NJ: Princeton University Press, 2005), viii, 411.

29. Aspray, "Was Early Entry a Competitive Advantage?" 66, 68.

30. I. Bernard Cohen, Gregory W. Welch, and Robert V. D. Campbell, *Makin' Numbers: Howard Aiken and the Computer* (Cambridge, MA: MIT Press, 1999).

31. Ibid., 186.

32. Aspray, "Was Early Entry a Competitive Advantage?" 52, 55.

33. Larry Owens, "Where Are We Going Phil Morse? Changing Agendas and the Rhetoric of Obviousness in the Transformation of Computing at MIT, 1939–1957," *IEEE Annals of the History of Computing* 18, no. 4 (1996): 34–41.

34. Aspray, "Was Early Entry a Competitive Advantage?" 49.

35. Ibid.

36. Ibid., 76.

37. Atsushi Akera, "Calculating a Natural World: Scientists, Engineers, and Computers in the United States, 1937–1968" (PhD diss., University of Pennsylvania, 1998).

38. Peter Galison, "Computer Simulations in the Trading Zone," in *The Disunity of Science*, ed. Peter Galison and David Stump (Stanford, CA: Stanford University Press, 1996), 118–157.

39. Dijkstra, "The Humble Programmer," 860.

40. Charles Yood, "Attack of the Giant Brains," *Research Penn State Online* 24, no. 3 (September 2003), available at http://www.rps.psu.edu/0309/brains.html.

41. David Parnas, "On the Preliminary Report of C3S" (letter to editor), *Communications of the ACM* 9, no. 4 (1966): 242–243.

42. John Backus et al., "The FORTRAN Automatic Coding System," in *Proceedings of the West Joint Computer Conference* (New York: ACM Press, 1957), 188–198.

43. Brent Jesiek, "The Sociotechnical Boundaries of Hardware and Software: A Humpty-Dumpty History," *Bulletin of Science, Technology, and Society* 26, no. 6 (2006): 497–509.

44. Anthony Oettinger, "President's Reply to Louis Fein," *Communications of the ACM* 10, no. 1 (1967): 1, 61.

45. William F. Atchison and John W. Hamblen, "Status of Computer Sciences Curricula in Colleges and Universities," *Communications of the ACM* 7, no. 4 (1964): 225–227.

46. Frank Harary, cited in Gerald M. Weinberg, *An Introduction to General Systems Thinking* (New York: Wiley, 1975).

47. Peter Wegner, "Undergraduate Programs in Computer Science," in *SIGCPR '66: Proceedings of the Fourth SIGCPR Conference on Computer Personnel Research* (New York: ACM Press, 1966), 121–129.

48. Ibid.

49. Herbert A. Simon, Allen Newell, and Alan Perlis, "Computer Science" (letter to editor), *Science* 157, no. 3795 (1967): 1373–1374; Simon, *The Sciences of the Artificial*.

50. In fact, although this quote is widely repeated and attributed to Edsger Dijkstra, it does not appear in any of his published writings. For one of many references, see Nick Parlante, "What Is Computer Science?" *SIGCSE Bulletin* 37, no. 2 (2005), 24.

51. Louis Fein, "Computer-Related Sciences (Synnoetics) at a University in 1975," *Datamation* 7, no. 9 (1961): 34–41.

52. Fein, "The Role of the University in Computers, Data Processing, and Related Fields."

53. ACM Curriculum Committee, "An Undergraduate Program in Computer Science: Preliminary Recommendations," *Communications of the ACM* 8, no. 9 (1965): 543–552.

54. "Will You Vote for an Association Name Change to ACIS?" (editorial), *Communications of the ACM* 8, no. 7 (1965): 424–426.

55. Michael Mahoney, "Computer Science: The Search for a Mathematical Theory," in *Science in the Twentieth Century*, ed. John Krige and Dominique Pestre (Amsterdam: Harwood Academic Publishers, 1997), 617–634.

56. Walter J. McNamara and John L. Hughes, "A Review of Research on the Selection of Computer Programmers," *Personnel Psychology* 14, no. 1 (1961): 41–42.

57. Christopher Shaw, "Programming Schisms," *Datamation* 8, no. 9 (1962): 32.

58. Atchison and Hamblen, "Status of Computer Sciences Curricula in Colleges and Universities."

59. Michael Mahoney, "Software as Science–Science as Software," in *Mapping the History of Computing: Software Issues*, ed. Ulf Hashagen, Reinhard Keil-Slawik, and Arthur Norberg (Berlin: Springer-Verlag, 2002), 25–48.

60. ACM Curriculum Committee, "An Undergraduate Program in Computer Science."

61. Claude Shannon and Warren Weaver, *A Mathematical Theory of Communication* (Urbana: University of Illinois Press, 1949).

62. Lily Kay, "Who Wrote the Book of Life? Information and the Transformation of Molecular Biology," *Science in Context* 8 (1995): 609–634; Ronald Kline, "Cybernetics, Management Science, and Technology Policy: The Emergence of 'Information Technology' as a Keyword, 1948–1985," *Technology and Culture* 47, no. 3 (2006): 513–535.

63. Karl Steinbuch, *INFORMATIK: Automatische Informationsverarbeitung* (Berlin: SEG-Nachrichten, 1957).

64. Thomas S. Kuhn, *The Structure of Scientific Revolutions* (Chicago: University of Chicago Press, 1962), 138.

65. Donald Ervin Knuth, *The Art of Computer programming, Volume 1: Fundamental Algorithms* (Reading, MA: Addison-Wesley, 1968).

66. Paul Ceruzzi, "Electronics Technology and Computer Science, 1940–1975: A Coevolution," *IEEE Annals of the History of Computing* 10, no. 4 (1989): 257–275.

67. Peter Wegner, "Three Computer Cultures: Computer Technology, Computer Mathematics, and Computer Science," *Advances in Computers* 10 (1970): 7–78.

68. Gupta, "Computer Science Curriculum Developments in the 1960s."

69. David Hemmendinger, "The ACM and IEEE-CS Guidelines for Undergraduate CS Education," *Communications of the ACM* 50, no. 5 (2007), 49.

70. Richard H. Austing, Bruce H. Barnes, and Gerald L. Engel, "A Survey of the Literature in Computer Science Education since Curriculum '68," *Communications of the ACM* 20, no. 1 (1977): 13–21.

71. *RAND Symposium* (1969), "RAND Symposia on Computing Transcripts," Charles Babbage Institute Archives, CBI 78, Box 3, Folder 4.

72. Sackman, "Conference on Personnel Research," 76.

73. Richard Hamming, "One Man's View of Computer Science," *Journal of the ACM* 16, no. 1 (1969), 3–12.

74. J. A. McMurrer and J. R. Parish, "The People Problem," *Datamation* 16, no. 7 (1970): 57.

75. Abraham Kandel, "Computer Science: A Vicious Circle," *Communications of the ACM* 15, no. 6 (1972): 470–471.

76. Robert Forest, "EDP People: Review and Preview," *Datamation* 18, no. 6 (1972): 68.

77. Fred Gruenberger, "Problems and Priorities," *Datamation* 18, no. 3 (1972): 49.

78. Mahoney, "Computer Science."

79. Daniel McCracken, "The Human Side of Computing," *Datamation* 7, no. 1 (1961): 9–11.

Chapter 6

1. "The Thinking Machine," *Time* magazine, January 23, 1950, 54–60.

2. J. Lear, "Can a Mechanical Brain Replace You?" *Colliers*, no. 131 (1953), 58–63.

3. "Office Robots," *Fortune* 45 (January 1952), 82–87, 112, 114, 116, 118.

4. Cheryl Knott Malone, "Imagining Information Retrieval in the Library: *Desk Set* in Historical Context," *IEEE Annals of the History of Computing* 24, no. 3 (2002): 14–22.

5. Ibid.

6. Ibid.

7. Thorstein Veblen, *The Theory of the Leisure Class* (New York: McMillan, 1899).

8. Thomas Haigh, "The Chromium-Plated Tabulator: Institutionalizing an Electronic Revolution, 1954–1958," *IEEE Annals of the History of Computing* 4, no. 23 (2001), 75–104.

9. James W. Cortada, *Information Technology as Business History: Issues in the History and Management of Computers* (Westport, CT: Greenwood Press, 1996).

10. Kenneth Flamm, *Creating the Computer: Government, Industry, and High Technology* (Washington, DC: Brookings Institution Press, 1988).

11. Thomas Alexander, "Computers Can't Solve Everything," *Fortune* 80, no. 5 (1969), 126–129, 168, 171.

12. Gordon Moore, "Cramming More Components onto Integrated Circuits," *Electronics* 38, no. 8 (1965), 114–117.

13. McKinsey and Company, "Unlocking the Computer's Profit Potential," *Computers and Automation* 16, no. 7 (1969): 24–33.

14. Alexander, "Computers Can't Solve Everything."

15. John Dearden, "How to Organize Information Systems," *Harvard Business Review* 43, no. 2 (1965): 65–73; John Dearden, "Myth of Real-Time Management Information," *Harvard Business Review* 44, no. 3 (1966): 123–132; John Dearden, "MIS is a Mirage," *Harvard Business Review* 50, no. I1 (1972): 90–99.

16. John Diebold, "Bad Decisions on Computer Use," *Harvard Business Review* 47, no. 1 (1969): 14–21.

17. David Hertz, *New Power for Management* (New York: McGraw-Hill, 1969).

18. Arnold Ditri and Donald Woods, *The End of the Beginning–The Fizzle of the "Computer Revolution"* (Touche Ross and Company, 1959).

19. McKinsey and Company, "Unlocking the Computer's Profit Potential."

20. Editorial, "Trouble . . . I Say Trouble, Trouble in DP City," *Datamation* 14, no. 7 (1968): 21.

21. William R. King and David I. Cleland, "The Design of Management Information Systems: An Information Analysis Approach," *Management Science* 22, no. 3 (1975): 286–297; E. Vanlommel and Bert De Brabander, "The Organization of Electronic Data Processing (EDP) Activities and Computer Use," *Journal of Business* 48, no. 3 (1975): 391–410; Bert De Brabander and Anders Edstrom, "Successful Information System Development Projects," *Management Science* 24, no. 2 (1977): 191–199; Michael J. Ginzberg, "Key Recurrent Issues in the MIS Implementation Process," *MIS Quarterly* 5, no. 2 (1981): 47–59.

22. Robert Patrick, "The Gap in Programming Support," *Datamation* 7, no. 5 (1961): 37; Daniel McCracken, "The Software Turmoil: Nine Predictions for '62," *Datamation* 8, no. 1 (1962): 21–22.

23. Brian Randall and John Buxton, *Software Engineering: Proceedings of the NATO Conferences* (New York: Petrocelli/Carter, 1976).

24. Thomas Haigh, "Software in the 1960s as Concept, Service, and Product," *IEEE Annals of the History of Computing* 24, no. 1 (2002): 5–13.

25. Richard Christian, "The Computer and the Marketing Man," *Journal of Marketing* 26, no. 3 (1962): 79–82; Robert Hayes, Ralph H. Parker, and Gilbert W. King, "Automation and the Library of Congress: Three Views," *Library Quarterly* 34, no. 3 (1964): 229–239; J. H. Spigelman, "Implications of Recent Advances in Electronic Data Processing," *Financial Analysts Journal* 20, no. 5 (1964): 137–143; Maurice Ronayne, "'Leads' to Pertinent ADP Literature for the Public Administrator," *Public Administration Review* 24, no. 2 (1964): 119–125; "Hardware And Software," *British Medical Journal* 1, no. 5449 (1965): 1509; "Abstracts of Papers for the Fourteenth Annual Meeting of the Radiation Research Society, Coronado, California February 13–16, 1966," *Radiation Research* 27, no. 3 (1966): 487–554; Allen Forte, "Review: Conference on the Use of Computers in Humanistic Research," *Computers and the Humanities* 1, no. 3 (1967): 110–112.

26. JoAnne Yates, "Application Software for Insurance in the 1960s and Early 1970s," *Business And Economic History* 24 (1) (1995): 123–134.

27. McKinsey and Company, "Unlocking the Computer's Profit Potential," 33.

28. John Golda, "The Effects of Computer Technology on the Traditional Role of Management" (master's thesis, Wharton School of Business, University of Pennsylvania, 1965), 34.

29. Gene Bylinsky, "Help Wanted: 50,000 Programmers," *Fortune* 75, no. 3 (1967): 141.

30. Charles Keelan, "Controlling Computer Programming," *Journal of Systems Management* 20, no. 1 (1969): 30–33; Hertz, *New Power for Management*; Richard Canning, "Managing the Programming Effort," *EDP Analyzer* 6, no. 6 (1968): 1–15; Charles Lecht, *The Management of Computer Programming Projects* (New York: American Management Association, 1967).

31. Malcolm Gotterer, "The Impact of Professionalization Efforts on the Computer Manager," in *Proceedings of 1971 ACM Annual Conference* (New York: ACM Press, 1971), 368.

32. Dallis Perry and William Cannon, "Vocational Interests of Computer Programmers," *Journal of Applied Psychology* 51, no. 1 (1967): 28–34.

33. W. R. Walker, "MIS Mysticism" (letter to editor), *Business Automation* 16, no. 7 (1969): 8.

34. Herbert Grosch, "Programmers: The Industry's Cosa Nostra," *Datamation* 12, no. 10 (1966): 202.

35. Richard Canning, "The Persistent Personnel Problem," *EDP Analyzer* 5, no. 5 (1967): 1–14.

36. Ibid.

37. Roger Guarino, "Managing Data Processing Professionals," *Personnel Journal* 48, no. 12 (1969): 972–975; P. Bradford and L. R. Cottrell, "Factors Influencing Business Data Processors Turnover: A Comparative Case History," in *Proceedings of the 1977 Annual Conference* (New York: ACM Press, 1977), 202–205.

38. H. V. Reid, "Problems in Managing the Data Processing Department," *Journal of Systems Management* 21, no. 5 (1970): 8–11; Richard Canning, "Managing Staff Retention and Turnover," *EDP Analyzer* 15, no. 8 (1977): 1–13.

39. Editorial, "EDP's Wailing Wall," *Datamation* 13, no. 7 (1967): 21.

40. Guarino, "Managing Data Processing Professionals."

41. John Fike, "Vultures Indeed," *Datamation* 13, no. 5 (1967): 12.

42. Deutsch and Shea, Inc., "A Profile of the Programmer," *Communications of the ACM* 6, no. 10 (1963): 592–594, 647.

43. Avner Porat and James Vaughan, "Computer Personnel: The New Theocracy—or Industrial Carpetbaggers," *Personnel Journal* 48, no. 6 (1968): 540–543.

44. Hertz, *New Power for Management*, 169.

45. McKinsey and Company, "Unlocking the Computer's Profit Potential," 33.

46. Jerry L. Ogdin, "The Mongolian Hordes versus Superprogrammer," *Infosystems* 19, no. 12 (1973): 20.

47. Editorial, "The Facts of Life," *Datamation* 14, no. 3 (1968): 21.

48. Hal Sackman, W. J. Erickson, and E. E. Grant, "Exploratory Experimental Studies Comparing Online and Offline Programming Performance," *Communications of the ACM* 11, no. 1 (1968): 3–11.

49. Edwin E. David, cited in Randall and Buxton, *Software Engineering*, 33.

50. Robert Gordon, "Personnel Selection," in *Data Processing, Practically Speaking*, ed. Stanley Naftaly and Fred Gruenberger (Los Angeles: Data Processing Digest, 1967), 88.

51. Joseph O'Shields, "Selection of EDP Personnel," *Personnel Journal* 44, no. 9 (1965): 472.

52. Perry and Cannon, "Vocational Interests of Computer Programmers."

53. Richard Brandon, "The Problem in Perspective," in *Proceedings of the 1968 23rd ACM National Conference* (New York: ACM Press, 1968), 332–334.

54. "Office Robots," *Fortune* 45, January 1952, 114.

55. See, for example, Gerald Weinberger, *The Psychology of Computer Programming* (New York: Von Nostrand Rheinhold, 1971).

56. Bylinsky, "Help Wanted: 50,000 Programmers," 141.

57. Lecht, *The Management of Computer Programming Projects*, 9.

58. Robert Gordon, "Review of Charles Lecht, *The Management of Computer Programmers*," *Datamation* 14, no. 4 (1968): 200.

59. John Backus, "Programming in America in the 1950s: Some Personal Impressions," in *A History of Computing in the Twentieth Century: A Collection of Essays*, ed. Nicholas Metropolis, Jack Howlett, and Gian-Carlo Rota (New York: Academic Press, 1980), 125–135.

60. Frederick Brooks, *The Mythical Man-Month: Essays on Software Engineering* (New York: Addison-Wesley, 1975), 7.

61. Donald Ervin Knuth, *The Art of Computer Programming. Addison-Wesley Series in Computer Science and Information Processing* (Reading, MA: Addison-Wesley, 1968); Donald Knuth, *Literate Programming* (Stanford, CA: Center for the Study of Language/Information, 1992).

62. P. Mody, "Is Programming an Art?" Software Engineering Notes 17, no. 4 (1992): 19–21; Steve Lohr, *Go to: The Story of the Math Majors, Bridge Players, Engineers, Chess Wizards, Maverick Scientists, and Iconoclasts—The Programmers Who Created the Software Revolution* (New York: Basic Books, 2001).

63. Carl Reynolds, cited in Gene Bylinsky, "Help Wanted: 50,000 Programmers," *Fortune* 75, no. 3 (1967), 142.

64. Daniel McCracken, "The Human Side of Computing," Datamation 7, no. 1 (1961): 9–11; Enid Mumford and Thomas Ward, *Computers: Planning for People* (London: B. T. Batsford, 1968); Gene Altshuler, "Programmers and Analysts" (letter to the editor), *Datamation* 16, no. 1(1970): 47; Raymond Berger, "Computer personnel selection and criteria development," in *Proceedings of the 2nd SIGCPR Conference on Computer Personnel Research* (New York: ACM Press, 1964), 65–77.

65. B. Conway, J. Gibbons, and D. E. Watts, *Business Experience with Electronic Computers: A Synthesis of What Has Been Learned from Electronic Data Processing Installations* (New York: Price Waterhouse, 1959), 81–83.

66. Felix Kaufman, "EDP and the Disenchanted," *California Management Review* 1, no. 4 (1959): 67.

67. Harold Leavitt and Thomas Whisler, "Management in the 1980s," *Harvard Management Review* 36, no. 6 (1958): 41–48.

68. Ibid., 44.

69. Philip Mirowski, *Machine Dreams: Economics Becomes a Cyborg Science* (Cambridge: Cambridge University Press, 2002).

70. Herbert Alexander Simon, *Administrative Behavior: A Study of Decision-Making Processes in Administrative Organization* (New York: Macmillan, 1947).

71. Herbert Alexander Simon, *The New Science of Management Decision* (New York: Harper, 1960), 22.

72. John Diebold, "ADP: The Still-Sleeping Giant," *Harvard Business Review* 42, no. 5 (1964): 64.

73. Thomas Haigh, "Inventing Information Systems: The Systems Men and the Computer, 1950–1968," *Business History Review* 75, no. 1 (2001): 18.

74. Thomas Whisler, "The Impact of Information Technology on Organizational Control," in *The Impact of Computers on Management*, ed. Charles A. Myers (Cambridge, MA: MIT Press, 1967), 48, 44.

75. L. R. Fiock, "Seven Deadly Dangers of EDP," *Harvard Business Review* 40, no. 3 (1962), 90.

76. "Is the Computer Running Wild?" *U.S. News and World Report*, February 1964.

77. Robert McFarland, "Electronic Power Grab," *Business Automation* 12, no.2 (February 1965), 30–39.

78. Michael Barnett, *Computer Programming in English* (New York: Harcourt, Brace and World, 1969), 3.

79. Rosemary Stewart, *How Computers Affect Management* (Cambridge, MA: MIT Press, 1971), 196.

80. Golda, "The Effects of Computer Technology on the Traditional Role of Management," 34.

81. Alexander, "Computers Can't Solve Everything," 169.

82. Michael Rose, *Computers, Managers, and Society* (Harmondsworth, UK: Penguin, 1969), 207.

83. Porat and Vaughan, "Computer Personnel," 542.

84. Editorial, "The Thoughtless Information Technologist," *Datamation* 12, no. 8 (1966): 21.

85. Haroun Jamous and Bernard Peliolle, "Changes in the French University Hospital System," in *Professions and Professionalisation*, ed. J. A. Jackson (Cambridge: Cambridge University Press, 1970), 111–152.

86. Barnett, *Computer Programming in English*, 5.

87. Perry and Cannon, "Vocational Interests of Computer Programmers."

88. Gotterer, "The Impact of Professionalization Efforts on the Computer Manager," 368.

89. Gordon, "Personnel Selection," 85.

90. Brian Rothery, *Installing and Managing a Computer* (London: Business Books, 1968), 83.

91. Editorial, "The Thoughtless Information Technologist," 21–22.

92. Ibid.

93. Walker, "MIS Mysticism," 8.

94. Editorial, "The Thoughtless Information Technologist," 21–22.

95. Hertz, *New Power for Management*, 169.

96. H. L. Morgan and J. V. Soden, "Understanding MIS Failures," *Database 5*, no. 2 (1973), 159.

97. Harry Larson, "EDP: A 20 Year Ripoff!" *Infosystems* (1974), 28.

98. Editorial, "Trouble . . . I Say Trouble, Trouble in DP City."

99. Golda, "The Effects of Computer Technology on the Traditional Role of Management," 34.

100. Larson, "EDP: A 20 Year Ripoff!" 26.

101. Hertz, *New Power for Management*, 169.

102. Robert Boguslaw and Warren Pelton, "Steps: A Management Game for Programming Supervisors," *Datamation 5*, no. 6 (1959): 13–16.

103. Gordon, "Personnel Selection," 200.

104. Keelan, "Controlling Computer Programming," 30.

Chapter 7

1. Editorial, "Editor's Readout: The Certified Public Programmer," *Datamation* 8, no. 3 (1962): 23–24.

2. Ibid.

3. Calvin Elliott, "DPMA: Its Function and Future," *Datamation* 9, no. 6 (1963): 35–36.

4. Ibid.

5. Report, "Certificate in Data Processing," *Datamation* 9, no. 8 (1963): 59.

6. Jerome Geckle, "Letter to the Editor," *Datamation* 11, no. 9 (1965): 12–13.

7. John A. Guerrieri, "Certification: Evolution, Not Revolution," *Datamation* 14, no. 11 (1973), 101; "DPMA Certificate Panel," (1964), CBI 46, "John K. Swearingen Papers, 1936–1993," Box 1, Folder 17, Archives of the Charles Babbage Institute, University of Minnesota, Minneapolis.

8. Richard Canning, "Professionalism: Coming or Not?" *EDP Analyzer* 14, no. 3 (1976): 1–12.

9. Richard Canning, "The Question of Professionalism," *EDP Analyzer* 6, no. 12 (1968): 1–13.

10. Richard Canning, "The DPMA Certificate in Data Processing," *EDP Analyzer* 3, no. 7 (1965): 1–12.

11. Charles M. Sidlo, "The Making of a Profession" (letter to editor), *Communications of the ACM* 4, no. 8 (1961): 366.

12. Hal Sackman, "Conference on Personnel Research," *Datamation* 14, no. 7 (1968): 74–76, 81.

13. Report, "Certificate in Data Processing," 38.

14. Editorial, "Learning a Trade," *Datamation* 12, no. 10 (1966): 21.

15. James Jenks, "Starting Salaries of Engineers Are Deceptively High," *Datamation* 13, no. 1 (1967): 13.

16. Louis Kaufman and Richard Smith, "Let's Get Computer Personnel on the Management Team," *Training and Development Journal* 20, no. 11 (1966): 25–29.

17. Bendix Computer Division, "Is Your Programming Career in a Closed Loop?" *Datamation* 8, no. 9 (1962): 86.

18. Mitre Corporation, "Are You Working Your Way toward Obsolescence?" *Datamation* 12, no. 6 (1966): 99.

19. Xerox Corporation, "At Xerox, We Look at Programmers . . . and See Managers" (ad), *Datamation* 14, no. 4 (1968).

20. Richard Canning, "Issues in Programming Management," *EDP Analyzer* 12, no. 4 (1974): 1–14.

21. Magali Sarfatti Larson, *The Rise of Professionalism: A Sociological Analysis* (Berkeley: University of California Press, 1977).

22. Harold Wilensky, "The Professionalization of Everyone?" *American Journal of Sociology* 70, no. 2 (1964): 137–158.

23. David Ross, "Certification and Accreditation," *Datamation* 14, no. 9 (1968): 183–184.

24. Canning, "Professionalism: Coming or Not?" 2.

25. Editorial, "Professionalism Termed Key to Computer Personnel Situation," *Personnel Journal* 51, no. 2 (1971): 156–157.

26. George Palmer, "Programming, The Profession That Isn't," *Datamation* 21, no. 4 (1975): 23–24.

27. Eric Weiss, "Publications in Computing: An Informal Review," *Communications of the ACM* 15, no. 7 (1972): 492–497.

28. Saul Gass, "ACM Class Structure" (letter to editor), *Communications of the ACM* 2, no. 5 (1959): 4.

29. "The Certificate and Undergraduate Program," (1959), CBI 88, "Data Processing Management Association records," Box 22, Folder 1, Archives of the Charles Babbage Institute, University of Minnesota, Minneapolis.

30. "RAND Symposium, 1959" (1959).

31. George DiNardo, "Software Management and the Impact of Improved Programming Technology," in *Proceedings of 1975 ACM Annual Conference Software Management and the Impact of Improved Programming Technology* (New York: ACM Press, 1975), 288–289.

32. Editorial, "The Cost of Professionalism," *Datamation* 9, no. 10 (1963): 23.

33. Anthony Oettinger, "On ACM's Responsibility" (president's letter to ACM membership 1966), *Communications of the ACM* 9, no. 8 (1966): 545–546.

34. Emphasis added. Paul Armer, "Thinking Big" (letter to editor), *Communications of the ACM* 2, no. 1 (1959).

35. Herbert Grosch, "Plus and Minus," *Datamation* 5, no. 6 (1959): 51.

36. Robert Payne, "Reaction to Publication Proposal" (letter to editor), *Communications of the ACM* 8, no. 1 (1965): 71.

37. Anthony Oettinger, "ACM Sponsors Professional Development Program" (president's letter to ACM membership), *Communications of the ACM* 9, no. 10 (1966): 712–713.

38. Bernard Galler, "The Journal" (president's letter to ACM membership), *Communications of the ACM* 12, no. 2 (1969): 65–66.

39. "Will You Vote for an Association Name Change to ACIS?" *Communications of the ACM* 8, no. 7 (1965): 424–426; Daniel McCracken, "Vote on ACM Name Change," (1978), CBI 43, "Daniel D. McCracken Papers, 1958–1983," Box 3, Folder 10, Archives of the Charles Babbage Institute, University of Minnesota, Minneapolis.

40. Anthony Oettinger, "President's Reply to Louis Fein," *Communications of the ACM* 10, no. 1 (1967): 1, 61.

41. Raymond Wishner, "Comment on Curriculum 68," *Communications of the ACM* 11, no. 10 (1968): 658; Report, "Curriculum 68," *Datamation* 14, no. 5 (1968): 114–116; Richard Hamming, "One Man's View of Computer Science," *Journal of the ACM* 16, no. 1 (1969), 3–12.

42. John Postley, "Letter to Editor," *Communications of the ACM* 3, no. 1 (1960): A6.

43. "Why Are Business Users Turned Off by ACM?" (1974), CBI 23, "George Glaser Papers, 1960–1989," Box 1, Folder 3, Archives of the Charles Babbage Institute, University of Minnesota, Minneapolis.

44. Ibid.

45. Ibid.

46. "Six Measures of Professionalism," (1962), CBI 88, "Data Processing Management Association records," Box 21, Folder 40, Archives of the Charles Babbage Institute, University of Minnesota, Minneapolis.

47. "Local Chapter CDP Publicity," (1964), CBI 46, "John K. Swearingen Papers, 1936–1993," Box 1, Folder 17, Archives of the Charles Babbage Institute, University of Minnesota, Minneapolis.

48. "Letter Re: Four Year Degree Requirement," (1970), CBI 116, "Institute for Certification of Computer Professionals Records, 1960–1993," Box 1, Folder 27, Archives of the Charles Babbage Institute, University of Minnesota, Minneapolis; R. Higgins, "Letter to the DPMA" (1973) CBI 46, "John K. Swearingen Papers, 1936–1993," Box 1, Folder 17, Archives of the Charles Babbage Institute, University of Minnesota, Minneapolis.

49. J. D. Madden, "Letter to Calvin Elliot," (June 27, 1967), CBI 88, "Data Processing Management Association records," Box 22, Folder 1, Archives of the Charles Babbage Institute, University of Minnesota, Minneapolis.

50. "Notes on ACM/DPMA merger" (1964), CBI 88, "Data Processing Management Association records," Box 22, Folder 2, Archives of the Charles Babbage Institute, University of Minnesota, Minneapolis; "Correspondence re: ACM/DPMA liason," (1966), CBI 88, "Data Processing Management Association records," Box 22, Folder 1, Archives of the Charles Babbage Institute, University of Minnesota, Minneapolis; "Discussion of DPMA/ACM Merger," (1970), CBI 88, "Data Processing Management Association records," Box 22, Folder 3, Archives of the Charles Babbage Institute, University of Minnesota, Minneapolis.

51. "RAND Symposium, 1975: Problems of the AFIPS Societies Revisited," (1975), CBI 78, "RAND Symposia on Computing Transcripts," Box 3, Folder 7, Archives of the Charles Babbage Institute, University of Minnesota, Minneapolis.

52. "CDP Advisory Council, Minutes of the Third Annual Meeting, Jan. 17–18, 1964," (1964), CBI 88, "Data Processing Management Association records," Box 22, Folder 3, Archives of the Charles Babbage Institute, University of Minnesota, Minneapolis.

53. "DPMA Certification Council minutes, 23rd meeting, April 1-4, 1970," (1970) CBI 116, "Institute for Certification of Computer Professionals Records, 1960–1993," Box 1, Folder 26, Archives of the Charles Babbage Institute, University of Minnesota, Minneapolis.

54. "DPMA Revises CDP Test Requirements," *Data Management* (1967): 34–35.

55. Higgins, "Letter to the DPMA."

56. Paul Armer, "Editor's Readout: Suspense Won't Kill Us," *Datamation* 19, no. 6 (1973): 53.

57. Robert Reinstedt and Raymond Berger, "Certification: A Suggested Approach to Acceptance," *Datamation* 19, no. 11 (1973): 97–100.

58. Alan Taylor, "DPMA Should be Saved Now, If At All Possible," *Computerworld* (1971), found in CBI 116, "Institute for Certification of Computer Professionals Records, 1960–1993," Box 1, Folder 30, Archives of the Charles Babbage Institute, University of Minnesota, Minneapolis; Alan Taylor; "Taylor Replies," *Computerworld* (1971), CBI 116, "Institute for Certification of Computer Professionals Records, 1960–1993," Box 1, Folder 30, Archives of the Charles Babbage Institute, University of Minnesota,

Minneapolis; William Claghorn, "Rough draft of a reply to Alan Taylor," (1971), CBI 88, "Data Processing Management Association records," Box 18, Folder 47, Archives of the Charles Babbage Institute, University of Minnesota, Minneapolis; "Letter to the editors of *Computerworld*," (1971, unpublished), CBI 88, "Data Processing Management Association records," Box 18, Folder 47, Archives of the Charles Babbage Institute, University of Minnesota, Minneapolis.

59. Alan Taylor. "Members Look More Like Markets From Park Ridge." *Computerworld* (April 14, 1971). CBI 116, "Institute for Certification of Computer Professionals Records, 1960–1993," Box 1, Folder 30, Archives of the Charles Babbage Institute, University of Minnesota, Minneapolis.

60. "SCDP Draft Legislation," (1974), CBI 116, "Institute for Certification of Computer Professionals Records, 1960–1993," Box 11, Folder 42, Archives of the Charles Babbage Institute, University of Minnesota, Minneapolis.

61. Ross, "Certification and Accreditation"; T.D.C. Kuch, "Unions or Licensing? or Both? or Neither?" *Infosystems* 20, no. 1 (1973): 42–43.

62. "SCDP Draft Legislation," CBI 116, Box 11, Folder 42.

63. D.J. MacPherson, "Letter to R. C. Elliot re: unauthorized use of CDP initials," (October 26, 1970), CBI 88, "Data Processing Management Association records," Box 18, Folder 22, Archives of the Charles Babbage Institute, University of Minnesota, Minneapolis.

64. Kenniston W. Lord, cited in Canning, "Professionalism: Coming or Not?"

65. "DPMA Board of Directors, 9th Meeting, March 11–12, 1966," (1966), CBI 88, "Data Processing Management Association records," Box 22, Folder 7, Archives of the Charles Babbage Institute, University of Minnesota, Minneapolis.

66. "DPMA Board of Directors, 12th Meeting, 1967 Las Vegas," (1967), CBI 88, "Data Processing Management Association records," Box 22, Folder 8, Archives of the Charles Babbage Institute, University of Minnesota, Minneapolis.

67. Ibid.

68. Malcolm Smith, "Complaint about Boston exam," (1969), CBI 116, "Institute for Certification of Computer Professionals Records, 1960–1993," Box 1, Folder 19, Archives of the Charles Babbage Institute, University of Minnesota, Minneapolis.

69. "The Certificate and Undergraduate Program," (1959); "The Certificate and Undergraduate Program," (1959), CBI 46, "John K. Swearingen Papers, 1936–1993," Box 1, Folder 13, Archives of the Charles Babbage Institute, University of Minnesota, Minneapolis.

70. "Notes on ACM/DPMA merger," CBI 88, Box 22, Folder 2.

71. "DPMA Board of Directors, 10th Meeting, 1966" (minutes), (June 19–20, 1966), CBI 88, "Data Processing Management Association records," Box 2, Folder 8, Archives of the Charles Babbage Institute, University of Minnesota, Minneapolis.

72. "Letter from Jack Yarbrough to John Swearingen," (1964), CBI 46, "John K. Swearingen Papers, 1936–1993," Box 1, Folder 17, Archives of the Charles Babbage Institute, University of Minnesota, Minneapolis.

73. "Response to Business Automation article on CDP," (1964), CBI 46, "John K. Swearingen Papers, 1936–1993," Box 1, Folder 16, Archives of the Charles Babbage Institute, University of Minnesota, Minneapolis.

74. "Notes on ACM/DPMA merger," CBI 88, Box 22, Folder 2.

75. Report, "Certificate in Data Processing," 59.

76. R. C. Heterick, "Letter to Ben Payne," (September 17, 1971), CBI 88, "Data Processing Management Association records," Box 18, Folder 22, Archives of the Charles Babbage Institute, University of Minnesota, Minneapolis.

77. "Computerworld Survey," (1970), CBI 88, "Data Processing Management Association records," Box 18, Folder 22, Archives of the Charles Babbage Institute, University of Minnesota, Minneapolis.

78. Herbert Grosch, cited in "New CDP Requirements 'Unduly Harsh' Professionals Protest," (1970), CBI 116, "Institute for Certification of Computer Professionals Records, 1960–1993," Box 1, Folder 27, Archives of the Charles Babbage Institute, University of Minnesota, Minneapolis.

79. Alex Orden, "The Emergence of a Profession," *Communications of the ACM* 10, no. 3 (1967): 145–146.

80. Sidlo, "The Making of a Profession," 367.

81. Edward Menkhaus, "EDP: Nice Work If You Can Get It," *Business Automation* 12, no. 3 (1969): 43.

82. Thomas White, "The 70's: People," *Datamation* 16, no. 7 (1970): 42–43.

83. Robert Forest, "EDP People: Review and Preview," *Datamation* 18, no. 6 (1972): 65–67.

84. Edward Markham, "Selecting a Private EDP School," *Datamation* 14, no. 5 (1968): 33.

85. "Executive Meeting Summary" (1966), CBI 46, "John K. Swearingen Papers, 1936–1993," Box 1, Folder 3, Archives of the Charles Babbage Institute, University of Minnesota, Minneapolis.

86. Charles Babbage Institute Archives, box 88, folder 18, file 28.

87. "Correspondence re: Improper Use of CDP Initials," (1966), CBI 88, "Data Processing Management Association records," Box 18, Folder 22, Archives of the Charles Babbage Institute, University of Minnesota, Minneapolis.

88. "Correspondence re: Academic and Experience Req's," (1966), CBI 88, "Data Processing Management Association records," Box 18, Folder 22, Archives of the Charles Babbage Institute, University of Minnesota, Minneapolis.

89. Canning, "The DPMA Certificate in Data Processing."

90. Ibid.; "Letter from Jack Yarbrough," CBI 46, Box 1, Folder 17.

91. Milt Stone, "In Search of an Identity," *Datamation* 18, no. 3 (1972): 53–54.

92. Fred Gruenberger, cited in "RAND Symposium, 1975: Problems of the AFIPS Societies Revisited," CBI 78, Box 3, Folder 7.

93. Ibid.

94. "DPMA Certificate Panel," CBI 46, Box 1, Folder 17.

95. Arthur Kaupe, "Letter to the Editors of *Computerworld*, March 1, 1972" (1972), CBI 116, "Institute for Certification of Computer Professionals Records, 1960–1993," Box 1, Folder 30, Archives of the Charles Babbage Institute, University of Minnesota, Minneapolis.

96. John Seitz, "Should DPMA Control Certification Process?" (letter to the editor), *Computerworld* (1971), CBI 116, "Institute for Certification of Computer Professionals Records, 1960–1993," Box 1, Folder 30, Archives of the Charles Babbage Institute, University of Minnesota, Minneapolis.

97. Willis Ware, "AFIPS in Retrospect," *Annals of the History of Computing* 8, no. 3 (1986): 304.

98. ARPA Survey, 1968, cited in "AFIPS Constitution Letter," *Communications of the ACM* 12, no. 3 (1969), 4.

99. Bernard Galler, "The AFIPS Constitution (President's Letter to ACM Membership)," *Communications of the ACM* 12, no. 3 (1969): 188.

100. Robert Rector, "Personal Reflections on the First Quarter Century of AFIPS," *Annals of the History of Computing* 8, no. 3 (1986): 261–269.

101. Richard Jones, "A Time to Assume Responsibility," *Datamation* 13, no. 9 (1967): 160.

102. "Survey on the Use of Service Bureaus," *Wall Street Journal* (November 4, 1969): 24.

103. RAND Symposium, "Is It Overhaul or Trade-in Time: Part I," *Datamation* 5, no. 4 (1959), 24–33.

104. Christopher Shaw, "Programming Schisms," *Datamation* 8, no. 9 (1962): 32.

105. Wolf Flywheel, "Letter to the Editor (on Professionalism)," *Datamation* 5, no. 5 (1959): 2.

106. Harry Tropp, cited in "AFIPS Presidents Discussion" (1985) CBI 114, "Walter M. Carlson Papers, 1960–1990," Box 1, Folder 4, Archives of the Charles Babbage Institute, University of Minnesota, Minneapolis.

107. Herbert Grosch, cited in RAND Symposium, "Is It Overhaul or Trade-in Time: Part I."

108. Editorial, "Professional Societies . . . or Technician Associations?" *Datamation* 11, no. 8 (1965): 23.

109. Hans A. Rhee, *Office Automation in Social Perspective: The Progress and Social Implications of Electronic Data Processing* (Oxford: Basil Blackwell, 1968), 118.

110. "Minutes of the Annual Meeting of the Certification Advisory Council" (1967).

111. Gotterer, "The Impact of Professionalization Efforts on the Computer Manager," 368.

112. Louis Fein, "ACM Has a Crisis of Identity?" *Communications of the ACM* 10, no. 1 (1967): 1.

113. John Backus, cited in Richard Wexelblat, ed., *History of Programming Languages* (New York: Academic Press, 1981), 69.

114. Canning, "Professionalism: Coming or Not?" 2.

115. "Why Are Business Users Turned Off by ACM?" (1974) CBI 23, Box 1, Folder 3.

116. George Glaser, "Letter to W. Carlson," (July 15, 1974), CBI 23, "George Glaser Papers, 1960–1989," Box 1, Folder 3, Archives of the Charles Babbage Institute, University of Minnesota, Minneapolis.

Chapter 8

1. Ronald Graham, cited in Peter Naur, Brian Randall, and John Buxton, ed., *Software Engineering: Proceedings of the NATO Conferences* (New York: Petrocelli/Charter, 1976), 32.

2. Robert Glass, "Is There Really a Software Crisis?" *IEEE Software* 15, no. 1 (1998): 104–105.

3. Robert Bemer, *Computers and Crisis: How Computers Are Shaping Our Future* (New York: ACM Press, 1971).

4. Robert Gordon, "Review of Charles Lecht, *The Management of Computer Programmers*," *Datamation* 14, no. 4 (1968): 200–202.

5. Ibid., 7.

6. Martin Campbell-Kelly and William Aspray, *Computer: A History of the Information Machine* (New York: Basic Books, 1996), 210.

7. W. Saba, "Letter to the Editor," *IEEE Computer* 29, no. 9 (1996): 10; Edward Nash Yourdon, ed., *Classics in Software Engineering* (New York: Yourdon Press, 1979); Herbert Freeman and Phillip Lewis, *Software Engineering* (New York: Academic Press, 1980).

8. M. Douglas McIlroy, cited in ibid, 7.

9. Douglas McIroy, cited in Naur, Randall, and Buxton, *Software Engineering*, 7.

10. Ibid.

11. Brad Cox, "There Is a Silver Bullet," *Byte* 15, no. 10 (1990): 209.

12. Frederick Winslow Taylor, *The Principles of Scientific Management* (New York: Harper and Brothers, 1911).

13. Richard Canning, "Issues in Programming Management," *EDP Analyzer* 12, no. 4 (1974): 1–14.

14. Stuart Shapiro, "Splitting the Difference: The Historical Necessity of Synthesis in Software Engineering," *IEEE Annals of the History of Computing* 19, no. 1 (1997): 25–54.

15. Gerald Weinberg, *The Psychology of Computer Programming* (New York: Van Nostrand Rheinhold, 1971).

16. Claude Baum, *The Systems Builders: The Story of SDC* (Santa Monica, CA: System Development Corporation, 1981), 52.

17. Ibid., 48.

18. Thomas C. Rowan, "The Recruiting and Training of Programmers," *Datamation* 4, no. 3 (1958): 16–18.

19. Baum, *The Systems Builders*, 47.

20. Philip Kraft, *Programmers and Managers: The Routinization of Computer Programming in the United States* (New York: Springer-Verlag, 1977), 39.

21. Philip Metzger, *Managing a Programming Project* (Englewood Cliffs, NJ: Prentice-Hall, 1973).

22. Richard Canning, "Issues in Programming Management," *EDP Analyzer* 12, no. 4 (1974): 1–14.

23. Joel Aron, *Part I: The Individual Programmer* (Reading, MA: Addison-Wesley, 1974); Joel Aron, *Program Development Process: The Programming Team* (Reading, MA: Addison-Wesley, 1983).

24. Canning, "Issues in Programming Management."

25. Richard Canning, "Professionalism: Coming or Not?" *EDP Analyzer* 14, no. 3 (1976): 1–12.

26. Brian Rothery, *Installing and Managing a Computer* (London: Business Books, 1968), 80.

27. Robert Gordon, "Personnel Selection," in *Data Processing: Practically Speaking*, ed. Stanley Naftaly and Fred Gruenberger (Los Angeles: Data Processing Digest, 1967): 85.

28. B. Conway, J. Gibbons, and D. E. Watts, *Business Experience with Electronic Computers: A Synthesis of What Has Been Learned from Electronic Data Processing Installations* (New York: Price Waterhouse, 1959), 81.

29. Ibid., 81–82.

30. Gene Bylinsky, "Help Wanted: 50,000 Programmers," *Fortune* 75, no. 3 (1967): 141.

31. H. V. Reid, "Problems in Managing the Data Processing Department," *Journal of Systems Management* 21, no. 5 (1970): 8–11; Richard Canning, "Managing Staff Retention and Turnover," *EDP Analyzer* 15, no. 8 (1977): 1–13.

32. Editorial, "EDP's Wailing Wall," *Datamation* 13, no. 7 (1967): 21.

33. Baum, *The Systems Builders*, 52.

34. Martin Campbell-Kelly, cited in Campbell-Kelly and Aspray, *Computer*, 144.

35. Thomas Wise, "IBM's $5,000,000,000 Gamble," *Time*, September 1966, 226.

36. Thomas Watson Jr., cited in Campbell-Kelly and Aspray, *Computer*, 199.

37. Frederick Brooks, cited in Campbell-Kelly and Aspray, *Computer*, 200; Emerson Pugh, Lyle Johnson, and John Palmer, *IBM's 360 and Early 370 Systems* (Cambridge, MA: MIT Press, 1991).

38. Frederick P. Brooks, *The Mythical Man-Month: Essays on Software Engineering* (New York: Addison-Wesley, 1975), 17.

39. Ibid., 31.

40. Ibid., 34–35.

41. Ibid., 42, 7.

42. Frederick P. Brooks, "No Silver Bullet: Essence and Accidents of Software Engineering," *IEEE Computer* 20, no. 4 (1987), 10–19.

43. F. Terry Baker and Harlan Mills, "Chief Programmer Teams," *Datamation* 19, no. 12 (1973): 198–199.

44. Ibid., 200.

45. Ibid., 201.

46. Clement McGowan and John Kelly, *Top-down Structured Programming Techniques* (New York: Petrocelli/Carter, 1975), 148.

47. Barbara Barry and John Naughton, *Structured Programming Series. Volume X. Chief Programmer Team Operations Description* (Gaithersburg, MD.: IBM Ferderal Systems, 1975), 12–13.

48. Stuart Shapiro, "Splitting the Difference," 25.

49. Barry Boehm, "Software Engineering," *IEEE Transactions on Computers*, no. 12 (1976): 349; Yourdon, *Classics in Software Engineering*, 63.

50. J. L. Ogdin, "The Mongolian Hordes versus Superprogrammer," *Infosystems* 19, no. 12 (1973): 23.

51. Daniel Couger and Robert Zawacki, "What Motivates DP Professionals?" *Datamation* 24, no. 9 (1978): 116–123; Canning, "Issues in Programming Management."

52. C. Anthony Hoare, "Software Engineering: A Keynote Address." In *Proceedings of the 3rd International Conference on Software Engineering* (Piscataway, NJ: IEEE Press, 1978): 1–4.

53. Carma McClure, *Managing Software Development and Maintenance* (New York: Van Nostrand Rheinhold, 1981), 77.

54. Ibid., 77–78, 86.

55. John Golda, "The Effects of Computer Technology on the Traditional Role of Management" (master's thesis, Wharton School of Business, University of Pennsylvania, 1965), 34.

56. Weinberg, *The Psychology of Computer Programming*, 56.

57. Ibid., 53.

58. Ibid.

59. Ibid.

60. Ibid.

61. Ogdin, "The Mongolian Hordes versus Superprogrammer," 23.

62. Canning, "Issues in Programming Management," 6.

63. Rudolph Hirsch, "Programming Performance: Monitoring, Maximization, and Prediction," in *Special Interest Group on Computer Personnel Research Annual Conference* (New York: ACM Press, 1972), 36–46.

64. Steve McConnell, *Code Complete: A Practical Handbook of Software Construction* (Redmond, WA: Microsoft Press, 1993), 287; Girish Parikh, *Programmer Productivity: Achieving an Urgent Priority* (Reston, VA: Reston Publishing, 1984), 209; Edward Yourdon, *Writings of the Revolution: Selected Readings on Software Engineering* (New York, Prentice Hall, 1986), 288.

65. Anthony Jay, *Corporation Man* (New York: Random House, 1971).

66. Douglas McGregor, *The Human Side of Enterprise* (New York: McGraw-Hill, 1960).

67. Ogdin, "The Mongolian Hordes versus Superprogrammer," 23.

68. Bo Sanden, "Programming Masters Break Out of the Managerial Mold," *Computerworld* (1986): 73.

69. Henry Lucas, "*On the Failure to Implement Structured Programming and Other Techniques*," in *Proceedings of 1975 ACM Annual Conference* (New York: ACM Press, 1975), 291–293.

70. McClure, *Managing Software Development and Maintenance*, 74–75.

71. Edsger Dijkstra, cited in Eloina Paleaz, "A Gift from Pandora's Box: The Software Crisis" (PhD diss., University of Edinburgh, 1988), 175.

72. Donald MacKenzie, "A View from the Sonnenbichl: On the Historical Sociology of Software and System Dependability," in *History of Computing: Software Issues*, ed. Ulf Hashagen, Reinhard Keil-Slawik, and Arthur L. Norberg (Berlin: Springer-Verlag, 2002): 97–122.

73. Friedrich L. Bauer, "Software Engineering: A Conference Report," *Datamation* 15, no. 10 (1969).

74. John N. Buxton, cited in Paleaz, "A Gift from Pandora's Box," 185.

75. Douglas Ross, cited in Paleaz, "A Gift from Pandora's Box," 182.

76. Campbell-Kelly and Aspray, *Computer*, 201.

77. Michael Mahoney, "The Roots of Software Engineering," *CWI Quarterly* 3, no. 4 (1980): 325–334.

78. Christopher Strachey, cited in Randall and Buxton, *Software Engineering*, 147.

79. Ibid.

80. Ibid.

81. Ann Dooley, "100% Over Budget," *Computerworld* (1987): 5.

82. Gary Chapman, "Bugs in the Program," *Communications of the ACM* 33, no. 3 (1990): 251–252.

83. David Morrison, "Software Crisis," *Defense* 21, no. 2 (1989): 72.

84. William Wayt Gibbs, "Software's Chronic Crisis," *Scientific American* 271, no. 3 (1994): 86.

Chapter 9

1. J. Jimms, "Could Y2K cause a global recession?" *Fortune* 138, no. 7 (1998): 172–176.

2. Fred Kaplan, "Military on Year 2000 alert," *Boston Globe* (June 21, 1998): A1.

3. David Edgerton, *The Shock of the Old: Technology and Global History since 1900* (Oxford: Oxford University Press, 2007).

4. B. P. Lientz, E. B. Swanson, and G. E. Tompkins, "Characteristics of application software maintenance," *Communications of the ACM* 21, no. 6 (1978): 466–471; Girish Parikh, "Software Maintenance: Penny Wise, Program Foolish," *SIGSOFT Software Engineering Notes* 10, no. 5 (1985): 89–98; Ruchi Shukla and Arun Kumar Misra, "Estimating Software Maintenance Effort: A Neural Network Approach," In *ISEC '08: Proceedings of the 1st Conference on India Software Engineering Conference* (Hyderabad, India: ACM, 2008), 107–112.

5. Richard Canning, "The Maintenance 'Iceberg,'" *EDP Analyzer* 10, no. 10 (1972): 1–13.

6. Gerardo Canfora and Aniello Cimitile, *Software Maintenance* (Technical report, University of Sannio, 2000).

7. Maurice Wilkes, *Memoirs of a Computer Pioneer* (Cambridge: MIT Press, 1985).

8. David Rine, "A Short Overview of a History of Software Maintenance: As It Pertains to Reuse," *SIGSOFT Software Engineering Notes* 16, no. 4 (1991): 60–63.

9. Canning, "The Maintenance 'Iceberg'" (1972).

10. E. Burton Swanson, "The Dimensions of Maintenance," in *ICSE '76: Proceedings of the 2nd International Conference on Software Engineering* (San Francisco: IEEE Computer Society Press, 1976), 492–497.

11. Girish Parikh, "What Is Software Maintenance Really? What Is in a Name?" *SIGSOFT Software Engineering Notes* 9, no. 2 (1984): 114–116.

12. Frederick Brooks, *The Mythical Man-Month: Essays on Software Engineering* (New York: Addison-Wesley, 1975), 7.

13. Bjarne Stroustrup, "A History of C++," in *History of Programming Languages*, ed. Thomas M. Bergin and R.G. Gibson (New York, ACM Press, 1996).

14. Michael Swaine, "Is Your Next Language COBOL?" *Dr. Dobbs Journal* (2008).

15. Andrew Pollack, "Year 2000 Problem Tests Professionalism of Programmers," *New York Times* (May 3, 1999): C1; Mark Manion and William M. Evan, "The Y2K Problem: Technological Risk and Professional Responsibility," *ACM SIGCAS Computers and Society* 29, no. 4 (1999): 24–29.

16. John Shore, "Why I Never Met a Programmer I Could Trust," *Communications of the ACM* 31, no. 4 (1988): 372.

17. Shoshana Zuboff, *In the Age of the Smart Machine: The Future of Work and Power* (New York: Basic Books, 1988).

18. Thomas Gieryn, "Boundary-Work and the Demarcation of Science from Non-Science: Strains and Interests in Professional Ideologies of Scientists," *American Sociological Review* 48, no. 4 (1983): 781–795.

19. Ibid.

20. Andrei P. Ershov, "Aesthetics and the Human Factor in Programming," *Communications of the ACM* 15, no. 7 (1972): 502.

21. Gieryn, "Boundary work," 792.

22. Harold Wilensky, "The Professionalization of Everyone?" *American Journal of Sociology* 70, no. 2 (1964): 137–158.

23. Nathan Ensmenger, "The 'Question of Professionalism' in the Computer Fields," *IEEE Annals of the History of Computing* 23, no. 4 (2001): 56–73.

24. Magali Sarfatti Larson, *The Rise of Professionalism: A Sociological Analysis*. (Berkeley: University of California Press, 1977).

25. Robert Zussman, *Mechanics of the Middle Class: Work and Politics among American Engineers*. (Berkeley: University of California Press, 1985).

26. "Professionalism Termed Key to Computer Personnel Situation," *Personnel Journal* 51, no 2. (1971): 156–157.

27. Wanda Orlikowski and Baroudi, Jack, "The Information Systems Profession: Myth or Reality?" *Office: Technology & People* 4 (1989): 13–30.

28. William Aspray, "The History of Computer Professionalism in America," (unpublished manuscript, 2001).

29. Philip Kraft, *Programmers and Managers: The Routinization of Computer Programming in the United States* (New York: Springer-Verlag, 1977), 26–28.

30. Joan Greenbaum, "On Twenty-five Years with Braverman's 'Labor and Monopoly Capital.' (Or, How Did Control and Coordination of Labor Get into the Software so Quickly?)," *Monthly Review* 50, no. 8 (1999).

31. Wanda Orlikowski, "The DP Occupation: Professionalization or Proletarianization?" *Research in the Sociology of Work* 4 (1988): 95–124.

32. Brian Rothery, *Installing and Managing a Computer* (London: Business Books, 1968), 152.

33. Kraft, *Programmers and Managers*, 26.

34. Enid Mumford, *Job Satisfaction: A Study of Computer Specialists* (London: Longman Group Limited, 1972), 175.

35. Robert Head, "Controlling Programming Costs," *Datamation* 13, no. 7 (1967): 141.

36. Andrew Friedman and Dominic Cornford, *Computer Systems Development: History, Organization, and Implementation* (Chichester, UK: Wiley, 1989); M. Beirne, H. Ramsay, and A. Panteli, "Developments in Computing Work: Control and Contradiction in the Software Labour Process," in *Developments in Computing Work: Control and Contradiction in the Software Labour Process*, ed. P. Thompson and C. Warhurst (New York: Macmillan, 1998), 142–162.

37. Andrew Abbott, *The Systems of Professions: An Essay on the Division of Expert Labor* (Chicago: University of Chicago Press, 1988); Paul DiMaggio, "Review of Andrew Abbott, *Systems of Professions*," *American Journal of Sociology* 95, no. 2 (1989): 534–535.

38. Nathan Ensmenger, "The 'Question of Professionalism' in the Computer Fields," *IEEE Annals of the History of Computing* 4, no. 23 (2001): 56–73.

39. Stephen Barley, "Technicians in the Workplace: Ethnographic Evidence for Bringing Work into Organization Studies," *Administrative Science Quarterly* 41 (1996): 404–441.

40. Ibid.

41. Stacia Zabusky and Stephen Barley, "Redefining Success: Ethnographic Observations on the Careers of Technicians," in *Broken Ladders: Managerial Careers in the New Economy*, ed. Paul Osterman (New York: Oxford University Press, 1996), 185–214.

42. Barley, "Technicians in the Workplace," 422.

43. Ibid., 430.

44. Ibid., 427.

45. Adele Mildred Koss, "Programming on the Univac 1," *IEEE Annals of the History of Computing* 25, no. 1 (2003): 48–59; Scott M. Campbell, "Beatrice Helen Worsley," *IEEE Annals of the History of Computing* 25, no. 4 (2003): 51–62.

46. Nathan Ensmenger, "Making Programming Masculine," in *Gender Codes: Women and Men in the Computing Professions*, ed. Thomas Misa (New York: Wiley, forthcoming).

47. Richard Canning, "Issues in Programming Management," *EDP Analyzer* 12, no. 4 (1974): 1–14.

48. Bruce Gilchrist and Richard Weber, "Enumerating Full-Time Programmers," *Communications of the ACM* 17, no. 10 (1974): 592–593.

49. Valerie Rockmael, "The Woman Programmer," *Datamation* 9, no. 1 (1963): 4.

50. Lois Mandel, "The Computer Girls," *Cosmopolitan* (April 1967): 52–56.

51. Ibid., 52.

52. Ibid., 51.

53. Ibid., 56.

54. Margaret Rossiter, *Women Scientists in America* (Baltimore: Johns Hopkins University Press, 1982); Jeffrey Hearn, "Notes on Patriarchy, Professionalization and the Semi-Professions," *Sociology* 16, no. 2 (1982): 184–202; Ruth Oldenziel, *Making Technology Masculine* (Amsterdam: Amsterdam University Press, 1999).

55. Claudia Goldin, Lawrence Katz, and Ilyana Kuziemko, "The Homecoming of American College Women," *Journal of Economic Perspectives* 20, no. 4 (2006): 133–156.

56. Thomas D'Auria, "ACM Membership Profile Report," *Communications of the ACM* 20, no. 10 (1977): 688–692.

57. Theodore Willoughby, "Psychometric Characteristics of the CDP Examination," *Proceedings of the Thirteenth Annual SIGCPR Conference* (New York: ACM Press, 1975), 152–160.

58. Gerald Weinberg, *The Psychology of Computer Programming* (New York: Van Nostrand Rheinhold, 1971).

59. Carol Cohn, "War, Wimps, and Women," in *Gendering War Talk*, ed. M. Cooke and A. Woolcott (Princeton: Princeton University Press Princeton, 1993), 227–246.

60. Ensmenger, "Making Programming Masculine."

61. Edith Martin and Albert Badre, "Problem Formulation for Programmers," in *Proceedings of the 7th SIGCSE Technical Symposium on Computer Science Education* (New York: ACM Press, 1977), 133–138.

62. Frederick Brooks, "No Silver Bullet: Essence and Accidents of Software Engineering," *IEEE Computer* 20, no 4 (1987): 18.

63. Jack Little, cited in RAND Symposium, "On Programming Languages, Part I," *Datamation* 8, no. 10 (1962): 29–30.

64. Morrison, "Software Crisis," 72.

65. Brad Cox, "There Is a Silver Bullet," *Byte Magazine* 15, no. 10 (1990): 209.

66. Maurice Black, "The Art of Code" (PhD diss., University of Pennsylvania, 2002); Scott Rosenberg, *Dreaming in Code: Two Dozen Programmers, Three Years, 4,732 Bugs, and One Quest for Transcendent Software* (New York: Crown Publishers, 2007).

67. James Paul and Gregory Simon, "Bugs in the Program: Problems in Federal Government Computer Software Development and Regulation," Staff Study for the House Committee on Science, Space, and Technology, September 1989.

68. Gibbs, "Software's Chronic Crisis."

Bibliography

Abbott, Andrew. *The Systems of Professions: An Essay on the Division of Expert Labor.* Chicago: University of Chicago Press, 1988.

"Abstracts of Papers for the Fourteenth Annual Meeting of the Radiation Research Society, Coronado, California February 13-16, 1966." *Radiation Research* 27 (3) (1966): 487–554.

ACM Curriculum Committee. "An Undergraduate Program in Computer Science: Preliminary Recommendations." *Communications of the ACM* 8 (9) (1965): 543–552.

"AFIPS Presidents Discussion" (1985) CBI 114, "Walter M. Carlson Papers, 1960–1990," Box 1, Folder 4, Archives of the Charles Babbage Institute, University of Minnesota, Minneapolis.

Aid to recovery: The economic impact of IT, software, and the Microsoft ecosystem on the global economy. Springfield, MA: Interactive Data Corporation, 2009.

Akera, Atsushi. "Calculating a Natural World: Scientists, Engineers, and Computers in the United States, 1937–1968." PhD diss., University of Pennsylvania, 1998.

Alexander, Thomas. *"Computers Can't Solve Everything."* Fortune 80 (5) (1969): 126–129, 168, 171.

Altshuler, Gene. "Programmers and Analysts" (letter to the editor) *Datamation* 16 (1) (1970): 47.

Anderegg, David. *Nerds: Who They Are and Why We Need More of Them.* New York: Jeremy P. Tarcher, 2007.

"Angels, Pins, and Language Standards." *Datamation* 9 (4) (1963): 23–25.

Armer, Paul. "Editor's Readout: Suspense Won't Kill Us." *Datamation* 19 (6) (1973): 53.

Armer, Paul. "Thinking Big" (letter to editor). *Communications of the ACM* 2 (1) (1959): 2–4.

Aron, Joel. *Program Development Process: The Individual Programmer.* Reading, MA: Addison-Wesley Reading, 1974.

Aron, Joel. *Program Development Process: The Programming Team.* Reading, MA: Addison-Wesley Reading, 1983.

Aspray, William. "Was Early Entry a Competitive Advantage? US Universities That Entered Computing in the 1940s." *IEEE Annals of the History of Computing* 22 (3) (2000): 42–87.

Atchison, William F., and John W. Hamblen. "Status of Computer Sciences Curricula in Colleges and Universities." *Communications of the ACM* 7 (4) (1964): 225–227.

Austing, Richard, Bruce Barnes and Gerald Engel. "A Survey of the Literature in Computer Science Education since Curriculum '68." *Communications of the ACM* 20 (1) (1977): 13–21.

Backus, John. "Automatic Programming Properties and Performance of FORTRAN Systems I and II." In *Proceedings of Symposium on the Mechanization of the Thought Processes*, 232–255. Middlesex, UK: National Physical Laboratory Press, 1958.

Backus, John. "Programming in America in the 1950s: Some Personal Impressions." In *A History of Computing in the Twentieth Century: A Collection of Essays*, ed. Nicholas Metropolis, Jack Howlett, and Gian-Carlo Rota. New York: Academic Press, 1980, 125–135.

Backus, John, Robert Beeber, Sheldon Best, Richard Goldberg, Lois Haibt, Harlan Herrick, Robert Nelson, et al. "The FORTRAN Automatic Coding System." In *Proceedings of the West Joint Computer Conference.* New York: ACM Press, 1957, 188–198.

Baker, F. Terry, and Harlan Mills. "Chief Programmer Teams." *Datamation* 19 (12) (1973): 58.

Bardini, Thierry. *Bootstrapping: Douglas Englebart, Coevolution, and the Origins of Personal Computing.* Stanford, CA: Stanford University Press, 2000.

Barley, Stephen. "Technicians in the Workplace: Ethnographic Evidence for Bringing Work into Organization Studies." *Administrative Science Quarterly* 41 (3) (1996): 404–441.

Barley, Stephen, and Gideon Kunda. *Gurus, Hired Guns, and Warm Bodies: Itinerant Experts in a Knowlege Economy.* Princeton, NJ: Princeton University Press, 2004.

Barley, Stephen, and Julian Orr, eds. *Between Craft and Science: Technical Work in US Settings.* Ithaca, NY: ILR Press, 1997.

Barnett, Michael. *Computer Programming in English.* New York: Harcourt, Brace and World, 1969.

Barry, Barbara, and John Naughton. *Chief Programmer Team Operations Description.* vol. X. Structured Programming Series. Gaithersburg, MD: IBM Federal Systems, 1975.

Bauer, Friedrich L. "Software Engineering: A Conference Report." *Datamation* 15, no. 10 (1969).

Baum, Claude. *The Systems Builders: The Story of SDC*. Santa Monica, CA: System Development Corporation, 1981.

Becker, Joseph. "Review: [untitled]." *Library Quarterly* 32 (1) (1962): 86–88.

Beirne, Martin, and Harold Ramsay and Androniki Panteli. "Developments in Computing Work: Control and Contradiction in the Software Labour Process." In *Developments in Computing Work: Control and Contradiction in the Software Labour Process*, ed. Paul Thompson and Chris Warhurst, 142–162. New York: Macmillan, 1998.

Bell, Daniel. *The Coming of Post-Industrial Society*. New York: Basic Books, 1973.

Bemer, Robert. *Computers and Crisis: How Computers Are Shaping Our Future*. New York: ACM Press, 1971.

Bendix Computer Division. "Is Your Programming Career in a Closed Loop?" (ad). *Datamation* 8 (9) (1962): 86.

Benington, Herbert. "Production of Large Computer Programs" (reprint). *IEEE Annals of the History of Computing* 5 (4) (1983): 350–361.

Berger, Raymond M. "Computer personnel selection and criteria development." In *Proceedings of the 2nd SIGCPR Conference on Computer Personnel Research*, 65–77. New York: ACM Press, 1964.

Berger, Raymond M., and Robert C. Wilson. "Correlates of Programmer Proficiency." In *SIGCPR '66: Proceedings of the Fourth SIGCPR Conference on Computer Personnel Research*, 83–95. New York: ACM Press, 1966.

Berkeley, Edmund Callis. *Giant Brains; or, Machines That Think*. New York: Wiley, 1949.

Black, Maurice. "The Art of Code." PhD diss., University of Pennsylvania, 2002.

Block, I. Edward. "Report on Meeting Held at University of Pennsylvania Computing Center" (1959).

Bloom, Allan. "Advances in Use of Programmer Aptitude Tests. In *Advances in Computer Programming Management*, ed. Thomas Rullo, 31–60. Philadelphia: Heyden, 1980.

Boehm, Barry. "Software and Its Impact: A Quantitative Assessment." *Datamation* 19 (5) (1973): 48–59.

Boehm, Barry. "Software Engineering." *IEEE Transactions on Computers* (12) (1976): 1226–1241.

Boguslaw, Robert, and Warren Pelton. "Steps: A Management Game for Programming Supervisors." *Datamation* 5 (6) (1959): 13–16.

Bowker, Geoffrey. "How to Be Universal: Some Cybernetic Strategies, 1943–1970." *Social Studies of Science* 23 (1) (1993): 107–127.

Bradford, P., and L. R. Cottrell. "Factors Influencing Business Data Processors Turnover: A Comparative Case History." In *Proceedings of the 1977 Annual Conference* (New York: ACM Press, 1977): 202–205.

Brandon, Richard. "The Problem in Perspective." In *Proceedings of the 1968 23rd ACM National Conference*, 332–334. New York: ACM Press, 1968.

Bromberg, Howard. "Survey of Programming Languages and Processors." *Communications of the ACM* 6 (3) (1965): 93–99.

Brooks, Frederick P. *The Mythical Man-Month: Essays on Software Engineering.* New York: Addison-Wesley, 1975.

Brooks, Frederick P. "No Silver Bullet: Essence and Accidents of Software Engineering." *IEEE Computer* 20 (4) (1987): 10–19.

Bureau of Labor Statistics. *U.S. Department of Labor, Occupational Outlook Handbook*, 2008–9 edition. Available online at http://www.bls.gov/oco/ocos258.htm (accessed December 16, 2009).

Bylinsky, Gene. "Help Wanted: 50,000 Programmers." *Fortune* 75 (3) (1967): 141–168.

Callahan, John. "Letter to the Editor." *Datamation* 7 (3) (1961): 7.

Campbell, Scott M. "Beatrice Helen Worsley." *IEEE Annals of the History of Computing* 25 (4) (2003): 51–62.

Campbell-Kelly, Martin. "The Airy Tape: An Early Chapter in the History of Debugging." *IEEE Annals of the History of Computing* 14 (4) (1992): 16–26.

Campbell-Kelly, Martin. "Development and Structure of the International Software Industry, 1950–1990." *Business and Economic History* 24 (2) (1995): 73–110.

Campbell-Kelly, Martin. *From Airline Reservations to Sonic the Hedgehog: A History of the Software Industry.* Cambridge, MA: MIT Press, 2003.

Campbell-Kelly, Martin, and William Aspray. *Computer: A History of the Information Machine.* New York: Basic Books, 1996.

Canfora, Gerardo, and Aniello Cimitile. *Software Maintenance.* Technical report. University of Sannio, 2000.

Canning, Richard. "The DPMA Certificate in Data Processing." *EDP Analyzer* 3 (7) (1965): 1–12.

Canning, Richard. "Issues in Programming Management." *EDP Analyzer* 12 (4) (1974): 1–14.

Canning, Richard. "The Maintenance 'Iceberg.'" *EDP Analyzer* 10 (10) (1972): 1–14.

Canning, Richard. "Managing Staff Retention and Turnover." *EDP Analyzer* 15 (8) (1977): 1–13.

Canning, Richard. "Managing the Programming Effort." *EDP Analyzer* 6 (6) (1968): 1–15.

Canning, Richard. "The Persistent Personnel Problem." *EDP Analyzer* 5 (5) (1967): 1–14.

Canning, Richard. "Professionalism: Coming or Not?" *EDP Analyzer* 14 (3) (1976): 1–12.

Canning, Richard. "The Question of Professionalism." *EDP Analyzer* 6 (12) (1968): 1–13.

"Careers in Computers" (ad). *Datamation* 8 (1) (1962): 80.

Carlson, Jack W. "On Determining C. S. Education Programs." *Communications of the ACM* 9 (3) (1966): 135.

Carter, Susan B., Scott Sigmund Gartner, Michael R. Haines, Alan L. Olmstead, Richard Sutch, and Gavin Wright, eds. *Historical Statistics of the United States Millennial Edition Online*. New York: Cambridge University Press, 2006.

"CDP Advisory Council, Minutes of the Third Annual Meeting, Jan 17–18, 1964" (1964), CBI 88, "Data Processing Management Association records," Box 22, Folder 3, Archives of the Charles Babbage Institute, University of Minnesota, Minneapolis.

"The Certificate and Undergraduate Program" (1959) CBI 46, "John K. Swearingen Papers, 1936–1993," Box 1, Folder 13, Archives of the Charles Babbage Institute, University of Minnesota, Minneapolis.

"The Certificate and Undergraduate Program" (1959), CBI 88, "Data Processing Management Association records," Box 22, Folder 1, Archives of the Charles Babbage Institute, University of Minnesota, Minneapolis.

"Certificate in Data Processing." *Datamation* 9 (8) (1963): 59.

Ceruzzi, Paul. "Electronics Technology and Computer Science, 1940–1975: A Coevolution." *IEEE Annals of the History of Computing* 10 (4) (1989): 257–275.

Chandler, Alfred. *The Visible Hand: The Managerial Revolution in American Business*. Cambridge, MA: Harvard University Press, 1977.

Chapin, Ned. "Teaching Business Data Processing with the Aid of a Computer." *Accounting Review* 38 (4) (1963): 835–839.

Chapman, Gary. "Bugs in the Program." *Communications of the ACM* 33 (3) (1990): 251–252.

Chinitz, M. Paul. "Contributions of Industrial Training Courses in Computers." In *Proceedings of the First Conference on Training Personnel for the Computing Machine Field*, ed. Arvid Jacobson, 29–32. Detroit: Wayne State University Press, 1955.

Christian, Richard C. "The Computer and the Marketing Man." *Journal of Marketing* 26 (3) (1962): 79–82.

Claghorn, William. "Rough draft of a reply to Alan Taylor," (1971), CBI 88, "Data Processing Management Association records," Box 18, Folder 47, Archives of the Charles Babbage Institute, University of Minnesota, Minneapolis.

Clippinger, Richard F. *A Logical Coding System Applied to the ENIAC (Electronic Numerical Integrator and Computer)*. Technical report. Ballistic Research Laboratories, Ordnance Department, Aberdeen Proving Ground, 1948.

Cohen, I. Bernard. *Howard Aiken: Portrait of a Computer Pioneer*. Cambridge, MA: MIT Press, 1999.

Cohen, I. Bernard, Gregory W. Welch, and Robert V. D. Campbell. *Makin' Numbers: Howard Aiken and the Computer.* Cambridge, MA: MIT Press, 1999.

Coleman, John S. "Computers as Tools for Management." *Management Science* 2 (2) (1956): 107.

"The Computer Personnel Research Group." *Datamation* 9 (1) (1963): 38–39.

Conway, B., J. Gibbons, and D. E. Watts. *Business Experience with Electronic Computers: A Synthesis of What Has Been Learned from Electronic Data Processing Installations.* New York: Price Waterhouse, 1959.

Correll, Quentin. "Letters to the Editor." *Communications of the ACM* 1 (7) (1958): 2.

"Correspondence re: Academic & Experience Req's" (1966), CBI 88, "Data Processing Management Association records," Box 18, Folder 22, Archives of the Charles Babbage Institute, University of Minnesota, Minneapolis.

"Correspondence re: ACM/DPMA Liason" (1966), CBI 88, "Data Processing Management Association records," Box 22, Folder 1, Archives of the Charles Babbage Institute, University of Minnesota, Minneapolis.

"Correspondence re: Improper Use of CDP Initials" (1966), CBI 88, "Data Processing Management Association records," Box 18, Folder 22, Archives of the Charles Babbage Institute, University of Minnesota, Minneapolis.

Cortada, James W. "Commercial Applications of the Digital Computer in American Corporations, 1945–1995." *IEEE Annals of the History of Computing* 18 (2) (Summer 1996): 18–29.

Cortada, James W. *Information Technology as Business History: Issues in the History and Management of Computers.* Westport, CT: Greenwood Press, 1996.

"The Cost of Professionalism." *Datamation* 9 (10) (1963): 23.

Cougar, Daniel, and Robert Zawacki. "What Motivates DP Professionals?" *Datamation* 24 (9) (1978): 116–123.

Cox, Brad. "There Is a Silver Bullet." *Byte Magazine* 15 (10) (1990): 209.

"Curriculum 68." *Datamation* 14 (5) (1968): 114–116.

DATA-LINK, editors of. "What's in a Name?" (letter to editor). *Communications of the ACM* 1 (4) (1958): 6.

D'Auria, Thomas. "ACM Membership Profile Report." *Communications of the ACM* 20 (10) (1977): 688–692.

Dauw, Dean. "Vocational Interests of Highly Creative Computer Personnel." *Personnel Journal* 46 (10) (1967): 653–659.

Davies, Margery W. *Woman's Place Is at the Typewriter: Office Work and Office Workers, 1870–1930.* Philadelphia: Temple University Press, 1982.

De Brabander, Bert, and Anders Edstrom. "Successful Information System Development Projects." *Management Science* 24 (2) (1977): 191–199.

Dearden, John. "How to Organize Information Systems." *Harvard Business Review* 43 (2) (1965): 65–73.

Dearden, John. "MIS Is a Mirage." *Harvard Business Review* 50 (11) (1972): 90–99.

Dearden, John. "Myth of Real-Time Management Information." *Harvard Business Review* 44 (3) (1966): 123–132.

DeNelsky, Garland, and Michael McKee. "Prediction of Computer Programmer Training and Job Performance Using the AAPB Test." *Personnel Psychology* 27 (1) (1974): 129–137.

Deutsch and Shea, Inc. "A Profile of the Programmer." *Communications of the ACM* 6 (10) (1963): 592–594, 647.

Dickmann, Robert A., and John Lockwood. "1966 Survey of Test Use in Computer Personnel Selection. Technical Report." In *Proceedings of the Fourth SIGCPR Conference on Computer Personal Research*. New York: ACM Press, 1966.

Diebold, John. "ADP: The Still-Sleeping Giant." *Harvard Business Review* 42 (5) (1964): 60–65.

Diebold, John. "Bad Decisions on Computer Use." *Harvard Business Review* 47 (1) (1969): 14–21.

Dijkstra, Edsger. "Communication with an Automatic Computer." PhD diss., University of Amsterdam, 1959.

Dijkstra, Edsger. "Go to Statement Considered Harmful." *Communications of the ACM* 11 (3) (1968): 147–148.

Dijkstra, Edsger. "The Humble Programmer." *Communications of the ACM* 15 (10) (1972): 859–866.

Dijkstra, Edsger. "Programming as a Discipline of Mathematical Nature." *American Mathematical Monthly* 81 (6) (1974): 608–612.

DiMaggio, Paul. "Review of Andrew Abbott, *Systems of Professions*." *American Journal of Sociology* 95 (2) (1989): 534–535.

DiNardo, George. "Software Management and the Impact of Improved Programming Technology." In *Proceedings of 1975 ACM Annual Conference Software Management and the Impact of Improved Programming Technology*, 288–290. New York: ACM Press, 1975.

"Discussion of DPMA/ACM Merger" (1970), CBI 88, "Data Processing Management Association records," Box 22, Folder 3, Archives of the Charles Babbage Institute, University of Minnesota, Minneapolis.

Ditri, Arnold, and Donald Woods. *The End of the Beginning–The Fizzle of the "Computer Revolution."* Touche Ross and Company, 1959.

Dooley, Ann. "100% over Budget." *Computerworld* 21 (7) (1987): 5.

"DPMA Board of Directors, 9th Meeting, March 11–12, 1966" (1966), CBI 88, "Data Processing Management Association records," Box 22, Folder 7, Archives of the Charles Babbage Institute, University of Minnesota, Minneapolis.

"DPMA Board of Directors, 10th Meeting, March 11–12, 1966" (1966), CBI 88, "Data Processing Management Association records," Box 22, Folder 7, Archives of the Charles Babbage Institute, University of Minnesota, Minneapolis.

"DPMA Board of Directors, 12th Meeting, 1967 Las Vegas" (1967), CBI 88, "Data Processing Management Association records," Box 22, Folder 8, Archives of the Charles Babbage Institute, University of Minnesota, Minneapolis.

"DPMA Certificate Panel" (1964), CBI 46, "John K. Swearingen Papers, 1936–1993," Box 1, Folder 17, Archives of the Charles Babbage Institute, University of Minnesota, Minneapolis.

"DPMA Certification Council minutes, 23rd meeting, April 1-4, 1970," (1970) CBI 116, "Institute for Certification of Computer Professionals Records, 1960-1993," Box 1, Folder 26, Archives of the Charles Babbage Institute, University of Minnesota, Minneapolis.

"DPMA Revises CDP Test Requirements." *Data Management* (1967): 34–35.

Dwyer, John. "Analysts Couched" (letter to the editor) *Datamation* 16 (1) (1970): 47.

Edgerton, David. *The shock of the old: technology and global history since 1900.* Oxford: Oxford University Press, 2007.

"Editor's Readout: The Certified Public Programmer." *Datamation* 8 (3) (1962): 23–24.

"Editor's Readout: A Long View of a Myopic Problem." *Datamation* 8 (5) (1962): 21–22.

"EDP's Wailing Wall." *Datamation* 13 (7) (1967): 21.

Eglash, Ron. "Race, Sex, and Nerds: From Black Geeks to Asian American Hipsters." *Social Text* 2 (20) (2002): 49–64.

Eilbert, Henry. "The Development of Personnel Management in the United States." *Business History Review* 33 (1959): 345–364.

11th RAND Symposium (1969), CBI 78, "RAND Symposia on Computing Transcripts," Box 3, Folder 4, Archives of the Charles Babbage Institute, University of Minnesota, Minneapolis.

Elliot, Richard. "Thinking Big: In Computer Software, the Reach Frequently Exceeds the Grasp." *Barron's National Business and Financial Weekly* 47 (40) (October 2, 1967): 3, 18–22.

Elliot, Richard. "Thinking Big: Profits in Computer Software Are Not What They Seem." *Barron's National Business and Financial Weekly* 47 (41) (October 9, 1967): 5, 8, 10, 12.

Elliott, Calvin. "DPMA: Its Function and Future." *Datamation* 9 (6) (1963): 35–36.

Englebardt, Stanley. "Wanted: 500,000 Men to Feed Computers." *Popular Science* (January 1965), 106–109.

Ensmenger, Nathan. "From 'Black Art' to Industrial Disciple: The Software Crisis and the Management of Programmers." PhD diss., University of Pennsylvania, 2001.

Ensmenger, Nathan. "Letting the 'Computer Boys' Take Over: Technology and the Politics of Organizational Transformation." *International Review of Social History* 48 (no. S11) (2003): 153–180.

Ensmenger, Nathan. Making Programming Masculine. In *Gender Codes: Women and Men in the Computing Professions*, ed. Thomas Misa. New York: Wiley; Forthcoming.

Ensmenger, Nathan. "The 'Question of Professionalism' in the Computer Fields." *IEEE Annals of the History of Computing* 23 (4) (2001): 56–73.

Ershov, Andrei P. "Aesthetics and the Human Factor in Programming." *Communications of the ACM* 15 (7) (1972): 501–505.

"Executive Meeting Summary" (1966) CBI 46, "John K. Swearingen Papers, 1936–1993," Box 1, Folder 3, Archives of the Charles Babbage Institute, University of Minnesota, Minneapolis.

"The Facts of Life." *Datamation* 14 (3) (1968): 21.

Fein, Louis. "ACM Has a Crisis of Identity?" *Communications of the ACM* 10 (1) (1967): 1.

Fein, Louis. "Computer-Related Sciences (Synnoetics) at a University in 1975." *Datamation* 7 (9) (1961): 34–41.

Fein, Louis. "The Role of the University in Computers, Data Processing, and Related Fields." *Communications of the ACM* 2 (10) (1959): 7–14.

Fike, John. "Vultures Indeed." *Datamation* 13 (5) (1967): 12.

Fiock, L. R. "Seven Deadly Dangers of EDP." *Harvard Business Review* 40 (3) (1962): 88–96.

"First Programmer Class at Sing-Sing Graduates." *Datamation* 14 (6) (1968): 97–98.

Flamm, Kenneth. *Creating the Computer: Government, Industry, and High Technology.* Washington, DC: Brookings Institution Press, 1988.

Flywheel, Wolf. "Letter to the Editor (on Professionalism)." *Datamation* 5 (5) (1959): 2.

Forest, Robert. "EDP People: Review and Preview." *Datamation* 18 (6) (1972): 65–67.

Forsythe, George E. "What to Do Till the Computer Scientist Comes." *American Mathematical Monthly* 75 (5) (1968): 454–462.

Forte, Allen. "Review: Conference on the Use of Computers in Humanistic Research." *Computers and the Humanities* 1 (3) (1967): 110–112.

Freeman, Herbert, and Phillip Lewis. *Software Engineering.* New York: Academic Press, 1980.

Friedman, Andrew, and Dominic Cornford. *Computer Systems Development: History, Organization, and Implementation.* Chichester, UK: Wiley, 1989.

Fritz, W. Barkley. "The Women of Eniac." *IEEE Annals of the History of Computing* 18 (3) (1996): 13–23.

Galison, Peter. Computer Simulations in the Trading Zone. In *The Disunity of Science*, ed. Peter Galison and David Stump, 118–157. Stanford, CA: Stanford University Press, 1996.

Galler, Bernard. "The AFIPS Constitution (President's Letter to ACM Membership)." *Communications of the ACM* 12 (3) (1969): 188.

Galler, Bernard. "Definition of Software." *Communications of the ACM* 5 (1) (1961): 6.

Galler, Bernard. "The Journal" (president's letter to ACM membership). *Communications of the ACM* 12 (2) (1969): 65–66.

Gass, Saul. "ACM Class Structure" (letter to editor). *Communications of the ACM* 2 (5) (1959): 4.

Geckle, Jerome. "Letter to the Editor." *Datamation* 11 (9) (1965): 12–13.

Gibbs, William Wayt. "Software's Chronic Crisis." *Scientific American* 271 (3) (1994): 86.

Gieryn, Thomas. "Boundary-Work and the Demarcation of Science from Non-Science: Strains and Interests in Professional Ideologies of Scientists." *American Sociological Review* 48 (4) (1983): 781–795.

Gilbert, Jean P., and David B. Mayer. "Experiences in Self-selection of Disadvantaged People into a Computer Operator Training Program." In *SIGCPR '69: Proceedings of the Seventh Annual Conference on SIGCPR*, 79–90. New York: ACM Press, 1969.

Gilchrist, Bruce, and Richard Weber, eds. *The State of the Computer Industry in the United States*. New York: American Federation of Information Processing Societies, 1972.

Gilchrist, Bruce, and Richard Weber. "Enumerating Full-Time Programmers." *Communications of the ACM* 17 (10) (1974): 592–593.

Gill, Brendan, and Andy Logan. "Talk of the Town." *New Yorker* 5 (January 1957): 18–19.

Ginzberg, Michael J. "Key Recurrent Issues in the MIS Implementation Process." *MIS Quarterly* 5 (2) (1981): 47–59.

Glaser, George. "Letter to W. Carlson" (July 15, 1974), CBI 23, "George Glaser Papers, 1960-1989," Box 1, Folder 3, Archives of the Charles Babbage Institute, University of Minnesota, Minneapolis.

Glass, Robert. "Is There Really a Software Crisis?" *IEEE Software* 15 (1) (1998): 104–105.

Golda, John. "The Effects of Computer Technology on the Traditional Role of Management." Master's thesis, Wharton School of Business, University of Pennsylvania, 1965.

Goldin, Claudia, Lawrence Katz, and Ilyana Kuziemko. "The Homecoming of American College Women." *Journal of Economic Perspectives* 20 (4) (2006): 133–156.

Goldstine, Adele. *A Report on the ENIAC (Electronic Numerical Integrator and Computer)*. Technical report, Moore School of Electrical Engineer, University of Pennsylvania, June 1, 1946.

Gordon, Robert. "Personnel Selection." In *Data Processing, Practically Speaking*, ed. Stanley Naftaly and Fred Gruenberger, 79–90. Los Angeles: Data Processing Digest, 1967.

Gordon, Robert. "Review of Charles Lecht, *The Management of Computer Programmers*." *Datamation* 14 (4) (1968): 200–202.

Gotterer, Malcolm. "The Impact of Professionalization Efforts on the Computer Manager." In *Proceedings of 1971 ACM Annual Conference*, 367–375. New York: ACM Press, 1971.

Gotterer, Malcolm, and Ashford W. Stalnaker. "Predicting Programmer Performance among Non-Preselected Trainee Groups." In *SIGCPR '64: Proceedings of the Second SIGCPR Conference on Computer Personnel Research*, 29–37. New York: ACM Press, 1964.

Granholm, Jackson. "How to Hire a Programmer." *Datamation* 8 (8) (1962): 31–32.

Greenbaum, Joan. "On Twenty-five years with Braverman's 'Labor and Monopoly Capital' (Or, How Did Control and Coordination of Labor Get into the Software So Quickly?)." *Monthly Review* 50 (8) (1999): 28–32.

Greenberger, Martin. *Management and the Computer of the Future*. Cambridge, MA: MIT Press, 1962.

Gregg, Charles R. "Personnel Requirements in Government Agencies in Machine Computation." In *Proceedings of the First Conference on Training Personnel for the Computing Machine Field*, ed. Arvid Jacobson, 9–14. Detroit: Wayne State University Press, 1955.

Grier, David Allan. "The ENIAC, the Verb to Program, and the Emergence of Digital Computers." *IEEE Annals of the History of Computing* 18 (1) (1996): 51–55.

Grier, David Allan. *When Computers Were Human*. Princeton, NJ: Princeton University Press, 2005.

Grosch, Herbert. *Computerworld* (August 19, 1970).

Grosch, Herbert. "Plus and Minus." *Datamation* 5 (6) (1959): 51.

Grosch, Herbert. "Magic Languages Debugged." *Datamation* 9 (2) (1963): 27–28.

Grosch, Herbert. "Programmers: The Industry's Cosa Nostra." *Datamation* 12 (10) (1966): 202.

Grosch, Herbert. "Software in Sickness and Health." *Datamation* 7 (7) (1961): 32–33.

Gruenberger, Fred. "Problems and Priorities." *Datamation* 18 (3) (1972): 47–50.

Guarino, Roger. "Managing Data Processing Professionals." *Personnel Journal* 48 (12) (1969): 972–975.

Guerrieri, John A. "Certification: Evolution, Not Revolution." *Datamation* 14 (11) (1973): 101.

Gupta, Gopal. "Computer Science Curriculum Developments in the 1960s." *IEEE Annals of the History of Computing* 29 (2) (2007): 40–54.

Hafner, Katie. *Cyberpunk: Outlaws and Hackers on the Computer Frontier, Revised.* New York: Simon and Schuster, 1995.

Haigh, Thomas. "The Chromium-Plated Tabulator: Institutionalizing an Electronic Revolution, 1954–1958." *IEEE Annals of the History of Computing* 4 (23) (2001): 75–104.

Haigh, Thomas. "Inventing Information Systems: The Systems Men and the Computer, 1950–1968." *Business History Review* 75 (1) (2001): 15–61.

Haigh, Thomas. "Software in the 1960s as Concept, Service, and Product." *IEEE Annals of the History of Computing* 24 (1) (2002): 5–13.

Haigh, Thomas. "Technology, Information and Power: Managerial Technicians in Corporate America: 1917–2000." PhD diss., University of Pennsylvania, 2002.

Halpern, Mark I. "Memoirs (Part 1)." *IEEE Annals of the History of Computing* 13 (1) (1991): 101–111.

Hamming, Richard. "One Man's View of Computer Science." *Journal of the ACM* 16 (1) (1969): 3–12.

"Hardware And Software." *British Medical Journal* 1 (5449) (1965): 1509.

Hayes, Robert M., Ralph H. Parker, and Gilbert W. King. "Automation and the Library of Congress: Three Views." *Library Quarterly* 34 (3) (1964): 229–239.

Head, Robert. "Controlling Programming Costs." *Datamation* 13 (7) (1967): 141–142.

Hearn, Jeffrey. "Notes on Patriarchy, Professionalization and the Semi-Professions." *Sociology* 16 (2) (1982): 184–202.

Heller, George. "Organizing a Local Program in Computing Education." *Datamation* 9 (1) (1963): 57–61.

Hemmendinger, David. "The ACM and IEEE-CS Guidelines for Undergraduate CS Education." *Communications of the ACM* 50 (5) (2007): 46–53.

Hertz, David. *New Power for Management.* New York: McGraw-Hill, 1969.

Heterick, R.C. "Letter to Ben Payne." (September 17, 1971) CBI 88, "Data Processing Management Association records," Box 18, Folder 22, Archives of the Charles Babbage Institute, University of Minnesota, Minneapolis.

Higgins, Robert. "Letter to the DPMA." (1973) CBI 46, "John K. Swearingen Papers, 1936–1993," Box 1, Folder 16, Archives of the Charles Babbage Institute, University of Minnesota, Minneapolis.

Hirsch, Rudolph. "Programming Performance: Monitoring, Maximization, and Prediction." In *Special Interest Group on Computer Personnel Research Annual Conference,* 26–36. New York: ACM Press, 1972.

Hoare, C. Anthony. "Software Engineering: A Keynote Address." In *Proceedings of the 3ʳᵈ International Conference on Software Engineering*, 1–4. Piscataway, NJ: IEEE Press, 1978.

Hollenbeck, George P., and Walter J. McNamara. "Cucpat and Programming Aptitude." *Personnel Psychology* 18 (1) (1965): 101–106.

Hughes, Thomas, and Agatha Hughes, eds. *Systems, Experts, and Computers: The Systems Approach in Management and Engineering, World War II and After*. Cambridge, MA: MIT Press, 2000.

Hunter, G. Truman. "Manpower Requirements by Computer Manufacturers." In *Proceedings of the First Conference on Training Personnel for the Computing Machine Field*, ed. Arvid Jacobson, 14–18. Detroit: Wayne State University Press, 1955.

Hurni, M. L. "Some Implications of the Use of Computers in Industry." *Accounting Review* 29 (3) (1954): 447–455.

IBM Corporation. "Are You the Man to Command Electronic Giants?" *New York Times*, May 13, 1956: 157.

"Is the Computer Running Wild?" *U.S. News and World Report*, February 1964.

Jacobson, Arvid, ed. *Proceedings of the First Conference on Training Personnel for the Computing Machine Field*. Detroit: Wayne State University Press, 1955.

Jamous, Haroun, and Bernard Peliolle. "Changes in the French University Hospital System." In *Professions and Professionalisation*, ed. J. A. Jackson, 111–152. Cambridge: Cambridge University Press, 1970.

Jay, Anthony. *Corporation Man*. New York: Random House, 1971.

Jenks, James. "Starting Salaries of Engineers Are Deceptively High." *Datamation* 13 (1) (1967): 13.

Jesiek, Brent. "The Sociotechnical Boundaries of Hardware and Software: A Humpty-Dumpty History." *Bulletin of Science, Technology, and Society* 26 (6) (2006): 497–509.

Jimms, J. "Could Y2K cause a global recession?" *Fortune* 138 (7) (1998): 172–176.

Johnsrud, John. "Computer Makers Set Up Own 'Universities'" *New York Times* (September 24, 1961): F1.

Jones, Richard. "Practical Control of Preparatory Programming Time for a Computer Installation." *NAA Bulletin* 43 (8) (1962): 71.

Jones, Richard. "A Time to Assume Responsibility." *Datamation* 13 (9) (1967): 160.

Kandel, Abraham. "Computer Science: A Vicious Circle." *Communications of the ACM* 15 (6) (1972): 470–471.

Kaplan, Fred. "Military on Year 2000 alert." *Boston Globe* (June 21, 1998): A1.

Kasson, John. *Civilizing the Machine: Technology and Republican Values in America, 1776–1900.* Harmondsworth, UK: Penguin, 1976.

Kaufman, Felix. "EDP and the Disenchanted." *California Management Review* 1 (4) (1959): 67–73.

Kaufman, Louis, and Richard Smith. "Let's Get Computer Personnel on the Management Team." *Training and Development Journal* 20 (11) (1966): 24–29.

Kaupe, Arthur. "Letter to the Editors of Computerworld," (March 1, 1972), CBI 116, "Institute for Certification of Computer Professionals Records, 1960-1993," Box 1, Folder 30, Archives of the Charles Babbage Institute, University of Minnesota, Minneapolis.

Kay, Lily. "Who Wrote the Book of Life? Information and the Transformation of Molecular Biology." *Science in Context* 8 (4) (1995): 609–634.

Keelan, Charles. "Controlling Computer Programming." *Journal of Systems Management* 20 (1) (1969): 30–33.

Keller, Arnold. "Crisis in Machine Accounting." *Management and Business Automation* 5 (6) (1961): 30–31.

Kessler-Harris, Alice. *Out to Work: A History of Wage-Earning Women in the United States.* New York: Oxford University Press, 1982.

Kevles, Daniel J. "Testing the Army's Intelligence: Psychologists and the Military in World War I." *Journal of American History* 55 (3) (1968): 565–581.

King, William R., and David I. Cleland. "The Design of Management Information Systems: An Information Analysis Approach." *Management Science* 22 (3) (1975): 286–297.

Kline, Ronald. "Cybernetics, Management Science, and Technology Policy: The Emergence of 'Information Technology' as a Keyword, 1948–1985." *Technology and Culture* 47 (3) (2006): 513–535.

Knoebel, Robert M. "The Federal Government's Role in the Education of Data Processing Personnel." In *SIGCPR '67: Proceedings of the Fifth SIGCPR Conference on Computer Personnel Research,* 77–84. New York: ACM Press, 1967.

Knuth, Donald Ervin. *The Art of Computer Programming, Volume 1: Fundamental Algorithms.* Reading, MA: Addison-Wesley, 1968.

Knuth, Donald Ervin. *Literate Programming.* Stanford, CA: Center for the Study of Language/Information, 1992.

Koss, Adele Mildred. "Programming on the UNIVAC 1." *IEEE Annals of the History of Computing* 25 (1) (2003): 48–59.

Kraft, Philip. *Programmers and Managers: The Routinization of Computer Programming in the United States.* New York: Springer-Verlag, 1977.

Kuch, T. D. C. "Unions or Licensing? or Both? or Neither?" *Infosystem* 20 (1) (1973): 42–43.

Kuhn, Thomas S. *The Structure of Scientific Revolutions.* Chicago: University of Chicago Press, 1962.

Larson, Harry. "EDP: A 20 Year Ripoff!" *Infosystems* 21 (11) (1974): 26–30.

Larson, Magali Sarfatti. *The Rise of Professionalism: A Sociological Analysis.* Berkeley: University of California Press, 1977.

Law, John. "Notes on the Theory of Actor-Network: Ordering, Strategy, and Heterogeneity." *Systems Practice* 5 (4) (1992): 379–393.

Law, John. Technology and Heterogeneous Engineering: The Case of the Portuguese Expansion. In *The Social Construction of Technical Systems: New Directions in the Sociology and History of Technology*, ed. Wiebe Bijker, Trevor Pinch, and Thomas Hughes, 111–134. Cambridge, MA: MIT Press, 1987.

Lawson, Charles. "A Survey of Computer Facility Management." *Datamation* 8 (7) (1962): 29–32.

Lear, J. "Can a Mechanical Brain Replace You?" *Colliers* 131, April 4, 1953, 58–63.

"Learning a Trade." *Datamation* 12 (10) (1966): 21.

Leavitt, Harold, and Thomas Whisler. "Management in the 1980s." *Harvard Management Review* 36 (6) (1958): 41–48.

Lecht, Charles. *The Management of Computer Programming Projects.* New York: American Management Association, 1967.

"Letter Re: Four Year Degree Requirement" (1970), CBI 116, "Institute for Certification of Computer Professionals Records, 1960-1993," Box 1, Folder 27, Archives of the Charles Babbage Institute, University of Minnesota, Minneapolis.

Levy, Steven. *Hackers: Heroes of the Computer Revolution.* Garden City, NY: Anchor Press, 1984.

Lewis, Ralph. "Never Overestimate the Power of a Computer." *Harvard Business Review* 35 (5) (1957): 77–84.

Lientz, B. P., E. B. Swanson, and G. E. Tompkins. "Characteristics of application software maintenance." *Communications of the ACM* 21 (6) (1978): 466–471.

"Local Chapter CDP publicity" (1964), CBI 46, "John K. Swearingen Papers, 1936–1993," Box 1, Folder 17, Archives of the Charles Babbage Institute, University of Minnesota, Minneapolis.

Lohr, Steve. *Go to: The Story of the Math Majors, Bridge Players, Engineers, Chess Wizards, Maverick Scientists, and Iconoclasts—The Programmers Who Created the Software Revolution.* New York: Basic Books, 2001.

Lucas, Henry. "On the Failure to Implement Structured Programming and Other Techniques." In *Proceedings of 1975 ACM Annual Conference*, 291–293. New York: ACM Press, 1975.

Lupton, Deborah. "The Embodied Computer User." *Body and Society* 1 (3–4) (1995): 97–112.

MacKenzie, Donald. "A View from the Sonnenbichl: On the Historical Sociology of Software and System Dependability." In *History of Computing: Software Issues*, ed. Ulf Hashagen, Reinhard Keil-Slawik, and Arthur L. Norberg, 97–122. Berlin: Springer-Verlag, 2002.

MacPherson, D. J. "Letter to R.C. Elliot re: unauthorized use of CDP initials." (October 26, 1970) CBI 88, "Data Processing Management Association records," Box 18, Folder 22, Archives of the Charles Babbage Institute, University of Minnesota, Minneapolis.

Madden, Don. "The Population Problem: Inexperience Will Dominate." *Datamation* 8 (1) (1962): 26.

Madden, J. D. "Letter to Calvin Elliot." (June 27, 1967). CBI 88, "Data Processing Management Association records," Box 22, Folder 1, Archives of the Charles Babbage Institute, University of Minnesota, Minneapolis.

Mahoney, Michael. Computer Science: The Search for a Mathematical Theory. In *Science in the Twentieth Century*, ed. John Krige and Dominique Pestre, 617–634. Amsterdam: Harwood Academic Publishers, 1997.

Mahoney, Michael. "In Our Own Image: Creating the Computer." In *The Changing Image of the Sciences*, ed. Ida Stamhuis, Teun Koetsier, and Kees de Pater, 9–27. Dordrecht: Kluwer Academic Publishers, 2002.

Mahoney, Michael. "The Roots of Software Engineering." *CWI Quarterly* 3 (4) (1980): 325–334.

Mahoney, Michael. "Software: The Self-Programming Machine." In *From 0 to 1: An Authoritative History of Modern Computing*, ed. Atsushi Akera and Frederik Nebeker, 91–100. New York: Oxford University Press, 2002.

Mahoney, Michael. "Software as Science—Science as Software." In *History of Computing: Software Issues*, ed. Ulf Hashagen, Reinhard Keil-Slawik, and Arthur Norberg. Berlin: Springer-Verlag, 2002, 25–48.

Mahoney, Michael. "What Makes the History of Software Hard." *IEEE Annals of the History of Computing* 30 (3) (2008): 8–18.

Malone, Cheryl Knott. "Imagining Information Retrieval in the Library: Desk Set in Historical Context." *IEEE Annals of the History of Computing* 24 (3) (2002): 14–22.

Mandel, Lois. "The Computer Girls." *Cosmopolitan*, April 1967, 52–56.

Manion, Mark, and William M. Evan. "The Y2K problem: technological risk and professional responsibility." *ACM SIGCAS Computers and Society* 29 (4) (1999): 24–29.

Markham, Edward. "EDP Schools: An Inside View." *Datamation* 14 (4) (1968): 22–27.

Markham, Edward. "Selecting a Private EDP School." *Datamation* 14 (5) (1968): 33–40.

Martin, Edith, and Albert Badre. "Problem formulation for programmers." In *Proceedings of the 7th SIGCSE Technical Symposium on Computer Science Education*, 133–138. New York: ACM Press, 1977.

Mayer, David, and Ashford Stainaker. "Selection and Evaluation of Computer Personnel: The Research History of SIG/CPR." In *Proceedings of the 1968 23rd ACM National Conference*, 657–670. New York: ACM Press, 1968.

McClure, Carma. *Managing Software Development and Maintenance*. New York: Van Nostrand Rheinhold, 1981.

McConnell, Steve. *Code Complete: A Practical Handbook of Software Construction*. Redmond, WA: Microsoft Press, 1993, 287.

McCracken, Daniel. "Is There FORTRAN In Your Future?" *Datamation* 19 (5) (1973): 236–237.

McCracken, Daniel. "The Human Side of Computing." *Datamation* 7 (1) (1961): 9–11.

McCracken, Daniel. "The Software Turmoil: Nine Predictions for '62." *Datamation* 8 (1) (1962): 21–22.

McCracken, Daniel. "Vote on ACM Name Change" (1978), CBI 43, "Daniel D. McCracken Papers, 1958–1983," Box 3, Folder 10, Archives of the Charles Babbage Institute, University of Minnesota, Minneapolis.

McFarland, Robert. "Electronic Power Grab." *Business Automation* 12 (2) (1965): 30–39.

McGowan, Clement, and John Kelly. *Top-down Structured Programming Techniques*. New York: Petrocelli/Carter, 1975.

McGregor, Douglas. *The Human Side of Enterprise*. New York: McGraw-Hill, 1960.

McKinsey and Company. "Unlocking the Computer's Profit Potential." *Computers and Automation* 16 (7) (1969): 24–33.

McMurrer, J. A., and J. R. Parish. "The People Problem." *Datamation* 16 (7) (1970): 57–59.

McNamara, Walter J. "The Selection of Computer Personnel: Past, Present, Future." In *SIGCPR '67: Proceedings of the Fifth SIGCPR Conference on Computer Personnel Research*, 52–56. New York: ACM Press, 1967.

McNamara, Walter J., and John L. Hughes. "A Review of Research on the Selection of Computer Programmers." *Personnel Psychology* 14 (1) (1961): 39–51.

Mengel, Milton E. "Present and Projected Computer Manpower Needs in Business and Industry." In *Proceedings of the First Conference on Training Personnel for the Computing Machine Field*, ed. Arvid Jacobson, 4–9. Detroit: Wayne State University Press, 1955.

Menkhaus, Edward. "EDP: Nice Work If You Can Get It." *Business Automation* 12 (3) (1969): 41–45, 74.

Metropolis, Nicholas, John Howlett, and Gian-Carlo Rota, eds. *A History of Computing in the Twentieth Century: A Collection of Essays*. New York: Academic Press, 1980.

Metzger, Philip. *Managing a Programming Project*. Englewood Cliffs, NJ: Prentice-Hall, 1973.

Meyers, G. J. *Software Reliability: Principles and Practices*. New York: John Wiley and Sons, 1976.

Milkman, Ruth. *Gender at Work: The Dynamics of Job Segregation by Sex during World War II.* Urbana: University of Illinois Press, 1987.

Mirowski, Philip. *Machine Dreams: Economics Becomes a Cyborg Science.* Cambridge: Cambridge University Press, 2002.

Mitchell, George W. "Exogenous Forces in the Development of Our Banking System." *Law and Contemporary Problems* 32 (1) (1967): 3–14.

Mitchell, Grace. *The 704 FORTRAN II Automatic Coding System.* Yorktown Heights, NY: IBM Research Center, 1959.

Mitre Corporation. "Are You Working Your Way toward Obsolescence?" *Datamation* 12 (6) (1966): 99.

Mody, P. "Is Programming an Art?" *Software Engineering Notes* 17 (4) (1992): 19–21.

Moore, Gordon. "Cramming More Components onto Integrated Circuits." *Electronics* 38 (8) (1965): 114–117.

Morgan, H. L., and J. V. Soden. "Understanding MIS Failures." *Database* 5 (2) (1973): 157–171.

Morrison, David. "Software Crisis." *Defense* 21 (2) (1989): 72.

Mumford, Enid. *Job Satisfaction: A Study of Computer Specialists.* London: Longman Group Limited, 1972.

Mumford, Enid, and Thomas Ward. *Computers: Planning for People.* London: B. T. Batsford, 1968.

Murray, Fergus, and David Knights. "Inter-managerial Competition and Capital Accumulation: IT Specialists, Accountants, and Executive Control." *Critical Perspectives on Accounting* 1 (2) (June 1990): 167–189.

Nadesan, Majia Holmer. *Constructing Autism: Unravelling the "Truth" and Understanding the Social.* London: Routledge, 2005.

Naftaly, Stanley. "How to Pick a Programming Language." In *Data Processing, Practically Speaking,* eds. Stanley Naftaly and Fred Gruenberger, 91–106. Los Angeles: Data Processing Digest, 1967.

Napoli, Donald S. "The Mobilization of American Psychologists, 1938–1941." *Military Affairs* 42 (1) (1978): 32–36.

Naur, Peter "The Science of Datalogy" (letter to editor). *Communications of the ACM* 9 (7) (1966): 485.

Naur, Peter, Brian Randall, and John Buxton eds. *Software Engineering: Proceedings of the NATO Conferences.* New York: Petrocelli/Charter, 1976.

Nelson, Daniel. "A Newly Appreciated Art: The Development of Personnel Work at Leeds & Northrup, 1915–1923." *Business History Review* 94 (4) (1970), 520–535.

Nesse, Arthur. "A User Looks at Software." *Datamation* 14 (10) (1968): 48–51.

"New CDP Requirements 'Unduly Harsh' Professionals Protest" (1970) CBI 116, "Institute for Certification of Computer Professionals Records, 1960-1993,"

Box 1, Folder 27, Archives of the Charles Babbage Institute, University of Minnesota, Minneapolis.

"Notes on ACM/DPMA merger" (1964), CBI 88, "Data Processing Management Association records," Box 22, Folder 2, Archives of the Charles Babbage Institute, University of Minnesota, Minneapolis.

"Not Quite All About MIS." *Datamation* 13 (5) (1967): 21.

Nugent, Benjamin. *American Nerd: The Story of My People.* New York: Scribner, 2008.

O'Shields, Joseph. "Selection of EDP Personnel." *Personnel Journal* 44 (9) (1965): 472–474.

Oettinger, Anthony. "ACM Sponsors Professional Development Program" (president's letter to ACM membership). *Communications of the ACM* 9 (10) (1966): 712–713.

Oettinger, Anthony. "The Hardware-Software Complexity." *Communications of the ACM* 10 (10) (1967): 604–606.

Oettinger, Anthony. "On ACM's Responsibility" (president's letter to ACM membership 1966). *Communications of the ACM* 9 (8) (1966): 545–546.

Oettinger, Anthony. "President's Letter to the ACM Membership." *Communications of the ACM* 9 (12) (1966): 838–839.

Oettinger, Anthony. "President's Reply to Louis Fein." *Communications of the ACM* 10 (1) (1967): 1, 61.

"Office Robots." *Fortune* 45, January 1952, 82–87, 112, 114, 116, 118.

Ogdin, Jerry L. "The Mongolian Hordes versus Superprogrammer." *Infosystems* 19 (12) (1972): 20–23.

Oldenziel, Ruth. *Making Technology Masculine.* Amsterdam: Amsterdam University Press, 1999.

Opler, Ascher. "Testing Programming Aptitude." *Datamation* 9 (10) (1963): 28–31.

Orden, Alex. "The Emergence of a Profession." *Communications of the ACM* 10 (3) (1967): 145–147.

Orlikowski, Wanda. "The DP occupation: professionalization or proletarianization?" *Research in the Sociology of Work* 4 (1988): 95–124.

Orlikowski, Wanda, and Jack Baroudi. "The Information Systems Profession: Myth or Reality?" *Office: Technology & People* 4 (1989): 13–30.

Osborn, Roddy. "GE and UNIVAC: Harnessing the High-Speed Computer." *Harvard Business Review* 32 (4) (1954): 99–107.

Oswald, H. "The Various FORTRANS." *Datamation* 10 (8) (1964): 25–29.

Oudshoorn, Nelly, and Trevor Pinch, eds. *How Users Matter: The Co-construction of Users and Technologies.* Cambridge, MA: MIT Press, 2003.

Owens, Larry. "Where Are We Going Phil Morse? Changing Agendas and the Rhetoric of Obviousness in the Transformation of Computing at MIT, 1939–1957." *IEEE Annals of the History of Computing* 18 (4) (1996): 34–41.

Paleaz, Eloina. "A Gift from Pandora's Box: The Software Crisis." PhD diss., University of Edinburgh, 1988.

Palmer, George. "Programming, The Profession That Isn't." *Datamation* 21 (4) (1975): 23–24.

Parikh, Girish. *Programmer Productivity: Achieving an Urgent Priority.* Reston, VA: Reston Publishing, 1984, 209.

Parikh, Girish. "Software maintenance: Penny wise, program foolish." *SIGSOFT Software Engineering Notes* 10 (5) (1985): 89–98.

Parikh, Girish. "What is software maintenance really? What is in a name?" *SIGSOFT Software Engineering Notes* 9 (2) (1984): 114–116.

Parlante, Nick. "What is computer science?" *SIGCSE Bulletin* 37 (2) (2005): 24–25.

Parnas, David. "On the Preliminary Report of C3S" (letter to editor). *Communications of the ACM* 9 (4) (1966): 242–243.

Paschell, William. *Automation and Employment Opportunities for Office Workers: A Report on the Effect of Electronic Computers on Employment of Clerical Workers.* Washington, DC: Bureau of Labor Statistics, 1958.

Patrick, Robert. "The Gap in Programming Support." *Datamation* 7 (5) (1961): 37.

Patterson Hume, J. N. "Development of Systems Software for the Ferut Computer at the University of Toronto, 1952 to 1955." *IEEE Annals of the History of Computing* 16 (2) (1994): 13–19.

Paul, James, and Gregory Simon. "Bugs in the Program: Problems in Federal Government Computer Software Development and Regulation." Staff Study for the House Committee on Science, Space, and Technology, September 1989.

Payne, Robert. "Reaction to Publication Proposal" (letter to editor). *Communications of the ACM* 8 (1) (1965): 71.

Perry, Dallis, and William Cannon. "Vocational Interests of Computer Programmers." *Journal of Applied Psychology* 51 (1) (1967): 28–34.

Perry, Dallis, and William Cannon. "Vocational Interests of Female Computer Programmers." *Journal of Applied Psychology* 52 (1) (1968): 31.

Polin, Terrence, Robert Morse, and John Zenger. "Selecting Programmers from In-Plant Employees." *Personnel Journal* 41 (8) (1962): 398–400.

Pollack, Andrew. "Year 2000 Problem Tests Professionalism of Programmers." *New York Times* (May 3, 1999): C1.

Popkin, Gary. "The Junior College as a Source of Programming Personnel." In *Proceedings of the Ninth Annual SIGCPR Conference*, 130–139. New York: ACM Press, 1971.

Porat, Avner, and James Vaughan. "Computer Personnel: The New Theocracy—or Industrial Carpetbaggers." *Personnel Journal* 48 (6) (1968): 540–543.

Postley, John. "Letter to Editor." *Communications of the ACM* 3 (1) (1960): A6.

Preliminary Report: Specifications for the IBM Mathematical Formula Translating System. New York: Programming Research Group, Applied Science Division, IBM Corporation, November 10, 1954.

"Professionalism Termed Key to Computer Personnel Situation." *Personnel Journal* 51 (2) (1971): 156–157.

"Professional Societies . . . or Technician Associations?" *Datamation* 11 (8) (1965): 23.

Pugh, Emerson, Lyle Johnson, and John Palmer. *IBM's 360 and Early 370 Systems.* Cambridge, MA: MIT Press, 1991.

Randall, Peggy. "Need for Warm Bodies." *Datamation* 9 (10) (1963): 14.

Randell, Brian. "The Origins of Computer Programming." *IEEE Annals of the History of Computing* 16 (4) (1994): 6–14.

Rector, Robert. "Personal Reflections on the First Quarter Century of AFIPS." *Annals of the History of Computing* 8 (3) (1986): 261–269.

Reid, H. V. "Problems in Managing the Data Processing Department." *Journal of Systems Management* 21 (5) (1970): 8–11.

Reinstedt, Robert N. "1966 Survey of Test Use in Computer Personnel Selection." In *Proceedings of the 4th Annual Computer Personnel Research Conference*, 1–8. New York: ACM Press, 1966.

Reinstedt, Robert N., and Raymond Berger. "Certification: A Suggested Approach to Acceptance." *Datamation* 19 (11) (1973): 97–100.

Reinstedt, Robert N., and Beulah C. Hammidi, Sherwood H. Peres, and Evelyn L. Ricard. *Computer Personnel Research Group Programmer Performance Prediction Study. Technical Report.* Santa Monica, CA: RAND Corporation Publications, 1964.

Remington Rand UNIVAC. *Introduction to Programming: Programming for the UNIVAC, Part 1.* (1949) Hagley Museum Archives, Accession 1825, Box 372.

Remington Rand UNIVAC. *An Introduction to Programming the UNIVAC 1103A and 1105 Computing Systems* (1958) Hagley Museum Archives, Accession 1825, Box 368.

"Report from the ACM Ad-hoc Committee on Private EDP Schools." (January 20, 1970) CBI 88, "Data Processing Management Association records," Box 21, Folder 38, Archives of the Charles Babbage Institute, University of Minnesota, Minneapolis.

"Response to Business Automation article on CDP" (1964), CBI 46, "John K. Swearingen Papers, 1936–1993," Box 1, Folder 16, Archives of the Charles Babbage Institute, University of Minnesota, Minneapolis.

Rhee, Hans A. *Office Automation in Social Perspective: The Progress and Social Implications of Electronic Data Processing.* Oxford: Basil Blackwell, 1968.

Rine, David C. "A short overview of a history of software maintenance: as it pertains to reuse." *SIGSOFT Software Engineering Notes* 16 (4) (1991): 60–63.

Rockmael, Valerie. "The Woman Programmer." *Datamation* 9 (1) (1963): 41.

Rojas, Raul, and Ulf Hashagen, eds. *The First Computers: History and Architectures.* Cambridge, MA: MIT Press, 2000.

Ronayne, Maurice F. "'Leads' to Pertinent ADP Literature for the Public Administrator." *Public Administration Review* 24 (2) (1964): 119–125.

Rose, Michael. *Computers, Managers, and Society.* Harmondsworth, UK: Penguin, 1969.

"Roseman Takes Firm Position against Private EDP Schools." *Communications of the ACM* 11 (3) (1968): 206–207.

Rosenberg, Scott. *Dreaming in Code: Two Dozen Programmers, Three Years, 4,732 Bugs, and One Quest for Transcendent Software.* New York: Crown Publishers, 2007.

Rosin, Robert. "Relative to the President's December Remarks." *Communications of the ACM* 10 (6) (1967): 342.

Ross, David. "Certification and Accreditation." *Datamation* 14 (9) (1968): 183–184.

Rossiter, Margaret. *Women Scientists in America.* Baltimore: Johns Hopkins University Press, 1982.

Rotella, Elyce J. *From Home to Office: U.S. Women at Work, 1870–1930. Volume No. 25.* Ann Arbor, MI: UMI Research Press, 1981.

Rothery, Brian. *Installing and Managing a Computer.* London: Business Books, 1968.

Rowan, Thomas C. "Psychological Tests and Selection of Computer Programmers." *Journal of the ACM* 4 (3) (1957): 348–353.

Rowan, Thomas C. "The Recruiting and Training of Programmers." *Datamation* 4 (3) (1958): 16–18.

Saba, W. "Letter to the Editor." *IEEE Computer* 29 (9) (1996): 10.

Sackman, Hal. "Conference on Personnel Research." *Datamation* 14 (7) (1968): 74–76, 81.

Sackman, Hal, W. J. Erickson, and E. E. Grant. "Exploratory Experimental Studies Comparing Online and Offline Programming Performance." *Communications of the ACM* 11 (1) (1968): 3–11.

Sammet, Jean. "Brief Summary of the Early History of COBOL." *IEEE Annals of the History of Computing* 7 (4) (1985): 203–288.

Sammet, Jean E. *Programming Languages: History and Fundamentals.* Englewood Cliffs, NJ: Prentice-Hall, 1969.

Sammet, Jean E. "Programming Languages History." *Annals of the History of Computing* 13 (1) (1991): 49.

Sanden, Bo. "Programming Masters Break Out of the Managerial Mold." *Computerworld* 20 (24) (1986): 73–78.

Saxon, James. "Programming Training: A Workable Approach." *Datamation* 9 (12) (1963): 48–50.

"SCDP Draft Legislation" (1974), CBI 116, "Institute for Certification of Computer Professionals Records, 1960–1993," Box 11, Folder 42, Archives of the Charles Babbage Institute, University of Minnesota, Minneapolis.

Schnaars, Steven P., and Sergio Carvalho. "Predicting the Market Evolution of Computers: Was the Revolution Really Unforeseen." *Technology in Society* 26 (1) (2004): 1–16.

Scranton, Philip. "None-too-Porous Boundaries: Labor History and the History of Technology." *Technology and Culture* 29 (4) (1988): 744–778.

2nd RAND Symposium (1959) CBI 78, "RAND Symposia on Computing Transcripts," Box 1, Folder 1, Archives of the Charles Babbage Institute, University of Minnesota, Minneapolis.

Seiner, J. P. "Programmer Aptitude and Competence Test Systems (PACTS)." In *Proceedings of the Ninth Annual SIGCPR*, 3–25. New York: ACM Press, 1971.

Seitz, John. "Should DPMA Control Certification Process?" (letter to the editor) Computerworld (1971). CBI 116, "Institute for Certification of Computer Professionals Records, 1960–1993," Box 1, Folder 30, Archives of the Charles Babbage Institute, University of Minnesota, Minneapolis.

17th RAND Symposium: Problems of the AFIPS Societies Revisited (1975), CBI 78, "RAND Symposia on Computing Transcripts," Box 3, Folder 7, Archives of the Charles Babbage Institute, University of Minnesota, Minneapolis.

Shannon, Claude, and Warren Weaver. *A Mathematical Theory of Communication.* Urbana: University of Illinois Press, 1949.

Shapiro, Stuart. "Splitting the Difference: The Historical Necessity of Synthesis in Software Engineering." *IEEE Annals of the History of Computing* 19 (1) (1997): 20–54.

Shapiro, Stuart, and Steven Woolgar. "Balancing acts: reconciling competing visions of the way software technologists work." In *Proceedings of the Eighth IEEE International Workshop on Incorporating Computer Aided Software Engineering*, 364–370. Los Alamitos, CA: IEEE Computer Society Press, 1997.

Shaw, Christopher. "Programming Schisms." *Datamation* 8 (9) (1962): 32.

Shneiderman, Ben. "The Relationship between COBOL and Computer Science." *Annals of the History of Computing* 7 (4) (1985): 348–352.

Shore, John. "Why I Never Met a Programmer I Could Trust." *Communications of the ACM* 31 (4) (1988): 372.

Shukla, Ruchi, and Arun Kumar Misra. "Estimating software maintenance effort: a neural network approach." In *ISEC '08: Proceedings of the 1st Conference on India Software Engineering Conference*, 107–112. Hyderabad, India: ACM, 2008.

Sidlo, C. M. "The Making of a Profession" (letter to editor). *Communications of the ACM* 4 (8) (1961): 366–367.

Silberman, Steve. "The Geek Syndrome." *Wired* 9 (12) (2001), 175–183.

Simon, Herbert Alexander. *Administrative Behavior: A Study of Decision-Making Processes in Administrative Organization.* New York: Macmillan, 1947.

Simon, Herbert Alexander. *The New Science of Management Decision.* New York: Harper, 1960.

Simon, Herbert A. *The Sciences of the Artificial.* Cambridge, MA: MIT Press, 1969.

Simon, Herbert A., Allen Newell, and Alan Perlis. "Computer Science" (letter to editor). *Science* 157 (3795) (1967): 1373–1374.

"Six Measures of Professionalism" (1962), CBI 88, "Data Processing Management Association records," Box 21, Folder 40, Archives of the Charles Babbage Institute, University of Minnesota, Minneapolis.

Smith, Malcolm. "Complaint about Boston exam" (1969) CBI 116, "Institute for Certification of Computer Professionals Records, 1960–1993," Box 1, Folder 19, Archives of the Charles Babbage Institute, University of Minnesota, Minneapolis.

"Social Science Notes." *Science News* 91 (13) (1967): 312.

"Software Gap: A Growing Crisis for Computers." *Business Week* 127 (November 5, 1966): 131.

Spigelman, J. H. "Implications of Recent Advances in Electronic Data Processing." *Financial Analysts Journal* 20 (5) (1964): 137–143.

Spigelman, J. H. "Implications of Recent Advances in Electronic Data Processing: Part II." *Financial Analysts Journal* 20 (6) (1964): 87–93.

Steinbuch, Karl. *INFORMATIK: Automatische Informationsverarbeitung.* Berlin: SEG-Nachrichten, 1957.

Stewart, Rosemary. *How Computers Affect Management.* Cambridge, MA: MIT Press, 1971.

Stone, Milt. "In Search of an Identity." *Datamation* 18 (3) (1972): 52–59.

Strom, Sharon Hartman. *Beyond the Typewriter: Gender, Class, and the Origins of Modern American Office Work, 1900–1930.* Urbana: University of Illinois Press, 1992.

Stroustrup, Bjarne. A History of C. In *History of Programming Languages,* ed. Thomas Bergin and R. G. Gibson. New York: ACM Press, 1996.

"Survey on the Use of Service Bureaus." *Wall Street Journal* (November 4, 1969): 24.

Swaine, Michael. *Is Your Next Language COBOL?* Dr. Dobbs Journal, 2008.

Swanson, E. Burton. "The dimensions of maintenance." In *ICSE '76: Proceedings of the 2nd International Conference on Software Engineering,* 492–497. San Francisco, IEEE Computer Society Press, 1976.

Swanson, E. Burton, and Cynthia Mathis Beath. "Departmentalization in software development and maintenance." *Communications of the ACM* 33 (6) (1990): 658–667.

RAND Symposium. "Is It Overhaul or Trade-in Time: Part I." *Datamation* 5 (4) (1959): 24–33.

RAND Symposium. "On Programming Languages, Part I." *Datamation* 8 (10) (1962): 25–32.

RAND Symposium. "On Programming Languages, Part II." *Datamation* 8 (11) (1962): 23–30.

Tanaka, Richard. "Fee or Free Software." *Datamation* 13 (10) (1967): 205–206.

Taylor, Frederick Winslow. *The Principles of Scientific Management*. New York: Harper and Brothers, 1911.

Taylor, Alan. "DPMA Should be Saved Now, If At All Possible." (Computerworld, 1971). CBI 116, "Institute for Certification of Computer Professionals Records, 1960–1993," Box 1, Folder 30, Archives of the Charles Babbage Institute, University of Minnesota, Minneapolis.

Taylor, Alan. "Members Look More Like Markets From Park Ridge." Computerworld (April 14, 1971). CBI 116, "Institute for Certification of Computer Professionals Records, 1960–1993," Box 1, Folder 30, Archives of the Charles Babbage Institute, University of Minnesota, Minneapolis.

Taylor, Alan. "Taylor Replies." (Computerworld, 1971). CBI 116, "Institute for Certification of Computer Professionals Records, 1960–1993," Box 1, Folder 30, Archives of the Charles Babbage Institute, University of Minnesota, Minneapolis.

"The Thinking Machine." *Time Magazine*, January 23, 1950: 54–60.

"The Thoughtless Information Technologist." *Datamation* 12 (8) (1966): 21–22.

Thurstone, L. L. *Primary Mental Abilities*. Chicago: University of Chicago Press, 1938.

Trimble, George, and Elmer Kubie. "Principles of Optimum Programming of the IBM Type 650." *IBM Applied Science Division Technical Newsletter* 8 (1954): 5–16.

Tropp, Henry S. "ACM's 20th Anniversary: 30 August 1967." *Annals of the History of Computing* 9 (3) (1988): 269.

"Trouble . . . I Say Trouble, Trouble in DP City." *Datamation* 14 (7) (1968): 21.

Tucker, Allan. *Programming Languages*. Reading, MA: Addison-Wesley, 1977.

Tukey, John. "The Teaching of Concrete Mathematics." *American Mathematical Monthly* 65 (1) (1958): 1–9.

Tukiainen, Markku, and Eero Mönkkönen. "Programming Aptitude Testing as a Prediction of Learning to Program." In *Proceedings of the 14th Annual*

Workshop of the Psychology of Programming Interest Group, eds. Jasna Kuljis and Lynne Baldwin and Rosa Scoble, 45–57. Berlin: Springer, 2002.

Turkle, Sherry. *The Second Self: Computers and the Human Spirit*. New York: Simon and Schuster, 1984.

Vanlommel, E., and Bert De Brabander. "The Organization of Electronic Data Processing (EDP) Activities and Computer Use." *Journal of Business* 48 (3) (1975): 391–410.

von Neumann, John. *First Draft of a Report on the EDVAC*. Technical report, contract no. W-670-ORD-4926. Philadelphia: Moore School of Electrical Engineering, University of Pennsylvania, June 30, 1945.

Walker, W. R. "MIS Mysticism" (letter to editor). *Business Automation* 16 (7) (1969): 8.

Ware, Willis. "AFIPS in Retrospect." IEEE *Annals of the History of Computing* 8 (3) (1986): 303–311.

Ware, Willis. "As I See It: A Guest Editorial." *Datamation* 11 (5) (1965): 27–28.

Webster, Bruce. "The Real Software Crisis." *Byte Magazine* 21 (1) (1996): 218.

Wegner, Peter. "Three Computer Cultures: Computer Technology, Computer Mathematics, and Computer Science." *Advances in Computers* 10 (1970): 7–78.

Wegner, Peter. "Undergraduate Programs in Computer Science." In *SIGCPR '66: Proceedings of the Fourth SIGCPR Conference on Computer Personnel Research*, 121–129. New York: ACM Press, 1966.

Weinberg, Gerald M. *An Introduction to General Systems Thinking*. New York: Wiley, 1975.

Weinberg, Gerald M. *The Psychology of Computer Programming*. New York: Van Nostrand Rheinhold, 1971.

Weinwurm, George F., ed. *On the Management of Computer Programmers*. New York: Auerbach Publishers, 1970.

Weiss, Eric. "Publications in Computing: An Informal Review." *Communications of the ACM* 15 (7) (1972): 492–497.

Weizenbaum, Joseph. *Computer Power and Human Reason: From Judgment to Calculation*. New York: Penguin, 1976.

Wexelblat, Richard, ed. *History of Programming Languages*. New York: Academic Press, 1981.

"What's Happening with COBOL?" *Business Automation* 14 (4) (1966): 42–43.

Whisler, Thomas. The Impact of Information Technology on Organizational Control. In *The Impact of Computers on Management*, ed. Charles A. Myers. Cambridge, MA: MIT Press, 1967, 16–48.

White, Thomas. "The 70's: People." *Datamation* 16 (7) (1970): 40–46.

"Why Are Business Users Turned Off by ACM?" (1974), CBI 23, "George Glaser Papers, 1960–1989," Box 1, Folder 3, Archives of the Charles Babbage Institute, University of Minnesota, Minneapolis.

Wiener, Norbert. *Cybernetics, or, Control and Communication in the Animal and the Machine.* Cambridge, MA: Technology Press, 1948.

Wilensky, Harold. "The Professionalization of Everyone?" *American Journal of Sociology* 70 (2) (1964): 137–158.

Wilkes, Maurice V. *Memoirs of a Computer Pioneer.* Boston: MIT Press, 1985.

Wilkes, Maurice, David Wheeler, and Stanley Gill. *Preparation of Programs for an Electronic Digital Computer.* Reading, MA: Addison-Wesley, 1951.

Willoughby, Theodore. "Are Programmers Paranoid?" In *Proceedings of the Tenth Annual Conference on SIGCPR,* 47–52. New York: ACM Press, 1972.

Willoughby, Theodore. "Staffing the MIS Function." *ACM Computing Surveys* 4 (4) (1972): 241–259.

Willoughby, Theodore. "Psychometric Characteristics of the CDP Examination." In *Proceedings of the Thirteenth Annual SIGCPR Conference,* 152–160. New York: ACM Press, 1975.

"Will You Vote for an Association Name Change to ACIS?" *Communications of the ACM* 8 (7) (1965): 424–426.

Wise, Thomas. "IBM's $5,000,000,000 Gamble." *Fortune* 74 (September) (1966): 118–123, 224, 226, 228.

Wishner, Raymond. "Comment on Curriculum 68." *Communications of the ACM* 11 (10) (1968): 658.

Wolfe, Jack. "Perspectives on Testing for Programming Aptitude." In *Proceedings of 1971 ACM Annual Conference,* 268–277. New York: ACM Press, 1971.

Xerox Corporation. "At Xerox, We Look at Programmers . . . and See Managers." Ad. *Datamation* 14 (4) (1968).

Yarbrough, Jack. "Letter from John Swearingen" (1964), CBI 46, "John K. Swearingen Papers, 1936–1993," Box 1, Folder 17, Archives of the Charles Babbage Institute, University of Minnesota, Minneapolis.

Yates, JoAnne. "Application Software for Insurance in the 1960s and Early 1970s." *Business And Economic History* 24 (1) (1995): 123–134.

Yates, JoAnne. *Control Through Communication: The Rise of System in American Management.* Baltimore: Johns Hopkins University Press, 1989.

Yates, JoAnne. *Structuring the Information Age: Life Insurance and Technology in the Twentieth Century.* Baltimore: Johns Hopkins University Press, 2005.

Yood, Charles. "Attack of the Giant Brains." *Research Penn State Online* 24 (3) (September 2003). Available at http://www.rps.psu.edu/0309/brains.html.

Yourdon, Edward. *Writings of the Revolution: Selected Readings on Software Engineering.* New York: Prentice Hall, 1986, 288.

Yourdon, Edward Nash, ed. *Classics in Software Engineering*. New York: Yourdon Press, 1979.

Zabusky, Stacia, and Stephen Barley. Redefining Success: Ethnographic Observations on the Careers of Technicians. In *Broken Ladders: Managerial Careers in the New Economy*, ed. Paul Osterman, 185–214. New York: Oxford University Press, 1996.

Zaphyr, P. A. "The Science of Hypology" (letter to editor). *Communications of the ACM* 2 (1) (1959): 4.

Zuboff, Shoshana. *In the Age of the Smart Machine: The Future of Work and Power*. New York: Basic Books, 1988.

Zussman, Robert. *Mechanics of the middle class: Work and politics among American engineers*. Berkeley: University of California Press, 1985.

Index

Egoless programming, 199, 212,
216–217
Electronic data processing (EDP),
16–17, 140
Elliot, Calvin, 164
ENIAC, 14, 15, 32–36
programmers, 14–15, 35–38
Ershov, Andrei, 1, 230

Fein, Louis, 118, 127, 173, 192

Galler, Bernard, 7, 105, 173
Gates, Bill, 3, 27
Gender, 2, 27–29, 89–90, 149,
236–240
masculinization, 12, 77–79,
239–240
women in computing, 12, 14–15,
73, 236–239
General Electric, 28
Gieryn, Thomas, 228–230
Gill, Stanley, 85
Goldstine, Herman, 15, 36
Gregg, Charles, 56
Grosch, Herbert, 107, 137, 144, 173,
184, 187, 190
Gruenberger, Fred, 135,
186–187

Hamming, Richard, 111, 134,
187
Hartree, Douglas, 27
Harvard Mark I, 33, 119–120
Harvard University, 55
Heterogeneous technology, 8, 10–11,
226, 241
Hierarchical management,
200–203
Hoare, C. A. R., 211
Holberton, Elizabeth (Betty) Snyder,
35, 37, 237
Honeywell, 28, 94, 99, 205
Hopper, Grace, 38, 73, 86–87, 94,
236–237
Hughes, John, 63
Hunter, Truman, 56, 58
Hypology, 118

IBM Corporation, 28, 51–54, 60, 71,
89, 99–100, 118–119, 137–138,
140, 171
IBM 650, 56
IBM 704, 90
IBM Federal Systems Division, 199,
202
IBM OS/360, 45–47, 205–206
IBM System/360, 45, 204–205
ICCP (Institute for the Certification
of Computing Professionals),
179–180
IEEE Computer Society, 179,
187–188
IFIP (International Federation on
Information Processing Societies),
188
Informatics, 130
Information science, 118, 130

Jay, Antony, 216
Jennings, Betty Jean, 35
Jurisdictional struggles, 234

Knuth, Donald, 10, 131–132, 151
Kuhn, Thomas, 130–132

Labor history, 231–233
Law, John, 8
Leavitt, Howard, 154
Legislation, 72, 181, 191
Lichterman, Ruth, 35

Mahoney, Michael, 129, 135, 220
Management
attitudes towards programmers, 22,
146, 150–151, 202
conflict with computerization, 144,
146, 152–154, 156–159
Management control, 147, 201–202
Management sciences, 22, 154
Management systems, 71, 140,
155–156
Management theory, 60–61,
216–217
Marx, Karl, 210
Marxist interpretation, 231–233

Printed in the United States
By Bookmasters